Moving Histories

Reappraisals in Irish History

Editors
Enda Delaney (University of Edinburgh)
Maria Luddy (University of Warwick)
Ciaran O'Neill (Trinity College Dublin)

Reappraisals in Irish History offers new insights into Irish history, society and culture from 1750. Recognising the many methodologies that make up historical research, the series presents innovative and interdisciplinary work that is conceptual and interpretative, and expands and challenges the common understandings of the Irish past. It showcases new and exciting scholarship on subjects such as the history of gender, power, class, the body, landscape, memory and social and cultural change. It also reflects the diversity of Irish historical writing, since it includes titles that are empirically sophisticated together with conceptually driven synoptic studies.

1. Jonathan Jeffrey Wright, *The 'Natural Leaders' and their World: Politics, Culture and Society in Belfast, c.1801–1832*

2. Gerardine Meaney, Mary O'Dowd and Bernadette Whelan, *Reading the Irish Woman: Studies in Cultural Encounters and Exchange, 1714–1960*

3. Emily Mark-FitzGerald, *Commemorating the Irish Famine: Memory and the Monument*

4. Virginia Crossman, *Poverty and the Poor Law in Ireland 1850–1914*

5. Paul Taylor, *Heroes or Traitors? Experiences of Southern Irish Soldiers Returning from the Great War 1919–39*

6. Paul Huddie, *The Crimean War and Irish Society*

7. Brian Hughes, *Defying the IRA?*

8. Laura Kelly, *Irish medical education and student culture, c.1850–1950*

9. Michael Dwyer, *Strangling Angel: Diphtheria and childhood immunization in Ireland*

10. Carole Holohan, *Reframing Irish Youth in the Sixties*

11. Lindsey Flewelling, *Two Irelands beyond the Sea: Ulster Unionism and America, 1880–1920*

12. Kyle Hughes and Donald MacRaild, *Ribbon Societies in Nineteenth-Century Ireland and its Diaspora: The Persistence of Tradition*

13. Ciarán McCabe, *Begging, Charity and Religion in Pre-Famine Ireland*

Moving Histories

Irish Women's Emigration to Britain
from Independence to Republic

JENNIFER REDMOND

LIVERPOOL UNIVERSITY PRESS

First published 2018 by
Liverpool University Press
4 Cambridge Street
Liverpool
L69 7ZU

British Library Cataloguing-in-Publication data
A British Library CIP record is available

ISBN 978-1-78694-167-1 (cased)
ISBN 978-1-78962-019-1 (limp)

Typeset by Carnegie Book Production, Lancaster
Printed and bound by TJ International Ltd, Padstow, Cornwall, PL28 8RW

For James, Sophia and Devin

Contents

Figures

Tables

Abbreviations

ATS	Auxiliary Territorial Service
BEA	British Empire Association
CPRSI	Catholic Protection and Rescue Society of Ireland
CSWB	Catholic Social Welfare Bureau
GFS	Girls' Friendly Society
ICGPS	International Catholic Girls' Protection Society
IHA	Irish Housewives' Association
IWWU	Irish Women Workers' Union
NSPCC	National Society for Prevention of Cruelty to Children
NVA	National Vigilance Association
PFI	'Pregnant from Ireland'
QAIMNS	Queen Alexandra's Imperial Military Nursing Service
SOSBW	Society for Overseas Settlement of British Women
SPCK	Society for the Promotion of Christian Knowledge
WAAF	Women's Auxiliary Air Force
WLA	Women's Land Army
WRNS	Women's Royal Navy Service

Acknowledgements

My first thanks go to Liverpool University Press for allowing me to develop this manuscript into a book for the Reappraisals in Irish History Series. Thanks especially to Alison Welsby, the editor, and the series editors Professor Enda Delaney, Professor Maria Luddy and Dr Ciaran O'Neill, for their faith in this project. My sincere thanks to the anonymous reviewers who offered judicious critique and great insights.

This book would not exist without the intellectual inspiration, the empirical knowledge base and the practical advice and guidance of many important individuals. Space constraints mean that I cannot name all inspiring scholars, but to all those who have laboured hard in archives and libraries across the world to contribute to our knowledge of Irish emigrants, I thank you.

This book is the result of archival work in Ireland, England and Scotland and I thank all archivists and librarians who assisted me. I was given special access to records along the way and I thank Canon G. O'Hanlon, Down and Connor Archives, Leslie McCartney, formerly of the King's Cross Voices project and Catriona Crowe, formerly of the National Archives of Ireland. I am also thankful to Adrienne Corless who shared letters and a travel permit belonging to her grandfather, to Joe Glennon who shared the travel permit used by his grandmother, Josephine Nestor, and to Patricia Marsh who shared the travel permit that belonged to her mother, Mary Henry. Thank you to the Irish Jesuit Archives for their assistance in sourcing images and their permission for reproducing them. Special thanks to Henrietta Ewart for sharing her fantastic PhD thesis which echoes some of the themes and findings in this book. The scholarly generosity is much appreciated. Such resources have enriched this work and I am thankful for the time and effort people expended.

Some inspiring advice from Donald Harman Akenson, generously given wisdom in response to an unsolicited email from me, helped to spur this project on. All errors and omissions remain my own, of course. Vincent Comerford has been a powerhouse of support; I thank him hugely for continuing to be a great mentor to me. Jackie Hill was a great mentor and an inspiring academic role model during my postdoctoral fellowship at Maynooth University and I also thank the Irish Research Council for their support of my work during that time. Thanks are due to the Royal Irish Academy who granted me a travel bursary through which some of this research was made possible. Supportive colleagues in Maynooth have helped see this book through to the end. Special thanks to Alison FitzGerald, Jonathan Wright, Michael Potterton, David Murphy, Marian Lyons and Jacinta Prunty for encouragement.

Friends and scholars Sonja Tiernan, Carole Holohan, Juliana Adelman, Mary McAuliffe, Sandra McAvoy, Judith Harford, Elaine Farrell, Sarah-Anne Buckley, Leanne McCormick, Laura Kelly, Ciara Breathnach, Georgina Laragy, Jennifer Kelly and Deirdre O'Donnell, among many others, have been inspirational and encouraging. I also thank my fellow members of the Women's History Association of Ireland for providing a stimulating forum and great support. A special mention here to Catherine Higgins for her beautiful friendship and unfailing interest. Thanks to Eric Pumroy for being a fantastic boss at Bryn Mawr College where I toiled on this throughout a stimulating CLIR postdoctoral fellowship.

To my friends and family, thanks for your patience and support while I conducted this research and was often absent (or worse, sober!) for many special occasions. My Mum has promised to read every word of this book, bless her! Last, but definitely not least, thanks to James O'Regan, my husband, great friend and former fellow emigrant; thanks for following me on this adventure and for all the dinners you cooked while I studied. This book is dedicated to you, Devin and Sophia, our beautiful transatlantic girl who helped us live my research.

Introduction

Water metaphors have always been used in discussing Irish emigration: a flood, a tide, a wave, a tsunami of people have left; there is a 'leakage' problem; Ireland is a 'leaky ship'; something must be done to 'stem the flow'. Long after boats have ceased to be the primary method for leaving Ireland, we still talk of people 'leaving our shores'. Sometimes, more sinisterly, these have morphed into images of blood: Ireland's population is 'haemorrhaging' young people; the 'life force' is draining away; we must stem the flow. It is as if Ireland's population is conceived of as so 'fluid' that metaphorical references are the only adequate ones to express our feelings about the loss of citizens. Ireland's population, in this metaphorical vein, has been slowly depleting since the Famine when the crisis reached its apogee in this watery, cultural imagination. Families, the potential anchor to all these turbulent population changes, have been eroded by the waves of emigration, and women, the life-givers, the soul of the family in traditional, nationalist rhetoric, abandoned ship in staggering numbers in search of new opportunities abroad.

This book looks at the impact women's migration had on Ireland in the crucial years of initial independence, from the partition of the island and the founding of the Free State to the declaration of a Republic. This period saw Ireland move from internal political instability in the 1920s to a more internationally focused country in the 1950s. However, emigration remained a constant feature and women's experiences have often been forgotten. The inevitability of emigration was a familiar trope in this period. By the 1940s, commentary in the *Irish Catholic* that young people of every class in Ireland over the previous century 'have regarded emigration as their natural destiny' resulting in 'too high a proportion of old people and that we, as a people, are committing national suicide' was a commonly held view.[1] The idea of race suicide was returned to repeatedly, and is a significant factor in what Liam

---

1 'A Voice for Emigrants in the Dáil?', *Irish Catholic*, 13 November 1947, p. 3.

Kennedy has termed 'MOPE' syndrome, or 'Most Oppressed People Ever',[2] although, as Delaney among others has argued, Ireland was not unique in terms of the experience of mass migration and rural depopulation.[3] 'MOPE' syndrome is also evident in the sentimentalising of emigration, evident in the tradition of the 'American wake' of the nineteenth century, but continuing in poems and ballads, often printed in national newspapers, such as this lament:

> Oh I pity the mother that rears up the child
> And likewise the father who labour and toils,
> To try and support them he will work night and day
> And when they are reared up they will go away.[4]

The 'MOPE' idea is linked to that of emigration as 'exile', a powerful trope that continued from Famine times until the late twentieth century and represents a complex theme in Irish historiography.[5] Declan Kiberd has observed the importance of the notion of exile in national identity, referring to the aphorism 'exile is the nursery of nationality'.[6] The history of women's emigration brings another dimension to this phrase, given their importance in sustaining the growth of the nation and the loss rendered by their emigration.

Why focus exclusively on women? The image of the navvy, the 'men who built Britain', looms large in the cultural imagination of interwar and post-Second World War migration and has become the archetype of the rational economic migrant who existed in popular imagination from the nineteenth century.[7] Examining the ways in which emigration was articulated in the press, by the government and the prominent welfare institutions in the era of the 'family wage', men's motivations for emigration were understood

---

2 Quoted by Mary Daly, 'Forty Shades of Grey? Irish Historiography and the Challenges of Multidisciplinarity', in Liam Harte and Yvonne Whelan (eds), *Ireland Beyond Boundaries: Mapping Irish Studies in the Twenty-First Century* (London: Pluto Press, 2007), p. 102.

3 See Enda Delaney, 'Placing Postwar Irish Migration to Britain in a Comparative European Perspective, 1945–1981', in Andy Bielenberg (ed.), *The Irish Diaspora* (Harlow: Longman, 2000), pp. 331–356.

4 Jenny Beale, *Women in Ireland: Voices of Change* (Dublin: Gill & Macmillan, 1986), p. 33.

5 The leading proponent of this theory is Kerby Miller in *Emigrants and Exiles: Ireland and the Irish Exodus to North America* (New York: Oxford University Press, 1985).

6 Declan Kiberd, *Inventing Ireland: The Literature of the Modern Nation* (London: Jonathan Cape, 1995), p. 2.

7 For a recent analysis of nineteenth-century emigration, see Sarah Roddy, *Population, Providence and Empire: The Churches and Emigration from Nineteenth-Century Ireland* (Manchester: Manchester University Press, 2014).

and accepted. Women, however, were spoken of in quite different terms. In the lament above, they are the mothers that stay at home to keen, but they were also the daughters who left. So, to paraphrase Virginia Woolf, Irish female emigrants need a book of their own.

The approach taken in this book is to demystify the female experience of migration to Britain, to separate rhetoric from reality and to investigate empirically, as far as is possible, the actuality of their immigrant lives. This book falls within the broad spectrum of diaspora studies as it focuses not just on the issue of migration from Ireland but also on the narratives of Irish immigrant lives in Britain. However, while this book encapsulates an analysis of diasporic elements of the Irish in Britain, it does not focus solely on the theoretical aspects of identity, location and belonging that is a feature of the work of Breda Gray, Mary Hickman and Bronwen Walter, all theorists embracing the history of the Irish in Britain from sociological and ethnicity perspectives. The empirical emphasis within *Moving Histories* is on the narratives of migration told at individual and state levels, in oral histories and government memos, in private correspondence and in national newspapers. This also differs from the thrust of recent work by Henrietta Ewart on policy responses to the Irish in Britain, although many of the conclusions reached are similar.[8]

It is over thirty years since pioneer Irish women's historian Mary Cullen argued that 'It has become almost a cliché to say that women are "invisible" in the past or have been "written out" of (male) history'.[9] While it may have appeared clichéd, issues of erasure persist. Irish migration is part of the narrative of Irish women's history and broader histories of Ireland in the nineteenth and twentieth centuries, yet no dedicated monograph on Irish women migrants to Britain in the first half of the twentieth century exists prior to this book. This is despite the fact that through the work of many scholars Irish women migrants to Britain are no longer one of Donald Akenson's 'great unknowns' of Irish migration history. However, increased scholarly attention has often been slight, and women's experiences remain peripheral or ignored completely in many general accounts of migration and the Irish diaspora. Two examples exemplify this trend: John Belchem's *Irish, Catholic and Scouse: The History of the Liverpool Irish, 1800–1939* does not include a comprehensive analysis of the vast network of activities Irish women in the city were engaged in.[10] This is

---

8 Henrietta Ewart, 'Caring for Migrants: Policy Responses to Irish Migration to England, 1940–1972' (PhD thesis, University of Warwick, 2012).

9 Mary Cullen, 'Telling it Our Way: Feminist History', in Liz Steiner-Scott (ed.), *Personally Speaking: Women's Thoughts on Women's Issues* (Dublin: Attic Press: 1985), p. 254.

10 John Belchem, *Irish, Catholic and Scouse: The History of the Liverpool Irish, 1800–1939* (Liverpool: Liverpool University Press, 2007).

despite a rich array of resources such as those used by Charlotte Wildman to reconstruct the Catholic world of interwar Liverpool and the part women played in that community in embracing modernity, consumerism and new roles for women.[11] Similarly, Martin Mitchell's edited collection *New Perspectives on the Irish in Scotland* described itself as a 'major reassessment of Irish immigration to Scotland'. Although the scholarship presented in this collection is of the highest standard, and in many ways the essays do offer an important reappraisal of accepted truths on the Irish in Scotland, the failure to include any contributions specifically related to women is disappointing, particularly given Irish women's visibility in the migrant flow to Scotland as workers, religious or as wives and mothers.[12] Thus, recent studies of Irish migrants continue to ignore women's specific experiences while claiming to be books about Irish immigrants (not books about Irish men, which indeed they are).

Whilst earlier works on Irish emigration had single chapters or sections that addressed the experience of women (for example, Robert Kennedy's *The Irish: Emigration, Marriage and Fertility*),[13] subsequent works have emerged that focus solely on women's experience of emigration. Female researchers and historians, interested in highlighting the unique nature of the Irish female emigration phenomenon, have primarily authored these texts. Louise Ryan, Breda Gray, Ide O'Carroll, Bronwen Walter, Mary Hickman, Sharon Lambert, Mary Muldowney, Hasia Diner and Janet Nolan, among others, have written specifically on Irish female emigrants, although their work has been on different time periods and distinct destination countries.[14]

---

11 Charlotte Wildman, 'Irish-Catholic Women and Modernity in 1930s Liverpool', in D.A.J. MacPherson and Mary J. Hickman (eds), *Irish Diaspora Studies and Women: Theories, Concepts and New Perspectives* (Manchester: Manchester University Press, 2014), pp. 72–91.

12 S. Karly Kehoe's comparative work on Irish women in religious orders in Scotland and Canada, for example, critically examines the role of ethnicity and race. See her chapter, 'Border Crossings: Being Irish in Nineteenth-Century Scotland and Canada', in MacPherson and Hickman, *Irish Diaspora Studies and Women* and her book, *Creating a Scottish Church: Catholicism, Gender and Ethnicity in Nineteenth-Century Scotland* (Manchester: Manchester University Press, 2010).

13 Robert E. Kenndy, *The Irish: Emigration, Marriage and Fertility* (Berkeley: University of California Press, 1973).

14 Ryan, Hickman, Walter and Gray focus on emigration to Britain, although in different time periods. Ryan's work focuses on the Free State period – for example, 'Irish Female Emigration in the 1930s: Transgressing Space and Culture', in *Gender, Place and Culture*, 8.3 (2001), pp. 271–282. Gray's work focuses on the resurgence of Irish emigration in the 1980s – for example, *Women and the Irish Diaspora* (Routledge: London, 2004). Both Walter and Hickman have addressed issues of identity, diaspora, ethnicity and second-generation status of the Irish in Britain – for example, Walter's work, *Outsiders Inside: Whiteness, Place and Irish Women* (London: Routledge, 2001) and Hickman, 'Locating

Enda Delaney's *Demography, State and Society* and *The Irish in Post-War Britain* both include a focus on female emigration to Britain from 1921, and he calls for more research in the area, as neither is a book solely on women's emigration. David Fitzpatrick's groundbreaking work on Irish emigrants' letters, *Oceans of Consolation*, includes a focus on women, as does his subsequent research on women and education in relation to migration.[15] Fitzpatrick's work, however, focuses predominantly on nineteenth- and early twentieth-century trends, thus pre-dating the focus of this book.[16] More recently, the joint scholarship of Patrick Fitzgerald and Brian Lambkin has recognised the value of gendered analyses of Irish migration, but although their book contains information on women their wider project was to study migration as a whole.[17] Thus, *Moving Histories* places itself within the historiography of Irish emigration that has utilised theoretical models and a multiplicity of source material, aiming to fill the gap in our specific knowledge and analysis of women's experiences of migration in the first decades of independence by making them centre stage.

This book focuses on Irish women's emigration to Britain in the first decades of Irish independence. It contends that female emigrants were neither consulted by the various experts who professed opinions about them, nor fully included in subsequent histories written about the Irish in Britain. For, like men, they too have been in the 'habit of going away' as observed as far back as the sixth century.[18] This book renders them visible and locates their socio-economic, cultural and emotional experiences in the canon of modern Irish history.

Most recently, Johanne Devlin Trew's work on migration from Northern Ireland in the twentieth century, *Leaving the North*, has taken a similar approach.[19] Interrogating collective and individual memories of migration,

the Irish Diaspora', in *Irish Journal of Sociology*, 11.2 (2002), pp. 8–26. Hickman and Walter have themselves created oral histories of the Irish in Britain, and Walter has interwoven and incorporated this data into *Outsiders Inside* in her analysis, as is done here, although it relates to a later period. O'Carroll and Nolan's work focuses on Irish female emigrants to America, in the nineteenth and twentieth centuries.

15 For example, see David Fitzpatrick, '"A Share of the Honeycomb": Education, Emigration and Irishwomen', *Continuity and Change*, 1.2 (1986), pp. 217–234 and *Oceans of Consolation: Personal Accounts of Irish Migration to Australia* (Ithaca, NY: Cornell University Press, 1994).

16 Angela McCarthy has also focused on letters from Irish emigrants in Australasia – see bibliography for further details.

17 Patrick Fitzgerald and Brian Lambkin, *Migration in Irish History, 1607–2007* (Basingstoke: Palgrave Macmillan, 2008).

18 Enda Delaney, *Demography, State and Society: Irish Migration to Britain 1921–1971* (Liverpool: Liverpool University Press, 2000), p. 1.

19 Johanne Devlin Trew, *Leaving the North: Migration and Memory, Northern Ireland 1921–2011* (Liverpool: Liverpool University Press, 2013).

Devlin Trew has sought to uncover hidden histories as a way of supplementing the available documentary evidence, although she has conducted oral histories, whereas this book examines the oral histories conducted by others. Strangely, personal narratives have often been ignored by historians despite the accessibility of recordings and transcripts in various repositories.[20] By giving us insight into larger historical events from a personal perspective, oral histories provide the historian with another prism through which to view the past, another piece of the jigsaw with which to build a narrative to explain past lives. They are no more or less subjective than a written letter or diary, and the act of committing the opinion, memory or conversation to a conventional, stylised piece of prose on paper does not give it superior authority. Every document has an author, and, as McKenna asserts, 'no form of record is "pure", capable of offering a truth untouched by author, intended audience or context'.[21] Many of the sources traditionally used by historians in the construction of histories are documents written by unnamed civil servants. The fact that they are not signed does not accord them an objective, disembodied status. It is just that the subjectivity of such documents is not as obvious and is rarely interrogated to the same extent as personal narratives. Indeed, as Ken Howarth, one of the leading figures in oral history methodologies, has argued: 'The strength of oral history lies in the fact that it complements written, printed and visual sources and can often clearly call into question those other sources'.[22] Oral histories have been recognised as important for constructing the histories of women because of their invisibility within standard documentary evidence.[23]

20 Reference here is made to the Irish Folklore Archives in University College Dublin, the online collections of University College Cork, the London Metropolitan University's Smurfitt Archive, the King's Cross Voices Project (http://camden.gov.uk/ccm/content/leisure/local-history/kings-cross-voices.en. After contacting the project I was allowed to access the database of interviews with residents of the King's Cross area of London. For this I am grateful to the project co-ordinator, Leslie McCartney) and the British Library Sound Archive. As part of the 'Breaking the Silence' project, the Irish Centre for Migration studies compiled interviews with those who did emigrate and with those who did not. These interviews are available in both text and aural format for those with access to the University College Cork intranet (http://migration.ucc.ie/oralarchive/testing/breaking/index.html). A collection of oral history interviews is also available as part of the Women's Oral History Project at https://repository.dri.ie/catalog/h9904j002. These interviews are accompanied by thematic texts on a range of contemporary issues such as employment for women. There is, however, increased interest in oral history; for example, the Irish Oral History Archive (www.ioha.co.uk/) and the Oral History Network of Ireland (https://www.oralhistorynetworkireland.ie/), which details even more resources.

21 Yvonne McKenna, *Made Holy: Irish Women Religious at Home and Abroad* (Dublin: Irish Academic Press, 2006), p. 4.

22 Ken Howarth, *Oral History: A Handbook* (Stroud: Sutton Publishing,1998), p. viii.

23 For an early treatise on the importance of oral history methods for women's history, see Sherna Gluck, 'What's So Special about Women? Women's Oral History', *Frontiers*, 2.2

This is particularly the case when studying the lives of working-class women (a major feature of this book).

There are, of course, drawbacks to oral history, namely the complex issues of subjectivity, bias and memory, yet the focus on the voice of the person is one of the strengths of the methodology. However, unlike statistical data or memorandums, which often follow a familiar format, interviews are non-standard, shaped by the dynamic that develops in the process. This can mean that questions are not fully answered or that the interviewee will dominate the process by revealing only what they wish to, or what they think the interviewer wishes to hear.[24] Telling one's life story in oral histories has led to a tendency to discuss major life events, with limited reflections on broader issues, or on the historiography of Irish emigration. One of the crucial elements most lacking in oral history collections to date is the specific questioning of emigrants on their awareness and views of public commentary on emigration issues. This would seem to be a particularly striking omission in collections that specifically focus on women's migration experiences given the abundance of contemporary publications that contained negative and often vitriolic commentary on women migrants.[25] The impetus is often to allow women's voices to be heard as a counterbalance to narratives of emigration that had previously ignored them.[26] While this is important, it is a lost opportunity to explore women's reflections on attitudes towards them as this is an ageing population whose experiences may soon be lost to history.

(1977), pp. 3–17. A case study approach utilising oral history for women's history can be seen in Judy Giles, 'Narratives of Gender, Class and Modernity in Women's Memories of Mid-Twentieth Century Britain', *Signs*, 28.1 (2002), pp. 21–41. For an examination of trends in Irish oral history methods, see Guy Beiner and Anna Bryson, 'Listening to the Past and Talking to Each Other: Problems and Possibilities Facing Oral History in Ireland', *Irish Economic and Social History*, 30 (2003), pp. 71–78.

24 See, for example, Louise Ryan's experience of interviewing Irish female emigrants, 'Passing Time: Irish Women Remembering and Re-Telling Stories of Migration to Britain', in Kathy Burrell and Panikos Panayi (eds), *Histories and Memories: Migrants and their History in Britain* (London: Tauris Academic Studies, 2006), pp. 192–209. For more on the methodological difficulties of using personal documentary evidence, see also June Purvis, 'Using Primary Sources When Researching Women's History from a Feminist Perspective', *Women's History Review*, 1.2 (1992), pp. 273–306. Added to this is the lack of an agreed set of standards for conducting interviews, resulting in an individualised approach, with researchers following guidelines and ethical procedures laid down by bodies often outside of the discipline of history, particularly in the Irish context.

25 Lennon, McAdam and O'Brien, *Across the Water*; Ryan's numerous articles are detailed in the bibliography; Dunne, *An Unconsidered People*.

26 This emphasis is particularly evident in Lennon, McAdam and O'Brien's work.

Moreover, oral sources allow us access to the views of those who are perhaps less likely to write autobiographies or engage in public commentary through the letters' pages of newspapers, particularly as most emigrants were unlikely even to conceive of leaving a personal archive. This brings us to the issue of class, an apposite concept given that much migration from Ireland was by people from the lower socio-economic classes, precisely those less likely to collate personal archives. The importance of paying attention to oral sources is further compounded when one considers that women are less likely to leave a chronicle of their lives than men. Indeed, this is the appeal of oral methodologies to feminist scholars in all fields, including history. Oral histories often allow a more nuanced, inclusive perspective to emerge when they are considered alongside the evidentiary pool of documentary sources. Combining sources in such a way provides both long- and short-range views; as Akenson argues, 'broad-based numerical description and tight narrative exposition are part of the same process'.[27] Or, in Devlin Trew's analysis, 'stories and memories of our individual lives also offer insights from social, psychological and geographical perspectives on larger historical contexts by uncovering hidden histories' which can 'supplement documentary evidence'.[28]

An analysis of newspapers, religious tracts and parliamentary debates reveals a repetitive narrative that the women of newly independent Ireland were not economic migrants of the same order as men, but rather they went to Britain against advice and for what might be termed 'trivial' or social reasons, such as a dislike of domestic service or the desire to marry. Such statements, appearing widely in articles in the daily, weekly, national, local and religious press, seem not only stereotypical but fundamentally unjust. The resulting impression was that while the best and brightest men were leaving, the worst kinds of women were becoming (or would quickly become) debased by going to British cities. This type of discourse was consistent despite the changes in political leadership in post-Civil War Ireland, and emanated from both sides of the confessional divide, although greater censure appears to have come from the Catholic Church than the Church of Ireland. *Moving Histories* charts the public rhetoric on migration and measures this against the evidence we have of the experiences of female migration; a less salacious, more mundane picture emerges – of women surviving, using migration to sustain themselves and to enter into full adulthood.

As has been much documented by historians, emigration had a long history by the inception of the Free State. Women had been migrating in large numbers from Ireland since the nineteenth century and had even been

---

27 Donald Harman Akenson, *Ireland, Sweden and the Great European Migration, 1815–1914* (Quebec: McGill-Queen's University Press, 2012), p. 3.

28 Devlin Trew, *Leaving the North*, pp. 1–2.

the specific focus of assisted emigration schemes.[29] However, while migration was part of the cultural condition of Irish life, discourses surrounding women's migration to Britain from the 1920s often created the impression that a new and calamitous movement was taking place. Ireland would be deprived of its future mothers and thus its viability was at stake (the future fathers are conspicuously absent in the rhetoric despite their similarly high rates of migration). It seems that independence brought about a peculiar sensitivity towards emigration, perhaps understandably given that the new state was meant to bring emigration to a halt, as if a political shift in government could magically alter the myriad reasons why a person might choose to leave. Yet emigration was not a surprising factor engendered by the creation of the new state: 'everyone knew the way the tides ran, even if they did not themselves choose to take to the sea'.[30]

Personal letters were sought through numerous public appeals, but were elusive, and in this I know I am not the only historian to have failed to discover such items.[31] Although letters between emigrants and their families were a common feature of life in pre-digital twentieth-century Ireland, they are difficult to locate and gain access to. The Irish Folklore Commission attempted to collect letters for the pre-1900 period as part of their national survey examining emigration to America. This part of their project proved unsuccessful. One collector claimed: 'Although I made enquiries over most of Inishowen I failed to get any old letters. I feel that, though people may have letters they are reluctant to part with them'.[32] Akenson, however, has posited

29 For more, see Gerard Moran, *Sending Out Ireland's Poor: Assisted Emigration to North America in the Nineteenth Century* (Dublin: Four Courts Press, 2004) and Perry McIntyre, *Free Passage: The Reunion of Irish Convicts and Their Families in Australia, 1788–1852* (Dublin: Irish Academic Press, 2010). Women were targeted in Vere Foster's scheme for assisted passage to North America as they were thought reliable remittance senders, a key way to increase the family income.

30 Akenson, *Ireland, Sweden and the Great European Migration*, p. 8.

31 Through public appeals I was allowed access to a series of letters by Adrienne Corless who possessed letters written by her grandmother, Josephine Nestor, to her grandfather, Paddy Corless, while he was working in England during the 1940s. I refer throughout to these letters as the Nestor–Corless letters. The Nestor–Corless letters offer a rare glimpse into the lives of young people in Ireland and Britain at this time, and reveal much about a range of issues, such as the permit system for migration in the Second World War, the travel options for getting from the West of Ireland to England and social events attended by both. They also provide proof of the existence of chain migration and the Irish-dominated parishes that emigrants were able to socialise in whilst in England. Unfortunately, I was not able to find any other such letters, despite regular and widespread appeals.

32 Quote from a Donegal collector, Connall C. O Deirn, Irish Folklore Archive MS 1411, *c.*1955. A group of thirty selected part-time and full-time collectors were sent to administer a questionnaire around the country, which included a question about letters. This project was reported to be for the assistance of Arnold Schrier, a research scholar

that it may be more the case that Irish families simply did not keep letters. Surveying the impressive collection and documentation skills of Kerby Miller, who found over 5,000 Irish emigrant letters, Akenson compares this to the excess of 50,000 letters preserved in the Swedish Emigrant Institute in addition to the collections held in regional repositories.[33] The failure to preserve letters (or, more accurately perhaps, the tradition of burning them) is a custom that appears to have persisted into the twentieth century.

Why did women's emigration provoke so much ire? Why were their reasons for migrating posited as being different from men's? Were they as vulnerable and flighty as newspapers depicted them? *Moving Histories* explores the issue of emigration by comparing and contrasting the public and private discourses and examining their emotive aspects, which are particular to women.

Overview of *Moving Histories*

The book begins in 1922 at the founding of the Free State, an event that heralded southern Ireland's entrée into independence from Britain and a new era of British–Irish relations that was to affect the position of the Irish in Britain.[34] It focuses on the first decades of independence, from the partition of Ireland to the declaration of a Republic. This key period, in which the political success of independence was contingent upon economic success, was deeply marked by the continued emigration of people which threatened the national project. Chapter 1 sketches the background to Irish women's emigration, arguing that their earlier migrations have been more fully researched than experiences in the twentieth century. America looms large in this historiography as Irish women achieved the notable status of being the largest female group of any in the Great European Migration of the nineteenth century to immigrate alone.[35] The shift in destination to Britain was driven by practical reasons, but attracted more opinionated and negative commentary as a land full of traps rather than opportunities.

from the USA. Schrier later published *Ireland and the American Emigration, 1850–1900* (New York: Russell & Russell, 1958).

33 Akenson, *Ireland, Sweden and the Great European Migration*, p. 252 n. 58. It is worth considering Miller's thesis that 'empty letters', or those without remittances, may have been burned and rarely admitted to.

34 See Mo Moulton, *Ireland and the Irish in Interwar England* (Cambridge: Cambridge University Press, 2014).

35 Between 1815 and 1930, Baines has estimated that approximately 51.7 million people left Europe; 7.3 million of these left Ireland. Dudley Baines, *Emigration From Europe, 1815–1930* (Cambridge: Cambridge University Press, 1995), p. 3.

The statistical evidence on post-independence migration is examined, alongside the theories developed to explain migratory patterns. How well these fit both an Irish and a gendered analysis of migration in this period is interrogated.

Chapter 2 offers an analysis of the public discourses on emigration to Britain in Irish political debates. Direct discussion of emigration was often avoided in the Oireachtas except as a political jibe or a shortcut critique by the opposition on the capabilities of the government. Constructive commentary or real debate was rare and no policy on emigration was ever formulated despite two official inquires in the 1930s and the 1940s.[36] The relaxed travel arrangements between Britain and Ireland allowed for politicians easily to claim they could do little to 'stem the tide'. Similarly, in Northern Ireland, the fact that the government there does not control its own national borders has given politicians a comparable excuse as to their helplessness in controlling emigration, or 'at least publicly, to maintain a "hands off" stance'.[37]

The gender dimension of the debates reveals how women emigrants were conceptualised differently and often denigrated at what was supposed to be the highest levels of discourse. They had few defenders. Women Senators and TDs were no more likely to stand up for female emigrants when negative commentary was made about them, nor did female representatives raise the issue of employment opportunities for women that lay at the heart of migration. The importance of the 'family wage' for men was an article of faith supported across the political spectrum. Historians have commented on the low profile of many of the women in the Oireachtas (apart from the vocal critiques of 1930s legislation and the Constitution) and this is merely another example. Chapter 2 also investigates the two government-sponsored inquiries into emigration: the 1937 Inter-Departmental Investigation into Seasonal Employment in Britain and the Commission on Emigration and Other Population Problems (1948–54). Women were virtually ignored in the former report but were substantially analysed in the latter, although, as Mary Daly has pointed out, without in fact being consulted as to what their views and experiences were.[38]

Safeguarding emigrant girls emerged as part of the panoply of philanthropic initiatives in this period run by affluent women along religious lines that were aimed at both the protection and betterment of working-class women and Chapter 3 addresses this. The early independence period is one

---

36 Delaney, *Demography, State and Society*, p. 296.
37 Devlin Trew, *Leaving the North*, p. 12.
38 Mary Daly, *The Slow Failure: Population Decline and Independent Ireland, 1920–1971* (Madison: University of Wisconsin Press, 2006), p. 168.

many would argue coincided with, and was facilitated by, a strong Catholic Church presence in welfare provision for the poor in Irish society in lieu of state-funded initiatives. This was particularly the case with emigrants, who successive governments in post-independence Ireland continuously lamented but did nothing constructive to help. Indeed 'at their worst, Irish official attitudes towards the emigrants layered smugness on top of moral censure'.[39]

Women were specifically targeted for moral assistance in their travels and were subject to scrutiny by such organisations as the Legion of Mary for their personal behaviour in Britain. Chapter 3 traces how both Catholic and Protestant organisations attempted to respond to what was viewed as a critical need in Irish society. Middle-class, older women offered advice and chaperoning to lower-class younger 'girls' – mostly from the country – en route to Britain to avoid trafficking (or the 'white slave trade', as it was known). Irish women predominated in the flow of immigrants to Britain, and, while their age and background matched their male contemporaries for the most part, they were often described by charitable workers in childlike terms as being ignorant, naive and foolish. As Ewart's work demonstrates, moral concerns for female emigrants extended beyond the 1950s, but were most intense in the decades covered in this book.[40]

Chapter 4 addresses evidence on the conduct of Irish women in Britain, revisiting the contentious issues of morality and sexual behaviour. As argued throughout the book, the focus on sexual immorality during the period was something that drew particular attention to Irish female migrants in Britain. Travelling to Britain to 'hide the shame' of an unplanned pregnancy was a solution that was sought by countless women, although the evidence base is fragmentary and unreliable. Issues that have been identified as 'hidden histories' have naturally attracted the attention of scholars, particularly those of women's history as part of the recovery of lost lives and stories. However, focusing on what was undoubtedly a minority experience without recognising it as such reinforces negative stereotypes of Irish women. This chapter explores the evidence base for Irish unmarried motherhood in Britain.

Chapter 5 widens the examination of personal behaviour to the more ordinary aspects of women's lived experience in Britain to contextualise the supposed phenomenon of the pregnant Irish immigrant. Irish men and women often married each other, congregating in suburbs with fellow Irish immigrants which allowed for socialising and sharing of their faith. The best evidence we have is related to those of the Catholic faith, and this chapter

39   Clair Wills, *The Best Are Leaving: Emigration and Post-War Irish Culture* (Cambridge: Cambridge University Press: 2015), p. 7.
40   Ewart, 'Caring for Migrants'.

also explores the widespread fears of the Irish in Britain becoming lost to the Church through lapsed attendance. It was argued that this could happen either because of the more secular environment (or, in the most negative discourses, the malign influence of 'pagan' Britain) or because Sunday work opportunities would create a barrier. For the most part, it seems that many emigrants clung to their faith as both an expression of their identity and because of a deep sense of belief, but a new environment also allowed for a new negotiation of faith for some.

Chapters 6 and 7 examine Irish women's employment. The context of work for women in Ireland is explored first in Chapter 6, before examining the available evidence on their working lives in Britain. Morality concerns persisted in newspaper articles about Irish women answering advertisements that could be traps set by unscrupulous gangs of white slavers, demonstrating how difficult it was for some to see women as independent, economic actors rather than potential victims of dangerous foreigners. Analysis of contemporary debates about women's reasons for leaving Ireland reveal a tension between those who recognised women's economic plight and those who identified more personal reasons, and this discord was replicated in other countries. Akenson, for example, has argued that migrants from Sweden and Ireland may have left in the post-Famine era for reasons that were cultural rather than material, or for a complex mixture of economic and non-economic reasons.[41] While I agree, looking specifically at women in twentieth-century Ireland, the economic reasons were paramount, but the overall decision may well have been shaped by cultural factors: the social approbation of married women working; the preference for providing work for men earning a 'family wage';[42] the contraction of traditional forms of income for rural women such as home spinning and the lack of a vibrant or lucrative alternative, particularly the dire conditions for most domestic servants. This is a complex nexus of competing reasons but is still concordant with Akenson's view that the 'truism that people migrate for a better life is merely silly if a better life is defined solely in economic terms'[43] – earning power allowed entry to the 'full adult' world, the opportunity to create a family, gain professional experience and send remittances home *as well as* a better individual quality of life.

41 This is developed in a number of Akenson's publications, most recently in *Ireland, Sweden and the Great European Migration.*
42 For an exposition of women's labour unionism and the arguments made against giving adult working women the same wage as their male peers, see Maria Luddy, 'Working Women, Trade Unionism and Politics in Ireland, 1830–1945', in Fintan Lane and Donal Ó Drisceoil (eds), *Politics and the Irish Working Class, 1830–1945* (Basingstoke: Palgrave Macmillan, 2005), pp. 44–61.
43 Akenson, *Ireland, Sweden and the Great European Migration*, p. 238.

Without access to employment, women remained a dependent burden, permanently inferior in status and power within traditional family structures. In the census, they would be counted as 'relatives assisting' on family farms, a laconic term that hides a wealth of meaning, or simply as unemployed. Women without income or a family to provide a dowry had little opportunities. Thus, as Maria Luddy and Dympna McLoughlin have argued, emigration for Irish women was a way in which to expand economic as well as personal opportunities:

> The possibility of an economically productive life, the fulfilment of personal aspirations, such as control over their own finances, the choice of a marriage partner, or indeed the choice not to marry at all, and the promise of a certain level of independence made emigration an attractive proposition for a large number of women.[44]

Emigration, therefore, was not a rejection by women of traditional family roles but rather the embracing of opportunities for fulfilling these as well as the opportunity for independence, if they wished. As Janet Nolan has argued, this is what motivated women's emigration to the USA and elsewhere for many decades prior to independence: 'The legions of young women leaving rural Ireland in the late nineteenth and early twentieth centuries were discarding their newly subservient and marginal positions, not their traditional expectations'.[45] It is also true that many emigrants left with their family's blessings because it allowed them to contribute to the family economy through remittances. Emigrants were also actively encouraged by family members and even neighbours to facilitate the migration of others: 'If I went home maybe some mother would come to me and ask me if I would bring her daughter over so I'd bring them over and get them a job in the hotel'.[46]

Although a facet of previous work on the Irish in Britain, the diversity of Irish female emigrants' occupations has been less well sketched. Walter has explored the positive stereotype of Irish nurses in Britain, but their employment in other areas, particularly domestic service, was viewed

---

44 Maria Luddy and Dympna McLoughlin, 'Women and Emigration from Ireland from the Seventeenth Century', in Angela Bourke *et al.* (eds), *The Field Day Anthology of Irish Writing*, vol. 5, *Irish Women's Writing and Traditions* (Cork: Cork University Press in association with Field Day, 2002), p. 569.

45 Janet A. Nolan, *Ourselves Alone: Women's Emigration from Ireland, 1885–1920* (Lexington: University Press of Kentucky, 1989), p. 92.

46 Interviewee quoted in Louise Ryan, 'Moving Spaces and Changing Places: Irish Women's Memories of Emigration to Britain in the 1930s', *Journal of Ethnic and Migration Studies*, 29.1 (2003), p. 78.

more problematically. These two dominant areas of employment feature in Chapter 7, as well as the less familiar roles they occupied in the British economy. Statistics derived from travel permit application forms submitted by Irish people in Britain during the Second World War form the basis of some of the new evidence presented.[47] The limited testimony on Irish women's direct participation in the British home front war effort is also explored, an area which has seen little previous research.

Women's economic emigration from the Free State was often framed within a distinctly gendered moral discourse which cast them in a simultaneously suspicious yet vulnerable light. Sharon Lambert concludes from her study of Irish women in Lancashire that there was no perceived social stigma for her respondents who had worked in factories before migrating to mainland Britain. This may indicate differences between the Free State and Northern Ireland, as most of those in her sample with factory experience had worked in Derry.[48] The cultural context of work, womanhood and migration can therefore never be underestimated. Finally, the concluding chapter threads together the insights from *Moving Histories*, arguing that the history of Irish women's emigration is substantively different from that of men's and deserves specific consideration on its own merits.

The theoretical framework adopted throughout this book emphasises the multiple facets of the history of Irish female emigration and the complexities of the discourses that surround it. Emigration was conceived of as a social problem to a far greater extent than as an economic or political one. As Nelson Phillips and Cynthia Hardy argue, 'social reality is produced and made real through discourses, and social interactions cannot be fully understood without reference to the discourses that give them meaning'.[49] In the context of this book, the 'social reality' of female emigrants as problematic, wayward, vulnerable and prone to sin cannot be understood without reference to the sources of public discourse that created this impression. This may be linked to discourses around what Hanne Blank has termed 'erotic virginity', in which 'holiness and sin are bound up' and which saw expression in visual and

---

47 This material is held in the Department of Foreign Affairs collection at the National Archives of Ireland and has been consulted exhaustively by the author between 2009 and 2011 as part of a Postdoctoral Fellowship in the Department of History, Maynooth University funded by the Irish Research Council for the Humanities and Social Sciences (now the Irish Research Council). Special permission was granted to research the collection and all files are dealt with anonymously.

48 Sharon Lambert, *Irish Women in Lancashire, 1922–1960: Their Story* (Lancaster: University of Lancaster, 2001), p. 18.

49 Nelson Phillips and Cynthia Hardy, *Discourse Analysis: Investigating Processes of Social Construction* (Thousand Oaks, Calif.: Sage Publications, 2002), p. 3.

written pornography, the lurid stories and magazines that partly prompted new censorship laws in Ireland in the 1920s.[50] However, as Fitzpatrick has warned, 'Since politicians and writers made it their business to "articulate" popular mentality, historians have been unduly influenced, for want of direct evidence, by these often biased or twisted "insights".[51] Thus, 'discourse analysis is both a perspective and a method' utilised within this book to interrogate different perspectives on emigrants, particularly women, and includes voices of the women themselves where possible.[52]

Migration is essentially a palimpsest of stories: life narratives that encapsulate successes and failures, change and continuity, challenges and opportunities. In Devlin Trew's analysis, thinking of migration through individual stories 'may also be helpful in getting beyond the economic discourse of migration to discover an alternative set of values, priorities and motivating factors'.[53] Importantly, *Moving Histories* also combines comparison of public discourses of both the Church of Ireland and the Catholic Church and state with private discourses of female emigrants. This approach is novel: most existing work focuses on discrete analyses of either public or private discourses. Women's personal recollections provide a fertile source to access a nuanced history of modern migration. Whilst methodological problems arise in terms of what is remembered and what is told, such collections are one of the only ways in which we can hear and incorporate the private voices of migrants.[54] Given the age at which many migrants undertook their journeys (more on this in the next chapter), oral histories offer insights from the period within the 'reminiscence bump', defined as 'a period of high memory encoding' that is 'said to occur between the ages of ten and thirty years'.[55] They can potentially offer lucid and reliable insights into the process of emigration from Ireland.

Similarly, when evaluating the use and bias of sources, Brian Conway has argued that scholars should exercise caution in examining 'the role of the media in perpetuating a dominant ideology or set of ideologies' because

---

50 Hanne Blank, *Virgin: The Untouched History* (New York: Bloomsbury, 2007), p. 196.
51 David Fitzpatrick, '"That Beloved Country That No Place Else Resembles": Connotations of Irishness in Irish-Australian Letters, 1841–1915', *Irish Historical Studies*, 27.108 (1991), pp. 324–351.
52 Phillips and Hardy, *Discourse Analysis*, p. 59.
53 Devlin Trew, *Leaving the North*, p. 15.
54 See Elizabeth Roberts, *A Woman's Place: An Oral History of Working Women, 1890–1940* (Oxford: Basil Blackwell, 1985) and Kevin Kearns, *Dublin's Lost Heroines: Mammies and Grannies in a Vanished City* (Dublin: Gill & Macmillan, 2004).
55 Devlin Trew, *Leaving the North*, p. 24. A further point on this is that recall is likely to be enhanced if duration in a location is five years or more, or if other important life cycle events occur concurrently, such as marriage, or when the relocation occurs with other relatives (ibid., p. 25).

'positing the media as a hegemonic force, has come under criticism for the lack of attention it pays to the agency of media audiences or consumers'.[56] An examination of Irish newspaper commentary on emigration during the period demonstrates that such commentary did *not* hold sway over audiences – emigration continued despite the voluminous printed warnings. Newspapers and public commentary are nevertheless interesting to study because they are indicative of the culture within which Irish people migrated. They are also a vital source of information on some of the emigrant welfare organisations discussed in the book.

While attempting to create a multi-method history, I also acknowledge the limitations and biases inherent in writing any history. As June Purvis has recognised, although feminist historians attempt to create narratives that illuminate women's lives in the past, they may in the process forget other groups who have been marginalised due to the limitations of both source materials and questions.[57] This book is no different. We have, as yet, only anecdotal evidence of Irish lesbians who migrated to Britain in this period (unlike the more modern period studied by Gray), and while sexuality is addressed in this study as an issue of some concern, the focus, following that of contemporary debates, is on heterosexuality. No public discourse existed on homosexuality in the Irish diaspora for the period under study, although undoubtedly there were women (and men) whose migration was prompted by feeling themselves to be outside the heteronormative framework of Irish society. It is a challenging topic in terms of source material, but it is hoped that future scholars will be able to include these narratives so that a fuller picture can emerge of motivations for migration.

Women's predominance at certain periods and the fact that many emigrated whilst single, unlike most other European female emigrants, drew much commentary and has been mentioned by many historians as a particularity of Irish demography. So why hasn't this book already been written? General histories of the period, while recognising the impact of emigration in some respects, have tended to focus on the internal political developments of the Free State, emigrants seemingly out of sight, out of mind. *Moving Histories* presents the case for the specific study of migration as impacting on Irish women's lives in the twentieth century and, it is argued, is an important consideration for charting social and demographic change in the modern period.

56 Brian Conway, 'Who Do We Think We Are? Immigration and the Discursive Construction on National Identity in an Irish Daily Mainstream Newspaper, 1996–2004', *Translocations*, 1.1 (2006), p. 82.

57 June Purvis, 'Doing Feminist Women's History: Researching the Lives of Women in the Suffragette Movement in Edwardian England', in June Purvis (ed.), *Women's History: Britain, 1850–1945* (London: Routledge, 2000), pp. 166–189.

Women had a particular experience of migration from Ireland in the decades under examination here; *Moving Histories* explores these lives, 'interpreting the weight given to loss and tragedy in narratives of emigration' in a specifically gendered way.[58]

---

58 Wills, *The Best Are Leaving*, p. 3.

1

Charting and Understanding
Irish Women's Emigration
in the Twentieth Century

S easonal, peripatetic and permanent migrations have been made by Irish people to all parts of Britain for centuries.[1] Women have always been part of the flow. This chapter will explore the background to twentieth-century female emigration to Britain, outlining the statistical evidence and analysing important geographical shifts in Irish migration. This highlights the extent and profile of female emigration. Finally, Irish women's experiences are examined in the context of established theoretical models which pose the question: how useful are such concepts in furthering our understanding of female migration?

Women's experiences of emigration in the nineteenth century have been better sketched than those of their counterparts in the twentieth. The historiography has focused on their compulsory migrations as paupers and convicted criminals, their independent migration to seek new opportunities, and their connectedness to families at home, often being the ones to send tickets and money to relatives in Ireland. Thus, emigration from Ireland was a long-established demographic feature of Irish life, yet it became an overtly political and moral problem when the Free State was founded in December 1922. Emigration, thought by many to be a colonial anomaly, was not eradicated upon independence. In fact, emigration increased, particularly, and most gallingly, to Britain, the former 'colonial oppressor'. Emigration was a factor that marked the Free State, but for the wrong reasons in the eyes of its leaders.

---

1 John Archer Jackson asserts that Irish settlements in Britain resulted from trading links, with Bristol having a settlement before 1200, but evidence of Irish missionaries in Scotland exists from the sixth century. See John Archer Jackson, *The Irish in Britain* (London: Routledge & Kegan Paul, 1963), pp. 6–7.

Statistical Evidence on Irish Women's Emigration

> Everything we know about the history of Irish women in the diaspora
> revolves around one cultural set of facts. One-half of the great Irish
> diaspora was female.[2]

In 1920, Ireland was in a unique position in the world, not because it had
been split into northern and southern territories, but because nearly half
(43 per cent) of the population of the Free State resided in other countries.
The 1926 Census of Population noted that in 1920–21 there were 1,037,234
Irish-born persons living in the USA, 367,747 living in England and Wales,
159,020 in Scotland, 105,033 in Australia, 93,301 in Canada, 34,419 in New
Zealand, 12,289 in the Union of South Africa and 8,414 in India, giving a
total of 1,817,457 persons born in Ireland or no less than 43 per cent of the
population of Ireland.[3] This was twice the proportion of Norway, second in
terms of global population scattering.[4] These kinds of exceptional facts came
to haunt politicians, eager to project a public image of Ireland as prosperous
and thriving in its independence. The high rates of Irish living abroad had
diminished from a peak in 1881 of 60 per cent of the population living in
Ireland to a more moderate figure in 1931 of 30 per cent. This was still
considered high by the Commission on Emigration and Other Population
Problems, who felt the figures threw 'into sharp relief the extent of the
emigration problem'.[5] Emigrants of Irish birth living in Great Britain came to
make up an increasingly large share of the ex-pat community: by 1951, it was
estimated that 722,000 Irish people were resident.[6] The population of Ireland
in 1951 was 2,960,593, making this the equivalent of almost one-quarter. The
fact that so many women were part of Ireland's global population dispersal
evoked lamentations, ire and at times sheer panic. The surplus of women in
relation to men in the nineteenth century was replaced by a deficit, as Table
1.1 shows. The emotional hand wringing, however, tempered fairly quickly

---

2 Akenson, *The Irish Diaspora*, p. 159.
3 Department of Industry and Commerce, *Census of Population, 1926*, vol. 1 (Stationery
   Office: Dublin, 1928), p. 8.
4 Although Coleman notes that other countries on the north-western fringes of Europe
   also had high emigration rates, Ireland's rates have been notable and exceptional over
   the last two centuries. See D.A. Coleman, 'Demography and Migration', in A.F. Heath,
   R. Breen and Christopher T. Whelan, *Ireland North and South: Perspectives from Social
   Science* (Oxford: Oxford University Press, 1999), p. 78.
5 Commission on Emigration and Other Population Problems, *Majority Report*, p. 121.
6 Ibid. Note that this figure includes England, Scotland and Wales. The Commission's
   report categorises England and Wales together, but Scotland separately. The number
   of Irish-born persons living in England and Wales alone was estimated to be 639,000 in
   1951. See *Majority Report*, Table 95.

Table 1.1   Population of Ireland, 1901–1951 (26 counties)

Year	Total population	Males	Females	Females per 100 males
1901	3,221,823	1,610,085	1,611,738	100
1911	3,139,688	1,589,509	1,550,179	97
1926	2,971,992	1,506,889	1,465,103	97
1936	2,968,420	1,520,454	1,447,966	95
1946	2,955,107	1,494,877	1,460,230	98
1951	2,960,593	1,506,597	1,453,996	96

Source: Data taken from Central Statistics Office, Population of Ireland 1841–2011 http://census.ie/in-history/population-of-ireland-1841–2006/.

into shoulder shrugging as successive governments failed to initiate policies that would make staying the more viable option.

The informal arrangements in existence before the common travel area[7] between Ireland and Britain after independence meant that migration to these parts could not be quantified in the same way as migration to other destinations. Various evaluations of emigration from Ireland based on different statistical models have been constructed.[8] The lack of clear data was a vexatious issue at the time, as well as being an irritant to historians. What is certain, however, is that Irish women, particularly since the turn of the twentieth century, constituted a significant and visible cohort within the emigration flow. In the 1930s, this was highlighted by statisticians who observed that there had been 'since the beginning of the century [...] a marked excess of females' in 'normal' migration. According to the Department of Industry and Commerce, this, coupled with 'the persistent male excess in "natural increase", has resulted in the exceptionally low proportion of females in the population of this country'.[9] The implication was that women were slowly but surely vanishing.

7   The common travel area includes Ireland, the United Kingdom, the Isle of Man, Jersey and Guernsey. Arrangements were not put down in legislation until the Treaty of Amsterdam in 1997. See Elizabeth Meehan, 'Free Movement between Ireland and the UK: From the "Common Travel Area" to The Common Travel Area', Studies in Public Policy, 4 (2000), pp. 1–112.
8   Most methods used in statistical analyses of emigration rely on Census data or on data derived from shipping companies. It was not possible to organise a census in 1921, thus there was a gap in this type of data being collected in Ireland between 1911 and 1926.
9   Department of Industry and Commerce, Census of Population, 1936, vol. 1 (Stationery Office: Dublin, 1938), p. 15.

Table 1.2   Net emigration by province, 1926–1936 (26 counties)

	Males	Females	Persons
Dublin County Borough, Dun Laoghaire Borough and remainder of County Dublin	12,450*	21,914*	34,364*
Rest of Leinster	15,832	23,721	39,553
Munster	34,861	43,855	78,716
Connacht	22,767	32,613	55,380
Ulster (part of)	13,200	16,831	30,031
Saorstát Éireann (Irish Free State)	74,210	95,106	169,316

* Net immigration.
Source: Department of Industry and Commerce, *Census of Population 1936*, vol. 1 (Dublin: Stationery Office, 1936), Table N (p. 19).

Census data reveals a consistent trend of women migrating to the Leinster region, particularly the greater Dublin area, from other parts of the country. Table 1.2 reveals that women were migrating to the Dublin area at a rate of nearly two to one in comparison with men and had higher rates of emigration from every province in Ireland in the 1930s.

The Commission on Emigration and Other Population Problems (1948–54), attempted to gather as much demographic information as possible about Ireland in the preceding decades.[10] They were hampered by the fact that there was no census taken in 1921 at the state's inception owing to the disturbances of the War of Independence, and the upturn in migration to Britain meant less documentary evidence. Official measures to count such persons were not adopted again until the Second World War, when security concerns enforced official identification, and hence counting, of travellers and migrants. Such measures were abandoned, however, within a few years of the conflict's end and the relaxed travel arrangements were resumed. The failure to keep adequate records of those emigrating is a loss and many historians, including Akenson, Delaney and Jackson advise caution when attempting to construct a quantitative analysis of Irish emigration given the weak nature of the data and the serious limitations of the existing sources.

The lack of concrete numbers of emigrants and their destinations was lamented by contemporary commentators. T.P. French, of the Catholic Young Men's Society, decried the insufficient data, asking, if accurate rates of migration were unknown, how could anything be done to stop it?

---

10 The political background to the establishment of the Commission is dealt with in the next chapter.

Furthermore, he contrasted the absence of regulation of persons to the plethora of documentation kept on food exports:

> according to the strict export regulations it is possible, even years afterwards, to identify the very cow that gave the milk that made the butter which was sold on the Manchester market on a given date. How many young Irish men and women leave here annually for the neighbouring countries? Where do they go? What do they work at? **We don't know**, and that fact alone betrays our own and our Government's interest. [...] while we are so exact regarding our produce, the real ambassadors of our nationality, our men and women, can go where, when and how they wish.[11]

Akenson speculated that this lack of record keeping may have been deliberate: 'One wonders if [...] the details of the heavy outflow to Britain were something that the authorities in the newly-independent twenty-six counties did not want to know'.[12] This is, of course, debatable. It is not known if a conscious decision was taken not to collect figures, or whether these activities became lost in the chaos of the Civil War and its aftermath. It is, however, interesting to speculate whether the unreliable, and at times unobtainable, data on emigration was a welcome reprieve for government ministers in the 'firing line' on questions about high emigration rates. As outlined in the next chapter, ministers often used the phrase 'such information is not available' to sidestep questions.

In the period 1911 to 1926, it is estimated that 405,029 people, or 8.8 per 1,000 persons, left Ireland.[13] Between 1926 and 1936, this lessened to 5.6 per 1,000 persons, or a total of 166,751. Rates from this period rose rapidly, to 187,111 persons leaving the state between 1936 and 1946 – a rate of 6.3 per 1,000. In the 1950s, a total of 119,568 people left Ireland, a rate of 8.2 per 1,000 persons in the population.[14] The war years thus saw a diminution in emigration rates that was quick to rise once the conflict ended. In contrast to the lack of information and the negative attitudes towards empire migration in the South, more accurate data is available for Northern Ireland. Between 1922 and 1937 over 94,000 people left Northern

---

11 *Irish Catholic*, 28 October 1937, p. 5. Emphasis in original.
12 Akenson, *The Irish Diaspora*, p. 57.
13 It must be noted that this period saw the removal of much of the British administration and military staff from the country as well as many Protestants, thus the figure does not represent solely Irish Catholic emigrants who made up the flow in subsequent periods. For more on this, see particularly Delaney, *Demography, State and Society*, pp. 69–83.
14 All data derived from W.E. Vaughan and A.J. Fitzpatrick, *Irish Historical Statistics: Population 1821 –1971* (Dublin: Royal Irish Academy, 1978), Table 56 (p. 266).

Table 1.3 Net emigration from Ireland, 1911–1951
(26 counties)

Intercensal period	Total persons	Males	Females	Number of females emigrating per 1,000 males
Average annual numbers				
1911–26	27,002	13,934	13,068	938
1926–36	16,675	7,255	9,420	1,298
1936–46	18,711	11,258	7,453	662
1946–51	24,384	10,309	14,075	1,365
Annual rate of emigration per 1,000 average population				
1911–26	8.8	9.0	8.7	
1926–36	5.6	4.8	6.5	
1936–46	6.3	7.5	5.1	
1946–51	8.3	6.9	9.7	

Source: *Report of the Commission on Emigration and Other Population Problems*, Table 86 (p. 111).

Ireland, the majority (50 per cent) going to Canada, where Prime Minister Craig had toured with his family in 1926.[15] Similar to trends in the South, Britain was to become the primary destination for Northern Irish migrants from the 1930s onwards.[16] Table 1.3 shows estimated emigration, from Census records, summarising the data by gender in both annual estimates and total numbers of emigrants in the intercensal periods.

As Table 1.3 reveals, female emigrants outnumbered males in both the 1926–36 and the 1946–51 periods.[17] If the rates across the period are averaged, the male emigration rate was 7.05 per 1,000, and the female emigration rate was slightly higher, at 7.5 per 1,000. The trend of high emigration of women from the Free State contrasts with the experience of women in Northern Ireland, where male migrants generally outnumbered females. Jackson suggests that this difference 'is largely accounted for by the fact that there are greater opportunities for female labour in Northern Ireland',[18]

15 Devlin Trew, *Leaving the North*, p. 39.
16 Ibid., p. 40.
17 It is necessary to note that these statistics, not being based on any official travel documentation for the most part, will have failed to capture many emigrants.
18 Jackson, *The Irish in Britain*, p. 18.

which again grounds emigration in economic necessity, an argument made strongly in Chapter 6.

The first Dáil issued a decree against emigration, attempting to impose restrictions on all citizens after 24 July 1920 'with the written sanction of the Government of the Republic' and requiring people to apply for permits.[19] The proclamation targeted IRA members, but also mentioned 'other citizens', hence the decree applied to everyone. The Dáil had been paying attention to emigration for some time at this point. On 29 June 1920, the report of the Department of Home Affairs was read by its Acting Secretary, who also presented statistics on emigration from Ireland for the period 12 January to 31 May 1920. According to this report, 3,836 people had emigrated, this being an increase of 2,963 when compared with the corresponding period of 1919. Interestingly, when Liam De Roiste (Cork City) moved as a further amendment that 'the Decree be not enforced pending the formulation of a scheme for providing employment in Ireland for intending emigrants', it was lost by 23 votes to 16.[20] This was a familiar pattern for the rest of the twentieth century – migrants were condemned for leaving but little was done to help them stay. It is interesting to also note that these views were shared by some of the local political bodies. According to the Minutes of the Municipal Council of the City of Dublin of May 1920, a letter from the Town Clerk of Cork proposed a resolution condemning emigration, 'excepting in those cases where idleness has long prevailed, and there is no absolute certainty of work; and further, that Booking Agents be prohibited carrying out their dastardly work of encouraging emigration for paltry commission'.[21] Furthermore, Cormac Ó Gráda has attributed this attitude to Patrick Pearse in 1916, who said the emigrant was 'a traitor to the Irish state, and, if he knew but all, a fool into the bargain'.[22] The IRA also adopted this attitude to the emigration of its members, arguing that those who emigrated were 'playing the enemy's game' by leaving the country in the early years of independence.[23] However, high unemployment rates and lack of opportunities meant that the policy of condemning emigration had to be abandoned in 1925, with the proviso that members had to join the IRA's Foreign Reserve.

19 Dáil proclamation available at the National Library of Ireland (Dublin: Department of Home Affairs, Dáil Eireann, 291920): http://catalogue.nli.ie/Record/vtls000266113.

20 Dáil Éireann debate, 6 August 1920: https://www.oireachtas.ie/en/debates/debate/dail/1920-08-06/.

21 The resolution originally came from Cove [sic] Urban District Council; Minute 436, May 1920.

22 Cormac Ó Gráda, A Rocky Road: The Irish Economy Since the 1920s (Manchester: Manchester University Press, 1997), p. 212.

23 Brian Hanley, The IRA, 1926–1936 (Dublin: Four Courts Press, 2002), p. 161 and a wider discussion in chap. 9.

While this permit system was not enforced – by the first Dáil or any other government session in the Free State period – the idea of emigration as desertion lingered in political rhetoric. For example, traces of this attitude are evident in de Valera's famous radio broadcast on St Patrick's Day, 1943:

> That Ireland which we dreamed of would be the home of a people who were *satisfied with frugal comfort* and devoted their leisure to things of the spirit – a land whose countryside would be bright with cosy homesteads, whose fields and villages would be joyous with the sounds of industry, with the romping of sturdy children, the contests of athletic youths and the laughter of comely maidens, whose firesides would be the home of a people living the life that God desires that man should live.[24]

Thus, de Valera's ideals of appropriate standards of living are intimately connected with the dream of an Irish nationalist sensibility that is in direct contrast with the emergent materialism of his day. Indeed, such comments are consistent with Daly's analysis that 'an Irish agenda for progress often entailed a backward glance'.[25] This attitude referenced days of higher rural population, a measure of success wholly inconsistent with the pace of industrialisation throughout the world in the twentieth century and having no regard for the poor quality of life experienced by both urban and rural dwellers. The inference is that happiness would come from a simplistic style of living, and emigration could therefore be lessened if expectations matched the 'frugal comforts' standard. There is a wilful denial in this rhetoric of the importance of emigrant remittances for sustaining many rural homesteads.[26]

Attitudes that framed emigration as somehow anti-nationalist or unpatriotic were not confined to politicians. The theme was taken up by the *Irish Independent* in 1923 when the editor commented that 'it is the duty of every patriot citizen not only to discourage emigration, but to remove the causes which give rise to it'.[27] The fact that migrants were, as Delaney

---

24 Maurice Moynihan (ed.), *Speeches and Statements by Eamon de Valera, 1917–73* (Dublin: Gill & Macmillan, 1980), p. 466. My emphasis. The idea of 'frugal living' had been used by Pope Leo XIII in *Rerum Novarum* in 1891.

25 Mary E. Daly, 'The Economic Ideals of Irish Nationalism: Frugal Comfort or Lavish Austerity?', *Eire–Ireland*, 29.4 (1994), p. 82. Gearóid Ó Crualaoich has argued also that de Valera's 'folk ideology' denied the extent to which Ireland was now a fully monetised country. See Ó Crualaoich, 'The Primacy of Form: A "Folk Ideology" in de Valera's Politics', in John P. O'Carroll and John A. Murphy *De Valera and His Times* (Cork: Cork University Press, 1983), pp. 50–51.

26 There is evidence to demonstrate that remittances sent through postal orders were being tracked by the government.

27 *Irish Independent*, 19 April 1923.

has pointed out, simply 'responding to a changing set of values' was not recognised or else blindly condemned by many.[28] The *Irish Times* offered a more realistic appraisal when it commented that if people 'cannot find work at home, mere sentiment will not keep them here'.[29] The irrational, or hyperbolic, however, was never far away. The spectre of 'race suicide' through emigration (and not contraception as in other countries at this time) loomed large. There was also a somewhat paradoxical strand within discourses on emigration that constructed emigrants as the 'best' of the nation, rather than those who were skulking from the country for their own selfish aims. In 1928, the *Irish Catholic* reported what they termed 'a striking sermon' by Rev. Fr Ignatius, CP, in which he decried the 'evil' of emigration and asked plaintively: 'Are we so unsympathetic in Catholic Ireland as to allow the race to deteriorate by emigration? If so, we will soon have nobody in the country but cripples and imbeciles. The strongest, the bravest and the best of our people are leaving the country'.[30] Thus the trope of 'race suicide' was referred to in a somewhat 'diluted' (although nonetheless discriminatory) form. This type of commentary generally blamed the emigrants themselves for their abandonment of the country rather than casting an eye on their circumstances and restricted set of choices.

Migrations to Britain were often meant to be temporary, such as in the case of seasonal agricultural workers. Their fluid movements, however, were not adequately captured by official statistics. An attempt was made to understand the scale and profile of seasonal migrants through the Inter-Departmental Committee on Seasonal Migration to Great Britain, 1937–38.[31] The Committee obtained a detailed statement from the Department of Agriculture of the numbers and types of persons who left the congested districts of Mayo, Galway, Roscommon, Sligo and Leitrim, West Donegal and Clare. According to this review, 9,783 persons migrated from those areas for seasonal agricultural work in 1937. Of these an estimated 1,787 migrated for potato lifting and 7,996 for general agricultural work; approximately 9,500 went to Britain to do this.[32] However, it was admitted by the authors that, given the ease of travel, and the fact that migrants may not have been honest when reporting whether they were migrating or holidaying, the figures must be viewed cautiously.

In terms of the age-distribution of Irish emigrants: historically, most migrants were aged between twenty and twenty-five; between 1852 and 1921,

---

28 Enda Delaney, *The Irish in Post-War Britain* (Oxford: Oxford University Press, 2007), p. 23.
29 *Irish Times*, 9 May 1923.
30 *Irish Catholic*, 25 August 1928.
31 The Committee examined internal migration as well as migration to Great Britain.
32 *Report of the Inter-Departmental Committee on Seasonal Migration to Great Britain, 1937–1938* (Dublin: Stationery Office, 1938), para. 21 (p. 31).

Table 1.4   Age and gender of migrants from
the Irish Free State, 1924–1939

Gender	Under 15 years	15–19 years	20–24 years	25–29 years	30 years and over	All ages
Male	9%	17%	35%	20%	19%	100%
Female	16%	28%	27%	13%	16%	100%

Source: Report of the Commission on Emigration and Other Population Problems, p. 117 n. 1.

over 40 per cent of emigrants from Ireland were in this age group.[33] The Commission on Emigration and Other Population Problems again provides the most comprehensive statistics, as can be seen in Table 1.4: girls under the age of fifteen and teenaged girls were emigrating in higher numbers than boys of the same age. Men and women over thirty emigrated in more equal numbers. However, the lack of detail presented in this data does not allow for a full analysis. Did men and women at forty or fifty differ in their migration behaviour from the way they did at thirty? Could differences have coincided with rates of marriages or family formation? Unfortunately, the lack of specifics leaves these as questions, but men's continued employment in seasonal, temporary and migratory work throughout the 1920s to the 1940s suggests they would perhaps have migrated at older ages than women. The substantial proportion of younger girls emigrating in comparison with boys is perhaps a contributory factor to the way in which they were discussed as impressionable and suggestible. While this may be true to a certain extent, many boys and girls at this time left school at either twelve or fourteen years of age to work, and thus their status as financially contributing family members is juxtaposed with the infantile depiction of naive young girls, a point to be discussed in further chapters.

As mentioned previously, from 1940 up to 1952, a system of travel permits for Irish migrants to Britain was established.[34] This allowed for more detailed information to be gathered on occupation, origins and destinations. Table 1.5 shows the numbers of new travel permits, identity cards and

33 Jackson, *The Irish in Britain*, p. 19.
34 The statistical data represents travel to Great Britain, including England, Wales and Scotland. The legislation adopted to create the travel restrictions will be discussed in greater detail in Chapter 2. Many evaded the official travel permit system and were caught without correct documentation. See Eunan O'Halpin, *Spying on Ireland: British Intelligence and Irish Neutrality During the Second World War* (Oxford: Oxford University Press, 2008), p. 122.

Table 1.5   Numbers of new travel permits, identity cards
and passports issued from the 26 counties, 1940–1951

| Year | To Great Britain and the Six Counties | | | Overseas | | | |
	Males	Females	Totals	Males	Females	Totals	Overall Totals
1940	17,080	8,884	25,964	No passports issued			25,964
1941	31,860	3,272	35,132	during war years			35,132
1942	37,263	14,448	51,711				51,711
1943	29,321	19,003	48,324				48,324
1944	7,723	5,890	13,613				13,613
1945	13,185	10,609	23,794				23,794
1946	10,547	18,956	29,503	282	249	531	30,034
1947	10,576	17,604	28,180	1,935	1,123	3,058	31,238
1948	15,804	14,486	30,290	5,918	3,867	9,785	40,075
1949	8,522	9,694	18,216	3,977	3,298	7,275	25,491
1950	6,326	6,442	12,768	2,188	2,400	4,588	17,356
1951	8,958	7,182	16,140	1,955	2,151	4,106	20,246

Figures in the first three columns relate to Great Britain only; no travel permits were needed for the Six Counties from 1947 onwards.
Source: Report of the Commission on Emigration and Other Population Problems, Table 96 (p. 128).

passports issued in the period 1940 to 1951. Male and female applicants for new travel documents outnumbered each other in different years according to the exigencies of the war in Britain and the Emergency in Ireland. In the years 1940–44, and in 1951, male applicants outnumbered females, but between 1946 and 1950, females outnumbered males. This was due to the lifting of work regulations for women in 1946 which led to the abandonment of the permit system for them. Men's labour continued to be regulated in Ireland and Britain, hence the permit system lasted longer. As with other statistics, however, the data is flawed, a fact noted by the Commission on Emigration and Other Population Problems:

The statistics refer to the total of new travel permits, identity cards or passports as the case may be and do not include renewals. There was, however, a certain amount of duplication. The same individual could have obtained a travel permit in one period, an identity card in another period, and finally a passport if proposing to travel outside the United Kingdom and would, accordingly, have been counted three times.[35]

Thus, the data fails to capture those who reapplied. Furthermore, the issuing of a travel permit did not equate with its use, thus, potentially, there were some who applied but never went. Despite these flaws, the data is useful in examining trends in migration to Britain during these years and the travel permit information emanating from applications and renewals made in Britain is the only data that supplies an accurate and detailed profile of Irish emigrants during the war.[36]

The applications for return journeys also reveal gendered trends in travel. Of the 23,040 travel permit applications made in Britain between 1940 and 1942, 15,252 (66.2 per cent) were from women, with the remaining 7,788 (33.8 per cent) from men. The overwhelming picture that emerges from these files is of a single, professional, urban-based young woman. A total of 10,734 stated they were single; the majority were engaged in nursing and based in London. While this may be influenced by those who had the means and time to travel, the information derived from travel permit applications confirms that Ireland had lost thousands of young women in the post-independence period, a fact not lost on politicians who lamented the dearth of future mothers.

From the USA to Britain:
Plus ça Change or a Momentous Difference?

Despite regular migration (both permanent and temporary) to Britain, the USA remained the favoured option for many until the post-independence era. According to Miller, from the early 1700s to the 1920s, at least 7 million people left Ireland for North America.[37] Their propensity for settling in urban locations is clear: by 1900, 'New York was second only to Dublin in the number of Irish residents'.[38] While men had predominated as migrants to the USA in the pre-Famine period, after 1851, women and men emigrated

---

35 Commission on Emigration and Other Population Problems, *Majority Report*, note (a) on Table 96 (p. 126).

36 The author's IRC postdoctoral research of Irish migrants' applications for travel permits to Britain is the only study of applications of this kind owing to the limitations currently placed on the records because of data protection issues.

37 Kerby A. Miller, *Ireland and Irish America: Culture, Class and Transatlantic Migration* (Dublin: Field Day, 2008), p. 7.

38 Thomas Bartlett, *Ireland: A History* (Cambridge: Cambridge University Press, 2010), p. 292.

in roughly equal numbers, and 'by the end of the nineteenth century, females outnumbered males in the Irish emigrant stream, reflecting the demand for domestic servants in the United States'.[39] The dramatic shift in the destination of Irish emigrants was stark: up to the 1920s, 84 per cent of emigrants from the Free State went to the USA; by the 1930s, 94 per cent went to the UK.[40]

The continued flow of emigrants from Ireland to Britain was due to a combination of factors. The limited employment opportunities available in the fledgling Free State and the difficult economic landscape of the 1930s limited opportunities for jobs at home. Importantly, this included the drastically altered economic opportunities for emigrants to the USA due to the Great Depression, precipitated by the 1929 Wall Street Crash. However, immigration restrictions were introduced by the US government in the 1920s, before the economic difficulties of the Depression, and were based on the principle of numerical limitation. Introduced first in an emergency act of 1921 the number of persons of any nationality annually entering the USA was limited to 3 per cent of that national group recorded as resident in the 1910 Census.

At that time, the United Kingdom of Great Britain and Ireland, treated as a single unit, was given an annual quota of 77,342. In May of 1924, the Immigration Act (the Johnson–Reed Act) reduced the quota from 3 per cent to 2 per cent, based on populations in the Census of 1890, and gave a separate annual quota of 28,567 to the Irish Free State, stipulating that immigration from all countries must take place uniformly over the whole year, and not more than 10 per cent of the annual quota would be admitted in any one month. These restrictions must be seen in context: the 1924 Act completely banned immigration from Asia, thus Irish migrants were still capitalising on ethnic privilege, despite being curtailed in comparison with the nineteenth century. In 1929, the quota for the Irish Free State was further reduced to 17,853. A year later, additional restrictions meant immigrants had to provide evidence of sufficient funds to ensure they did not become a charge on the state. This was the fall-out from the Wall Street Crash and, naturally, it made the USA a less attractive destination for emigrants from this point.[41] The 'Hungry Thirties' meant the era of penniless emigrants seeking their fortunes in America was over for the time being and despite economic recovery America never regained its primacy as a destination country for Irish emigrants.

39 Delaney, *Demography, State and Society*, p. 27.
40 Louise Ryan, 'Sexualising Emigration: Discourses of Irish Female Emigration in the 1930s', *Women's Studies International Forum*, 25.1 (2002), p. 52.
41 See Commission on Emigration and Other Population Problems, *Majority Report*, Appendix 5 for a comprehensive account of the immigration restrictions and procedures to America.

Both the economic conditions and the immigration restrictions imposed by America meant that Britain became a more practicable destination for those seeking a better life, from seasonal workers to professionals. Britain also had some additional advantages over other destinations: it was relatively close; there were inexpensive, established travel routes; generally, no documentation or proof of economic status was required;[42] and, probably of most importance, emigration to Britain did not mean having to plan a permanent migration. As Ewart has phrased it, the 'psychic costs of migration from Ireland to Britain were low'.[43] Although permanent residence was often the *result* of migration to Britain, psychologically, the option to go 'home', at some point, meant there was a potential way out if plans went awry. Indeed, the idea of return was always a potent myth.

The destination of most migrants in this period, coupled with the high rates of emigrant women, created a discourse that was both more moralistic and fatalistic than that of previous periods. Concerns expressed over emigration in the 1920s were overt expressions of a sense of unease about the place of Irish immigrant identity in contrast with notions of British identity. Irish and British identities were variously posited in the two countries both as extremely different and broadly similar. For example, this writer to the *Church of Ireland Gazette* in 1922 felt that an 'Irishman going to live in England, or an Englishman coming to live in Ireland does not feel that he is going to a foreign country'.[44] Yet it appears the prevailing nationalist agenda in Ireland favoured a discourse of cultural difference and this had historical roots. As Bhavsar and Bhugra's work on the mental health of Irish immigrants in the nineteenth century has shown, the poorer classes of Irish immigrants in Britain were often cast as degenerate and subnormal, being 'viewed by some as fundamentally different from their English hosts' due to their perceived criminality, workplace tensions and sporadic rioting in major towns and cities.[45]

In contrast, Irish political and Catholic Church leaders often exhorted the Irish public to beware the nefarious influences of modern British culture, and proffered Irish women as the ultimate model of Christian virtue and decorum, a trope that plays into the idea of 'the best' as the ones who were leaving. The Catholic clergy in Britain also subscribed to this view at times,

---

42 Travel documentation was not ordinarily required and was introduced during the Second World War as a security measure. Travel documentation was used in the period 1939–51 and regulated men and women in different ways.

43 Ewart, 'Caring for Migrants', p. 3.

44 Letter from Dudley Fletcher, Coolbanagher Rectory, Portarlington, *Church of Ireland Gazette*, 20 January 1922, p. 41.

45 Vishal Bhavsar and Dinesh Bhugra, 'Bethlem's Irish: Migration and Distress in Nineteenth-Century London', *History of Psychiatry*, 20.2 (2009), p. 185.

with the Archbishop of Liverpool, Dr Downey, for example, referring to 'birds of prey ready to pounce on young, unprotected girls' whereas 'boys on the whole do well enough abroad'. In Dr Downey's opinion, 'girls must be protected from themselves'.[46] This infantilising, gendered depiction of male and female Irish emigrants is typical not just of the *Irish Catholic* publication in which it is quoted but also of the era. Similar sentiments could be found in the national press. Louise Ryan has come to a similar conclusion in her work on Irish newspapers, suggesting that high moral standards for women were not expected to be matched by men.[47]

Where commentaries were made relating to male migrants, their tone is rather one of concern and pity when referring to their lack of success at getting jobs or else it is complementary or non-judgemental, as Dr Downey's remarks above illustrate. Warnings were given to men not to emigrate when jobs were perceived to be scarce. But men were not warned about the potential immorality of their workplaces or the dangers of the dance hall. This reveals the strict gendered identities and relations that were idealised at the beginning of the Free State, which identified men with the public sphere and women with the private, and thus moral, sphere continued in debates on migrants.[48] Under these strictures, even when women left Ireland they were still discursively conceptualised as embodying the ideals of the new nation.

The debate on Irish female emigration also seemed to focus on the most negative or most exceptional accounts of their lives in Britain – both hypothetical and real. This served to conjure a rather skewed image of what female emigration was in practice. Accounts from Irish female migrants reveal a picture of immigrant life as more focused on a new negotiation of identity, religion and cultural practices, in contrast to the frenzied, 'Dionysic' abandonment of faith and morals in pursuit of pleasure and amusement often depicted by the press and the Catholic hierarchy. Nor do the personal narratives in oral history collections reveal that Irish girls were easily manipulated and gullible when in Britain. While there *are* recorded cases of women who engaged in 'immoral' behaviour, namely sexual relations outside marriage, such stories are not representative of the 'norm' of female migrant experience, a fact not conveyed in most of the public statements of the time. Why were reports on female migrants framed in this way? The following chapters will explore this in greater detail, but it seems that the female emigrant, by being an active agent, challenged notions of

46 *Irish Catholic*, 15 August 1936.

47 Louise Ryan, *Gender, Identity and the Irish Press, 1922–1937: Embodying the Nation* (Lewiston, NY: Edwin Mellen Press, 2002), p. 125.

48 For more on the public/private debate in relation to women, see Maryann Valiulis, 'Power, Gender and Identity in the Irish Free State', *Journal of Women's History*, 6.4/7.1 (1995), p. 129.

womanly passivity and acceptance of their fate that was deeply unsettling to conservative swathes of opinion in Irish society.

The exodus of Irish people at a monumental point in the evolution of an independent state was a blow. Reasons why the rates continued to be so high were sought and explanations often focused on gender. As Ryan argues: 'At an important phase in the process of nation building, the apparent exodus of so many people warranted serious attention and explanation'.[49] There was no commentary emanating from either the Catholic Church or the state that men were leaving to lead sexually active, profligate lifestyles or to pursue lives inspired by the adventures portrayed in Hollywood films. Nor was it stated anywhere that Irish men were fleeing the country to avoid the shame of having fathered an illegitimate child. It seems absurd even to suggest this. However, all of these reasons were posited as motivational factors for Irish women emigrants.

Concern over female emigrants came from many sectors in Irish life. The list of those involved, in some form or another, in the discourses on Irish female emigration to Britain, and emigration in general, is extensive. This demonstrates the widespread perception that emigration was a 'crisis' of national concern. The statistical evidence on migration rates from Ireland reveals this perception to have some truth: everyone knew someone who was no longer at home.

Theoretical Discourses on Irish Female Emigration

Why were people leaving? More specifically for the purposes of this study, why were women leaving, and in such large numbers? The theoretical literature developed from geographic, demographic, sociological and historical research is discussed here to explore the ways in which these theories account for women and how well they fit Irish women's experiences of migration.

E.G. Ravenstein's theories of the 1880s remain a touchstone for migration historians in examining motivations for leaving one's home place.[50] Although his classifications may be too rigid to apply to *all* instances of migration, they constitute a useful paradigm. The economic reasons for migration are privileged in his schema, and while Irish

---

49 Ryan, 'Sexualising Emigration', p. 52.
50 E.G. Ravenstein, 'The Laws of Migration', *Journal of the Statistical Society of London*, 48.2 (1885), pp. 167–235. Ravenstein's theories have been summarised in D.B. Grigg, 'E.G. Ravenstein and the "Laws of Migration"', *Journal of Historical Geography*, 3 (1977), pp. 42–43 and reproduced in Delaney, *Demography, State and Society*, p. 9 and in Everett S. Lee, 'A Theory of Migration', *Demography*, 3.1 (1966), p. 48.

women's economic motivations for migrating were denigrated, they were nevertheless paramount and therefore consistent with the theories. Economic opportunities were admitted as much greater in number and more attractive in remuneration in Britain by the Commission on Emigration and Other Population Problems:

> Large numbers of girls emigrate to domestic service in Great Britain because they consider the wages, conditions of work and also the status of domestic service in this country are unsatisfactory. Many others emigrate because the possibility of obtaining factory or office work are better than here, and in the nursing profession numbers leave the country because the remuneration, facilities for training, pension schemes and hours of work in this country are considered to be unattractive.[51]

The Commission's observations assumed that female emigrants had sufficient information to compare economic opportunities in both countries. Their assessment was fair; the economic opportunities that attracted women from the Free State to Britain were far wider in scope and better in conditions, and information filtered through from advertisements, letters and visits home from emigrants. Unlike their counterparts in Northern Ireland who enjoyed a greater range of industrial occupations, many women from the Free State had to leave their homes for comparable work.

Irish people in general defied some of the schema by their migration choices; for example, although Ravenstein posited that most migrants go only a short distance, for Irish migrants it was perhaps more common to make more radical choices than simply rural to urban migrations. The choice to go to New York, London or Toronto was considered more quickly by many than simply migrating to Dublin. However, the expression 'across the water' to describe journeys to Britain is evocative of the psychological framing of Britain as near, reflecting the close geographic borders and shared heritage of Ireland and Britain. Irish migrants did conform to Ravenstein's suppositions that most migrants were adult, and went to major industrial centres from rural locations. However, the 'law' that most obviously does not fit with the Irish female experience is Ravenstein's observation that women generally made shorter journeys than men. Irish women migrated abroad rather than just internally in common with, and at times outnumbering, their male counterparts. This is, in fact, a remarkable and unique feature of

---

51 Commission on Emigration and Other Population Problems, *Majority Report*, para. 303.

Irish migration, and not necessarily a fault of Ravenstein's 'laws'. The Irish migrant flow differed in this respect from many others.[52]

However, the conception of Britain as a place of 'foreign' migration is complex given its proximity, and it is questionable if emigration to Britain was viewed in the same light as migrations to destinations further afield. This may have been a matter of political persuasion than a strict consideration of geographical or political boundaries. The Protestant Girls' Friendly Society, for example, did not appear to count Britain as a migration destination and did not keep figures on the number of its members who went there, as they did for Canada, the USA, Australia and other places.[53] Walter has observed that the geographic myopia that excludes Britain from understandings of the diaspora 'implicitly reinforce[s] a colonial perspective in which Ireland remains attached to Britain' with movements of persons 'seen as simply an internal movement between the two' countries.[54] While this is true, emigrants themselves may not have considered migration to Britain in the same sense as a move to America. This is indicated by the number of persons who recorded their shock at finding themselves officially excluded from the Irish register of citizens as a result of lengthy residence in Britain after the Irish Nationality and Citizenship Acts of the 1930s.[55]

Donald Harman Akenson's *The Irish Diaspora: A Primer*, a seminal text on Irish emigration, posits that there are two types of migration: forced and volitional. The former is defined as migration that occurs to save one's life, because of political or religious persecution, because there is no other option. The contemporary refugee crisis involving primarily Syrian citizens is an example of such a movement. Volitional migration accounts for migrant choices made in freer circumstances. Akenson qualifies this latter definition by stating that volitional migrants are 'always reacting to the constraints that surround their lives'.[56] However, he maintains that 'they

---

52 For more on other emigration flows in comparison with the Irish experience, see Delaney, 'Placing Postwar Irish Migration to Britain in a Comparative European Perspective, 1945–1981', pp. 331–356.

53 The Girls' Friendly Society had an Emigration Committee whose activities are reported in the Girls' Friendly Society, Executive Minutes, October 1920–December 1938, Representative Church Body Library MS 578/4/4. It seems that emigration was broadly conceived of as anywhere *but* Britain by the members of this group.

54 Walter, *Outsiders Inside*, p. 78.

55 Under the terms of the Irish Nationality and Citizenship Acts 1935 to 1937, Irish citizens not domiciled in the twenty-six counties at the founding of the State in 1922 were required to pay a fee to have their name officially registered as a citizen. Travel permit applications made in Britain reveal that many were ignorant of the requirements of the Acts and were outraged to find that they were not legally considered Irish citizens, despite sometimes long residences in Britain.

56 Akenson, *The Irish Diaspora*, p. 37.

have the choice of staying or leaving. In Irish history there has been very little forced emigration. The chief exceptions in our time period were the common criminals and political nationalists who were sent to Australia'.[57] This definition of volitional migration, therefore, precludes women and men who migrated to Britain during the first decades of independence. There were no instances of famine, genocide or other extreme circumstances that would be compatible with Akenson's binary schema, although the War of Independence and Civil War may have come close to this experience for some.

According to Akenson, then, to conceptualise the Irish as forced migrants diminishes 'their dignity as intelligent, self-aware responsible persons, each of whom made a conscious decision to leave Ireland'.[58] In fact, Akenson argues, to conceptualise Irish *women* as forced migrants is 'doubly demeaning'.[59] By this it appears Akenson means that it would be derogatory to portray women as passive victims in the migration process because they were so obviously active in making choices about their lives through the act of migrating. However, the distinction between forced and volitional migrants in the case of Ireland seems too rigid to explain the complex motives for migration in the post-independence era. There are diverse types and degrees of force operating on a person facing the prospect of leaving their native land: direct or threatened violence, political or religious persecution, economic imperatives or incentives, direct or indirect compulsions. There are also diverse types of volition. Some emigrants may not have a *realistic* choice to stay, if staying meant starving, living on the bare minimum to survive for the rest of their lives, or diminishing their family's chances for survival by being unable to contribute income. Some emigrants might also have more choices than others – the choice to go to America, Canada or Britain, for example. The stark polarisation of migrants into 'forced' or 'volitional' categories doesn't fully account for the fact that some migrants had better choices than others. If a person had the choice, for example, of marriage, financial support from extended family, or job prospects available to them as well as emigration, they are in a much more fortunate and 'volitional' position than an individual who has none of these. Akenson's comparative research on Irish and Swedish migrants in the nineteenth century explores motivations for migration in more nuanced terms, considering the cultural context. Thus, a more expansive version of 'volitional' migration would appear to be more appropriate for men and women in post-independence Ireland.

---

57 Ibid.
58 Ibid.
59 Ibid., p. 159.

The trope of emigration as exile, as in Miller's seminal work on Irish migrants to America, has been influential yet contested, particularly by Akenson.[60] This theory asserts that emigration was experienced as a kind of banishment, with the subsequent lamentations in letters proof of a widespread resentment towards migration. Others have recognised that the 'narrative of exile, however, has undoubtedly obscured a more complex picture of multidirectional movements of individuals and family groups over time', as Devlin Trew put it.[61] This connects with the theoretical paradigm of 'push' and 'pull' factors, developed by scholars such as Everett S. Lee and utilised by historians to explain Irish migration. This theoretical schema proposes negative factors that act to drive migration from a country, and other, positive ones that pull or draw migrants to a particular country or centre. Lee acknowledges the fluidity within the 'push–pull' model, with migrants responding to the different compulsion factors according to their circumstances, some positively and some negatively selected.[62] Lee's theories emphasise the importance of taking into account personal resources and characteristics that together determine attitudes to migration and create a dynamic whereby 'for some individuals, there must be compelling reasons for migration, while for others little provocation or promise suffices'.[63] Thus, networks, personal resources and an individual's interpretation of their circumstances can all influence migration decisions.[64] As Fitzgerald and Lambkin have observed, the tension in the 'push' and 'pull' dynamic results from economic conditions at home and abroad that are being compared by the emigrant.[65] What we know of the wage differentials, particularly for women doing similar work in Ireland and Britain, is just one example of how the 'push–pull' model worked.

60 Kerby A. Miller, *Emigrants and Exiles: Ireland and the Irish Exodus to North America* (Oxford: Oxford University Press, 1988).

61 Devlin Trew, *Leaving the North*.

62 Lee, 'A Theory of Migration', p. 56.

63 Ibid., p. 51.

64 For a further discussion of the 'push/pull' model and of Lee's work, see Delaney, *Demography, State and Society*, pp. 8–11. See David Fitzpatrick 'The Irish in Britain: Settlers or Transients?', in Patrick Buckland and John Belchem (eds), *The Irish in British Labour History* (Liverpool: University of Liverpool, 1993), pp. 1–10. See also Enda Delaney and Donald M. MacRaild, 'Irish Migration Networks and Ethnic Identities since 1750: An Introduction', *Immigrants and Minorities*, 23.2–3 (2005), pp. 127–142; Monica Boyd, 'Family and Personal Networks in International Migration: Recent Developments and New Agendas', *International Migration Review*, 23.3 (1989), pp. 638–670.

65 Patrick Fitzgerald and Brian Lambkin, *Migration in Irish History, 1607–2007* (London, Palgrave Macmillan, 2008).

Theoretical models used to explain emigration are useful in understanding the Irish migration flows although they do not always coalesce with Irish women's experiences. Irish women's motivations in leaving were consistent with Ravenstein's theory that economic motives are primary. Other theoretical models, such as the 'push–pull' theory, also have elements that resonate with Irish women: limitations of life at home and opportunities abroad variously 'pushed' and 'pulled' female emigrants. While we can't be certain of how individuals reacted to their circumstances, it is certain, however, that most male and female emigrants who have been interviewed in various studies regard themselves as having been 'pushed' from the country rather than lured or pulled by opportunities. For many women in the early decades of independent Ireland, there was little to 'pull' them to stay, and much to 'push' them to leave.

The 'core/periphery' model privileges economic factors. Simply put, migrants are drawn from areas that are peripheral in terms of resources, development, services or opportunities and drawn towards central or core areas which have these. As Delaney noted, this model corresponds with the Irish experience of emigration driven by rural–urban migration patterns.[66] It is also true that the 'cores' may shift as globalised markets develop and centres of production change. The core may also be different for men and women according to the gendered nature of industrial occupations. For example, towns or cities renowned for heavy industry will undoubtedly be viewed as more 'core' areas for men than women. Women may be drawn to 'cores' of female-dominated employment such as nursing, teaching and domestic service. A sub-division of the core may exist on gendered 'lines' of demarcation, even within the one city. Men and women may therefore experience different geographies of migration and this is an area that requires further interdisciplinary and theoretical attention for scholars of Irish migration.

The final theoretical model considered useful by historians originated in Hirschman's Exit-Voice Polarity hypothesis, responses an individual may have to their circumstances.[67] As Delaney has highlighted, these simple terms refer to the actions of leaving or staying and protesting, each response affected by the degree of loyalty the individual possesses. This can have applicability to migration if one is to view it as a response to national and economic circumstances, although critics have highlighted the role of the

---

66 Delaney, *Demography, State and Society*, p. 17.
67 Albert O. Hirschman, *Exit, Voice, and Loyalty: Responses to Decline in Firms, Organizations, and States* (Cambridge, Mass.: Harvard University Press, 1970). For further discussion on Hirschman's theories and their subsequent development and application, see Delaney, *Demography, State and Society* and Fitzgerald and Lambkin, *Migration in Irish History*.

state in determining the movements of its persons, as happened during the Emergency in Ireland. However, the term 'loyalty' is problematic when applied to the often emotionally fraught decision to migrate. Is loyalty really the mitigating factor between exit and voice, or could it be lack of resources, familial influence or personal courage? For women, who in post-independence Ireland did not have a strong united public voice and few political champions, was 'voice' a realistic option? If women had protested or rioted in response to their poor economic position, would their concerns have been taken seriously? Was their decision to leave due to lack of loyalty, lack of agency or lack of choice? It seems that Hirshman's theories may have different implications for women than men.

The Commission on Emigration and Other Population Problems recognised the multiple reasons why people left Ireland: 'While the fundamental cause of emigration is economic, in most cases the decision to emigrate cannot be ascribed to any single motive but to the interplay of a number of motives'.[68] No one theory has emerged definitively to explain Irish migration, but some Irish migrants, if not the majority, could be categorised as compulsory economic migrants. This does not diminish agency in deciding to leave Ireland. Nor does it cast migrants as passive victims of circumstance. Rather, it is more appropriate to expand the point that emigrants were reacting to their circumstances. In the context of the legislative, economic and ideological restrictions characteristic of the Irish Free State, this was particularly true for women. DeLaet has argued for attention to be paid to the potential gender differences in the theoretical discussions of why people migrate: 'Although no consensus emerges [...] female migration is neither driven by exactly the same determinants as male migration nor do women experience migration in precisely the same way as men'.[69] Many women chose to leave because of the limited personal, social *and* economic/professional opportunities available to them that they *would* be able to pursue in Britain. They could change neither the economy nor the laws of the Free State that continually encroached on their employment opportunities, but they *could* leave.

The characterisation of Irish migrants as economically motivated fits with most migrants internationally, both historically and currently, apart from those fleeing persecution. As Annie Phizacklea argues, 'Nearly all labour migration is characterised by economic *compulsion* due to the decomposition of backward productive sectors, principally agriculture [...]

68 Commission on Emigration and Other Population Problems, *Majority Report*, para. 290.
69 D.L. DeLaet, 'Introduction: The Invisibility of Women in Scholarship on International Migration', in G.A. Kelson and D.L. DeLaet (eds), *Gender and Immigration* (New York: New York University Press, 1999), p. 2.

and the higher nominal and real wages offered in the dominant capitalist formation' (i.e. the host society).[70] Applying Phizacklea's theorisation to the Irish migration experience contextualises the stream of Irish women migrating from rural locations with limited economic opportunities within broader trends for women globally in the twentieth century. The experience of migration due to higher cash rewards also relates to Irish women's experience as even at domestic servant level they could obtain wages higher in both nominal and real terms in Britain. The fact Phizacklea uses the term 'compulsion' in relation to economic migrants also strengthens the argument for viewing such individuals as *compelled* or *forced* by economic circumstances to leave. Phizacklea also connects the trends in labour migration with modern economic practices that privilege a cash economy rather than trade in kind:

> Various studies have indicated how the penetration of the cash economy in the sending societies results in women, not men, becoming a relative surplus population. Girls are thus dispatched to earn cash which they will send home in the form of remittances.[71]

This is an interesting connection, and one that would seem to correspond with Ireland's slow modernisation which increasingly relied on trade and monetary transactions rather than a bartering system, and so emigrants' remittances were vital. Remittances were recognised by the Commission as being 'an important item in the national economy' that 'partly redress the adverse balance of trade' which could also stimulate production, or, more negatively, cause some inflation, but overall their 'social effect is to bring about greater equality in the distribution of wealth'.[72]

Phizacklea's assertion that female migrants may have fled 'patriarchal oppression' in their home countries is one that has received attention in the other major works written about female emigration.[73] Although many of these concern migration to the USA, they are worth considering. Hasia Diner's *Erin's Daughters in America* addresses female emigrant experiences of mid- to late nineteenth-century America.[74] Diner examined both quantitative and qualitative accounts of Irish women's lives in America,

70 Introduction, in Annie Phizacklea (ed.), *One Way Ticket: Migration and Female Labour* (London: Routledge & Kegan Paul, 1983), pp. 1–11. My emphasis.

71 Ibid., p. 7.

72 Commission on Emigration and Other Population Problems, *Majority Report*, para. 310.

73 For example, Lennon *et al.*, *Across the Water*.

74 Hasia R. Diner, *Erin's Daughters in America: Irish Immigrant Women in the Nineteenth Century* (Baltimore, Md.: Johns Hopkins University Press, 1983).

concluding that migration was a liberating experience for women, coming
from a country of late marriage and high celibacy rates, to a land where
they could work and fulfil family ambitions also, if they chose to. Diner's
thesis has been criticised by some for diminishing the extent to which
emigrants are released from their 'cultural baggage' on arrival in a new
land.[75] Socialisation and conditioning of people in their native lands will not
simply be erased by stepping on a boat or plane. In fact, cultural difference
is often retained and asserted by immigrants, particularly Irish immigrants
in Britain due to the ethnically similar appearance between English and
Irish people which led to a conscious effort to assert 'Irishness'. This
was achieved through socialising with other Irish people at Irish clubs,
engagement in the Catholic Church and participation in traditional social
activities such as féiseanna and ceilí, aspects of Irish experience dealt with
in Chapter 5.

Ide O'Carroll similarly examined the migration of Irish women in
the post-independence period, in *Models for Movers*. O'Carroll argued
that women were fleeing poverty and lack of economic opportunities, but
were also utilising emigration to escape the patriarchal system of power.
O'Carroll's thesis is akin to Diner's as both historians position female
emigrant women as active social agents, reacting to ideological and cultural
constraints imposed on them by a male dominated society. Similarly,
Hickman and Walter's argument that many 'Irish women emigrated as a
direct or indirect result of their low status at home'[76] implies that women
sought to flee oppression in some way, although it is not possible to 'prove'
this thesis in a definitive way. David Fitzpatrick has argued that women
reacted in different ways to the restriction of their social and economic
roles in Ireland either by 'glorifying the rôle of unpaid mother-manager,
or by trying to escape'.[77] Together, these works outline a history of steadily
increasing male domination of Irish life in the nineteenth century, which
resulted in a constriction of women's social and cultural roles. This left
many with no choice but to emigrate, for ideological or economic reasons.
This is quite a different model from those which view emigrants as less
aware of the ideological underpinnings of their position in society, and more
responsive to their immediate circumstances.

Janet Nolan's examination of the Irish female emigrant phenomenon
between 1885 and 1920 also relates post-Famine changes in social relations

---

75 See, for example, the review of Diner's work by Brenda Collins in *Irish Economic and
    Social History*, 12 (1985), pp. 143–144.
76 Mary J. Hickman and Bronwen Walter, 'Deconstructing Whiteness', *Feminist Review*,
    50 (1995), p. 13.
77 Fitzpatrick, "'A Share of the Honeycomb'", p. 217.

to women's decision to leave Ireland. Nolan argues that women experienced a constriction in their autonomy and in the social roles available to them after the Famine due to shifts in inheritance traditions and cultural practices, such as late marriage and high celibacy rates. She concluded that women did not emigrate to radically change their lives, or to flee patriarchy, but to fulfil their traditional expectations of life such as marriage and motherhood: 'The emigration of this generation did not represent a rejection of traditional female roles, nor did it mean a passive transference abroad of intact female roles. Instead, these women emigrated so that they could actively recover their lost importance in Irish life'.[78]

This argument refutes claims that female emigrants were more radical ideologically (that is, in rejecting patriarchy). Rather, it seems that women, in common with men, were seeking better life opportunities. The greater prospects outside Ireland would assist them in fulfilling their aspirations of becoming workers, wives and mothers, roles that had become increasingly unavailable to them in Ireland. This is, of course, a heterosexual paradigm of adult women's lives, and doesn't account for migrations based on fleeing the heteronormative culture of Ireland that surely characterised lesbian experience in the past.[79] Kerby Miller contends that Nolan and Diner are both right, but only if considered together. He argues that, at least in the case of American immigrants, both economic freedom and marriage opportunities were motivating factors.[80] The evidence from oral history collections suggests that Miller's qualification applies regardless of the migration destination. It is also difficult to conceptualise female emigration as a radical break from familial and cultural constraints, given that the initial decision to migrate was often made with the family, migrants often went to areas where they had friends or family, they facilitated chain migration of relatives, and frequently visited home. As Lambert points out, 'female emigration from Ireland cannot be simply explained as a conscious rejection of family duties, since family involvement and networks were crucial to the emigration process'.[81]

---

78 Nolan, *Ourselves Alone*, p. 8.

79 For more on this point, see Jennifer Redmond, 'The Politics of Emigrant Bodies: Irish Women's Sexual Practice in Question', in Jennifer Redmond, Sonja Tiernan, Sandra McAvoy and Mary McAuliffe (eds), *Sexual Politics in Modern Ireland* (Dublin: Irish Academic Press, 2015), pp. 73–89.

80 See Miller, Doyle and Kelleher, '"For Love and Liberty": Irish Women, Migration and Domesticity in Ireland', in Patrick O'Sullivan (ed.), *The Irish World Wide, History, Heritage, Identity: Irish Women and Irish Migration*, vol. 4 (London: Leicester University Press, 1997), pp. 53–54.

81 Sharon Lambert, 'Irish Women's Emigration to England, 1922–1960: The Lengthening of Family Ties', in Alan Hayes and Diane Urquhart (eds), *Irish Women's History* (Dublin: Irish Academic Press, 2004), p. 159.

Louise Ryan's work on constructions of femininity in the Irish Free State and female emigration includes many facets of female migration experiences: gendered notions of space and culture; the characterisation of female emigrants as vulnerable and at risk; the gendered discourses on migration; female chain migration (in particular, through nursing); and the experiences of women who emigrated in the Free State period. Ryan's argument that Irish 'women's emigration was represented through the lens of sexuality, reproduction, and maternity'[82] emphasises the multifaceted nature of the female migrant experience. The historical phenomenon of Irish female migration cannot be understood through a singular, overarching paradigm. What this work seeks to add to Ryan's scholarship is an analysis of emigrants' stories in relation to the wider public discourses.

Ryan has asserted that women were connected to the conceptualisation of the unemployment problem in Ireland;[83] however, the repeated failure to address female unemployment and the strength of the 'family wage' rhetoric pushed women's economic needs out of the picture.[84] Indeed, women's economic motivations for emigration were continuously questioned; only male migrants appeared to be able to claim the 'respectability' of economic forces. Women's status within the domestic sphere (even as unpaid farm workers) did not allow them to access the legitimating discourses of economic necessity even though they were unable to claim unemployment assistance as their rural brothers were. Women were often viewed as neither economically active nor productive. However, Ryan's analysis does highlight the fact that female emigration was discursively reproduced within an inherently moral framework, including anxieties about sexual behaviour, fertility, nationalism, religion, economics and the rejection of the traditional female roles of wife and mother.

Conclusion

Emigration rates underwent peaks and troughs, with the 1920s and the 1950s experiencing the higher rates of emigration from Ireland. The sustained flow of people from Ireland in the early years of the new state, with the rise in numbers leaving even after a quarter of a century of native rule, contributed to the pessimistic discourses on migration. It also influenced the negative

---

82 Ryan, 'Sexualising Emigration', p. 51.
83 Ryan, *Gender, Identity and the Irish Press*, p. 112.
84 Reference is made here to such legislation as the 1925 Civil Service Act and the Conditions of Employment Act 1936, which curtailed and regulated employment opportunities for women.

discourses on emigrants themselves as 'unpatriotic deserters' or materialistic and greedy. The statistical data available, although flawed, allows for the analysis of trends in migration to Britain and shows the considerable proportion of women emigrants in all time periods. This may partly explain why there was such a volume of discourse on female emigrants. As will be discussed in the following chapters, such discourses reflected traditional, patriarchal attitudes of the time, which suggested that female emigrants needed both control and protection. No such attitude was adopted in relation to male migrants, despite similarities in age, background and motivation. Thus, the gendered nature of Irish migration must be interrogated. As Dobrowolsky and Tastsoglou have argued:

> examining closely how gender is implicated in processes of migration is a must. Gender differences arise from the subordinate status of women in society which acts as a 'filter', gendering structural forces and influencing the experiences of men and women differently.[85]

The theoretical debates and paradigms offered to explain contemporary and historical migration emanate from a range of disciplines and are essential in understanding Irish women's migration. Recent scholarship has engaged with this rich literature, although the gender dimensions to the theoretical frameworks could be further explored by historians.

While the primacy of economic motivations has been established in most theoretical studies of migration, in the Irish context women were often excluded from identifying themselves as economic migrants. Elected representatives often played up to public sensibilities and spouted populist jargon that diminished Irish women's right to be viewed as economic actors, as will be seen in the next chapter.

---

85 Dobrowolsky and Tastsoglou, 'Crossing Boundaries and Making Connections', p. 17.

2

The Rhetorical, Political and Legislative Framing of Irish Women Emigrants

In twenty-six years, we have had three Governments, each of which took office loudly (and sincerely) announced its determination to tackle for once and for all the emigration and rural depopulation problems. The first two of those Governments first began to 'postpone', then proceeded to hedge and compromise and discover difficulties and, in the course of a few years in power, became strong apologists for and firm supporters of both emigration and rural depopulation. The present Government shows every sign of following the same course.

> Memorandum, 'Origin and Development of the Present Emigration Mania and Catastrophe', submitted by the playwright Michael J. Molloy, Milltown, Co. Galway, to the Commission on Emigration and Other Population Problems.[1]

Will any Deputy on the opposite side say that it is a good thing that young girls should be allowed to put themselves in a position in which they may find themselves without any control, that they should go to England or any other country without anybody to look after them?

> Quote from a speech by Éamon de Valera, *Dáil Éireann Debates*, vol. 97, col. 2449, 13 July 1945.

---

1 Arnold Marsh papers, Trinity College Dublin MS 8305. The document is not dated but most probably comes from 1948, as a follow-up interview took place that year. Molloy was referring to the first coalition government who were in power at this time.

From examining the statistical profile of Irish women's migration, we turn now to consider the rhetorical pronouncements made on emigration in general, and women's migration in particular, in the post-independence era. Emigration was debated in the Dáil and Seanad in discussions on the economy, rural depopulation, employment policy and 'national policy', sometimes in heated exchanges.[2] Unfortunately, there is no evidence that governmental debates or expressions of opinion by political parties have been raised in interviews with emigrants themselves. We don't know, therefore, what emigrants made of the many public pronouncements on their motivations, behaviours, experiences and desires. The parliamentary debates on emigration have not featured strongly in historical work on the area, despite being mined extensively by those examining the Anglo-Irish Treaty and the 1937 Constitution, for example.[3] They are a fruitful area of research in tracing dominant attitudes at the highest level of government, opinions across political parties and from deputies representing diverse areas, many of which were the key emigration sending sites. Unlike the aims of successive British governments, Irish governments had no interest in promoting emigration for the benefit of the nation;[4] the paradigm for discussing emigration was always one centred on loss, and any suggestions to the contrary were met with rather hysterical condemnation.

Akenson has observed, 'difficult as it is to assess historically, culture counts' and examining political discussions of emigration in Ireland allows us to analyse the interplay between national policies and societal attitudes.[5] Although women are not mentioned with the same frequency as men in government debates featuring migration, there appears to be a consensus regarding them. TDs and Senators from different sides of the political divide and in different decades often agreed that certain restrictions should be placed on women's emigration, while arguing fervently against any restrictions for men.

How was the issue of emigration raised? What kind of language was used? Why was women's emigration denigrated or seen as dangerous in comparison with men's? Emigration was a topic many politicians raised

---

2 This is similar to parliamentary and cabinet debates analysed by Devlin Trew in Northern Ireland; see *Leaving the North*, p. 44.

3 Parliamentary debates are vital sources for the study of emigration but appear under-utilised in most studies.

4 For more on British empire migration, in particular the contrasting history of Northern Ireland's involvement in imperial schemes, see Devlin Trew, *Leaving the North*, chap. 2. It is important to note that migration policy for Northern Ireland remained under the control of the Westminster government although a certain level of local control and application existed.

5 Akenson, *Ireland, Sweden and the Great European Migration*, p. 85.

periodically within the Oireachtas, but the issue failed to inspire effective action so much as grandstanding, rhetoric and political point-scoring. The frustration this caused for some was adeptly summed up in a memorandum to the Commission on Emigration and Other Population Problems from which the opening quotation was taken. The reluctance of successive governments to address the problem of emigration effectively (or at all) meant that it was raised repeatedly, almost habitually, within Oireachtas debates but almost always superficially. At such times the regional, economic, social and gender dimensions to the issue were cited, but little constructive dialogue ensued, resulting in stagnation for the entire period under examination.

Emigration as an election issue is examined first, tracing the ways in which various parties addressed, avoided, made promises or otherwise referred to the issue, before moving to an examination of what parties did once in power.

Emigration as a (Non) Election Issue

During each election from the 1920s to the 1950s it might be thought that emigration policies would feature among the promises of the contending political parties; this was not the case. If emigration in general was principally ignored, the reader may have guessed that the issue of women's emigration was completely absent in any campaign slogans. Women were a voting constituency that could have been appealed to from the beginning of the state, if any of the parties had had the ingenuity to do so.[6]

In August 1923, the main election issues covered in both the *Irish Times* and *The Irish Independent* concerned the Land Bill and the Public Safety Bill, reflective of the recurrent concern over land ownership and the recent Civil War instability. It may not be surprising that at this crisis point emigration was not a priority, but Delaney has observed that it also failed to feature in numerous political pamphlets produced for the 1927 and 1932 elections:

> Clearly, the acknowledgement of the 'problem' of migration was not perceived as a practical vote-winner, yet outlining policies which might 'stem the flow', as it were, was a ploy used fairly effectively by the Fianna Fáil party to increase its support.[7]

---

6 Women and men in Ireland aged over twenty-one had full voting rights under the 1922 Constitution.

7 Delaney, *Demography, State and Society*, p. 60.

The major focus –and indeed drama – of the 1927 election campaign was the danger or benefit (depending on your political persuasion) of abandoning the Cumann na nGaedheal administration in favour of the new Fianna Fáil party. No proper outline of Cumann na nGaedheal policies or goals for government were provided, the electorate merely being asked to vote on ideology, not issues. The 1932 election also saw this strategy and emigration failed to feature as a significant issue for any party. This was a tense and hotly contested election given that Fianna Fáil was now in a viable position to take over government.[8] Emigration was mentioned in an election poster for the aspirant Fianna Fáil in the 1932 election campaign, but reduced to a slogan and thus amounting to little more than vapid electioneering propaganda. Fianna Fáil stressed the connection of the party to the land in the slogan 'Speed the Plough', with 'stop to emigration' as a mere bullet point at the bottom.[9]

Ferriter has argued that such tactics can be viewed as characteristic of Fianna Fáil's political style: their 'approach to the electorate [...] was utterly pragmatic and often deliberately ambiguous'.[10] Electioneering propaganda promising to stop emigration was not committed to in policy. Women were not the focus of the appeal; when it came to conceiving women's role in Irish society, the various parties agreed on this more than they did on other issues.[11] The Labour Party also placed advertisements that similarly failed to engage specifically with the issue of emigration, despite their avowal of 'commonsense politics'.[12] Emigration did not become what Delaney terms a 'live political issue' until after the Second World War when rates increased, particularly to Great Britain due to the reconstruction work it needed and the abolition of travel restrictions.[13] Thus, according to Pauric Travers, in the run up to the election in 1948, emigration received the greatest attention ever seen before or since,[14] although Mary Daly has argued that emigration was

8   Michael Gallagher has highlighted the fears about Fianna Fáil coming to power because of their statements on dismantling the political institutions of the state. This led Cumman na nGaedheal to offer 'no policies at all' in their election campaign of 1932, 'merely invoking the tradition of suffering and sacrifice in the cause of Religion'. Warner Moss, quoted in Gallagher, *Electoral Support for Irish Political Parties, 1927–1973* (London: Sage Publications, 1976), p. 21.

9   *Irish Independent*, 5 February 1932, p. 7.

10 Diarmaid Ferriter, *The Transformation of Ireland: 1900–2000* (London: Profile Books, 2005), p. 18.

11 An example is the ban on married women working in the public sector and in teaching. For more on the latter, see Jennifer Redmond and Judith Harford, '"One Man One Job": The Marriage Ban and the Employment of Women Teachers in Irish Primary Schools', *Paedagogica Historica*, 46.5 (2010), pp. 639–654.

12 *Irish Independent*, 13 February 1932, p. 6.

13 Delaney, *Demography, State and Society*, p. 202.

14 Pauric Travers, '"The Dream Gone Bust": Irish Responses to Emigration, 1922–60', in Oliver MacDonagh and W.F. Mandle (eds), *Irish-Australian Studies: Papers Delivered*

not the dominant issue, but appeared alongside partition, the cost of living and the dangers of a coalition government.[15] The point to stress, however, is that it had barely featured in previous campaigns, so its inclusion in the election rhetoric was significant. Clann na Poblachta, with its emphasis on economic issues, placed emigration at the forefront of its campaign.[16] In a speech made in Cork by Seán MacBride, the government was challenged to deny that it had pursued a duplicitous policy of publicly condemning emigration but privately facilitating it through the Labour Exchanges, as it had done during the Emergency. Furthermore, he stated:

> If that [emigration] was allowed to continue for another 25 years this nation would be in a position from which it would never recover. It has been suggested that emigration was inevitable. Clann na Poblachta did not believe that nor did they believe that this country, as had been suggested, was not able to support more people.[17]

The rhetoric used by Clann na Poblachta candidates may have seemed fresh and vital, coming as it did from an entirely new political party. The ever-present spectre of emigration may have been thought to be finally seeing the proper light of political debate. This sense of change may also have been influenced by the promise of the outgoing government to investigate emigration and rural depopulation, discussed further below.[18]

The omission of emigration from election campaigns can be hypothesised in three ways: first, emigration was strongly linked to employment, thus promises to increase employment were automatically understood to be connected to the need to reduce emigration; second, emigration was a particularly thorny matter and promises to reduce it may have been seen as infringements on liberties or freedom of movement; and third, emigration was seen as a large problem, but an inevitable one, too big to tackle and hence too large to make election promises about. Such reluctance to address the issue was also evident in debates. What is noteworthy, and perhaps expected, is that women's economic needs and their role in emigration culture were not

    at the Fifth Irish-Australian Conference (Canberra: Australian National University, 1989), pp. 326–327.

15 See Daly, *The Slow Failure*, p. 158.

16 Clann na Poblachta ('Family or the People of the Republic') was set up by a small group of republican figures on 6 July 1946. Seán MacBride became party leader. Kevin Rafter, *The Clann: The Story of Clann na Poblachta* (Cork: Mercier Press, 1996).

17 *Irish Independent*, 30 January 1948, p. 6.

18 Although the Commission was established by the coalition government, it was proposed by James Ryan, Minister for Social Welfare in December 1947. Daly argues that it may have been instituted to 'placate the Catholic hierarchy and Clann na Poblachta', *The Slow Failure*, p. 161.

mentioned in campaign slogans and posters. The inevitable conclusion is that women were not a constituency thought to be worth wooing; it seems women were invisible to the major parties.

Dáil and Seanad Debates on Emigration

Emigration was not addressed within debates in the Dáil and Seanad with any more action or vigour than in election campaigns. The debates did, however, alter according to the varying trends throughout the period. Issues that arose in the Dáil and Seanad consequently changed from concerns over the rigorous medical inspections emigrants on the Cunard–Anchor line had to endure in the 1920s[19] to specific questions about the numbers and destinations of emigrants to Britain. A politician's gender did not seem to influence whether they involved themselves in the issue, or their stance on female emigrants. Women TDs did not champion the cause of female emigrants, or the issues that drove women to migrate. There were also few women in the Oireachtas: between 1922 and 1948, of the 518 elected representatives, only 12 (or 2.3 per cent) were women,[20] with an average of only four women deputies in each Dáil or 3 per cent of the total number of TDs,[21] meaning a critical mass was lacking. While this was undoubtedly an influencing factor, the tenor of their role in government in this era is worth noting. As Daly has commented, the sparse numbers of female representatives 'owed their election to kinship with dead nationalist heroes rather than to independent political credentials'; given this, they could perhaps be expected to tow the party line in relation to emigration.[22] Furthermore, no woman served as a minister between 1922 and 1979,[23] and, even if they had, it is unlikely they would have focused on women's issues given the political climate.

19 Major Cooper asked the Minister for External Affairs, Desmond FitzGerald, why emigrants had tougher medical inspections at Moville than those carried out at Glasgow and Greenock. The Minister replied that there might be some difference in interpretation of rules by doctors in different ports. *Dáil Éireann Debates*, vol. 10, col. 196, 13 February 1925.

20 R.K. Carty, 'Women in Irish Politics', *Canadian Journal of Irish Studies*, 6.1 (1980), p. 92. Carty asserts, however, that when women managed to be elected they were often successful in keeping their seats for a long time. It is also necessary to note that women have been more numerous in the Seanad than the Dáil.

21 Meadbh McNamara and Paschal Mooney, *Women in Parliament: Ireland, 1918–2000* (Dublin: Wolfhound Press, 2000), p. 16.

22 Mary E. Daly, 'Women in the Irish Free State, 1922–1939: The Interaction between Economics and ideology', *Journal of Women's History*, vol. 6/7 (1995), p. 99.

23 Dermot Keogh, *Twentieth-Century Ireland: Nation and State* (Dublin: Gill & Macmillan, 1994), p. 38.

Many women TDs had no previous experience of serving in political life. They may have been motivated by economic reasons due to the lack of pensions for relatives of TDs,[24] and were often 'sent to the Dáil as surrogates for the male members of their families' in a process known as 'male equivalence'.[25] Hilda Tweedy, co-founder of the Irish Housewives' Association, remarked of these widows that they were generally installed on a 'sympathy vote' and that: 'Little was heard from them, or of them. We called them the "silent sisters", but perhaps that was a hasty judgement. They probably proved their worth on the various committees then deemed suitable for women, but their work was not reported'.[26] If this is the case on emigration, their work has been lost to history completely. Once in office, such women rarely adopted as vocal a stance as their male counterparts; giving 'priority to their constituency activity over their legislative function [...] their contributions to debates were infrequent'.[27] Women in the Seanad were often more vocal and united in their opposition to the legislative assaults to women's equality than they were on migration, yet no woman senator adopted the issue of female emigration as a major campaign.

This silence leads us back to the idea of the O Gráda paradox framed by Akenson, but in this context the question is: there was some discussion of emigration, but given the enormity of the outflow, why wasn't there more?[28] As has been noted by Delaney and Daly, emigration did not arise as an issue in political debates or election campaigns with the frequency that one would expect given that high rates were a consistent feature of the time.[29] Ferriter attributes this lack of public discourse to be a sign of a somewhat fatalistic attitude:

Emigration did not become a significant part of political and public discourse in Ireland during these years [1923–32], which seemed to indicate an acceptance of its inevitability, and this, no doubt, was the sentiment in so many of Ireland's large families.[30]

24 Dermot Keogh, *Twentieth-Century Ireland*, p. 38.
25 Carty, 'Women in Irish Politics', p. 94.
26 Hilda Tweedy, *A Link in the Chain: The Story of the Irish Housewives Association, 1942–1992* (Dublin: Attic Press, 1992), p. 22.
27 Ibid. The exception to this is the example of women such as Fianna Fáil Senator Helena Concannon, who supported and vociferously defended the conservative politics of her party.
28 Akenson discusses Cormac Ó Gráda's thesis that while migration from Ireland was at an unprecedented scale during and after the Famine, it is curious that there was not even more given the state of the country. See Akenson, *Ireland, Sweden and the Great European Migration*, p. 27.
29 Delaney, *Demography, State and Society*; Daly, *The Slow Failure*.
30 Ferriter, *The Transformation of Ireland*, p. 330.

It may also be true that emigration did not emerge as a major issue because Irish people were not required to give up their citizenship to live and work in Britain. If they had, it is interesting to speculate whether there would have been greater attention to legislative and constitutional provisions built around the retention of Irish citizenship and hence stopping migration (a topic to which we will return later in the chapter).

Debating Emigration Statistics

The most frequent way in which emigration was used to score political points was in questioning the Minister in government about precise rates of emigration or specific information on emigrants to Britain: as all knew, these could not be answered. These enquiries were posed periodically by the opposition, an example being Seán Lemass's (Fianna Fáil) detailed questioning of Cumman na nGaedheal's Deputy McGilligan, Minister for Industry and Commerce, on how many emigrants there had been in the Intercensal period 1911–26 and specifically, how many there were in 1922, 1923, 1924, 1925 and 1926.[31] Lemass appeared to want to emphasise the government's lack of complete data and its 'record' on migration since assuming office, before his own political party had been formed. In McGilligan's reply, he admitted that the number of emigrants from Saorstát Éireann between the censuses was not known and that neither was there any information for the years 1922 or 1923, nor any data available on emigration to Great Britain or Northern Ireland.[32]

Interestingly, the same two deputies again engaged in the topic of emigration when Fianna Fáil were in office for what appears to be similar motives. In April 1932, Deputy McGilligan questioned Lemass, then Minister for Industry and Commerce, as to the detailed history of immigration, migration outside Europe, an average over the last five years of migration to Great Britain, the number of seasonal migrants, and their average duration of employment while there.[33] Clearly, McGilligan, having been in government and held this specific ministerial appointment, knew that this information was impossible to give. In response, Seán Lemass provided a similarly lengthy response as had McGilligan five years previously, outlining the available immigration information, which was more accurate than that on emigration. Tit for tat indeed.

Requests for statistical information emerged numerous times and were always responded to with the same formulaic answer – that whilst some

31 *Dáil Éireann Debates*, vol. 21, col. 948, 8 November 1927.
32 Ibid.
33 *Dáil Éireann Debates*, vol. 41, col. 327, 21 April 1932.

information was available, it was incomplete, and no mechanism existed or could be envisaged that would correct the data gap. The lack of comprehensive information led to claims about the extent of emigration from either side of the debate that could not be substantiated.[34] Deputy McDermott's rather vexatious response in one of these debates is apposite to consider: 'Is not a knowledge of the volume of our emigration to Great Britain a matter of vital importance to this country in view of the possible implications of Government policy?' This would have been true if there had actually been a government policy on emigration at any point.[35]

Despite Fianna Fáil's stated campaign commitment to eliminating the need for emigration, little was done to effect such a radical change after they assumed office in 1932 and Fine Gael lost no opportunity to question the government on its record.[36] During the Economic War in 1937 the issue resurfaced. Professor O'Sullivan of Fine Gael highlighted that Fianna Fáil no longer raised the issue of emigration, but he saw it very clearly escalating within his own constituency:

> When this question of emigration to England was first mentioned in the Dáil, Ministers refused to listen. They suggested that we [Fine Gael] were drawing on our imaginations. In answer to that, all that I can say is that all the people of Kerry must be drawing on their imaginations, because they know perfectly well what is occurring. The people cannot find work at home, and they are deserting the land at the present moment.[37]

Deputy Richard Mulcahy (Fine Gael) went further: he argued that the government was pursuing a policy of forced emigration, particularly in the case of women. Citing a case he had recently been informed of, he told the house that a girl had been refused her 'dole' money because she declined to accept work that was offered through the Labour Exchange in a British factory making paper coronation hats.[38] While Lemass was probably

---

34 For example, during a debate in the Dáil in 1936, Deputy McDermott queried if the government could initiate a system for counting migrants. The inevitable answer was that statistics were regularly collected, but that emigration rates could not be calculated for Great Britain due to 'the large volume of regular passenger movement between the two countries'. *Dáil Éireann Debates*, vol. 63, col. 2726, 13 August 1936.

35 Delaney has argued that the policy of the government in the inter-war period was 'essentially one of non-intervention', which translated as inaction. See Delaney, 'State, Politics and Demography: The Case of Irish Emigration, 1921–1971', *Irish Political Studies*, 13 (1998), p. 46.

36 For more on this point, see ibid.

37 *Dáil Éireann Debates*, vol. 65, col. 1285, 4 March 1937.

38 *Dáil Éireann Debates*, vol. 65, col. 1323, 4 March 1937.

truthful in asserting that this was an obvious administrative mistake, the point was made that employment in Britain was being offered by Irish Labour Exchanges, and that this could be viewed as both an indictment of the national economic policy and a means by which women were facilitated to leave the country. That the work offered was related to celebrations of the British monarchy was not explicitly commented upon, but may have been the reason this specific case was raised.

During this debate, the gender composition of the flow of emigrants was also raised. This was not a mere statistical question, but was raised as a matter of national policy that, the opposition argued, should be of concern to the government. Lemass and Mulcahy traded claims about the diminishing population, with Mulcahy asserting that 'this country was injured economically by the circumstances brought about by the Ministry'.[39] The point raised regarding the declining female population was carried over to further debates, with opposition deputies arguing that female rates of emigration should be taken seriously, but that large numbers of rural men were also leaving. Lemass refused to withdraw his assertion that mostly women were emigrating, blithely stating, 'Then the men must be going out in disguise, disguised as women'.[40] Lemass also joked when questioned again by Mulcahy on how many women had been helped to find jobs in the paper hat factory. When Mulcahy asked whether he would raise the issue again on the adjournment, Lemass queried whether he would be 'Wearing an appropriate paper hat?'[41] This jocular, derogatory tone conveys the lack of concern about women and the superficial dismissal of Fine Gael deputies' arguments on the problem of emigration itself.

Fianna Fáil deputies countered the claims of the opposition throughout the 1930s that the economy and emigration were serious problems, arguing that the country was not in such a bad state as was claimed. They also rightly pointed out that Fine Gael had yet to propose any alternative programme for government that would solve economic difficulties. Furthermore, Fianna Fáil repeatedly claimed that not all emigration was due to purely economic factors. Fianna Fáil TD Seamus Moore stated that 'there was always a very considerable amount of emigration which was not due to economic causes, but which was due to a genuine desire to move, to change, to see more of the world'.[42] The denials evident in such claims were rebutted by Fine Gael deputies who pointed out that Fianna Fáil members would not have argued for a less serious view of emigration when in opposition. This was the

---

39 *Dáil Éireann Debates*, vol. 65, cols. 1327–1328, 4 March 1937.
40 *Dáil Éireann Debates*, vol. 65, col. 1529, 10 March 1937.
41 *Dáil Éireann Debates*, vol. 65, col. 1604, 11 March 1937.
42 *Dáil Éireann Debates*, vol. 65, col. 1494, 10 March 1937.

crux of the issue: emigration, and particularly concerns over women, were more likely to be raised as policy or political issues when either side was in opposition, and *not* when the party was in government. This tactic suggests that much of the rhetoric on the issue was not entirely serious.

The criticism that Fianna Fáil did not try to capitalise on the value of Irish emigration in its various economic negotiations with Great Britain has some legitimacy. This was raised by Deputy Cogan in 1947 during his contribution to the debate on the Anglo-Irish Trade Agreement:

> Did our Ministers ask the British Ministers what they were going to pay for the 250,000 men and women that we have sent over to build up the British nation? Did that matter come up for discussion? While our cattle may be good for the British people, and our poultry products may be very desirable, I think there is nothing we have given to Great Britain that is of such immense value as the young men and women we have exported to that country during the past ten years.[43]

The value of Irish emigration to the British economy was not taken up in the debate by other deputies. The Taoiseach, de Valera, instead insisted that there were plenty of jobs in Ireland and that 'a good deal of psychological matter – it is not solely economic matters – is responsible'.[44] Emigrants themselves may have agreed with Fine Gael's views that Fianna Fáil were simply not doing enough. When Catherine Dunne asked her interviewee, Joe Dunne, 'Did you, and any of the Irish people you were friends with, blame anybody for the fact that you had to emigrate in the fifties?', Joe replied, with certain bitterness: 'I blame de Valera. My mother was a de Valera woman but I blame him for everything. He had a vision of what Ireland should be – his vision, only *his* vision. One man shouldn't have a vision like that for all the people'.[45]

Emigration, Legislation and the Emergency

Legislation passed by the Fianna Fáil government in the 1930s sought to define Irish citizenship and can be considered part of the strategy for building an independent, post-colonial nation.[46] The formulation of a

---

43 *Dáil Éireann Debates*, vol. 108, col. 2119, 20 November 1947.

44 *Dáil Éireann Debates*, vol. 108, col. 2133, 20 November 1947.

45 See Catherine Dunne, *An Unconsidered People: The Irish in London* (Dublin: New Island Books, 2003), p. 225. This is a rare instance of political reflection in oral history accounts as many others do not mention government actions.

46 The legislation referred to includes the 1935 Aliens Act and the 1935 Irish Nationality

legislative 'imagined community' defined who was inside and outside the new nation, and informed the strict measures on emigration and travel instituted in response to the outbreak of the Second World War. The Emergency Powers Act (1939) came into effect on 3 September 1939 and regulated the movements of Irish citizens across the Irish Sea. Travel was strictly controlled or prohibited according to the exigencies of the war. Journeys across the Irish Sea had been banned during the First World War for safety and political reasons.[47] The regular movement of people within the travel area established between Britain and Ireland meant that the permit system of the Second World War was the first regulated form of travel experienced by passengers since the inception of the Irish Free State. The state could 'authorise and provide for the prohibition, restriction or control of the entry or departure of persons into or out of the State and the movements of persons within the State'. Under the scope of the Act men and women wishing to travel had to obtain a permit from the British Permit Office and an identity card from their local Garda station. Furthermore, certain categories of persons were strictly prohibited from migrating as the war progressed: any man with previous experience in agriculture or turf cutting; all persons under the age of twenty-two;[48] and all persons leaving for employment had to prove there were no jobs available in their area. Eldest sons who were head of households in economic need were also exempt – no such provision was made for eldest daughters of such families.

Muldowney argues that the war made the problem of looking after emigrants seem less urgent as other national concerns took over, and the government *could* for once claim that they were regulating emigration through travel permits.[49] During the war, emigration arose infrequently in the Dáil; however, one particular speech by de Valera in July 1945 is memorable and was commented upon by newspapers. The government proposed extending the strict controls contained in the 1939 Act based on two concerns: that it was still dealing with the effects of the Emergency and that such controls provided a safeguard to people accepting employment from Britain without adequate knowledge. However, even those who opposed

---

and Citizenship Act, the 1937 Amendment to the Irish Nationality Act and the 1939 Irish Nationality and Citizenship Regulations.

47 Sonja Tiernan details the difficulties Irish women had in obtaining an exit permit to travel to The Hague for the International Congress of Women in 1915. See Tiernan, *Eva Gore-Booth: An Image of Such Politics* (Manchester: Manchester University Press, 2012), pp. 150–151.

48 Travel was permitted for those under twenty-two for the purposes of training, such as for nursing, teaching and midwifery, and for religious instruction as priests or nuns.

49 Mary Muldowney, 'The Impact of the Second World War on Women in Belfast and Dublin: An Oral History', 2 vols (PhD thesis, Trinity College Dublin, 2005), vol. 1, p. 151.

emigration felt the restrictions were objectionable. Deputy Cogan's dramatic language is indicative of both the emotional resonance the issue had and the opposition many felt to controlling the movement of citizens who wished to seek employment in Britain:

> Probably no Deputy has spoken so frequently as I have against the evil of emigration. I regard the emigration of our young people as an open gash in the nation's main artery, through which the nation is bleeding to death. Nevertheless, I do not hold that the way to stop emigration is [...] by a ruthless coercion measure prohibiting our people from leaving.[50]

However, Fianna Fáil again argued that their actions were instituted to protect workers, and accused those against the measures of encouraging emigration.[51] De Valera contended that the restrictions worked well and were a counterpoint to inducements to leave by fellow emigrants already settled in Britain. His famous expression, that 'cows far away have long horns and young people can be played upon',[52] captured the attention of the *Irish Times*, which commented that the 'speech was particularly interesting, inasmuch as hitherto the Taoiseach has been curiously quiet on this all-important subject of emigration'.[53] Indeed, it seemed as if suppression of debate occurred particularly if the benefits of emigration were alluded to. Those who strayed from framing the issue in tragic terms encountered criticism at a very personal level.

Much of the rhetoric in debates on the Bill focused on men's employment. In fact, the divide was based on whether men should be allowed the freedom to work wherever they wished or whether they should be restricted from leaving the country to satisfy Ireland's 'manpower' needs. Female emigrants, in contrast, were framed within the debates as in need of control and restriction. Female domestic servants were particularly highlighted as a counterargument to those who stated that emigration was due to unemployment:

> There is no need, for instance, for any domestic servant to leave this country. There is a shortage of domestic servants in the City of

50 *Dáil Éireann Debates*, vol. 97, col. 2437, 13 July 1945.
51 Fianna Fáil's Bernard Butler argued that those who were against the Bill *wanted* emigration: 'the Opposition Parties [...] are, apparently, trying to encourage, or at least facilitate, young people in leaving the country.' *Dáil Éireann Debates*, vol. 97, col. 2434, 13 July 1945.
52 *Dáil Éireann Debates*, vol. 97, cols. 2449–2450, 13 July 1945.
53 *Irish Times*, 14 July 1945, p. 3.

Dublin, and any good domestic servant can get good wages, very good food and very much better homes, social and moral surroundings than probably she will get in Britain or possibly any other country.[54]

This assertion, as will be explored further in Chapter 4, was simply not true, given the very large wage differences and conditions of service between Ireland and Great Britain in domestic work.

Women were also accused of leaving their children as a charge on the state when they went to join their husbands in Britain. Micheál Ó Cléirigh of Fianna Fáil and the Taoiseach both referred to this, with de Valera arguing that restricting such women was simply common sense:

> Have we not the right to say to the mother: 'No, you must take your children with you. If you want to join your husband and if you take your family, well and good, but you are not going to desert your children and leave them here'? Is it not obvious that you must have controls of that sort?[55]

No statistics or substantiating evidence was given to explicate this claim. The apparent attitude was that it was the mother's sole fault and responsibility for leaving the children, despite the fact that men were conceived of as heads of households at this time, and, in this example, had also left the country. William Norton, leader of the Labour Party, similarly failed to include women in his analysis of the needs of Irish citizens to earn a living. While rejecting the Bill, he supported the proposals on restricting women's emigration, expressing his warm agreement with the Taoiseach:

> The Taoiseach made the case – I quite agree with a couple of the cases he made – that it is not desirable to allow a woman to go to England and leave her children behind her; that it may not be desirable to let a young girl go to England without the consent of her parents, and mix with a community with which she is not normally identified. These are just commonplace matters about which there should be some type of control.[56]

Commonplace matters, not biases based on gendered assumptions or blindness as to the economic role played by women in Irish society. Norton

---

54 *Dáil Éireann Debates*, vol. 97, col. 2434, 13 July 1945. References to domestic servants appeared sporadically within Dáil debates and will be referred to in detail in Chapter 4.
55 *Dáil Éireann Debates*, vol. 97, col. 2449, 13 July 1945.
56 *Dáil Éireann Debates*, vol. 97, col. 2462, 13 July 1945.

also voiced his concern with men's right to employment, conflating men with citizens:

> If the State would recognise, *in respect of every citizen*, the right to a decent family wage to enable him to keep his wife, children and himself in decency, one could probably justify the retention of our citizens here because by their efforts they would help not only to create wealth but to diffuse it here.[57]

Here a family wage is argued for, taking little account of single females who contributed to their family economy.[58] This ignored the fundamental role, recognised by anthropologists Arensberg and Kimball, for women in the family as workers, household organisers, traders in eggs and butter. Many women were vital, reciprocal contributors to rural family units.[59]

It was also implied within some of the speeches of the 1940s that women had no business emigrating. Deputy Coburn, a Fine Gael representative who opposed the Bill on the grounds that it restricted liberty, argued that it 'takes a manly man to make up his mind to travel. When he does it shows that there is something in him'.[60] This assertion of a type of 'emigrant masculinity' does not emerge anywhere in its opposite form in discussions on women. The fortitudinous female emigrant simply does not exist; her passive sister was a much stronger archetype.

De Valera appeared to equate *controls* on female emigration with *help*, as outlined in the opening quotation to this chapter.[61] How can this rhetoric be taken seriously when the government of the time neither facilitated women's employment in Ireland nor developed or supported welfare measures to ensure female emigrants were looked after? While the social mores of the period may have made specific economic policies to boost women's employment impossible to conceive, it seems absurd that politicians repeatedly ignored the fact that many women worked, many women needed to work, and thus many women emigrated to fulfil this need. There are significant, yet silent, class biases within this rhetoric, much like the 1937 Constitution which conceptualises a space for women unburdened by economic necessity and

---

57 *Dáil Éireann Debates*, vol. 97, cols. 2462–2463, 13 July 1945. My emphasis.
58 The rhetoric here can be seen to be simply a continuation of that which led to the Conditions of Employment Act in 1936.
59 Conrad Arensberg and Solon T. Kimball, *Family and Community in Ireland* (Cambridge, Mass.: Harvard University Press, 1940). This study refers extensively to the duties and expectations that consume the whole family and the particular role women played in the family economies they observed.
60 *Dáil Éireann Debates*, vol. 97, col. 2443, 13 July 1945.
61 *Dáil Éireann Debates*, vol. 97, col. 2449, 13 July 1945.

free to labour solely within her home.[62] The heteronormativity of these formulations of 'modern' womanhood are also apparent. These attitudes, not coincidentally, appear to have been influenced by Catholic ideologies of womanhood and its social teachings which also appear in the Constitution thanks in part to the Jesuit Order who convened a committee to 'advise on certain matters connected with the Constitution' and whose direct influence in its subsequent form has been traced by Gerard Hogan, although, as Hogan observed, there are also secular, liberal elements to the document.[63]

Prior to the Bill, in July 1942, Archbishop of Dublin, Most Rev. Dr John Charles McQuaid, gave his opinions on the restriction of emigration to the Minister for Justice, Gerald Boland. He claimed high numbers of teenagers were emigrating and proposed further regulating the travel permit system, with a view to both restricting the numbers of people leaving the country and obtaining more detailed information on those who left.[64] This included furnishing the Catholic Social Welfare Bureau (CSWB; more on this organisation in the next chapter) with the names, destinations and employment details of all those who applied for a passport. Clearly, McQuaid felt that the CSWB deserved to be accorded the same status and rights to information as a government department, and, as Delaney has remarked, 'the request does shed some interesting light on the consensual nature of church–state relations in Ireland at this time'.[65] As with other issues, McQuaid's views were considered seriously and investigations began. Boland's department probed the Archbishop's claims but found a lack of evidence, as revealed in a letter to de Valera:

> Dr. McQuaid was able to give information in regard to only two cases of children under sixteen leaving the country for employment. The Shipping Companies couldn't give us any information, and as we couldn't approach the British on the strength of two cases, arrangements

62 Article 41.2.1 states that 'In particular, the State recognises that by her life within the home, woman gives to the State a support without which the common good cannot be achieved', while Article 41.2.2 continues: 'The State shall, therefore, endeavour to ensure that mothers shall not be obliged by economic necessity to engage in labour to the neglect of their duties in the home': 1937 Constitution, *Bunreacht na hÉireann*.

63 Gerard Hogan, *The Origins of the Irish Constitution, 1928–1941* (Dublin: Royal Irish Academy, 2012), p. 210. The quotation comes directly from Minutes of the Jesuit Constitution Committee, first Meeting, 24 September 1936, JA, J55/65/1.

64 Letter from Boland to the Taoiseach, Éamon de Valera, 14 July 1942, NAI, DTS 11582A. McQuaid was particularly interested in the loophole that existed in regulations whereby under sixteens could emigrate without any restrictions if they were with a family member.

65 Enda Delaney, 'Irish Migration to Britain, 1921–1971: Patterns, Trends and Contingent Factors' (PhD thesis, Queen's University of Belfast, 1997), p. 229.

have been made to have the outgoing traffic at Dunlaoghaire [*sic*] inspected by the police for a few days in order to ascertain whether many children under sixteen are in fact leaving the country.[66]

The matter was subsequently dropped.[67] However, the government considered banning emigration again in 1944, revealing a distinct difference in their conception of male and female economic emigration:

> people who are quite prepared to admit the necessity of emigration in the case of men who have families to support and cannot obtain work here, cannot see any present or future good in allowing young people, particularly young girls, to go straight from the severe, but salutary, restraints of their home environments into the hectic wartime atmosphere of British cities and towns, for the sake of earning artificially high rates of wages which they have neither the experience nor the knowledge of the world to be able to spend to their own moral and material advantage.[68]

The end of the Second World War saw a relaxation of travel restrictions and the end of the regulation of women's employment in Britain, which led to the ending of restrictions on Irish female travel in 1946. With this came renewed calls on the Irish government to restrict women's emigration. In 1947, the government considered a memorandum on the possibility of reinstituting the ban on women by following three directions: a ban on women under twenty-two years of age; the introduction of a quota system based on pre-war averages adjusted to suit current conditions; or to issue each woman with a travel permit card and leaflet warning them of the dangers and difficulties they were likely to encounter in Britain.[69]

Concern was not only for the welfare of women but the demographic impact their migration had on the country. Furthermore, there was an

---

66 Letter from Boland to the Taoiseach, Éamon de Valera, 14 July 1942, NAI, DTS 11582A. Boland indicated that the issuing of information from the passport office to the CSWB was being investigated by the Department of External Affairs but that the final decision would 'no doubt be submitted to you for decision', indicating that de Valera may have ultimately refused to supply the information.

67 McQuaid's efforts in this area, however, went beyond bending the ears of sympathetic politicians; his concern over female emigrants led him to take a more hands-on approach: initiating the CSWB.

68 Department of External Affairs, Memorandum to the government dated 9 May 1944, NAI, DTS 11582B: 'New Proposals Regarding Restrictions on Travel Permit Issues to Workers'.

69 Department of External Affairs, Memorandum dated 30 August 1947, NAI, DFA 402/25.

emphasis within the memorandum on the fact that even before controls were lifted in July 1946 there was a steady rise in the number of women emigrating, a trend which provoked 'deep public unease'.[70] How this 'unease' was measured is not made clear. The restrictions on male workers were still in existence, thus banning women could have been publicly justified in terms of a regulation of workers rather than specifically a control on women. However, after a number of postponements, the issue was struck off the cabinet's agenda. Delaney has posited that 'perhaps the Fianna Fáil government of the day found these issues too uncomfortable to contemplate'.[71] Instituting a ban would require an explicit articulation of the morally dubious behaviours or circumstances the government feared Irish women might find themselves engaged in. The embarrassment of this prospect may have outweighed the perceived benefits. It is perhaps a shame that this debate did not get a public airing as it meant that such attitudes towards women latently persisted, unchallenged in any public arena and therefore liable to reappear.

The issue, however, lingered. Further calls for an emigration ban came in 1948 when the Commission on Emigration and Other Population Problems considered the subject at the request of the Clann na Poblachta party. Delaney has argued this was driven by Seán MacBride, then Minister for External Affairs. MacBride was clearly in agreement with (if not prompted by) fellow party member and Commissioner Aodh de Blácam who wrote a memorandum on the issue in the same year in which he argued that:

> The primary cause of emigration is not an economic but a spiritual one – the people's loss of the natural instinct to survive. A patriotic Government resolved to save the nation from extinction could revive national aspirations and so create conditions in which the economic measures necessary to stop emigration could be effective.[72]

The Commission did not, however, recommend a ban on emigration for either men or women in their final report.[73] Thus, as Delaney has highlighted, banning women from emigrating was a measure considered (and subsequently rejected) by both Fianna Fáil and Clann na Poblachta, two radically different political parties. This indicates a general tenor of

---

70 Department of External Affairs, Memorandum: 'New Proposals Regarding Restrictions on Travel Permit Issues to Workers'.
71 Delaney, *State, Politics and Demography*, p. 38.
72 Aodh de Blácam, 'Emigration, Cause and Cure', NAI, DTS 14249/Annex.
73 The report will be discussed further in relation to attitudes to women and employment in Chapter 4. Aodh de Blácam died before the end of the Commission and perhaps if he had lived he would have insisted on inserting a recommendation of this kind, or else a minority report, as did other dissenting commissioners.

belief in the appropriateness – on moral grounds – of banning women from exercising their own will in matters of emigration. It is interesting also to note that such arguments were refuted by members of the Catholic hierarchy (apart from McQuaid) because it not only interfered with parental authority but the autonomy of minors themselves. It seems that banning, as opposed to guiding, controlling, assisting and being informed, was one step too far under Catholic moral reasoning.

For those who dared to outline any positive aspects of emigration, strict censure followed. In February 1946, TD Richard Mulcahy argued cogently that the government policy on wages did not match up with their supposed aspirations to keep people on the land.[74] The Minister for Local Government, Seán MacEntee, dismissed Mulcahy's remarks, stating that his speech could be likened to 'the country grocer who had the advertisements of the steamship lines in his shop' and called him an 'emigrating agent or a recruiting sergeant for another country', accusing him of dishonesty about 'the real conditions' in Britain.[75] MacEntee's branding of Mulcahy as an 'emigration agent' received much publicity and sparked similar criticism of him within the press.[76] Interestingly, in an analogous vein, James Craig, Prime Minister of Northern Ireland, was forced to issue a statement to counter claims that his holiday to Canada in 1926 was designed to promote the emigration of young rural Protestants.[77] Paranoia over being considered an 'emigration agent' appears to have been a cross-border issue.

In all of this debate, however, it is to be remembered that concern was expressly articulated for *men's* ability to earn a living to support their family. State schemes to provide employment and greater production policies in agriculture and industry were proposed to solve the problem of male emigration; for example, the Construction Corps developed during the Emergency.[78] While this was certainly the norm in terms of international government policies and attitudes, women's need to earn a living was ignored, either in itself or as a reason for their emigration to Britain, and this one-sided rhetoric indicates a case of ideology trumping reality. Patriarchal norms did not allow for the promotion of women's work outside the home and the nature of the economy at the time may also have been an influencing factor. Agriculture was thought to be essential to the economy and government policy retained a commitment to developing the sector throughout the 1920s

---

74 *Dáil Éireann Debates*, vol. 99, col. 1083, 14 February 1946.

75 *Dáil Éireann Debates*, vol. 99, cols. 1118–1119, 15 February 1946.

76 The term 'emigration agent' was not coined by MacEntee and seems to have been in common usage.

77 Devlin Trew, *Leaving the North*, p. 44.

78 For more on this, see Bryce Evans, 'The Construction Corps, 1940–1948', *Saothar*, 2 (2007), pp. 19–31.

to the 1950s, with secondary efforts directed towards developing industry. The majority of agricultural (paid and unpaid) workers were men, which is why male emigration evoked more concern than female. Time and again the necessity to provide for 'farmers, farmers sons or farm labourers'[79] was articulated, but rarely the need to provide for farmers' daughters.

During the 1942 debate, Senator Helena Concannon, in an exceptional display of gender awareness on migration, referred to the 'constant flow of young men from the country', but Concannon was also concerned about female rates and stated she did 'not know whether any inquiry was made as to the conditions under which these girls would work or the dangers to which they might be exposed and what is to become of them when the war ends and they come back to us'.[80] Concannon's speech demonstrates the parallel discourses that surrounded male and female emigrants: male emigration was accepted as a fact, female emigration required the articulation of a wealth of welfare concerns.

As might be expected, the issue of emigration arose in debates related to finances, an instance of this being the Finance Bill of 1947. Domestic servants arose again as a topic, this time contradicting assertions, such as those mentioned above, that there was no need for them to emigrate. Deputy Dominick Cafferky of Clann na Talmhúain argued that domestic servants had three grievances: 'Firstly, the long hours, secondly, the small rate of wage, and, thirdly, the disrespect held for them in the household'.[81] Despite this alteration in tone, defending rather than condemning women's emigration, Deputy Cafferky's concerns over 'the dangers from the moral and religious point of view'[82] can be viewed as within the mainstream of discourse on women, positing them as more vulnerable than male emigrants. What is most significant, however, is his point that:

nothing [is] being done by the Government to alleviate or to remove these dangers by providing suitable employment for these people in their own country and by seeing that these ladies who could be given employment here and who would take up employment here if they were properly treated would get it.[83]

This speech is one of the very few times where the *need* for female employment of any kind is expressed by a TD or Senator. Deputy Cafferky's

79 Deputy Corry, *Dáil Éireann Debates*, vol. 108, col. 1472, 6 November 1947.
80 *Seanad Éireann Debates*, vol. 26, col. 1937, 23 July 1942.
81 *Dáil Éireann Debates*, vol. 108, col. 1499, 6 November 1947.
82 Ibid.
83 Ibid.

arguments were endorsed by Deputy Dockrell,[84] who argued that 'in spite of years of native Government, we still have this tragic drain of many of our best men and women and [...] nothing is being done to stop it'.[85]

(Non) Debates on the Inter-Departmental Committee Report on Seasonal Emigration and the Commission on Emigration and Other Population Problems Report

On 23 September 1937, the Inter-Departmental Committee on Seasonal Migration to Great Britain was instituted to investigate the scale and conditions of recruitment, accommodation and employment of Irish workers who travelled seasonally to work in agricultural areas of Great Britain.[86] This was in response to a tragedy on 10 September 1937 in which ten seasonal male workers from Achill Island had been killed when a fire broke out in the wooden shed in which they were sleeping at a farm in Kirkintilloch in Scotland. The total group consisted of men, young boys and girls who had gone to pick potatoes. The Dáil was not in session when the committee was instituted by Seán Lemass, and the Seanad was at that time still in dissolution.[87] Thus no debate was conducted as to the terms of reference, composition or procedural remit of the committee. Furthermore, it was staffed solely by civil servants. Given the massive outcry of public sympathy after the tragedy, one may have expected the report to have had wider influence on policy or debate. The legal limitations on the government in restricting seasonal emigration and its economic importance to families in the West were stressed. The report did not result in any changes in government policy.

The report found that practically all the migrants from Clare and West Galway went to East Galway hiring fairs, and some of the migrants from West Donegal went to fairs at Strabane and Letterkenny where they were hired for casual employment. The number of migrants to Great Britain in

---

84 It is not clear which Deputy Dockrell is being referred to here as there were two Fine Gael TDs with the same name: Henry Morgan Dockrell and Maurice Edward Dockrell.

85 *Dáil Éireann Debates*, vol. 108, col. 1570, 6 November 1947.

86 The Committee was set up by the Minister for Industry and Commerce and included the following: Mr Sean Moylan TD, Parliamentary Secretary to the Minister of Industry and Commerce; Mr J.J. Keane, Chief Employment Officer, Department of Industry and Commerce; Mr F.H. Boland, Principal Officer, Department of Industry and Commerce; Mr T. O'Connell, Chief Inspector, Department of Agriculture; Mr J.C. Gamble, Senior Inspector, Land Commission; Mr Sean Moran, Director, Gaeltacht Services, and Mr Leon O'Brien, Assistant Principal, Department of Finance.

87 The second Seanad was not instituted until 1938.

1937 was reckoned at approximately 9,500.[88] Women were included in these groups, though they constituted a minority of the workers and generally worked as part of family groups.[89] 'The normal group consists of about twenty-five workers and a "gaffer" [foreman]. Of this group of twenty-five workers, probably only a few are male adults, the remainder being women, boys and girls'.[90] Considering women's share of this workforce, their contribution to the finances of their communities was significant. It was estimated that the aggregate earnings of these migrants was approximately £200,000 per annum.[91] Such groups were engaged almost exclusively in picking potatoes, with general farm work and other harvesting also regular activities. The report does *not* make any comments on moral concerns over women involved in this type of migration.[92] This suggests either that it was not investigated or was not thought important.

This lack of attention, despite fervent interest at the time in the newspapers and by the Catholic Church in the status of female migrants, may be because women were encased within a traditional, patriarchal unit, working as wives, sisters, daughters or relatives alongside boys and men. Although female agricultural workers were not a large group within the overall female migrant flow, they were a continual presence. It is therefore interesting that these female seasonal workers were not subject to the same type of censure, analysis and critique as were women working in other occupations.

The Commission on Emigration and Other Population Problems was initiated by William Norton, Minister for Social Welfare, on 5 April 1948, following a promise by the outgoing Fianna Fáil administration to set up a body to investigate what was viewed as the chronic problem of Ireland's skewed demography. It produced much useful statistical and qualitative data. Chaired by Dr James P. Beddy, an economist and public servant who became the first Chairman of the Industrial Development Authority, it contained representatives from both the Protestant and Catholic faiths, with experts in policy, medicine, academia and statistics. Many of the men had written articles or letters in the press about emigration, women and morality issues in Irish life. Just two women, Mrs Agnes McGuire and Mrs Frances

---

88 *Report of the Inter-Departmental Committee on Seasonal Migration to Great Britain, 1937–1938* (Dublin: Stationery Office, 1938), para. 21.

89 These groups of seasonal migrants were often known as 'Achill Workers' due to the predominance of workers from Achill Island, off the coast of Mayo in the west of Ireland and the surrounding regions.

90 *Report of the Inter-Departmental Committee on Seasonal Migration*, para. 19.

91 Ibid., para. 28.

92 Although such groups were small, there were probably many engaged in seasonal migration. It is impossible to know the exact number of women engaged in this kind of seasonal employment.

Wrenne, were included in the Commission, out of a total of twenty-three original members. While an improvement on the composition of the seasonal migration inquiry (to which women could not be appointed because they did not occupy posts at the higher level of the civil service), it was still a very low number. It also appears that the women were there as mere tokens. Frances Wrenne, née Cunningham, was a trained domestic science teacher who wrote recipes and tips for the *Fold*, the monthly magazine for the Diocese of Cork and Ross. Wrenne was close to fellow Commissioner Dr Cornelius Lucey, establishing the 'Tabernacle fund' to encourage donations of gold jewellery towards the tabernacles of a circle of new churches – known as the rosary of churches – being built by the Bishop in Cork.[93] Although little documentary evidence is extant, it is likely that Wrenne conducted some of the 'on the ground' investigations in Cork which fed into Lucey's submissions. Wrenne submitted a brief Reservation to the report in which she objected to paragraph 184, which asserted the inheritance rights of eldest sons (which she felt could be to the detriment of widows), and she wished a revision of Chapter 9 on Population to assert more strictly Catholic principles that would reflect the religious preference of the majority of the country.[94] Lucey, in comparison, submitted a thirty-page Reservation.

Mrs Agnes McGuire was noted as being from the Department of Social Science in University College Dublin, although there is no record of her in the College Calendars and as the teaching staff came from different departments in the Faculties of Arts and Medicine she is particularly difficult to trace.[95] McGuire did not write an individual Reservation, unlike Wrenne, although neither woman features as a strong presence in the notes and memorandums that have survived in Commissioner Arnold Marsh's papers.[96] Thus, both women remain a shadowy presence in the report and neither appears to have asserted themselves as advocates for women emigrants. Indeed, their presence is so quiet that they are often not included in lists of the Commissioners.[97]

The Commission's aim was to investigate the demographic trends in Ireland such as fertility, marriage rates, emigration and internal migration and other matters thought to affect Ireland's population. Daly has argued

---

93 My thanks are due to Wrenne's grand-nephew, Laurence J.F. Wrenne, for biographical details on her life, provided after contact was made in 2013 through the IR-D (Irish Diaspora) Listserv.

94 Frances Wrenne, Reservation Number 12, *Majority Report*, p. 254.

95 My thanks to University College Dublin archivist Kate Manning for this information.

96 Thus far these are the only surviving personal papers and are housed in the Manuscripts Department, Trinity College Dublin.

97 Neither woman is listed in the recent extensive treatment of the Commission by Clair Wills in *The Best Are Leaving*, for example.

that the Commission may have been established as a 'safety valve' to alleviate pressure posed by the Catholic Church and some of its supporters in the 1940s to restrict the right to emigrate.[98] Given the absence of serious commentary or parliamentary debate on the report, and the disappointing lack of action on the Commission's policy recommendations, this appears to be an apt judgement. The publication of the Commission's findings was, *ostensibly*, eagerly awaited if one is to judge this by the frequent Dáil questions on when it was to be published which emerged from 1952 onwards (years before it was actually published). As questions arose, so too did vested interests, none of which addressed the Commission's view that 'a steadily increasing population should occupy a high place among the criteria by which the success of national policy should be judged'.[99] This statement, however, must be viewed as aspirational, as no concrete recommendations were given as to how to achieve this. The Commission did not propose a ban on emigration, but it did recommend that the government become more actively involved in providing emigrant assistance. The final report recommended that:

> some type of social bureau should be established in Great Britain to look after the welfare of our emigrants there. We realise that young people, and especially girls, recruited singly into employment through newspaper advertisements and by other means, may well find themselves in jobs which they should and would give up if they know where to look for prompt aid and guidance. [...] We are of the opinion that the suggestion is a good one and we think that, in the event of a request for a conference to establish such a committee, the appropriate Government Department should arrange for consultations to ensure that the committee was a thoroughly representative one.[100]

This last point touches on the issue of ecumenical welfare cooperation which will be a feature of the next chapter, though this practical suggestion was, like many, ignored by successive governments, preferring instead to leave this to existing ecclesiastical networks and voluntary lay organisations.

Most of the recommendations, however, did not propose ideas that could be tackled practically by any government. The opportunity was missed,

---

98 Daly, *The Slow Failure*, p. 162. Delaney has suggested appointing a commission was 'an age-old method of kicking issues to touch': *State, Politics and Demography*, p. 37.

99 Commission on Emigration and Other Population Problems, *Majority Report*, para. 472. For a thorough discussion of the views of the Commission and its reception, see also Delaney, *Demography, State and Society* and *The Irish in Post-War Britain* as well as Daly, *The Slow Failure*.

100 Commission on Emigration and Other Population Problems, *Majority Report*, para. 328.

therefore, to address the problem of emigration even after new statistical evidence was gathered and rigorous policy and economic and social analysis by experts had occurred. It is also indicative of governmental attitudes to emigration in the time period that no TD, Senator or political party attempted to formulate more actionable policy recommendations on the basis of the report. Thus, by 1960, Seán Lemass was able to claim that the report had sunk without trace, stating that it 'made very little impact on Irish public opinion when published and was now almost forgotten'.[101]

Conclusion

Emigration was a topic that often attracted sporadic, emotional and irrational rhetoric rather than serious discussions or deliberations in the Oireachtas. The issue of emigration assumed a 'jibe' status, being regularly hurled to and fro between the government and opposition parties. It seems the topic was raised as an issue particularly because it was known that nothing would be done by any government of any political persuasion. This is in stark contrast to the pre-independence policy of the first Dáil which banned emigration on the grounds that it was unpatriotic to leave the land during the national struggle, as outlined in Chapter 1.[102]

Emigration was, at the same time, one of the key indicators of success or failure: a booming population would have indicated a healthy economy and a nation with confidence in its ability successfully to support itself. It seems this would have also further legitimised independence, a process continuously worked upon throughout the 1920s and the 1930s under both Cumman na nGaedheal and Fianna Fáil, culminating in the declaration of a republic in 1948 by the first coalition government. In contrast, the consistently high rates of emigration appeared to indicate what was – to use Daly's expression – a 'slow failure' in the Irish economy to develop itself sufficiently once the shackles of colonialism had been thrown off. Indeed, as Ferriter has commented: 'More than anything else [...] it was emigration that made a mockery of any idealisation of rural life, providing successive governments in the 1930s and 1940s with evidence of the failure of policies designed to keep people on the land'.[103] This was recognised in a wider context by TD Richard Mulcahy, who pointed out that the issue went beyond economics; the government's vision for the nation was at stake: 'This is not a matter of

---

101 Daly, *The Slow Failure*, p. 182.
102 Ferriter, *The Transformation of Ireland*, p. 211. The policy could not, in practice, be enforced.
103 Ibid. p. 381.

mere wages. It is a question of what the Government expect men and women to live in Ireland for, who have struggled to set up an Irish Parliament and an Irish Government representative of themselves'.[104]

It seems that debates on emigration constituted little more than political grandstanding and those that did occur within the Dáil focused on such issues as welfare, the appropriateness of restricting freedom of movement, rural depopulation and the effect of emigration on the economy. There are only brief moments of realistic commentary, such as Deputy Coburn's observation in 1945:

> I believe all the crocodile tears shed in regard to emigration are nothing but pure hypocrisy. I never regarded emigration as a thing to be ashamed of, as a thing to be avoided or scorned, and I never felt that legislation should be introduced in order to prevent it. I think that emigration during the past five or six years has been a great safety valve for this country. It was a very good thing that so many people were able to go away.[105]

When official reports emerged, however, political parties did nothing to act on the evidence, merely making empty assertions about the plight of emigrants or remaining silent. No elected official emerged as a champion of emigrants in the post-independence period, and women representatives did not demonstrate an interest in either developing arguments on the necessity for women to work or defending female emigrants from charges of moral wantonness. Two observations can be made in relation to female public representatives. First, although they were not as vocal as their male counterparts, this may reflect the 'political climate which was inimical to the participation of women' in political life.[106] Second, women TDs' silence on emigration also indicates the lack of wider public debate in Ireland. Emigration may, in fact, have been too obvious to comment upon. Akenson declared that in the first half of the nineteenth century, having 'a cousin on the near coast of North America became an ordinary part of the family furnishings';[107] if this is the case, having a cousin in Britain in the twentieth century was like having them in the next room.

The special attention paid to female emigrants and their moral needs is nowhere more evident, however, than in the discourses on emigrant welfare, as will be discussed in the next chapter.

---

104 *Dáil Éireann Debates*, vol. 99, col. 1233, 20 February 1946.
105 *Dáil Éireann Debates*, vol. 97, col. 2442, 13 July 1945.
106 McNamara and Mooney, *Women in Parliament*, p. 17.
107 Akenson, *Ireland, Sweden and the Great European Migration*, p. 106.

3

Travelling
and the Morality of Moving

We are glad to report that the White Slave Traffic through
Liverpool, especially with the United States, has been considerably checked […] The evil, however, still exists, and is worse
in some other countries, but its progress has been impeded
and frequently frustrated by the work of the Society and other
Vigilance Associations in Great Britain.

Liverpool Port and Station Work Society, Annual Report 1923.

In 1923, the National Vigilance Association (NVA) in Britain wrote to the
Irish High Commissioner, James McNeill, urging him to address the
problem of Irish women coming to Britain.[1] Such women were stated to
be often without money, luggage or a job, or, alternatively, completely unfit
for jobs they were accepted for and hence quickly lost. Mr Sempkins, head
of the NVA, pointed out that although many women were helped in their
travel arrangements by the International Catholic Girls' Protection Society
(ICGPS) in Cork and Dublin, he:

would suggest that the girls for whom special protection is most
needed are not the girls who seek the help of these two Societies; but
are rather those girls who either come over in entire ignorance of the
dangers and difficulties awaiting them, or those who think they are
quite capable of taking care of themselves.[2]

1 James McNeill (1869–1938), brother of Eoin McNeill, acted as High Commissioner
  from 1923 and was later Governor General of the Irish Free State, replacing Timothy
  Healy in 1928.
2 Letter from Mr Sempkins to Irish High Commissioner in London dated 10 August
  1923, Women's Library, File 4NVA/04/02 Box FL098. Emphasis in original.

The message from many involved in helping emigrant women was that above all they needed guidance and the 'special protection' offered by welfare associations during their journeys.

The vulnerability of Irish girls travelling to and living in Britain was a consistent theme in the post-independence period. As I have argued elsewhere, morality, keeping 'respectable' and upholding the religious values imbued in Ireland were markers of success for women in a way they were not for men.[3] In a nutshell, where financial achievement was a hallmark of the 'right type' of male emigrant, sexual purity before marriage was such for women – a quality more difficult to 'police' when a woman was abroad. This is where emigrant philanthropy, primarily of a religious nature, stepped in: organisations designed to protect women on their journeys, the largest recipients of such attention being Irish women. Thus, on both sides of the Irish Sea, women were continually framed as needful of assistance, yet while small numbers actively called on the services of voluntary organisations, many thousands more ignored them.

This example from the Liverpool Vigilance Association files from 1954 is typical of the way in which the problematic Irish emigrant girl is narrated:

> It is amazing the number of girls who arrive here without any knowledge of the sort of place to which they are going. Even a place the size of London seems beyond the comprehension of some of these young Irish girls from remote rural areas. How they would fare if I were not on hand to help I do not know. One day a girl whom I was helping said that she was going to St. Joseph's Hospital, London. I pointed out that London was a very big place and the difficulties of finding it with only this address would be tremendous. The girl said she was sure to be all right as a friend was meeting her. But there was always the chance that the friend would not be at Euston Station to meet her, this I explained to the girl who then realised she would be in a very awkward position. She searched through her handbag to see if she had a letter from her friend with the full address and fortunately was successful. The girl left in a very grateful mood.[4]

This encounter, narrated from the perspective of the station worker, Mrs Blyth, is framed as her compassionate help for a naive country girl who was sure to go drastically wrong without her intervention. To re-imagine creatively this scenario from the perspective of the female traveller, however,

---

3 For more, see Jennifer Redmond, '"Sinful Singleness?" Discourses on Irish Women's Emigration to England, 1922–1948', *Women's History Review*, 17 July 2008, pp. 455–476.

4 Liverpool Vigilance Association, Annual Report 1954, unpaginated.

it could be narrated thus: the girl had full knowledge of where she was going, had assured the station worker that she didn't need help, humoured her by producing a letter with the full address on it and left rolling her eyes at the quaint maternal preaching she had just received.

This chapter looks at the narratives that surrounded women emigrants, focusing on their travel arrangements and the perceived dangers that awaited them on their journeys from rural homesteads to urban centres. From the vantage point of the Catholic and Protestant emigrant philanthropic organisations, women's journeys were tinged with precariousness in a way that was different from men. Their physical vulnerability and the widespread misperception that women were emigrating for social rather than economic reasons led to a hyperbolic discourse about women's bodies and their sexual and moral behaviour.

The conservative social tone surrounding sexual matters in Ireland was couched in moralistic terms and was deeply influenced by religious beliefs about the role of sex for procreation rather than pleasure. Mary Hazard's *Sixty Years a Nurse* reflects on her life as a teenager in the 1950s, having come to Britain to train as a nurse, and her sentiments are echoed in the memoirs and oral histories of both men and women of this era. Interestingly, Hazard admitted that although she had rejected 'so much of Catholicism intellectually', issues of sexual behaviour, which were mortal sins in Catholic teaching, 'went deep' and could not be shaken off despite the modernising trends in relationships in the post-war period.[5] The key question is thus: if we can generally accept that Irish women were largely uneducated about sexual matters and had received messages from both home and church about the damnation that sexual experimentation before marriage would bring, why was the assumption that so many girls would be so quick to abandon long held morals? Why would emigration result in sexual liberation?

This was also a time, as has been discussed by many historians, when nation building involved an intense interest in sexuality and morality, with several commissions being established to examine 'the moral conduct of the nation' that 'reported on how Irish social behaviour should be disciplined', which led to a raft of legislation 'designed to give the state and its various bodies the power to intervene into the sexual lives of its citizens'.[6] This 'architecture of containment', as Smith describes it,[7] was to impact heavily

---

5 Mary Hazard (with Corinne Sweet), *Sixty Years a Nurse* (London: Harper Element, 2015), p. 129.

6 Una Crowley and Rob Kitchin, 'Producing "Decent Girls": Governmentality and the Moral Geographies of Sexual Conduct in Ireland (1922–1937)', *Gender, Place and Culture*, 15.4 (2008), p. 355.

7 James M. Smith, *Ireland's Magdalen Laundries and the Nation's Architecture of Containment* (Notre Dame, Ind.: University of Notre Dame Press, 2007).

on understandings of female emigrants and largely shaped the fears that existed about what would become of Irish women in Britain: 'that evil, Protestant Godforsaken country', as described by Mary Hazard's mother.[8]

White Slavers and Emigrant Women: Campaigns, Reform and Hyperbole

As part of the panoply of private philanthropy initiatives cultivated in the nineteenth century, specific welfare organisations for women emigrants were created by both Protestant and Catholic groups to guide such women safely in their transition from Ireland to Britain and elsewhere. Such services continued in the post-independence era, with a sustained belief that middle-class women of faith were needed for moral guidance. For a brief time, there was ecumenical cooperation in acting on this firmly held belief. This was to change with the narrowing of lay women's opportunities to provide such services, culminating in the wholesale takeover of Catholic welfare provision with the advent of Archbishop McQuaid's tenure in Dublin, when Catholic services were strengthened and brought under the direct control of the Church.[9] However, the tendency of the state to bestow responsibility for the social (and in many cases this was understood as equating with moral) welfare of its citizens on private, religious organisations was established in the nineteenth century and continued into the post-independence era, leading to the rise of the Catholic Church's influence in this area.[10] These organisations did not operate as coherent groups at national level, unlike the larger philanthropic organisations such as the National Society for the Prevention of Cruelty to Children, which developed 'a strong alliance with the legal agencies of the state'.[11] However, they attracted interest from prominent women in Irish society throughout their existence.

The organisations provided experienced women welfare workers, although they lacked any formal qualifications. These women, wearing identifiable pins, badges and arm bands, acted as kindly figures to help and guide women

---

8 Hazard, *Sixty Years a Nurse*, p. 2.

9 For more on this, see Jennifer Redmond, '"Safeguarding Irish Girls": Welfare Work, Female Emigrants and the Catholic Church, 1920s–1940s', in Christina S. Brophy and Cara Delay (eds), *Women, Reform, and Resistance in Ireland, 1850–1950* (New York: Palgrave Macmillan, 2015), pp. 79–106.

10 See Joe Moran, 'From Catholic Church Dominance to Social Partnership Promise and Now Economic Crisis, Little Changes in Irish Social Policy', *Irish Journal of Public Policy*, 2.1 (2010). Available online at http://publish.ucc.ie/ijpp/2010/01/moran/01/en.

11 Maria Luddy, 'The Early Years of the NSPCC in Ireland', *Éire-Ireland*, 44.1–2 (2009), p. 64.

who became lost, directing them to trains, assisting at ports, and, in cases of emergency, providing contact with appropriate hostels, which were usually provided by affiliated religious groups. All organisations, regardless of religion, were interested in one thing: prevention. In this sense, prevention was always centred on moral behaviour: a single girl at a station was a remarkably vulnerable archetype invoked repeatedly in funding appeals. Setting these girls on the right geographical *and* moral path was the mission of all emigrant philanthropy organisations. Symbolically, the presence of welfare workers also operated as a warning to those who would do harm to girls travelling. The port and station workers were therefore an emblem of womanly propriety and a beacon of hope for the distressed woman traveller. Despite a common goal of protection and prevention, however, these organisations did not sustain their cooperation in Dublin. A contrast between Catholic and Protestant approaches can be seen. While there was intermittent cooperation followed by sectarian clashes, there were more seminal differences in the approach to emigration itself that appeared to have religious and political overtones, as a comparison between the Church of Ireland Girls' Friendly Society and the Catholic groups, the International Catholic Girls' Protection Society and the Catholic Social Welfare Bureau, reveals.

The laws in Ireland concerning the abolition of the white slave trade were enacted in the pre-independence period due to pressure from activists who connected this phenomenon with that of domestic prostitution in Britain. Investigations into European brothels by the Quaker journalist Alfred Dyer had found an active trade in British girls into the regulated brothels of Belgium in the 1870s.[12] This exposé led to the establishment of the Select Committee of the House of Lords on the Law Related to the Protection of Young Girls, which investigated the matter and published its report between 1881 and 1882. As a result of the findings and the vigorous campaigning of journalist W.T. Stead,[13] British activist Josephine Butler and other social purity and feminist activists sought 'to mobilize popular opinion during a moral panic over "white slavery" in the 1880s' and the Criminal Law Amendment Act (1885) came into being, followed by the Criminal Law Amendment (White Slave Traffic) Act of 1912.[14] This was not a uniquely British problem; concern for women disappearing into the white slave trade

---

12 Julia Laite, *Common Prostitutes and Ordinary Citizens: Commercial Sex in London, 1885–1960* (Basingstoke: Palgrave Macmillan, 2012), p. 8.

13 Stead also did his own exposé of juvenile prostitution in a serialised account, 'The Maiden Tribute of Modern Babylon', which appeared in the *Pall Mall Gazette* in July 1885.

14 Ian Christopher Fletcher, 'Opposition by Journalism? The Socialist and Suffragist Press and the Passage of the Criminal Law Amendment Act of 1912', *Parliamentary History*, 25.1 (2006), p. 88.

occurred across the world and was concomitant with debates on moral purity, women's suffrage rights and welfare reform, as Maria Luddy's work on prostitution has highlighted.[15]

What led to the spectre of white slavery as a threat to Irish women in twentieth-century discourses? Irish societies involved in helping emigrant women may have been influenced by contacts with British moral welfare organisations such as the National Vigilance Association, who will be discussed in greater detail further on. The global attention to the issue culminated in the International Convention for the Suppression of the Traffic in Women and Children, by the League of Nations, in 1921, which was signed by thirty-three countries.[16] Ireland was not one of them.[17]

As Luddy has noted, there is little evidence of the impact of Stead's campaign in Ireland, or that white slavery was a problem:

The Chief Commissioner of the DMP [Dublin Metropolitan Police] reported that he was unaware of any traffic in young girls between Ireland and England. Such a traffic, he noted, could not 'be carried on without the knowledge of the detective department as there is no class with whom we are more frequently brought into contact in the discharge of our duties than female servants, brothel keepers and prostitutes'.[18]

However, the issue persisted, and white slavery, prostitution and emigration were intermingled in discourses in both northern and southern Ireland and

---

15 Maria Luddy, *Prostitution and Irish Society, 1800–1940* (Cambridge: Cambridge University Press, 2008). Luddy attributes the perpetuation of the mythical prevalence of the white slave trade and prostitution to Irish suffragists who sustained arguments about it for their own political purposes.

16 For a full discussion of the background to legislation in this area, see Jean Allain, 'White Slave Traffic in International Law', *Journal of Trafficking and Human Exploitation*, 1.1 (2017), pp. 1–40.

17 The convention referred to, adopted on 30 September 1921, came into force on 15 June 1922. Given political events in Ireland, it is not surprising that it was not ratified at the time. The signatory countries were: 'Albania, Germany, Austria, Belgium, Brazil, the British Empire (with Canada, the Commonwealth of Australia, the Union of South Africa, New Zealand and India), Chile, China, Colombia, Costa Rica, Cuba, Estonia, Greece, Hungary, Italy, Japan, Latvia, Lithuania, Norway, the Netherlands, Persia, Poland (with Danzig), Portugal, Romania, Siam, Sweden, Switzerland and Czechoslovakia'. It is unclear if it ever was ratified in Ireland. However, a memorandum from the Department of External Affairs, 'New Proposals Regarding Restrictions on Travel Permit Issues to Workers', quotes Article 6 and states that Ireland is a party to the convention and has obligations to protect women using employment agencies. Memorandum dated 9 May 1944, NAI, DFA 402/25.

18 Luddy, *Prostitution and Irish Society*, p. 153.

Figure 3.1   John Regan, 'Crimes of the white slavers and the results: a
vivid exposé of the methods used by this unscrupulous band of vampires
in their nefarious business, portraying the snares laid for the unwary
girl to force her into a disreputable life and bring dishonour into the
family circle', published by The Purity League, Chicago, *c.*1912.
Reproduced with permission by Bryn Mawr College Library.

by mainstream as well as religious papers that created the image of the 'vulnerable girl' under threat from perverse male sexuality.[19]

Despite the lack of firm evidence that a problem existed, white slavery as a threat to Irish women persisted as a topic of concern for welfare agencies (Figure 3.1). The International Catholic Girls' Protection Society (ICGPS) reiterated their concerns in frequent newspaper articles containing dramatic language: 'We also solemnly warn all intending emigrants to be on their guard against the agents of the white slave traffic, who, we have good reason to believe, are always trying to carry on their nefarious work on most of the outgoing transatlantic liners'.[20] The files of the NVA in Britain contain a copy of a letter with the subject 'Suspected White Slave Traffic in Irish Girls in Great Britain' sent from police in Dublin to the Chief of Police in London:

> It appears it has been suggested to the Authorities that the traffic is being carried on mainly at Liverpool, but probably at other large centres also, they have no definite information, but as the Authorities are greatly concerned, the Officers asked me to bring the matter to your notice and to ask you that you Officers are instructed to keep a watch on young girls arriving by Irish connecting trains, in case the people concerned in the traffic are accosting or intercepting them at various large centres and termini, notably Liverpool and London.[21]

Although this indicates the problem was regarded seriously by police as well as welfare organisations, it seems it was still largely perceived as a 'foreign' phenomenon. No measures were taken by post-1922 Irish governments at any point to provide funding for welfare work to prevent Irish women from being targeted. Again, this may be because of the assumption that welfare work of this kind was more properly within the remit of the Catholic Church. It may also be because some felt such claims were grossly overstated. There is no specific evidence available on this issue at government level that would allow for a definite conclusion to be reached.

In the 1930s, the Liverpool Vigilance Society, however, argued that most 'people associated the white slave traffic with Buenos Aires. It was not necessary to go that far afield. In every large city there were birds of prey ready to pounce on young unprotected girls'.[22] The intimation in the

---

19 Ibid., p. 166.
20 *Irish Catholic*, 24 May 1930, p. 7.
21 Letter from Inspector E.R. Neal, Police Department, North Wall, Dublin 1 to Chief of Police, Euston dated 27 October 1931, Women's Library, File 4NVA/04/02 Box FL098.
22 *Irish Catholic*, 8 August 1936, p. 6.

article was that Irish girls were also vulnerable because the society dealt with so many of them coming in to Liverpool. Oral history evidence suggests this opinion may have filtered into 'common sense' advice given to female emigrants by friends and family. Bridget Dantu, for example, emigrated from Limerick to London in 1946 with advice from two female neighbours that 'if you hear anyone with a foreign accent, run, because you'll be sold to the white slave traffic'.[23] 'Maureen', in an interview with Louise Ryan, reported she had 'heard stories where young girls coming to London were met at train stations and people offered to take them places. I heard that but I didn't know any of them'.[24] Joan, interviewed by Sharon Lambert, appears to have been extremely frightened by the prospect of white slavers when living in Britain:

> We were warned before I left home about the South American er? … ye'd get an injection and ye'd end up in South America in the white slavery. *Oh it was common knowledge* … I remember once, I wanted to see a picture in the daytime … And them cinemas used to be very dark. And there was only one seat down the side, and the girl put me into it. I couldn't see who it was that was next to me but oh, I wasn't long sitting down there when I heard it was a man next to me. I thought 'Oh, a white slaver! This injection is coming any time!' I had sense enough to get up, and I went back until I got another seat. I think I kicked out at him or something. I nearly died.[25]

It is clear from this quotation that even after many years Joan felt that it was simply 'common knowledge' that women could be snatched into slavery so easily. Clearly, for some, the 'danger' theme within public discourses about Irish female emigrants was potent. Yet it is hard to view this strand of concern as anything other than what Luddy has concluded – titillation for a public who enjoyed being horrified by the shocking stories created in this trope: 'For the reading public the appeal of white slavery was its lurid and melodramatic stories of intrigue, crime, seduction and sex. Such tales provided virtually pornographic entertainment to the reading audience'.[26] It may have also been easy for the Irish public to countenance these claims given the wider discourses on female emigrants as young, foolish, inexperienced and perhaps seeking (mis)adventure through their migrations.

23 From interview by Matthew Linfoot with Bridget Dantu, Millennium Memory Bank Interview Collection, C900/05026 C1, BLSA.
24 Ryan, 'Moving Spaces and Changing Places', p. 76.
25 Joan emigrated to Kent from Mayo in 1933; see Lambert, *Irish Women in Lancashire*, p. 89. Ellipses in the original; my emphasis.
26 Luddy, *Prostitution and Irish Society*, p. 163.

Travel

Historians of emigration have tended to gloss over the travel arrangements of emigrants, despite the available archival evidence and the opportunity to investigate travel arrangements in oral interviews. There are a number of questions that could have been usefully asked, such as: were they frightened of travelling to Britain? Did they travel alone or in a group? What were their opinions about the threat of the white slave trade? It is possible that, in the linear narrative form many accounts take, such information is viewed as less vital or interesting and may be left out in favour of the more 'active' vignettes relating to how the person found accommodation or a job. Either way, it is, unfortunately, another missed opportunity to explore in greater depth the social discourses surrounding emigration by comparing them with first-hand accounts. Travelling to their destination was the first, often monumental, step for emigrants in their new lives, many of whom (men *and* women) had never travelled outside their localities.

What is the evidentiary base for concern for women travelling? The passenger-movement statistics available to historians differ from the census-related data outlined in Chapter 1 in that they track individual journeys which may or may not have been migrations. They do, however, plot general trends. As demonstrated in Table 3.1, the numbers of persons leaving Ireland fluctuated throughout the 1920s to the 1940s, with some years seeing an inflow of persons whilst others seeing an outflow.[27] As with Census data on migration, the imprecise nature of these statistics must be highlighted given that journeys for holiday or business purposes skew the figures relating to emigrants. They also relate specifically to the Free State and do not allow us any insight into passenger movements from Northern Ireland.

The escalation in passenger movements in the mid to late 1930s corresponds with the global economic depression. The brief return traffic at the beginning of the Second World War was counteracted by an even greater outward flow of Irish immigrants pursuing war work in Britain and partially prompted the launch of the CSWB. The substantial increase in the numbers of persons leaving the country between 1946 and 1947 relates the lifting of wartime restrictions on female employment and travel. The last date in the table, movements for 1948, shows only a small number of excess movements of persons out of the country, indicative of the fact that restrictions on men's travel were still in place.

---

27 The earliest figures available are for the 1926 period when first collated by the Department of Industry and Commerce. This function was later taken over by the Central Statistics Office (CSO). The reports vary in detail, including information on travel permits in relevant years.

Table 3.1   Passenger movements to and from Ireland,
1926–1948 (26 counties)

Year	Number of passengers *from* Saorstát Éireann to Great Britain and Northern Ireland	Number of passengers *to* Saorstát Éireann from Great Britain and Northern Ireland	Balance outward
1926	322,200	317,917	4,283
1927	349,591	340,023	9,568
1928	361,526	350,104	11,422
1929	374,904	364,323	10,581
1930	370,361	363,842	6,519
1931	377,138	371,899	5,239
1932	376,579	369,719	6,860
1933	364,195	356,464	7,731
1934	394,822	381,834	12,988
1935	433,869	416,131	17,738
1936	489,318	462,401	26,917
1937	534,168	506,116	28,052
1938	539,480	520,068	19,412
1939	432,529	448,419	+15,890
1940	94,504	106,138	+11,634
1941	126,831	108,998	17,833
1942	168,397	142,925	25,472
1943	209,190	183,208	25,982
1944	136,545	137,853	+1,308
1945	282,444	276,889	5,555
1946	483,155	482,770	385
1947	479,674	471,055	8,619
1948	728,763	728,114	649

Note: Figures appearing with a + indicates a net *inward* movement to Ireland.
Source: Calculations made from tables in Department of Industry and Commerce, *Statistical Abstract, 1926–1948* (Dublin: Stationery Office).

Transportation by sea had a long history: the first ferry services operated from Dublin and Cork in the 1820s, primarily to Liverpool, and journeys in the nineteenth century could sometimes be made free of charge, as empty coal ships needed passengers as ballast for their return journeys.[28] Routes were well known and the journey for emigrants appears to have been relatively easy logistically, if uncomfortable, even from rural parts of Ireland, to Britain. According to Josephine Nestor, trains were frequent from Galway to Dublin in the post-war 1940s. She used this information as a prompt to get Patrick Corless to return home, so they could resume their courtship: 'The trains are running four days a week from Dublin on Mondays, Tuesdays, Fridays and Saturdays. So you will chance getting to Tuam all right'.[29]

Many women (and men) used the cheapest form of transport available to them to get to Britain – going on the cattle boats. As Fitzgerald and Lambkin have noted, the steamers from Ireland to Liverpool 'gave priority to baggage and livestock, carrying passengers on the open deck',[30] an experience recounted by emigrant Noreen Hill: 'Do I remember the journey over? Do I heck! It was one of those old cattle boats, you know, where the cattle were underneath and the passengers on top – you could hear the cattle as you travelled on top'.[31] A contributor to the *Irish Catholic* felt that the passengers themselves were treated like livestock in the way they were dealt with at Customs, such as the following description of disembarkation: 'Travellers were then herded into wooden pens like cattle and were eventually allowed to file into sheds where their papers and luggage were thoroughly examined'.[32] Considering the lengthy waiting times and exhaustion experienced by emigrants described in the article, it is again curious that such stories rarely feature in oral histories.

Gertrude Gaffney's now famous series of articles charting Irish migrants in Britain (subsequently issued as a pamphlet) appeared in the *Irish Independent* in 1936 and detailed both the perils and safeguards that existed for women in their journeys 'across the water'. The general tone of her articles cast a negative light on all aspects of emigration. However, Gaffney did admit that the stewards and stewardesses provided by shipping companies looked after

28 Roger Swift (ed.), *Irish Migrants in Britain, 1815–1914: A Documentary History* (Cork: Cork University Press, 2002), p. 5.

29 Nestor–Corless letters, 7 September 1944, kindly shared with the author by Adrienne Corless. The Corless travel permit is now held by Trinity College Dublin Manuscripts Department.

30 Patrick Fitzgerald and Brian Lambkin, *Migration in Irish History, 1607–2007* (Basingstoke: Palgrave Macmillan, 2008), p. 27.

31 Lennon *et al.*, *Across the Water*, p. 94.

32 Kevin O'Dwyer, 'Advice to Intending Emigrants', *Irish Catholic*, 7 February 1946, p. 3.

young Irish women 'as if they were their own children'.[33] This language indicates not only the particular attention they received on their travels, but also the infantilised conception of such 'girls' that is often characteristic of contemporary newspaper articles and public discourses.[34] Veiled insinuations of moral danger are referred to by Gaffney in the 'almost certain disaster' that came of women taking lifts in lorries from Liverpool to London.[35] Gaffney also warned of the practice of buying 'half' of a day return ticket from someone who would sell it cheaply but may sell a ticket that was not valid for the whole of the person's journey. In this case, the worry was that they would be thrown off the train if caught, not that they would get into moral danger.

This characterisation of girls as excessively naive and vulnerable had roots in the previous century when female emigrant philanthropy first flourished. Sectarian tensions in Ireland in this sector, and key denominational differences in attitudes towards migration, are discussed next.

The Girls' Friendly Society

The Girls' Friendly Society (GFS) was a Church of Ireland organisation designed to involve women in parish life and to promote Christian ideals. Established in 1877 by Mrs Mary Elizabeth Townsend, the GFS motto was: 'Bear ye one another's burdens' (Galatians 6:2). Its rules of membership indicate that it favoured a certain type of girl: those who could afford a total annual subscription of not less than 6*d.*, and those who had 'borne a virtuous character'. If the latter was 'lost', the member had to forfeit her card. It had 12,000 members in Ireland in 1927, for example, down from 16,432 reported in 1912, reflecting perhaps the declining Protestant population in Ireland overall.[36] It was actively involved in assisting emigrants and in port and station work, focusing its energies on helping rural women navigate these spaces. Like other organisations, it fundraised for its activities in newspapers, principally the *Church of Ireland Gazette* and the *Irish Times*, which also had a significant Protestant readership. An editorial in the *Church of Ireland Gazette* urged people to support an arts and crafts fair by the

---

33 Gertrude Gaffney, *Irish Independent*, 8 December 1936, p. 8. There is little detail in her articles about specific arrangements on the ships for providing protections.

34 The British government provided a reception officer at Holyhead during the war, 'specifically to deal with Irish labour, and a further two welfare officers were stationed at Crewe to cut down on the numbers of lost and overwhelmed travellers'. Wills, *That Neutral Island*, p. 320.

35 Gaffney, *Irish Independent*, 7 December 1936, p. 5.

36 Figure for 1927 noted in *Church of Ireland Gazette*, 17 June 1927, p. 346; Annual Report of the Girls' Friendly Society 1912, p. 3.

GFS with the assertion that 'we know the need that it is meeting in keeping our Protestant girls in a wholesome moral and spiritual atmosphere and in shepherding girls away from home'.[37] As Luddy has outlined, the GFS was also concerned about the white slave trade. Middle-class, mature women shepherding younger or working-class women was an idea not confined to the GFS, though, and was an ethos shared by many organisations offering welfare assistance.

Each Diocesan Branch of the organisation had a dedicated Head of Emigration whose job it was to find out which members were emigrating and to assist them by formally 'commending' them to their destination parish and their local GFS branch (even if they were migrating with their families). It was considered a serious breach to allow a member to emigrate 'uncommended'. In this, it appears that the GFS were attempting to protect their members and provide them with a ready-made network. Furthermore, the GFS commendation system required the local branch to write back to assure them of the girls' whereabouts and safety, a rule that irked some international branches who did not see the necessity. The insistence on this rule by the Irish GFS is testament, perhaps, to the enduring importance attached to reputation and character in Irish life, necessary attributes for employment and social respectability.

As well as offering a 'protective' service for women, the GFS appears to have involved itself in tracking 'wayward' migrants. For example, in 1929, it was noted that on 15 May a letter was received from Mrs Dunphy of Cookstown, Tyrone in relation to Minnie Purvis who was at an address in West Perth, Australia and reported as 'lost for 18 months'. Ongoing investigation of the Purvis case is recorded throughout 1929 and on 5 November it was recorded that Miss Edwards had found Purvis, now Mrs W. Jenkins, and contact was re-established. The capacity for tracing women over long distances was obviously a benefit to relatives, and although this does not appear frequently in the ledgers of the Emigration Department it is likely that members used the networks informally for such needs.

A factor that substantially differentiates the GFS from the ICGPS and the CSWB in terms of its attitude to female emigration is that it appears not to have considered moving to Britain as emigration. Rates of emigration by GFS members presented in Table 3.2 for years when consecutive reports gave figures do not include Britain but rather focus on migration to Canada, the USA, Australia, New Zealand and India.[38]

Although the figures are low, the higher number of GFS members emigrating in the early years of the Free State confirms the findings

---

37 *Church of Ireland Gazette*, 31 March 1923, p. 162.
38 Some reports are missing or else do not give figures.

Table 3.2   Numbers of Irish Girls' Friendly Society Members
emigrating, 1924–1935

Year	Numbers migrating
1924	43
1925	44
1926	66
1927	56
1928	75
1929	62
1930	50
1931	3
1932	0
1933	1
1934	0
1935	1

Source: Girls' Friendly Society, Annual Reports,
Representative Church Body Library MS 578/19.

of other studies – that the Protestant population in Ireland experienced
increased emigration at that time, as referred to in Chapter 1. The lessening
of GFS member migration does not reflect overall trends in Protestant
women's emigration, but rather the lagging system of referrals that the GFS
constantly strove to maintain. Their membership profile would also have
failed to take in working-class women unable to afford their subscription fees
who were more likely to migrate.

The records of the GFS indicate that its members availed themselves
of British empire settlement schemes, a clear difference to the reports of
the ICGPS, which had little experience (at least in Dublin) with overseas
migrations. In 1906, the published report stated that 'The G.F.S. Emigration
Secretary in England will work in future in the Office of the B.E.A. [British
Empire Association] in London, where all arrangements for G.F.S. Members
joining protected parties to Canada, Australia etc. will be made'.[39] In 1909,
the Emigration Secretary's report mentions that she attended a session on
'Women in our Colonies' at the Meeting of the National Union of Women
Workers in Portsmouth. Naturally, the 'our' includes Irish women at this

39 'Report of the Emigration Department', Annual Report of the Girls' Friendly Society
1906, p. 12.

moment, although their rhetoric reveals no recognition of any domestic tensions regarding Home Rule, nationalism or otherwise.

Indeed, it appears that GFS members were being specifically targeted for such migration, as indicated in the 1911 report:

> We know that pressure is being put upon our Members, as well as on other young girls, by Emigration Agents to go to the Colonies without any satisfactory knowledge of where or to whom they are going, and many warnings have been sent out on the subject. Whenever an opportunity offers, girls should be warned not to think of emigrating without consulting their Associate. There are more protected parties than ever to be sent this year, and at all ports increased arrangements have been made for safeguarding girls.[40]

In 1913, the GFS noted that the migration of 120 members meant a loss to the Irish branch but 'it is a gain to the G.F.S. in our Dominions beyond the seas and in other distant lands, where we trust the principles of faithfulness, purity and helpfulness, as inculcated by our Society – may bear good fruit in the lives and influence of our Members'.[41]

This, it seemed, was their definition of migration: leaving Ireland for the colonies, not leaving Ireland to 'cross the water'. There was also a certain enthusiasm for GFS members being part of the colonial enterprise. During the First World War, it reported that some Irish members had taken advantage of the heavily subsidised fares offered by the Australian Colonies of New South Wales and Victoria for unemployed women, including factory workers and domestic servants. Even after independence, the GFS signalled their interest and involvement with the project of empire settlement. The Society for Overseas Settlement of British Women (or SOSBW) was set up to respond to the economic needs of 'surplus women' in post-First World War Britain. The GFS were on the executive council of the SOSBW from the beginning, along with representatives from other faiths and the labour movement. It is intriguing that there was a potential cadre of Protestant women without adequate opportunities in Ireland who may have been interested in prospects overseas. Who they were, what they did and where they went is difficult to research. They were invisible to contemporary commentators, unlike their Catholic peers. Irish Protestant women's migration to Britain was therefore framed in the GFS mindset – both before and after independence – as an internal migration of sorts, standing in stark contrast in importance to overseas settlement. Although it sought to help

40 Annual Report of the Girls' Friendly Society 1911, pp. 13–14.
41 Annual Report of the Girls' Friendly Society 1913, p. 3.

these women in the same way as it did girls coming from country areas to Dublin, it did not view them as comparable migrants to those journeying outside the UK.

The Mothers' Union and the GFS united in 1912 to undertake 'vigilance work' in ports and stations. They had a joint fundraising appeal which raised £325 and thereafter issued yearly appeals. A Station Worker was appointed to protect women 'from accepting help from strangers, which has, alas! so often ended in disastrous results', and initially this person worked alongside the ICGPS workers, cooperating to direct girls to the appropriate religious organisation for help.[42] The different societies appeared to collaborate under an umbrella group, the Girls' Protection Crusade. The Mothers' Union and the GFS were reported in 1913 as having representatives on the Committee of the ICGPS and they contributed financially to that organisation in recognition of their cooperation in producing flyers, placards and helping to direct girls to the GFS lodge. However, tensions between the different lay organisations in their quest best to help young women emigrating from Ireland emerged in the 1920s.[43] This ecumenical alliance seems to have faltered, perhaps due to the GFS association with the Irish Women Police Patrols who employed both Catholic and Protestant workers in their port and station work. This led to serious tensions and although it is undocumented is probably the reason for the splintering of emigrant welfare efforts in the post-independence era.

The International Catholic Girls' Protection Society

The International Catholic Girls' Protection Society (ICGPS) was a lay Catholic welfare organisation committed to helping girls in their journeys, particularly to take up employment.[44] The work of the ICGPS was brought to Ireland in 1902 by an Australian woman, Miss Austice Baker, who collaborated with the Sisters of St Vincent de Paul in North William Street in Dublin to set up an Information Bureau for intending emigrant women.[45] Women who encountered difficulties in their journeys were often sent by

---

42 Annual Report of the Girls' Friendly Society 1912, p. 4.
43 Little documentary evidence remains but it appears that joint financial arrangements existed between Catholic and Protestant organisations to fund port and station work in conjunction with the Irish Women Police Patrols prior to 1922. Relations appear to have soured in the early 1920s and funding for workers was separated along religious lines. My thanks to John Johnston-Kehoe for helpful discussions on this matter.
44 In Ireland, the International Catholic Girls' Protection Society operated under the title of 'the Catholic Bureau' and 'Traveller's Aid' at times.
45 Undated information booklet in the ICGPS file, Down and Connor Diocesan Archives.

railway workers to the nuns. The Information Bureau was run on a charitable basis between 1902 and 1908. Subsequently it was officially established in Dublin by Mrs Power Lalor with a branch at 42 Mountjoy Square, with the aid of £100 donated by the Archbishop of Dublin, William Joseph Walsh.[46] A branch also operated in Cork harbour, assisting women going to America. The Belfast Branch of the ICGPS was inaugurated at a much later date – it held its foundational meeting on Thursday, 21 January 1943 at the home of the first President, Mrs McGarry, at 84 Dublin Road, Belfast.[47]

The details of their activities in Dublin and Cork, such as they can be traced, have been sketched elsewhere.[48] The important aspect to stress is that as a lay organisation the ICGPS was under the patronage (and goodwill) of the Bishop, and relied on priests and the Catholic press to communicate their services. Although the Society was active, they struggled to carve out a niche for themselves in Ireland in the care of Catholic women, striving at first to gain regular funding from the Archbishop of Dublin and then to receive regular subscriptions from ordinary Catholics throughout Ireland. The committee membership also set the tone for the organisation and harked back to nineteenth-century notions of philanthropy of the positive influence that middle- and upper-class women could have on their working-class 'sisters'. This class awareness was also something the society wished their fellow citizens would pay attention to. In their 1925–26 report, they had this to say to the Irish middle-class, who they felt had a duty to inform women emigrants of the work of the ICGPS:

> As to these emigrants, they could be saved so much hardship if only their well-to-do neighbours would interest themselves on their behalf. If these would realise that if they cannot stop them from going, it would be more Christian to make that going less hard and dangerous for them.[49]

46 Archbishop Walsh was Archbishop of Dublin from August 1885 until his death in 1921.
47 The few records of the Belfast Branch of the ICGPS were kindly provided to me by Canon G. O'Hanlon of the Down and Connor Archives, Belfast. This consisted of a small amount of correspondence, annual reports and notes on activities of the Belfast branch.
48 Redmond, 'Safeguarding Irish Girls'. There is no clear indication of when the ICGPS stopped its work, but it appears to have slowly dwindled between the 1950s and the 1970s. The 1956 Liverpool Vigilance Association Annual Report notes with regret that the Dublin branch had stopped its work that year, although the last published report of the ICGPS in the Down and Connor Diocesan Archives dates from 1971 and does not contain any indication that it is ceasing operations, thus it is likely that it continued further into the 1970s. Liverpool Port and Station Work, Annual Report 1956 (unpaginated), Women's Library, File 3AMS/17/01.
49 ICGPS, Annual Report 1925–26, p. 5.

Help given at the stations was provided for a small fee according to the 1950 annual report, although in earlier periods it seems to have been given free of charge; in the 1920s, the ICGPS had stated that those who 'travel in search of a livelihood are not able to pay for the luxury of being saved from dangers and anxieties to soul and body'.[50] Their assistance could range from giving simple directions, to housing women in their dedicated hostel. Most importantly, the ICGPS took pains to point out that their work was not undertaken to facilitate emigration: 'We wish it to be distinctly understood, however, that we are not an emigration society, nor do we encourage emigration in any way; on the contrary, we do what lies in our power to keep the girls at home'.[51] This rather defensive assertion must be seen in the context of the vitriolic discourses, referred to in discussion of the 'emigration agent' in Chapter 2, directed towards anyone who was seen to be encouraging or facilitating emigration in any way, despite the economic exigencies of the time. It also sets them apart from the GFS and their interest in populating the British empire.

The Belfast Branch, like the Dublin branch, sought the patronage of the local Bishop, Most Rev. Dr Mageean, for both financial aid and support in promoting the organisation. It is unclear why this work only migrated to Belfast four decades after it began in the south; a plausible reason was the greater working opportunities that led to less emigration by women in Ulster. It is interesting to note that all the women helped by the Belfast Branch were from southern not northern Ireland. Some may have been using the Belfast port to get to destinations in Scotland, such as postulants entering convents in Glasgow and Lanark. It appears curious, however, that the Belfast ICGPS did not encounter any women from the six counties who may have needed assistance. This is particularly so given that the war made travel more difficult (Table 3.3).

Outside of Ireland, correspondence between the ICGPS and British welfare societies demonstrate they were well networked. They reported figures to the European ICGPS head office in Fribourg and kept abreast of international conferences on women, trafficking and migration.[52] Evidence of liaison with League of Nations committees investigating the phenomenon of trafficking and prostitution show that the ICGPS submitted memorandums on their experience of the issue.[53] Given the society's stature in international

---

50 ICGPS, Annual Report 1923–24, p. 5.
51 ICGPS, Twenty-Eighth Annual Report 1941. Copy supplied by Canon O'Hanlon, Down and Connor Archives, Belfast.
52 For more on the international context of efforts to combat the 'white slave trade', see Katarina Leppänen, 'Movement of Women: Trafficking in the Interwar Era', *Women's Studies International Forum*, 30 (2007), pp. 523–533.
53 See files in Women's Library, File 3AMS/B/11/02, Box Number 071, League of Nations 2, 1934–44 folder.

Table 3.3   Summary of work undertaken by Belfast
International Catholic Girls' Protection Society in 1943

Name	Address	Travelling To	Date	Reason of Travelling
Mary Connolly (17)	Wexford	Convent of Mercy, Glasgow	4/3/43	Entering as a postulant
Brigid McBride (18)	Tipperary	Convent of Mercy, Glasgow	4/3/43	" "
Kathleen Dunne	Mayo	Convent of Mercy, Lanark	1/5/43	" "
Denis Smyth (12)	Glasgow	Dublin	4/5/43	To reside with an Uncle
Kathleen Mullen	Clones	England	18/5/43	Employment
Nora Bailie	Dublin	Edinburgh	30/6/43	Employment
Mary Mallon	Dublin	Glasgow	21/9/43	Employment
Annie Walsh	Dromod, Eire	Aberdeenshire	11/10/43	Employment
Mary Garrett	Cork	Perthshire	20/10/43	Employment
Cath. Cusack	Cavan	Glasgow	9/11/43	Employment
Mary Lambe W.A.A.F.	Tullamore	Aldergrove	28/10/43	Join the Air Force
Ellen Goodwin (15½)	Dublin	Scotland	3/11/43	Entering as a postulant
Annie Leonard	Cork	Belfast	16/12/43	To join the A.T.S. [Auxiliary Territorial Service] but was rejected. Escorted back to the train.

Note: Headings in the table have been kept as they appear in the original documen-
tation. Ages are not given for all persons. For further information on Irish women in the
British military auxiliary forces, see Chapter 7.
Source: Documentation provided to the author by Canon G. O'Hanlon, Down and
Connor Archives, Belfast.

circles, it is surprising that it never gained significant recognition in Ireland.
The branches in Ireland seem to have struggled to gain a legitimate space
for themselves in the plethora of Catholic lay organisations. The frequent
appeals to gain attention and funds reflected a sense of invisibility in the case
of both the Dublin and Cork branches. In 1941, twenty-eight years since the
ICGPS was first established, the Cork branch annual report stated that 'we

still find that there are many people who do not even know of its existence at all, and others have only the haziest, if any, ideas of what our work really is'.[54] The report goes on to say:

> Some people are inclined to make little of this Society, and say that there is no need for it in Catholic Ireland. All our experience and information goes to prove that the need for an active branch of such a Society in Cork was never more urgent or insistent than at present.[55]

This statement is curious in light of their work being so well known to counterparts in Great Britain, the USA and continental Europe, with whom they liaised closely.

The ICGPS also struggled continuously with finances, with frequent public appeals in newspapers and mention of the issue in every annual report that is extant. The ICGPS seems to have received an annual donation from Archbishop Byrne of Dublin, although this was also tenuous, as indicated by letters in the archive which reveal polite, repeated, reminders.[56] The insecure status of the ICGPS may have been a sore point for them, and may also explain why the society has not been written about in the history of emigration despite their contemporary significance.[57] Daly's claim that the welfare arrangements organised for emigrants by lay organisations were 'ad hoc and not coordinated' is only true in the sense that they were not systematically funded or government controlled.[58] The claim made by Miss O'Donohoe of the Dublin branch in a letter to the Liverpool Port and Station Work Society in 1931 that 'the Authorities here will not allow any girl to be sent out of the country by the Registry Office where the situation was found, without the girl going through our Society and being looked after by us'[59] is not backed up by any reference in government documentation and is clearly a boast to her Liverpool colleagues. There was also no state control of emigration for either men or women. Thus, claims for restricting women from migrating unless they were going to 'suitable' jobs are false, but neither

54 ICGPS, Twenty-Eighth Annual Report 1941.
55 Ibid.
56 Letter from Angela Boland, Honorary Treasurer of the ICGPS, to the Archbishop of Dublin, 29 May 1930, thanking him for the annual donation; uncatalogued files, Down and Connor Diocesan Archives, Belfast.
57 For example, there is no mention of ICGPS activities in Ryan's *Gender Identity and the Irish Press* and only a brief mention of the fact that they were active in the 1920s in Daly's *The Slow Failure* (p. 277).
58 Daly, *The Slow Failure*, p. 277.
59 Letter from Liverpool Port and Station Work Society (unsigned) to Mr Sempkins of the National Vigilance Association, 16 November 1931, Women's Library, File 4NVA/04/02 Box FL098.

is it true, as Caslin has speculated, that arrangements between Irish- and Liverpool-based moral purity organisations may have been accidental.[60] The successive committees demonstrated professionalism, organisation and resolve in pursuing their work and consistently communicated with their British counterparts. Despite this international profile, the efforts of the ICGPS were directly challenged by the setting up of the Catholic Social Welfare Bureau.

The Catholic Social Welfare Bureau

Concern for emigrant women, particularly unmarried mothers, simmered throughout the 1930s. Richard Mulcahy, TD, appears to have had a genuine concern for the plight of female emigrants and was interested in setting up an information bureau on Irish welfare services. Aimed particularly at pregnant Irish women to stop them fleeing to Britain, it never came to fruition.[61] However, as the decade wore on, it was evident that the government was not going to do anything either to hinder or help emigrants, and thus the Catholic Church, in the form of Archbishop John Charles McQuaid, decided to intervene. The CSWB, established by McQuaid in Dublin in 1942, utilised the Legion of Mary and was essentially a rival organisation to the International Catholic Girls' Protection Society. McQuaid achieved more control than his role in the ICGPS allowed, an approach consistent with his attitude to maternity welfare provision. As outlined in Earner Byrne's work, McQuaid used the Catholic Social Services Conference facilities to oust non-Catholic groups and to centralise his personal control over what he viewed as 'a sphere proper to ourselves, caring for our own poor'.[62]

The history of these organisations has not been well attended to in the spectrum of historical research on emigrants or on philanthropic endeavours. Archival material, not previously examined by other historians, is used here to outline the extent of the welfare networks for women travelling between

60 Samantha Caslin, '"One Can Only Guess What Might Have Happened if the Worker Had Not Intervened in Time": The Liverpool Vigilance Association, Moral Vulnerability and Irish Girls in Early- to Mid-Twentieth-Century Liverpool', *Women's History Review*, 25:2 (2016), pp. 254–273.

61 Letter from Josephine McNeill (wife of the Governor General), Vice Regal Lodge, to Mrs Caseau, 21 January 1930, Women's Library, File 4IBS/6/094/ Box FL 115/Co 34.

62 Lindsey Earner-Byrne, 'Managing Motherhood: Negotiating a Maternity Service for Catholic Mothers in Dublin, 1930–1954', *Social History of Medicine*, 19.2 (2006), p. 267; quotation by McQuaid from an internal memorandum. See also Earner Byrne's *Mother and Child: Maternity and Child Welfare in Dublin, 1922–1960* (Manchester: Manchester University Press, 2007).

Ireland and Britain and the religious tensions and struggles for power that characterised this work in the post-independence period.[63] Interestingly, despite the fuss made about the need for services to assist safe travel, very few emigrants report using them. This may be, as Patrick Duffy has suggested, because 'letters from emigrants contained detailed instructions, based on first-hand experience, on each stage in the outward journey'.[64]

The nexus of emigrant welfare groups assisting with travel arrangements was one of the distinct ways in which male and female migrants were differentiated in public discourses throughout the twentieth century. No public statements were ever made that posited travelling to Britain as a dangerous pursuit for men; the 'danger' of possible moral corruption was gendered. It is important to look at travel arrangements and associated welfare work because it was of major concern to the Catholic Church, the Church of Ireland and their associated lay organisations. Improper behaviour or incautious conversations with strangers on the way to Britain was thought to be a significant factor in the 'downfall' of some women who emigrated.[65] Ryan posits that the tendency for unmarried Irish women to migrate, combined with their youth, 'helped to shape the image of the archetypal "emigrant girl" and the many concerns that were vocalised about her in the 1930s' and indeed beyond.[66] It appears that youth, single status and agency crystallised as a trifecta of attributes seen as dangerous or undesirable in young women. This conception of the Irish female emigrant is at odds with many reported experiences of migration: women often travelled with family or friends, or made arrangements with their employer, much the same as their male counterparts. The issue of travel and welfare therefore contextualises some of the moral discourses on women's behaviour whilst they were in Britain – a bad start would have signalled potential 'moral trouble' in the long run.

Part of the historiographical silence on the issue of women's travel arrangements may be because the concerns raised in the contemporary rhetoric of post-independence Ireland may appear so patently absurd as to warrant ignoring. This rhetoric, uttered in the public sphere, was, however, a powerful determinant in the popular construction of what Ryan has

---

63 More recent work has been conducted by Henrietta Ewart, but on a later era. See Ewart, 'Protecting the Honour of the Daughters of Eire: Welfare Policy for Irish Female Migrants to England, 1940–70', *Irish Studies Review*, 21.1 (2013), pp. 71–84.

64 Patrick Duffy, 'Literary Reflection on Irish Migration in the Nineteenth and Twentieth Centuries', in Russell King, John Connell and Paul White (eds), *Writing Across Worlds: Literature and Migration* (London: Routledge, 1995), p. 25.

65 See Maria Luddy, 'Sex and the Single Girl in 1920s and 1930s Ireland', *Irish Review*, 35 (2007), pp. 79–91.

66 Duffy, 'Literary Reflection on Irish Migration', p. 25.

termed the 'wild Irish girl' and what Archbishop of Dublin, John Charles McQuaid, saw as a group of emigrants in *particular* need of care, although his vision of the moral problems associated with emigration extended beyond women, unlike the other organisations.[67] Furthermore, the large body of correspondence on the issue of travel arrangements between Irish and British Catholic lay organisations, and between the Church hierarchy in each country, reveals this was an important contemporary topic. Newspapers regularly featured articles on the work of lay organisations in addition to warnings of the dangers to women travelling on their own. Articles even occasionally used the 'hook' of the endangered female emigrant in stories that had no content relating to women.[68] Hyperbole and sensationalism were characteristic of many newspaper headlines on the 'vulnerable emigrant girl'. These discourses, and welfare work itself, were complicated by parallel and sometimes overlapping efforts to assist 'PFIs', or women who were 'Pregnant from Ireland'.[69] This, it seems, was the reason why the problem of illegitimate pregnancy was conflated with female emigration.

Emigrant Women in Britain: Leisure and Behaviour

McQuaid, utilising the Legion of Mary, extended his reach into emigrant communities in Britain in a form of assistance that appears to have been part concern, part control. Emigration carried connotations of sexual freedom and adventure, as well as sexual danger and loss. Away from the scrutiny of families, local priests and small communities, Irish women could test or violate the sexual boundaries they had been raised with, with less risk of social repercussions that at home.[70] Unsurprisingly, the behaviour of

---

67 For more on the trope of the wild Irish girl, see Ryan, *Gender, Identity and the Irish Press*. John Charles McQuaid was Archbishop of Dublin from November 1940 until retirement in 1971, after which he was Archbishop Emeritus until his death in 1973. McQuaid opened the CSWB with the words that women needed 'particular' care as emigrants.

68 An example is of the front-page headline 'Irish Emigrant Girls: Measures for the Protection, Work of the Mission of Our Lady of the Rosary', which detailed the new immigration restrictions America had imposed. *Irish Catholic*, 31 January 1925, p. 1.

69 For more, see Paul Michael Garrett, 'The Hidden History of the PFIs: The Repatriation of Unmarried Mothers and Their Children from England to Ireland in the 1950s and 1960s', *Immigrants and Minorities*, 19.3 (2000), pp. 25–44. See also Jennifer Redmond, 'In the Family Way and Away from the Family: Examining the Evidence in Irish Unmarried Mothers in Britain, 1920s–1940s', in Elaine Farrell (ed.), *'She Said She Was in the Family Way': Pregnancy and Infancy in the Irish Past* (London: Institute of Historical Research, 2012), pp. 163–185.

70 Howes, 'Public Discourse, Private Reflection', p. 928.

men, their private lives and relationships, was little commented upon in the atmosphere of sexual double standards that persisted throughout this period.

Sexual morality, sexual crime, illegitimacy and unmarried motherhood in Ireland have attracted substantial scholarly attention in historical research in recent years, from Luddy and Buckley's studies of the NSPCC, prostitution and unmarried mothers in Ireland, to Earner Byrne's examination of maternity welfare and poverty, to Rattigan's and Farrell's studies of infanticide and Ferriter's review of Ireland's sexual culture in the twentieth century. The darker parts of Irish history have now had significant light thrown upon them. There is considerable justification for focusing on this part of Irish history; as Luddy's work has shown, it was an area of continuous concern to successive Irish governments and to society at large, despite the suppression of open discourse.[71]

One of the key gender differences in the representations of male and female emigrants to Britain centred on their morality, particularly sexual morality, as distinct from their working experiences, as outlined in the next chapter. Three of the key elements in discourses on the perceived social and moral dangers for Irish female emigrants were: (1) illegitimate pregnancy as a reason for, or consequence of, migration; (2) marriage as motivation for migration, resulting in the categorisation of women as 'absent' wives and mothers in Ireland; and (3) the 'leakage' problem or the thorny issue of emigrants falling away from their religion in Britain. This triad are related because they all focus on women and the allegation of their emigration as the pursuit of selfish desires. It was often claimed that Irish women were motivated to emigrate to escape parental control, to hide illegitimate pregnancies (which were exclusively their fault in the 'logic' of the time) or to pursue 'modern' lifestyles that were sexually promiscuous. Within all this, of course, there are paradoxes and counter discourses which will also be explored.

Discourses on moral behaviours can be broadly categorised as revolving around different 'gendered axes' for men and women. For women, moral behaviours associated with sexual activities were of paramount concern, whereas for men, where such discourses existed, they tended to focus on the suitability of accommodation, their drinking habits and their tendency to work on Sundays (taking them away from regular religious practice). Furthermore, while there was deep concern for 'lost' Irish mothers because of emigration, there was no such parallel concern for the loss of fathers. The widely held belief that 'hordes' of girls were fleeing to hide sexual misconduct in Ireland was a common trope in post-independence Ireland, reflecting both Irish gender relations and the misguided opinions that existed about female emigrants. This idea also raises the question of what kind of people

---

71 Luddy, 'Sex and the Single Girl', pp. 79–91.

emigrated from Ireland. Were they the best and brightest? Or were they the kind who desperately wanted to break free from parental control and community censure? Was cultural deviancy, as explored in Akenson's work in the nineteenth century, still at play in the twentieth? Many thought the best men were leaving, or, as Deputy Coburn put it, 'a manly man'.[72] In contrast, the 'worst' women were emigrating because they were allegedly doing so for selfish or immoral reasons. This again is a result of the paradigm that posited men as economic and women as non-economic migrants.

Leisure Facilities for Female Emigrants Employed in Britain

In addition to the networks initiated by the ICGPS and the NVA to help Irish women reach their employment safely and to check the suitability of their situation, newspaper reports reveal that the Catholic Church in Britain attempted specifically to cater for their leisure needs. For example, Bishop Butt, Vicar-General of the Archdiocese of Westminster, announced the official launch of St Patrick's Club in Soho Square (in St Patrick's parish, Soho), in the *Irish Catholic*, due to take place on 25 March 1934.[73] The girls' club had previously existed in limited form, being open just once a week, and having 160 members, 55 of whom were Irish. The new club was to open nightly, and was aimed 'mainly for girls who are employed in hotels and boardinghouses or domestic service'. The fact that there was a modest fee to join (6*d*.), plus small charges for refreshments, means it was most likely frequented by girls who had obtained better paid positions and had the freedom to go often. Interestingly, the opening was attended by Mr Dulanty, High Commissioner for the Irish Free State, demonstrating the interest of the Irish government in provisions being made for Irish women. This report also indicates, paradoxically, that while the Free State government (at this time under de Valera) was happy publicly to support such ventures, it was not prepared to do so financially.

The motivation for providing entertainment for domestic servants may have been to keep them safe while enjoying themselves, but it was also useful in retaining them within the occupation. The 1923 investigation into why British women were fleeing domestic service found that it was the status of the job as well as the isolation that made women seek other employment. One witness to the Labour Ministry commission thought the provision of

---

72 See Chapter 2 for reference to Deputy Coburn's comments.

73 'Surely this will be a good work for these girls who have work of an interesting nature and no home in London'. *Irish Catholic*, 17 March 1934, p. 6. The article was written in advance of the opening.

a gramophone might alleviate the girls' boredom, but the *Irish Independent* derided such a comment: 'unless a gramophone can be constructed so as to carry on an intelligent conversation the problem will remain unsolved. The constant repetition of "Old Pal, Why Don't You Answer Me?" on the gramophone would become as irritating as the daily "Do this" or "Why did you do that?"'.[74] The Girls' Friendly Society Lodge in Dublin made a point of providing refreshments, music and reading materials for girls (domestics and shop or office workers) to use, recognising the need for comfortable surroundings for girls who had no home for their own.

Little research has thus far been conducted on the leisure pursuits of Irish immigrants in Britain, although oral histories often refer to dances, the cinema, going for tea and joining sodalities and guilds (more on the latter below). Emigrants were undoubtedly interested in British popular culture; the 93 million cinema admissions in 1934 must have included a significant number of Irish men and women.[75] Similar discourses existed in Ireland and Britain on the 'jazzing flapper' and her lowering of moral standards, although Pugh argues that the decline in prostitution and alcoholism after the First World War meant that Britain was actually becoming *more* not less moral.[76] O'Leary has argued that an awareness of modern conveniences and a better standard of living in the 1950s emanating from popular culture drove migration as 'rising levels of individual and collective dissatisfaction at both the cost and standard of living began to undermine national consensus' in Ireland.[77] Clearly, times were changing, and frugal comfort was not enough to satisfy many citizens.

Concern with moral issues is often depicted in Irish history as peculiarly Irish, but a comparative perspective reveals that similar concerns existed in Britain. Debates about divorce and contraception also raged in Britain, although access to both was easier than in Ireland.[78] Acknowledging shared moral concerns also challenges the contemporary assumption that Irish

---

74 *Irish Independent*, 16 May 1923, p. 6.

75 Martin Pugh, *State and Society: British Political and Social History, 1870–1992* (London: Edward Arnold, 1994), p. 198.

76 Ibid., p. 199.

77 Eleanor O'Leary, 'Desperate Housewives: Social Change and the Desire for Modern Lifestyles in 1950s Ireland', in Rebecca Anne Barr, Sarah-Anne Buckley and Laura Kelly (eds), *Engendering Ireland: New Reflections on Modern History and Literature* (Newcastle upon Tyne: Cambridge Scholars Publishing, 2015), p. 14.

78 Pugh makes the point that advice on contraception was not authorised to be given in local authority clinics until the Church of England and the British Medical Association backed down on the issue in 1930. Up to this point, Marie Stopes was allowed to operate her voluntary clinics. However, even as late as 1937, only 95 of 423 local authorities provided contraceptive advice, and this was restricted to married women who faced health risks from more pregnancies. Pugh, *State and Society*, p. 201.

migrants would find themselves at sea in Britain, unable to cope with the modernity and paganism they found, when in fact both countries shared many concerns over morality and women's place in society.

Newspaper focus on leisure pursuits for Irish emigrants mainly centred on domestic servants, probably because they had the least resources and generally worked singly, in contrast to nurses or factory workers. In 1946, Rev. John Foster of Our Lady of Victories Presbytery appealed to readers of the *Irish Catholic* for funds to set up new premises for their girls' club in Kensington to cater for 'the enormous number of young girls from Ireland working in hotels or living in apartment houses who find it very difficult to meet the right company and often have nowhere to go or meet their friends when they are off-duty'.[79] The club planned to have a restaurant, reading and games rooms and facilities for socialising. The idea that, yet again, English Catholics were supporting welfare work for Irish Catholic women in Britain was alluded to in the letter, which claimed that due to wartime damage the parish itself was unable to come up with the necessary £1,000. The letter ended with the appeal: 'Perhaps the parents or relations of our Irish girls, realising the need for such a club, would like to help us?'[80] No help appeared to be forthcoming from the Irish government, despite protestations at the embarrassment of having young women wandering around without the care of any organisation. This again brought up the spectre of sexual misconduct, the ultimate marker between 'good' and 'bad' girls and between successful and unsuccessful emigrants.

Conclusion

Travelling and the moral welfare of young girls were issues that revealed the gendered paradigms in understandings of, and attitudes towards, migrants in twentieth-century Ireland. These attitudes stand in marked contrast to the lack of concern shown towards men of the same ages, backgrounds, religions and classes. As men could not conceivably be duped and sold into 'white slavery' as could women, this may explain the lack of attention to issues of public safety while travelling. Men were vital to sustaining the population, both as fathers and workers, yet we do not see the same level of concern for their absence or their moral welfare.

79 *Irish Catholic*, 18 April 1946, p. 7.
80 It is important to acknowledge the possibility that some of the parishioners may have been Irish immigrants, although the tone of the letter suggests that Foster felt the burden was being faced by the local parish with the inference that these were not all Irish.

There may have been denominational differences between the welfare organisations created to assist female emigrants from Ireland, but they appear united on their distrust of public spaces and the malignant influence of modern attitudes to girls that allowed them greater freedom. The GFS Executive Committee Minutes, Wednesday, 18 October 1933, are revealing in this respect: 'it was agreed that the following recommendation be sent to the Central Council. "That having regard to the increased liberty of young girls and the consequent moral dangers the Council is asked to concentrate for next year on Conferences, meetings and literature with a view to helping our members to be true to the G.F.S. object and that the Conference in Synod week should bear on this subject"'.[81]

Examining these issues also reveals religious and political differences in attitudes towards migration. The GFS's interest in British empire migration is in the starkest opposition to attitudes elsewhere in post-independence Ireland. For example, in 1937, Deputy McDermott asked Éamon de Valera in Dáil question time whether, in recognition of the fact that empire migration schemes were open to Éire nationals, the government would 'take a full share in Imperial Conferences in dealing with problems of Empire migration'.[82] The suggestion that the government would in any way facilitate emigration was met with fierce resistance. De Valera gave a stern and unequivocal response:

> The aim of the Irish Government is not to provide facilities for the emigration of our people to the States of the British Commonwealth or elsewhere. Its aim is to concentrate on utilising the resources of this country and so improving the conditions of life here that our people will not have to emigrate, but will be able to find a livelihood in their own country.[83]

The idea of populating the British empire with Irish citizens was anathema to the government, and migration to England itself a sore spot, so the GFS's position puts them at odds with dominant ideologies, not simply of where to migrate to and the appropriateness of empire migration. They were also out of step in their conception of what constituted migration. In 1937, Helen Moore, the Central Head of Emigration, suggested her position be abolished 'due to the fact that there was so little emigration'.[84] This comment is rather

---

81 Girls' Friendly Society, Executive Minutes, 18 October 1933, Representative Church Body Library MS 578/4/4.
82 *Dáil Éireann Debates*, vol. 65, cols. 331–332, 17 February 1937.
83 Ibid.
84 Girls' Friendly Society, Executive Minutes, October 1920–December 1938, Representative Church Body Library MS 578/4/4.

strange: Ireland was in the midst of the Economic War and migration was in full flow. In the 1926–36 census period, it was estimated that 166,751 left the country, increasing to 187,111 persons between 1936 and 1946.[85] To claim that migration was down was to ignore Britain as a destination.

For GFS members, ideas of national belonging appear to have been wider than the narrow confines of the island of Ireland and their minute books point to a sense of themselves as global citizens, bounded only perhaps by the geographical limits of the British Empire. Foster has referred to 'the tiny Protestant minority' who were 'in the new state a dwindling and infinitesimal proportion', and this even smaller minority of GFS members are certainly not representative of all attitudes to migration within the Church of Ireland community.[86] They are, however, one of the main protagonists in female emigrant welfare and are interesting to consider on this basis.

It is only since 2014 that the Irish government created the role of Minister for Diaspora affairs; prior to this, successive administrations avoided taking responsibility for emigrant welfare.[87] The ways in which emigrants – male or female – travelled to their destination was little discussed by politicians, the emphasis being on the rates of migration, as outlined in Chapter 2. A possible reason is that how emigrants got to their destination and what happened to them whilst there appears to have been largely conceived of as a pastoral matter for the Catholic Church. Most welfare-related services from the 1920s to the 1950s (and beyond) were controlled and administered by the Catholic Church and its associated lay organisations.[88] Ewart's analysis highlights some practical reasons for this stance: Irish governments had limited resources that in the opinion of many should properly stay at home rather than go to emigrants who were enjoying greater access to health and social welfare services in Britain.[89]

In the first half of the twentieth century, the trafficking of women was a significant international concern, and this infused opinions about women travelling. Women's reasons for migrating were scrutinised frequently in the press and independent travel was repeatedly remarked upon. As Leppanën has commented: 'A woman travelling on her own was suspicious, whatever the motives for her movement'.[90] What transpires from a review of the evidence

---

85 Data from Vaughan and Fitzpatrick, *Irish Historical Statistics*, Table 56 (p. 266).
86 Roy Foster, *Modern Ireland: 1600–1972* (London: Allen Lane, 1988), p. 534.
87 For a detailed exposition of the efforts to establish a welfare bureau for emigrants in Britain, see Daly, *The Slow Failure*.
88 See, for example, Earner Byrne, *Mother and Child* for more on the involvement of the church in maternity services.
89 Ewart, 'Caring for Migrants', p. 210.
90 Leppanën, 'Movement of Women: Trafficking in the Interwar Era', *Women's Studies International Forum*, 30 (2007), p. 529.

is the widespread impression that Irish women were particularly vulnerable and naive. What also emerges is evidence of a latent power struggle over who was most appropriate to 'look after' such young women, with religious and class tensions abounding. When the Archbishop of Dublin, John Charles McQuaid, 'the most formidable and successful episcopal proponent of the Catholicisation of public life',[91] decided to open the Catholic Social Welfare Bureau in 1942,[92] this effectively set the Catholic Church as the predominant force for emigrant welfare in Ireland. The CSWB had close ties to the government, eventually leading to the direct provision of services to the Irish in Britain, particularly through the Emigrant Chaplaincy Scheme of the 1950s.[93] The tensions that had abounded between Protestants and Catholics in this realm were effectively muted as cooperation ceased and the efforts of Catholic lay women were overshadowed, to the extent that their archives are negligible and may have been destroyed.[94] By the 1950s, the panic over female migrant safety had significantly declined and the reach of organisations such as the CSWB was lessened with the deregulation of wartime emigration. McQuaid could no longer claim the CSWB had 'a national co-ordinating role' and the focus shifted towards providing support for the Irish in Britain through a chaplaincy scheme rather than repelling 'white slavers' in Ireland.[95] Morality, behaviour and migration were intertwined in the minds of many throughout the first decades of independence, demonstrated in attitudes towards female migrants once they arrived in Britain, as the next chapter will explore.

---

91 R.V. Comerford, *Ireland: Inventing the Nation* (London: Hodder Arnold, 2003), p. 117.

92 The Catholic Social Welfare Bureau operated from 1942 until 1982. The Emigrant Welfare Bureau continued to operate until 1987 when it was reformed as Emigrant Advice. See https://www.migrantproject.ie/.

93 For more on this, see Kennedy, *Welcoming the Stranger*.

94 Reference is made here to the scant material available on the work of the prolific and long-standing Irish branch of the International Catholic Girls' Protection Society.

95 Ewart, 'Caring for Migrants', p. 64.

4

Morality and Immorality: The Temptations of City Life

In the evidence presented to us, there were many references to the moral dangers to which emigrants are exposed. That these dangers exist cannot be denied. The majority of emigrants are young and inexperienced and have lived comparatively sheltered lives before emigrating. An abrupt change to a new environment, lacking the discipline and restraint of home surroundings and the vigilance of parents, constitutes in itself a real danger. In receipt of relatively large earnings to which they are unaccustomed, and often living in crowded hostels and lodging-houses, they may succumb to the temptations of city life.

Commission on Emigration and Other Population Problems,
Majority Report, para. 318.

I was very much an innocent then, on the sexual front. I'd had it drummed into me over and over, since the year dot, that things carnal were a mortal sin, and I had visions of the most terrible things that would happen to me if I transgressed … the message went deep into my soul.

Mary Hazard, *Sixty Years a Nurse*, p. 129.

The post-independence era saw a more overt emphasis on the behaviour of Irish citizens, most particularly because of the importance of nation-building and solidifying ideas of citizenship. Consequently, most historians agree that notions of appropriate behaviour circulated more consciously at this time than in previous decades.[1] Akenson's assertion that the Catholic Church played a significantly under-appreciated role in influencing the 'ideology of reproductive suppression upon generation after generation' is persuasive in explaining not just the post-Famine demographic trends he has focused on but also the subsequent panic in post-independence Ireland that legitimate fertility and the growth of the nation were at stake.[2] Had Irish Catholics learned the lessons of the church too well by then? Given high emigration, the low number of marriages and high celibacy rates, the high fertility rates within marriage were not enough to counteract population decline and it might have indeed seemed to some that Ireland was vanishing.[3]

The dominance of the Catholic Church in such matters has been extensively researched and it is generally accepted that, as Angela Martin has argued, in the early decades of the Irish state the Church was involved in the 'discursive regulation of sexuality'.[4] The Church of Ireland shared many of its concerns, however, particularly about sexual morality, as examination of the GFS reveals. The government was lobbied to a greater extent by individual Catholic clergy, however, such as the indomitable R.S. Devane, a Jesuit social worker who wrote frequently on issues related to sexual matters in the Catholic press of the time.[5] He also liaised with Alison Neilans, the General Secretary of the British Association for Moral and Social Hygiene, asking particularly for her views on the draft Criminal Law Amendment Bill in 1934, the campaigns in Britain on such matters having already occurred.[6] This again demonstrates the connections between British and Irish moral and social purity activists on issues of sex.

---

1   See, Ferriter, *Occasions of Sin*, and Cliona Rattigan, *'What Else Could I Do?':* *Single Mothers and Infanticide, Ireland, 1900–1950* (Dublin: Irish Academic Press, 2011).

2   Akenson, *Ireland, Sweden and the Great European Migration*, p. 200.

3   John A. O'Brien (ed.), *The Vanishing Irish: The Enigma of the Modern World* (London: W.H. Allen, 1955). See also Enda Delaney, 'The Vanishing Irish? The Exodus from Ireland in the 1950s', in Dermot Keogh, Finbarr O'Shea and Carmel Quinlan (eds), *The Lost Decade: Ireland in the 1950s* (Cork: Mercier Press), pp. 80–86.

4   Angela K. Martin, 'Death of a Nation: Transnationalism, Bodies and Abortion in Late Twentieth-Century Ireland', in Tamar Mayer (ed.), *Gender Ironies of Nationalism: Sexing the Nation* (London: Routledge, 2000), p. 67. Margaret O'Callaghan argues that the Church 'sought an extended moral control in compensation for the loss of its historical role as the "public voice of a wronged nation"' after independence, 'Women and Politics in Independent Ireland, 1921–68', in Angela Bourke *et al.* (eds), *The Field Day Anthology of Irish Writing*, vol. 5, p. 125.

5   R.S. Devane, SJ was among those who campaigned for stricter censorship in Ireland during the 1920s. See Michael Adams, *Censorship: The Irish Experience* (Dublin: Scepter Books, 1968).

6   Neilans appears to have thought the draft bill quite good, although she made objections to clauses related to prostitution as they only penalised women. She refused to comment

Pregnancy outside of marriage was one of the major topics of debate concerning Irish women's emigration. To escape the shame of an illegitimate pregnancy, many women fled to Britain, on the pretext of finding work, to have their children in secrecy. The other 'solutions' to illegitimate pregnancy were: immediate marriage; concealing the pregnancy and passing the child off as a sibling; institutionalisation in Ireland; infanticide; 'adoption' (although the fees had to be paid for by the mother up until the legalisation of adoption in 1952, so this was less popular); or, in rarer cases, keeping the child. Why was this so shameful? Earner Byrne's explanation is convincing: the concept of illegitimacy extended in practice, if not in name, to the unmarried mother: she was an 'illegitimate mother'.[7] The boat to Britain was therefore an escape from severe social censure for the girl and her family.[8] The history of pregnant Irish emigrants is a vital part of what was to become the 'abortion trail' from 1967. However, an examination of the available evidence reveals that the scale of the problem was consistently overstated, by both the press and welfare organisations. The experience of illegitimate pregnancy – either before or after emigration – was a minority one. The vast majority of female emigrants did not experience pregnancy as part of the process of emigration.[9]

The Catholic Church and the Church of Ireland adopted similar strategies in their assistance to unmarried mothers. The first Magdalen Asylum was founded in 1765 by Lady Arabella Denny, daughter of the Earl of Kerry, at Leeson Street, Dublin. It accepted Protestant women from any part of Ireland on the following conditions: the 'young, and the young only, on their first lapse, are received into the Institution; and thus the danger of companionship with hardened and experienced sinners does not exist'.[10] Girls contributed to their accommodation costs according to their means. The women were expected to do all the housework within the Asylum (even when heavily pregnant) and to participate in classes in Bible reading, sewing, singing and domestic skills. Having given birth, they were expected to find employment to support their children in foster homes, or in Protestant-run orphanages. Originally, mothers and babies were separated immediately, but in 1919 the decision was made to keep

---

in her official capacity on the clauses related to birth control. In the original letter from Devane, dated 9 August 1934, he indicates that Neilans has been very helpful in the past. Correspondence is contained in the archival holdings of the Women's Library, File 3AMS/D/14, Box Number 114 (Eire) Ireland 1934–1949.

7 Earner Byrne, *Mother and Child*, p. 172.
8 Welfare payments for unmarried mothers were not introduced in Ireland until 1973.
9 See Jennifer Redmond, 'In the Family Away and Away from the Family'.
10 Report of the Guardians of the Magdalen Asylum, 1915, Representative Church Body Library MS 551/12, p. 4.

them together for six months within the Asylum. The overall length of stay expected by women was originally between eighteen months and two years; however, by the end of the period examined here, this had become six months, with the Governesses reporting some occasional difficulties in getting girls to stay even this long. Between 1915 and 1950, a total of 805 women were reported as having been in the Asylum, with an average of twenty-five inhabitants each year.[11]

The regime, while restrictive, does not appear to have been as prohibitive or punitive as in Catholic-run institutions, although to modern eyes the use of the term 'inmate' and the lack of privacy and freedom are horrifying, particularly as the men who made the young women pregnant suffered no such consequences.[12] The development of the Magdalen system in Britain and Ireland was mirrored in other countries. Kunzel has outlined the development of maternity homes for unmarried mothers in the USA by evangelical women's philanthropic endeavours throughout the nineteenth century. There are many parallels between homes in Ireland and America, including the utilisation of a rehabilitative framework that provided a 'maternal, religious and domestic influence that made up the redemptive tonic of womanly benevolence'.[13] For those able to afford it, private nursing homes existed to shield one from the harshest regimes, but for the most part women without resources had to accept whatever help was offered by charitable and state institutions.[14]

Women in unmarried mothers' homes continued to be segregated by whether they were 'first-time offenders' or 'repeat offenders' and some homes, like the Magdalen Asylum on Leeson Street, would only accept women on their 'first fall'. The former group were housed in three special institutions for first-time unmarried mothers to be 'rehabilitated' away from the bad

11 Figures calculated from Magdalen Asylum Annual Reports, Representative Church Body Library MS 551/12. Of this figure, 62 were reported as leaving to go home, 111 as being placed in employment (usually domestic service), 1 girl was repatriated (although it does not specify where to), 4 died and 3 emigrated.

12 The state of the house is mentioned often: at times they had infestations of rats. Guardians of the Magdalen Asylum, Minute Books, Representative Church Body Library MS 551/2/4.

13 Regina G. Kunzel, *Fallen Women, Problem Girls: Unmarried Mothers and the Professionalization of Social Work, 1890–1945* (New Haven, Conn. and London: Yale University Press, 1993), p. 8.

14 Support came in the form of grants to Mother and Baby Homes and in the government's subsidy for illegitimate children who were 'boarded out' or fostered. For more on the system of payments, see Ann Marie Graham, 'Unmarried Mothers; The Legislative Context in Ireland, 1921–79' (MLitt thesis, Maynooth University, 2012), pp. 48–50. See also Donnacha Seán Lucey, '"These Schemes Will Win for Themselves the Confidence of the People": Irish Independence, Poor Law Reform and Hospital Provision', *Medical History*, 58.1 (2014), pp. 46–66.

influence of the latter. 'Repeat offenders' were sent to the local county homes and Magdalene Asylums run primarily by Catholic religious orders. Upon examination of the arrangements, it is easy to see why women shunned this experience in favour of going to Britain. Pregnancy was framed by the Irish welfare system as an offence, with women being incarcerated, referred to as 'inmates' and strictly regulated in their actions and behaviour. This general perception of the punitive consequences of premarital sex is indicated in the following quotation:

> I was naïve actually … All I'd ever heard about girls having babies before they were married, as we put it in those days, was when they were put into the place called The Good Shepherd Convent, and they were left there until somebody claimed them out. And this is what you were threatened with if you weren't home at night by ten o'clock.[15]

Similarly, in Sharon Lambert's case study of Irish women in Lancashire, the disgrace of illegitimate pregnancy loomed large in the women's narratives: 'Without exception, respondents [...] reported that the greatest shame they could have brought upon their families in Ireland was to have had an illegitimate child'.[16] One of Lambert's interviewees, 'Siobhan', provided a dramatic analogy as to how unmarried mothers were viewed: 'If a girl had a child and she wasn't married they treated her worse than if she had took a gun and murdered half a dozen people'.[17]

The policies adopted by the Catholic Church and the Irish government to deal with illegitimate pregnancies were both gender and class specific, and this also influenced the framing of female emigrants' sexual vulnerability. As has been recently revealed in the preliminary work of the Mother and Baby Homes Commission of Investigation, the relationship between the state and the vast number of institutions providing care for unmarried mothers and their children, is complex. The *Second Interim Report*, for example, found that while the state gave capitation grants it did not exercise authority over the institutions and in some cases appears to have sought little documentation. The Department of Health has no files for Bessboro, the Cork mother and baby home, for example, despite it receiving funding for over eighty years.[18]

15 Lennon *et al.*, *Across the Water*, quotation from Noreen Hill who left Cork in 1945, p. 92. Hill was referring to the Good Shepherd Convent in Cork.
16 Lambert, 'Irish Women's Emigration to England, 1922–60', p. 156.
17 Ibid.
18 Mother and Baby Home Commission of Investigation, *Second Interim Report*, September 2016, p. 8. Available at www.mbhcoi.ie/MBH.nsf/page/LPRN-ALCFND1238712-en/ $File/MBHCOI%202nd%20Interim%20Report.pdf.

Women were generally held in Catholic-run institutions for between eighteen and twenty-four months unless they had money to leave early.[19] The length of time women were held was felt by some to render them 'psychologically unsuitable for social integration', and this is illustrated most heart-rendingly in the following quotation from one of Kevin Kearns's interviewees:

> I know of one poor girl (who) had a baby and she was put into the convent. A hard life, a *hard life*. I went to see her in the convent. Her hair was cut tight and you wore a big heavy convent skirt and a pair of big boots and you were made to work like a slave, and water (perspiration) dripping out of her. Her baby was given out for adoption. And that poor girl was going around the streets, her poor mind gone. And do you know what? She used to put an old cat in a little pram and drive it around, God love her. Cause her mind went. And she was a lovely girl.[20]

While we may think that the history of 'Magdalen women' has only recently been 'revealed', evidence such as this highlights that contemporaries were aware of the hardships that existed for unmarried mothers. As Smith points out, the prominent geographical locations of such institutions made them well known: they 'functioned as a constant reminder of the social mores deemed appropriate in Catholic Ireland and the consequences awaiting transgressors of those standards'.[21]

It would be incorrect, however, to suggest that the government or Catholic hierarchy imposed their teachings on an unruly or unwilling populace. Rather, as suggested by many historians, people accepted Catholic doctrinal teachings on sexual behaviour because this suited their aspirations for living standards and their family inheritance practices.[22] Marjorie Howes argues convincingly that

---

19 See Sarah-Anne Buckley, 'The Catholic Cure for Poverty', Jacobinmag.com, 27 May 2016: https://www.jacobinmag.com/2016/05/catholic-church-ireland-magdalene-laundries-mother-baby-homes.

20 Kearns, *Dublin's Lost Heroines*, p. 122. The words in brackets are Kearns's explanatory insertions. Emphasis in original.

21 Smith, *Ireland's Magdalen Laundries and the Nation's Architecture of Containment*, p. xiv.

22 For further discussion of these issues, see Whyte, *Church and State in Modern Ireland*; Ann Rossiter, 'Bringing the Margins into the Centre: A Review of Aspects of Irish Women's Emigration from a British Perspective', in Ailbhe Smyth (ed.), *Irish Women Studies Reader* (Dublin: Attic Press, 1993), pp. 177–202; Mary E. Daly, *Social and Economic History of Ireland Since 1800* (Dublin: The Educational Company, 1981); Kennedy, *The Irish*.

The church was most successful in enforcing its doctrines when other factors, like the familistic structure of rural life, also encouraged conformity. Many priests encouraged early and universal marriage and were ignored. Irish Catholicism's emphasis on chastity and sexual morality, which became woven into post-revolutionary efforts to define and assert the national character, was more the result than the cause of Irish rural bourgeois values.[23]

Thus, mores surrounding sexual purity and the systems adopted for managing digressive behaviour were tacitly condoned by the community if not fully complied with, as the evidence from the Carrigan Report appeared to suggest.

An emphasis on sexual morality was not restricted to the Catholic Church, as Protestant pamphlets also stressed the importance of restraint and often exemplified a similar gender bias in considering women as weaker willed. A pamphlet aimed at men dating from 1929 is revealing:

Every girl is a Princess, because she is a child of God. Who is the King of kings. God had placed her in a strong castle – the castle of her purity. But the dragon of sin is still abroad. [...] What man worthy of the name will take the side of the dragon in that cruel conflict? What chivalry have we unless we fight in defence of that castle, resisting both the evil passions within ourselves and also the corruption that is in the world around us? God has made man stronger than woman. Why? To be her protector, not her tyrant; to shield her, not to shame her.[24]

Moreover, there was a general sharing of moral beliefs by both the Catholic and Protestant Church in the Free State up until 1930 when the Lambeth Conference declared acceptance for the use of contraceptives in certain circumstances (for example, within marriage where a wife suffered ill health).[25] This divergence did not, however, affect the passing of legislation banning contraceptives, thereby prohibiting them for all, regardless of personal moral viewpoints (much like divorce).

Ireland's 'containment culture', the term coined by Smith to describe the contemporary focus on repressing sexual behaviour, is attested to by other historians and is also recounted in oral histories.[26] Michael Brazil, for

---

23 Howes, 'Public Discourse, Private Reflection, 1916–70', p. 926.
24 Rev. Spencer H. Elliott, 'A Woman's Honour: A Straight Talk to Men', Straight Talk Series No. 5 (London: Society for Promoting Christian Knowledge, 1929), p. 9.
25 McAvoy, 'The Regulation of Sexuality', p. 255.
26 Smith, 'The Politics of Sexual Knowledge', p. 209.

example, recalled that the Christian Brothers in Waterford taught the boys
to beware of women. He felt their mission was:

> to warn us of the perils that were waiting for a young man in the wide,
> wide world, especially women. One of women's main missions in life
> was to steer us young men and drag us down to their level, and open
> the gates of hell, and do all kinds of naughty things. We weren't sure
> what they were supposed to do, but we were terrified of girls. And we
> were warned to keep away from them. And I believe that the girls were
> warned by the nuns about us boys.[27]

This quotation illustrates the ignorance and fear that was engendered in many
through their school education in relation to sexual matters. Smith argues
that the repressive 'containment culture' operating in Ireland around sexual
matters was solidified in the early Free State period through the Carrigan
Commission, its report and the subsequent legislation, the Criminal Law
Amendment Act (1935).[28] This served to create a 'sanitised moral landscape'
in Ireland based on Catholic principles of morality.[29]

The Catholic Church imposed a moral orthodoxy within Ireland about
knowledge of sexual matters that kept many in ignorance, a stance 'which
assumes that the mere possession of knowledge will inevitably lead to sin'.[30]
Consequently, it was felt by some that Irish women were less knowledgeable
about sexual matters than their English counterparts and that this would
leave them at a disadvantage when in Britain. Witnesses to the Carrigan
Commission argued girls should be given education about human sexuality
and reproductive biology because they were 'physically more immature than
those of equal age abroad and temperamentally they were more trusting
and simple', according to the Irish Women Citizens and Local Government
Association.[31] This lack of knowledge is testified to by some oral histories
that mention such sensitive matters, although of course no baseline data for
sexual knowledge will ever be available to test these assumptions against. A
case study in sexual ignorance, however, is provided in the oral testimony
of Maira Curran (née O'Rourke), who emigrated to Britain in 1947. Curran

---

27 Pam Schweitzer (ed.), *Across the Irish Sea* (London: Age Exchange Theatre Company,
    2001), p. 12.
28 Smith, 'The Politics of Sexual Knowledge', p. 209.
29 Crowley and Kitchin, 'Producing "Decent Girls"', p. 355.
30 Howes, 'Public Discourse, Private Reflection, 1916–70', pp. 929–930.
31 Dr Angela Russell represented the Irish Women Citizens and Local Government
    Association (IWCLGA) at the hearings. This attitude was also espoused by Mrs
    J.M. Kettle of the Dublin County Union. See Smith, 'The Politics of Sexual Knowledge',
    pp. 225–226.

went to train as a nurse, sent by nuns in the convent where she grew up after her father died. Curran's sheltered upbringing in the convent had not prepared her for the reality of nursing, particularly the intimacy it required with men's bodies. Curran had been given a book to read on the 'facts of life' before she left but she got a big shock when she first saw a naked male patient:

> The first day I was on the ward, the sister said to me, 'Come along, Nurse O'Rourke, and help me with this patient'. It was a men's ward and Mr. Jones was his name. I went in and she was taking his stitches out and she pulled the bedclothes back and he was uncovered and I suddenly saw his private parts. Well, I never knew that men and women were different, and I let out a scream. She put her hand across and slapped me round the face and said, 'Control yourself, Nurse O'Rourke'. She didn't know why I was screaming, and I never told her, but I shall never forget that though, when I saw that, oh my God, you know.[32]

Curran, however, is not the only trainee nurse to have been ignorant or inexperienced in sexual matters. Extreme embarrassment was also reported by Mrs Maden, an English nurse, who said that they coped with it by 'just treating them as bodies'.[33] Mrs Pearce, another English nurse, said that her embarrassment lasted two weeks until she just 'had to get over it'.[34] The naivety of Irish women about sexual matters is also alluded to by Mary Muldowney's interviewees. When Muldowney asked Frances was she aware of the discussions about dangers for Irish women living in Britain, Frances responded: 'I wasn't even told the facts of life'.[35] It is interesting that when questioned about dangers for women Frances immediately connected the answer to sex. Similarly, in Muldowney's interview with Meta, a woman from Northern Ireland, it emerged that during her time as a nurse she was promoted prematurely to Matron because 'there had been an episode there with the Matron and another older assistant nurse. I didn't know anything about those sort of relations, in my education there had been no mention of lesbians or such things'.[36] There is thus no reason to assume that women who

32 Ibid.
33 Interview with Mrs Maden, Royal College of Nursing History Group Interviews, British Library Sound Archive, C545/21/01.
34 Interview with Mrs Pearce, Royal College of Nursing History Group Interviews, British Library Sound Archive, C545/26/01-02.
35 Muldowney, 'The Impact of the Second World War on Women in Belfast and Dublin', vol. 2, 'Interview Transcripts', p. FS8.
36 Ibid., p. ML2.

emigrated were any more knowledgeable than women who stayed at home, or were *motivated* by a desire to explore sex, particularly if it was largely portrayed in such frightening terms.

Most Irish emigrants went to the largest cities in Britain. By 1951, one-third of Irish immigrants were living in Greater London.[37] City life was depicted in many newspaper articles and religious sermons as having a deleterious effect on both male and female emigrants because, as they came mostly from rural backgrounds, they were thus ill-equipped for the freedoms and pitfalls it contained. This concern has some merit given the fact that many may never have spent time in Dublin let alone in larger cities such as London. However, the success, failure, danger or safety of Irish women in English cities hinged on their 'sexual integrity', a facet of the discourses completely absent in relation to men.[38] The alien nature of the city and the dangers this posed for Irish people, who would find themselves in the minority, was referred to in advice from the Bishop of Elphin:

> If you have to go to England or Scotland do not do so without bringing a letter of introduction from your priest. I would advise you, however, not to go to these countries, for everywhere throughout England there are snares that will beset you – especially for Catholic girls. If you find you must have to leave Ireland, go to America, where your Catholic brethren are more numerous and influential.[39]

The indirect allusion to 'snares' for girls, undoubtedly refers to those of a sexual nature (that is, illegitimate pregnancy, immorality or prostitution) and the word is used repeatedly in articles such as this.[40] The convergence of geography, religion, politics and influence are thus viewed in this instance as creating 'snares' or traps that will most particularly endanger Irish girls.

It was not just Catholic girls who were thought of as being vulnerable in the city. The London Female Preventive and Reformatory Institution regularly placed advertisements in the *Church of Ireland Gazette* detailing their work and asking for donations. One such advertisement, appearing in March 1939, told the story of a young woman who came to them at 12.25 a.m. in distress after being left alone in the house with her master. Further details

37 Irish immigrants also followed this pattern in America where nine out of ten of Irish born persons in 1940 lived in urban areas and more than half of these lived in five large cities: New York, Chicago, Philadelphia, Boston and San Francisco. Kennedy, *The Irish*, p. 75.

38 Henkes 'Maids on the Move', p. 239.

39 *Standard*, 11 May 1929, p. 1.

40 For example, reporting of the 1930 Lenten Pastorals in the *Irish Catholic* also refer to 'snares for the unwary', *Irish Catholic*, 8 March 1930, p. 8.

are not divulged but it seems the reader is to assume she was thus vulnerable to improper advances from her employer. The story, an illustration of the cases they dealt with, is closed with the petition: 'Please help us to continue this most necessary work among young women and girls stranded in London, some from Ireland'.[41]

Although there may be snares 'set up' for Irish girls, the blame lies with them for so stupidly falling for them, according to journalist Gertrude Gaffney. Their willingness to associate with the wrong kind of people would inevitably get them into trouble:

> The great danger to the younger and more flighty of these girls is not, I found, commercialised vice [i.e., prostitution] but the unscrupulous loose-living men they meet in the street. It seems quite impossible to keep them from talking to anybody who wishes to talk to them. As all of the social workers in turn declared, they are bright and gay and far more fond of dress and life and dancing than the English girls, and with their fresh, pretty complexions, their easy manner and unmistakable Irish faces and beautiful eyes, they attract the wrong kind of man. This is how many of them come to grief.[42]

Gaffney's article confirms that fears of white slave traders were generally unfounded, but that the silliness, flightiness and love of fashion are what really got Irish women into trouble. She also drew clear distinctions between women who would be able to cope with city life and those who would not:

> I would say to all who take any part in securing posts for Irish girls in England not under any circumstances to permit, if they can prevent it, the very young girl, the sub-normal girl, the girl who is stolid to the point of stupidity, or the giddy girl, to emigrate. The only girl who should be assisted is the girl who is known to be clean, capable and tidy in her own home and well-equipped with neat clothes and uniform and enough money to keep her until she can get another situation if that to which she goes is unsuitable.[43]

These stereotypical and derogatory characterisations of Irish women were to be continually invoked in the series. Gaffney was not the only one to refer to 'sub-normal' Irish girls. Cardinal Hinsley of Westminster, generally a sympathetic voice in discussion of Irish women, made similar

---

41 *Church of Ireland Gazette*, 17 March 1939, p. 153.
42 Gaffney, *Irish Independent*, 9 December 1936, p. 7.
43 Gaffney, *Irish Independent*, 14 December 1936, p. 5.

comments in a letter to his counterpart in Ireland, Cardinal MacRory, when he recommended that:

> girls who are not of strong character and good intellect should be discouraged from undertaking the adventure of Emigration, which entails their separation from their natural protectors, family and friends. These girls are exposed here to temptations which they have not the necessary fortitude and prudence to resist. I find that many of the girls who find their way to my Moral Welfare Office are of feeble, or at least sub-normal intellect. Such girls should never have been allowed to leave their homes.[44]

An annotation in the margin of the letter (presumably by MacRory) stated one word to summarise this observation: 'weaklings'.

Delaney has remarked that 'it was perceived that young women were more likely to "fall by the wayside", despite the fact that evidence to substantiate this unscientific conjecture was rarely cited'.[45] Evidence, it seems, was less important in such discourses than the power of suggestion. The Commission on Emigration and Other Population Problems referred to the commentary on 'moral dangers' in their report, as noted in the quotation opening this chapter. Tracey Connolly has highlighted the overt concern displayed in submissions to the Commission, which 'echoed a fear in public circles throughout the late 1940s and early 1950s, especially felt by the Catholic church, for the moral well-being of emigrants'.[46] However, acceptance of these fears as based on 'fact' is to assume that Irish emigrants were all easily influenced, or would somehow seek out mischief, or needed strict forms of outside control to behave themselves respectably.

Much rhetoric reveals a fear of modernity that resonates with anti-materialist discourses outlined in the following chapter. Modernity brought with it questionable, and even objectionable, moral behaviours. This was a sentiment shared by some in the Church of Ireland. In the reports of the Protestant Magdalen Asylum on Leeson Street, modern life is also blamed for its ruinous effect on women's virtue: 'the freedom enjoyed by girlhood, the literature available for all, the attractive Cinema, each is good

---

44 Letter from Cardinal Hinsley to Cardinal MacRory, letter undated, but notation says it was received on 26 May 1939. Folder No. 1, 'Correspondence Concerning Who Come to England Seeking Employment'. MacRory papers, Tomas O Fiaich Library.

45 Enda Delaney, 'Gender and Twentieth-Century Irish Migration, 1921–1971', in Pamela Sharpe (ed.), *Women, Gender and Labour Migration: Historical and Global Perspectives* (London: Routledge, 2001), p. 215.

46 Tracey Connolly, 'The Commission on Emigration, 1948–1954', in Keogh, O'Shea and Quinlan, *The Lost Decade*, p. 95.

in its measure, yet each too often brings with it a temptation for a girl to take the one wrong step which handicaps her for life'.[47] The dance hall, as has been well covered in the field of Irish women's history, attracted much attention as a site of sin in the Free State and the dance hall in Britain was also singled out for particular attention.

A Catholic pamphlet from the early 1950s, *Handbook for the Catholic Emigrant to England*, addressed temptation, demonstrating the issue persisted even into an era in which social mores were changing. The pamphlet warned the reader that drinking was especially tempting to lonely emigrants, but they should never get drunk. While 'dancing is good in itself as a recreation' emigrants should 'have nothing to do with halls which permit or encourage sin. Remember that the full marriage act is not the only thing to be avoided by the unmarried. The Sixth Commandment forbids whatever is contrary to holy purity in looks, words or actions'.[48] The pamphlet referred to the particular responsibility women had regarding 'occasions of sin'. In the English dance hall it was argued:

It is here that the Irish girl has a great responsibility. She it is who will dictate whether sin is to be committed or not. She is failing in her solemn duty if she allows a man to be impure with her by word or action. She has little chance of avoiding such sins if she takes to drinking in public houses.[49]

Women were proscribed from entering public houses in Britain in the same way as in Ireland, although the assumption seems to be that they might actually do this in Britain. The admonitions given here show little had changed in Catholic attitudes towards women's social behaviour since Gilmartin's statement over twenty years previously: 'If the girls are good so will the boys'.[50]

Despite the prevalent attitudes towards the susceptibility of emigrants to temptations, the Commission on Emigration and Other Population Problems tempered this view of the 'big bad city':

We believe that the large majority of Irish emigrants lead lives very like those of their own generation at home and similar to those of the average citizens of corresponding ages and occupations in their

47 Report of the Guardians of the Magdalen Asylum, 1924, Representative Church Body Library MS 551/12, p. 2.
48 Catholic Truth Society, *Handbook for the Catholic Emigrant to England* (1953), pp. 16–17. Available from the National Library of Ireland.
49 Ibid.
50 *Irish Catholic*, 16 May 1931, p. 5.

new country [...] We consider that there is a good deal of exaggerated comment on the point, based for the most part on statements by welfare workers and others who, in the course of their work, come into closer contact with individual cases of moral delinquency than with the behaviour of emigrants as a whole.[51]

The Commission's report also noted that evidence on the prevalence of sexual immorality came exclusively from welfare workers who *only* dealt with such cases, and thus had no experience of emigrants who did not get themselves into problematic situations. The Commission conceded that 'while moral and religious deterioration among emigrants may not be very extensive and may indeed affect only a small percentage of the many thousands of emigrants, nevertheless, the number of such cases was sufficient to be disturbing and to merit attention'.[52] Given their remit, their composition and the cultural mores of the time, perhaps nothing less than an admonition to monitor such 'disturbing' behaviour could be expected.

Illegitimate Pregnancy:
Girls Leaving Ireland to 'Hide Their Shame'

A girl's 'character' is her chief social as well as economic asset. Her sexual conduct becomes the concern of the community and the loss of her 'character' brings disgrace not on her alone but on family and kin [too] [...] Emigration may in this way provide an answer to the pregnant girl who can be sent to England to have her baby without anyone knowing [...] [and] return when all is over without an apparent blemish on her character, her child having been adopted.[53]

Archival evidence suggests that the problem of Irish women going to Britain to hide pregnancies was constant throughout the post-independence era, such that the term 'PFI' or 'Pregnant from Ireland' had become part of the vocabulary of social workers in Britain, by the 1950s.[54] This section will demonstrate, however, that while this was a significant problem, in the context of the large flows of emigrant Irish women, illegitimate pregnancy was a minority experience.

51 Commission on Emigration and Other Population Problems, *Majority Report*, para. 319.
52 Ibid.
53 Jackson, *The Irish in Britain*, pp. 32–33.
54 Garrett, 'The Hidden History of the PFIs', p. 26. This is also referred to in an issue of *Spare Rib* featuring a special article dedicated to Irish women in England. See *Spare Rib*, 94 (May 1980), pp. 52–55.

Records such as those in the Dublin Diocesan Archives illustrate the intense interest in the potential moral or immoral implications of single and sometimes married Irish women's lifestyles in Britain. This was a topic frequently returned to in Lenten pastorals and public statements of the Catholic Bishops in Ireland such as Dr Gilmartin, Archbishop of Tuam. Referring to the immoral behaviours at dance halls across the country in 1931, Dr Gilmartin stated bluntly that girls were 'doing what they liked then fleeing to Britain to hide their shame'.[55] Gilmartin's statement implies a knowingness, and a flouting of cultural and moral orthodoxy that is wholly damning to Irish women, and does not take into account either their own ignorance in sexual matters or the equal culpability of Irish men. The shame is theirs and theirs alone. Throughout the 1920s and the 1930s, regular letters were received by Archbishop Byrne from English charitable organisations asking for assistance in dealing with pregnant women fleeing Ireland. For example, a letter from Florence Russell, Honorary Secretary of the Liverpool Port and Station Work Society in 1924, requested help. Russell, herself an Irish woman, claimed the Society had helped twenty-six girls in the previous nine months; again, quite a small number, although felt to be alarming and by Russell to 'bring disgrace on our religion and our country'.[56] What is interesting to note is Russell's declaration that 'this is not a Rescue Society'. The normal work of the Society was to assist women in their travel arrangements, like the work of the ICGPS, though they had a more overt emphasis on stopping the 'white slave traffic'.[57]

The Port and Station Work Society claimed they had difficulty accommodating unmarried mothers in Liverpool despite the existence of Catholic-run unmarried mothers' homes. Consequently, if they could pay, they sent women to a home in Leeds, and if not, they entered the Poor Law Institutes. If entering the latter, as in Ireland, they needed to be claimed by someone to be released. Russell asserted that this fate was tragic as they were often claimed by 'undesirable women' and became 'the companions of prostitutes' in 'common lodging houses'.[58] Occasionally a charity would send one of them

---

55 *Irish Catholic*, 16 May 1931, p. 5.
56 Letter from Florence Russell to Archbishop Byrne, 30 June 1924 in Archbishop Byrne papers, Dublin Diocesan Archives, Lay Organisations (2).
57 The full name of the Liverpool Port and Station Work Society included the subtitle, 'The Liverpool Society for the Prevention of International Traffic in Women and Children'. The Society was an interdenominational coalition of the Catholic Church, the Mayors of surrounding cities, the Jewish community and was affiliated to the National Vigilance Association. Miss Edith Rose appears to have worked for both the NVA in Liverpool and the Port and Station Work Society.
58 Russell also referred to the large number of Irish women 'on the streets' of Liverpool (that is, in prostitution), although she does not quantify this. Again, what is more important than actual numbers is the impression it gives to English people that 'the

home, although Russell does not mention whether this was with their child or alone. Russell's point was that under the current ad hoc system not only was the Liverpool Port and Station Work Society distracted in their proper work, but Liverpool ratepayers were incurring the cost of housing these women in institutions. A note scrawled at the bottom of the letter, which appears to have been added by Archbishop Byrne, says simply that the letter had got his attention; however, '[we] regret thus we cannot see how to stop this evil'. This rather passive response meant that English Catholic charities continued to take on the burden of welfare work for pregnant Irish women.

Vast, intricate networks of contacts between the Irish hierarchy and English welfare groups developed around Irish women emigrants. It is possible, however, that the intense interest obscured the extent to which Irish female emigrants represented a problem. A document from the Liverpool Port and Station Work Society claimed that between 1922 and 1927 alone it assisted 2,292 Irish women, the highest number of any nationality.[59] However, assistance was counted as having taken place if station workers merely gave directions, and this does not in any way reflect the number of women who sought help because they were pregnant. Records in the Dublin Diocesan Archives reveal that communications were received in the 1920s from eight associations and institutions helping unmarried mothers.[60] Over a period of four years, it was reported that a total of 1,203 women were given assistance. Of this figure, 376 had become pregnant in Ireland and were attempting to conceal it. A further 155 became pregnant in Britain; the remaining 672 represented a combination of both. Cardinal Hinsley of Westminster reported in 1939 that his Moral Welfare Committee were helping approximately one hundred women a year up to that time, far lower rates than earlier figures suggest.[61] While the data is imprecise, it is interesting to note that it showed a *decreasing* trend in the numbers of pregnant women assisted. This was not the impression one gets reading the newspaper coverage or the ecclesiastical correspondence. All one can conclude from this is either that the figures are fundamentally flawed or that the intensity of the discourse was in inverse proportion to the trends.

boast of the purity of Irishwomen is not a true one'. Letter from Florence Russell to Archbishop Byrne, 30 June 1924, in Archbishop Byrne papers, Dublin Diocesan Archives, Lay Organisations (2).

59   From papers in the Dublin Diocesan Archives, Lay Organisations (2).

60   These organisations were: St Pelagia's Home, London; Guardian Angels' Home, London; Catholic Women's League Rescue Committee, London; the Manchester Union; St Vincent's Home, Manchester; the Leeds Diocesan Rescue and Protection Society; the Crusade of Rescue, London; and the Liverpool and County Catholic Aid Society.

61   Letter from Cardinal Hinsley to Cardinal MacRory, letter undated, but notation says it was received on 26 May 1939. Tomas O Fiaich Library.

In 1932, another investigation into the problem of Irish unmarried mothers was conducted in Britain, with correspondence flowing this time through the National Vigilance Association. Edith Rose, Secretary of the Liverpool branch outlined to the national NVA Secretary Mr Sempkins, that the Crusade of Rescue, often quoted by Irish ecclesiastics, wilfully overstated the numbers of Irish women who sought help in Liverpool:

> The Crusade of Rescue, and Homes for Destitute Catholic Children' London, have been making strong appeals in Ireland, and grossly overstating the need and numbers of the Irish expectant mother and baby in London. I was mixed up with this Society last July, because I stated at a Catholic Conference in Liverpool, that the numbers of expectant mothers arriving in Liverpool from Ireland, had, within the last three years, been very small. This had been thoroughly investigated and I was proved right. The Society in London was very wrath with me, as they thought my statement would hinder their appeal in Ireland.[62]

The reasons why the Crusade would overstate the numbers of women it helped, other than to obtain self-sustaining resources or perhaps praise, are hard to fathom.

If the figures reported in the 1920s were remotely accurate, it is evident that welfare work for Irish unmarried mothers was a continuous drain on the resources of English charities. However, this was not evidence of an epidemic; the extant archives rather suggest there was a continuously small number of women assisted. This may explain the nonchalant attitude exhibited by the Irish hierarchy in addressing the concerns of their English counterparts and charity workers in the 1920s. To examine the issue in more detail, the correspondence relating to Liverpool is analysed here.

Lucy Desmond of the Liverpool and County Catholic Aid Society reported that they had assisted a small number of Irish women in the latter half of the 1920s.[63] Between 1924 and 1925, just nineteen Irish women were helped;[64] between 1925 and 1926, a total of twenty-seven Irish women were admitted to the West Derby Union, a local poor law institution, five of whom

---

62 Letter from Edith Rose of the Port and Station Work Society in Liverpool, 22 January 1932, Women's Library, File 4NVA/04/02 Box FL098.

63 Undated typed letter from Lucy Desmond of the Liverpool and County Catholic Aid Society in Archbishop Byrne papers, Dublin Diocesan Archives. All figures appear to have been provided by Desmond and relate both to the West Derby Union and the Liverpool and County Catholic Aid Society.

64 A total of forty-six women are reported for the period between September 1924 and June 1926.

were having their second child. Furthermore, between March 1927 and June 1929, thirty-one Irish women were admitted there. Of these, five were assisted to return home, four were discharged to domestic service, thirteen returned to Ireland by their own arrangement, three were discharged to relatives in Liverpool, one got married to the father of her child and five were still in the institution in 1929. Lastly, the Liverpool and County Catholic Aid Society reported that they assisted thirty Irish women between 1928 and 1929.[65] Desmond reported collaboration with Miss Cruice of St Patrick's Guild in Dublin, again emphasising the point that welfare organisations in Ireland and Britain were intimately networked. A total of six women had been sent home, seven had paid for their own confinement and treatment, and seventeen entered the West Derby Union. Crucially, Desmond made the following statement: 'I cannot say that these cases are on the increase – we have waves of them'. It was perhaps not the *number* so much as the continued 'waves' of Irish women coming over that caused the sense of panic, shame and alarm, particularly within the Catholic press.

It is evident from the above data that the seventeen Irish women assisted by the Society are most probably included in the total given for the West Derby Union itself and to regard them as separate serves to inflate the number of cases. In fact, it is not unlikely that women helped by welfare societies were counted multiple times. For example, a woman travelling through Dublin may have been counted by the Irish Catholic Girls' Protection Society. On her arrival in Liverpool she may have been assisted by the Liverpool Port and Station workers. If she was pregnant, she may have been referred on to the Liverpool and County Catholic Aid Society or directly to an institution such as the West Derby Union. In this hypothetical example, one female traveller could have been counted three to four times.

In assessing the figures, therefore, one must be careful to distinguish their accuracy. This has wider applicability in the popular reporting of cases of unmarried Irish mothers. Ryan's analysis of the *Catholic Women's League Magazine* revealed that between 1935 and 1937 the Westminster diocese of London helped 800 pregnant unmarried Catholic women.[66] The proportion of Irish women in this report is not given, but Ryan posits that the publication frequently referred to 'pregnant Irish girls'.[67] Not giving the specific number creates the impression that they were perhaps all Irish, or the majority were Irish. The difficulty partially lies in attempting to assess

65 The Society helped a total of 105 women in this period; under one-third were Irish. See letter dated 22 January 1932 to Sempkins of the NVA, Women's Library, File 4NVA/04/02 Box FL098.
66 Ryan, '"A Decent Girl Well Worth Helping"', p. 147.
67 Ibid.

the extent of the issue by only speaking with those involved in rescue work, as was done by Gertrude Gaffney of the *Irish Independent*. It seems that those who were asked to provide opinions '*only* came into contact with so-called deviant women, resulting perhaps in a tendency to exaggerate its extent and to see deviancy to a greater degree than was actually warranted'.[68]

The NVA records provide many case studies of Irish women they dealt with in the 1920s. Table 4.1 gives details of Irish women who either migrated to Britain due to pregnancy or became pregnant after commencing work. The diversity of the women is interesting: some are noted as 'middle class', others have experienced multiple pregnancies; some have received financial and moral support from family members at home, and, as suggested by Ferriter in *Occasions of Sin*, some migrated at the urging of their mother, who kept their secret for them. In the case of 'K.M.', it appears that her mistress brought her to Britain. The main point of the record keeping seems to have been to monitor cases from Ireland the NVA and their associates had spent money on. There is little in the way of sympathetic commentary, or empathy, and, although the fathers are mentioned (unlike in similar documentary evidence), in most cases the men were not held accountable. Cardinal Hinsley's comments to Cardinal MacRory in 1939 expressed frustration that women were so eager to give up their children in such cases; but, despite his condemnation, he wanted to help and had this to say of the women he met:

> It may be said of the unmarried mothers generally that contact with them breeds strong sympathy. Very few are vicious and if they had received the opportunity of marriage with the man concerned they would have done well. Their wretched position and feelings of intense shame, combined with the bad advice they receive, leads however to much equivocation and reluctance to shoulder responsibility.[69]

Ryan's oral history research with twelve Irish women who emigrated in the inter-war period suggests the interviewees believed that illegitimate pregnancy occurred more often in Ireland than England.[70] None of Ryan's participants had experienced pregnancy outside marriage, but two had unmarried sisters who became pregnant in Ireland. In one case, the girl was despatched to an aunt in Manchester to have her child, where she remained for the rest of her life. In the other, the younger sister had been placed in a Magdalen Asylum and the participant went home and brought her back

---

68 Redmond, 'In the Family Way', p. 171.
69 Letter from Cardinal Hinsley to Cardinal MacRory, letter undated, but around 26 May 1939, MacRory papers, Tomas O Fiach Library.
70 Ryan, '"A Decent Girl Well Worth Helping"', pp. 149–150.

Table 4.1   Case studies of Irish women
helped by the National Vigilance Association (1921–1923)

Girls Initials	Nationality	Where trouble occurred and what done for case
A.O.	Irish	Came to England as servant for Irish lady, then went to Hotel service. Father of child a Swede – staying in hotel. In workhouse but in touch with her mother in Ireland. Spent £10 on her.
M.H.	Irish	Well educated of middle class – got work as pianist. Trouble in England. Back at work – but Catholic Women's League are partly paying for the child! Money help given and continues.
M.K.	Irish	Age 27. Came over to be mental nurse. Father of child American soldier – knows nothing of him. Child with foster mother. Her mother in Ireland now helps. Some money given.
P.C.	Irish	Trouble in Ireland came over to hide it – work in Drapers' shop. Is supporting child herself. £5 spent on her.
M.O'C	Irish Co. Clare	Age 27. One baby in Ireland. Came to service in Hotels here. Father of 2nd baby Australian. Working in a Hotel.
P.O'C	Irish ” ” Sister of above	Father of baby Australian. Working in Hotel to support baby. (helped with money).
M. O'L	Irish	Came to service. Went wrong quite soon. Sent to Guardian Angels. In service again. Father of baby soldier infected her with V.D. Had saved £5 and then in workhouse Infirmary.
A.C.	Irish	Sent over by mother to hide her condition. Went into service. Very ignorant girl. Father of her child an Irish married man working on her father's Farm – now in St. Pelagia's Home.
O'R. 'Annie'	Irish	Found in Protestant Rescue Home having been sent over by mother to hide condition. Sent to Guardian Angels. After the birth her mother sent her fare to return to Ireland with child. Some money help given.
M.C.	Irish	Came to England in service. Now supports her child.
O.G.	Irish	Came to service in Boarding House and trouble in England. Baby died. Disappeared and cannot be traced. Money spent on her.

Girls Initials	Nationality	Where trouble occurred and what done for case
K.M.	Not stated	Now in Oxford Workhouse. First child born in Ireland. Father married man on neighbouring farm. Brought to England by Irish mistress. She went abroad and placed her in a good situation in Oxford. Went wrong almost at once. Taken to Protestant Rescue Home – confined in workhouse Infirmary – several men cited for paternity: no claim allowed. Still in workhouse.[1]

Note: Headings in the table have been kept as they appear in the original documentation.
[1] This is the only case which is from 1923, all others are from 1921.
Source: Women's Library, File 4NVA/04/02 Box FL098.

to Britain. Incidences of Irish women becoming pregnant while working in Britain do, of course, exist; indeed, Moulton's conclusion has been that this was the predominant experience, rather than arriving pregnant.[71] One of Ryan's participants, Annie (a pseudonym), worked with an Irish girl in a hotel where they also lived. The girl had a boyfriend and decided to leave the hotel to spend more time with him. Some time later, Annie visited her in a bedsit and found a dead baby concealed in a wardrobe.[72] In another account, Catherine Ridgeway recalled working with a chambermaid in London in the 1930s who became pregnant and refused to marry the father. Without telling anyone, she gave birth to a stillborn child and put it in a suitcase. Ridgeway was instructed by the housekeeper to take the girl to get medical help after she looked unwell one morning and carried the suitcase out of the hotel without knowing the baby's corpse was inside.[73] These are the most graphic and tragic of the stories related in oral history accounts and show the extreme level of shame and fear that many Irish women experienced regarding illegitimate pregnancy. These examples point to the fact that emigrants may have known women who 'got into trouble' during their time in Britain. However, there are far fewer of these examples than of those who pursued the more 'normal' route of courtship, marriage and then children.

Gaffney's series of articles at the end of 1936 addressed the problem of female emigrants 'getting into trouble' in Britain. She cautioned the reader

71 Moulton, *Ireland and the Irish*, p. 289.
72 Ibid., p. 150.
73 In Lennon *et al.*, *Across the Water*, p. 50. The girl later broke down at a friend's house and confessed. She was put on trial but let off on probation as they felt she 'had already suffered her punishment'.

in the first article: 'I want you to bear in mind all through these articles that these girls who come to grief are the minority, but that they are a rapidly growing minority'.[74] However, despite some further brief provisos, the focus of the articles was on girls who indulged in immoral behaviours, and her tone is often judgemental. While Gaffney interpreted the secrecy as 'a vast and endless web of conspiracy', perpetrated by Irish female emigrants, the fact that such incidents were hidden illustrates their taboo nature.[75] Furthermore, historians have used her arguments problematically to demonstrate evidence of pregnancy outside marriage.[76]

The conclusion to this corpus of woeful tales is that while there is evidence that some Irish female immigrants did 'slip' in their moral standards in Britain, as Gaffney outlined, oral histories of Irish female migrants also reveal a much more mundane experience than was conveyed in the press. Such girls were generally not attempting to live modern, gregarious lifestyles, and their pregnancies do not refute this; rather, they reveal the girls' ignorance of sexual matters. Gaffney's claims that girls who went 'to the bad' lacked principle, character and religious training ignored the profound lack of knowledge many had of their own reproductive functions.[77] Emigrants carried with them Irish sexual mores of behaviour, much as they did other social conventions, such as those related to food, clothes, working and socialising. Implying that immorality was a common experience is an overstatement.

In the 1930s, the Irish government established a repatriation scheme after persistent calls from British welfare agencies for assistance in dealing with Irish unmarried mothers who came to Britain to have their children in secret. A 'behind the scenes' approach was adopted, with Irish High Commissioner Dulanty involved.[78] The details of the scheme have been traced elsewhere and will be outlined only briefly here.[79] Only first-time unmarried mothers who had conceived their children in Ireland were eligible for the scheme, which paid for their passage back to Ireland where they

74 *Irish Independent*, 7 December 1936, p. 5.
75 *Irish Independent*, 11 December 1936, p. 6.
76 See Ryan, *Gender, Identity and the Irish Press*; Earner Byrne, '"Moral Repatriation"'.
77 *Irish Independent*, 14 December 1936.
78 According to a memo by Alice Litster, 'Unmarried Mothers, in Great Britain and at Home' (undated), Dulanty arranged an informal conference of Catholic social welfare societies in London in November 1931. Department of Health and Children Records Management Unit files (DH&C) 22.4.3, Clandillon papers (489778), UK–Ireland Repatriation Scheme, 1939–50). Litster was the Lady Inspector at the Department of Local Government and Public Health responsible for liaising with the Catholic Protection and Rescue society for repatriation arrangements. She also undertook inspection of homes for unmarried mothers.
79 See Redmond, 'In the Family Way'.

and their child would be looked after by Catholic welfare organisations and homes, primarily the Catholic Protection and Rescue Society of Ireland (CPRSI). The insistence on the place of conception reveals the concern with helping only Irish citizens – children with foreign paternity would not be accommodated by the scheme. Mothers and babies usually went to their local county home and the Irish government paid 50 per cent of the costs. Control of the scheme was largely left to the Catholic Church, which eventually took it over completely in August 1940 and administered it through the CPRSI for a further thirty years.[80]

Further into the 1930s, the Irish government appears to have been most eager to deflect any criticism about female emigrant welfare on to the Catholic Church. Following a letter from Cardinal Hinsley to J.W. Dulanty in 1938, the government made enquiries as to whether the Irish bishops had previously discussed the issue through Cardinal McRory, who had communicated in 1937 with Hinsley. McRory assured Hurson, Secretary of the Department of Local Government and Public Health, that the Irish bishops had discussed Hinsley's concerns in 1937 and that they would be 'willing to do anything they could do to help'.[81] Upon hearing this, Hurson's colleague J.P. Walshe at the Department of External Affairs was quick to suggest that 'it is time for us to put the responsibility for this matter where it really belongs, namely, on the shoulders of the clergy'.[82] The government clearly felt that this was a pastoral affair and pondered over how to get the Catholic hierarchy to institute an organisation along the same lines as that presided over by Hinsley, in Westminster, the Moral Welfare Committee. This, it felt, was imperative, if 'we are to preserve any reputation at all vis-à-vis the English Catholics'.[83]

Dulanty was a key figure in the management of this particularly odious image problem the Irish government and Catholic hierarchy faced. Further research is needed to establish to what extent Dulanty's role as High Commissioner in London was used to resolve welfare issues rather than matters of diplomacy as may be expected of such a high-ranking office. There are numerous letters and memorandums from both Dulanty and Catholic organisations in Britain responding to Dulanty's requests for information on Irish unmarried mothers. For example, lists of pregnant Irish women between 1937 and 1940, including their names, ages, dates of arrival and

---

80 See 'Memorandum on Repatriated Irish Girls' prepared by the Catholic Protection and Rescue Society, 20 May 1941. DH&C, Clandillon papers. Also see Earner Byrne, '"Moral Repatriation"' and Paul Michael Garrett, 'The Abnormal Flight'. According to Garrett (p. 340), the repatriation scheme ended in 1971.
81 Letter from Cardinal McRory to J. Hurson, 26 July 1938. DH&C, Clandillon papers.
82 J.P. Walshe to J. Hurson, 25 October 1938. DH&C, Clandillon papers.
83 J.P. Walshe to J. Hurson, 27 May 1939. Walshe was quoting de Valera in this letter. DH&C, Clandillon papers.

county of origin are contained in the files of the Department of Health and Children.[84] These lists, where possible, detail where conception took place and the nationality of the father. It is likely that the women were not aware that such personal information was being given to the Irish government and their right to privacy is never referred to in the documents.

Given that these lists were sent back to the Taoiseach's office, it appears that the Irish government wanted to keep abreast of the situation, despite being reluctant to assume financial or organisational responsibility for the problem. Why was this so? Was it perhaps to assess the true extent of the problem? In a report of her visit to London in 1938, Alice Litster, an inspector with the Department of Health, stated that she deduced a reduction in the numbers of pregnant women leaving Ireland.[85] However, she was informed by Canon Craven of the London Crusade of Rescue that the number was actually 'rapidly on the increase'. Litster comments of this assertion: 'He adduced no figures in support of his contention, but undertook to forward data, which so far has not been received'.[86] Were these investigations and data keeping undertaken to provide the government with leverage in their bids to get the Irish hierarchy to take over the welfare arrangements for Irish female emigrants?

Inaction on the issue persisted. Cardinal Hinsley forwarded a second report on welfare work for pregnant Irish women in his diocese in May 1939, this time directly to de Valera.[87] Hinsley again referred to the fact that many emigrants were a 'credit to their country', but there was a minority element that was not. Among these included girls who emigrated to conceal their pregnancy and girls who through 'sheer weakness of intellect and

---

84   These lists were provided to Dulanty by the Legion of Mary, the Lancaster Diocesan Protection and Rescue Society, the Leeds Diocesan Rescue and Protection Society and the Liverpool Catholic Children's Protection Society and were forwarded on to the Department of External Affairs. Note that in copies that I have obtained from the DH&C, surnames of the women have been redacted to protect their privacy, but these were contained in the original documentation. DH&C, Clandillon papers.

85   Report by Alice Litster, untitled, but addressed to the Secretary, most likely Hurson, dated 10 November 1938. DH&C, Clandillon papers.

86   Ibid.

87   Letter from Cardinal Hinsley to de Valera, 25 May 1939. DH&C, Clandillon papers. Hinsley was aware his statements would not be viewed kindly in Ireland. Cooney has noted that during the Second World War Hinsley was censored in the Irish press because he outspokenly railed against Nazism and Fascism, but he thought he was silenced because he had been involved with helping Irish unmarried mothers. In a letter to McQuaid, he stated: 'Am I blacklisted in Eire because I have spent money – my own and that of charitable persons zealous for the salvation of souls and the good name of Catholic Ireland – in an endeavour to prevent the scandal of Irish girls and Irishmen who have left their unwanted babies to be maintained by us?' John Cooney, *John Charles McQuaid: Ruler of Catholic Ireland* (Dublin: The O'Brien Press, 1999), p. 143.

character combined with inexperience' fell pregnant after arriving. Despite continued reports of numbers of Irish women seeking assistance to return at the end of the 1930s, it was not until the advent of John Charles McQuaid as Archbishop of Dublin that the issue of female emigrants was taken up with zealous enthusiasm. McQuaid was to tackle the issue by increasing connections with the English hierarchy and by providing support for female emigrants as they were leaving Ireland through the CSWB.

Tensions existed between the Irish and English welfare organisations responsible for repatriation. Alice Litster reported that the English societies appeared so hasty in getting rid of Irish girls that they did not inform them properly of the conditions of the scheme: 'girl after girl has returned from Great Britain through these societies expecting that her baby will be "adopted" immediately and that she will be able to return at once to her work on the other side. This makes the problem of dealing with the repatriate doubly difficult'.[88] The suggestion is that they did not fully inform the women to ensure they would comply in leaving Britain. It seems knowledge of what the scheme entailed must have filtered through to Irish women as the numbers taking up the option remained low; it was clearly the very last resort for many. Litster's report in 1948 revealed that relatively few women were availing themselves of (or were perhaps eligible for) the repatriation scheme; from 1940 to 1948, there were just 150 cases dealt with by the Catholic Protection and Rescue Society, although in 1940 they also enlisted the help of St Patrick's Guild, due to difficulties in managing the number of repatriation cases, according to Ewart.[89] In contrast, 2,652 cases of Irish unmarried mothers applied for help from Catholic organisations in Britain during 1947 alone.[90] It is impossible to assess definitively what proportion of these women became pregnant in Ireland or Britain. It is also interesting to speculate whether the high numbers reported in 1947 represented a significant increase upon previous years or not, given the lack of reliable figures. The lack of response to the repatriation scheme is evident even in wartime. A study of the Irish travel permit applications has revealed just 18 unmarried mothers, 12 of whom were participating in the scheme, out of a cohort of over 20,000 permit applications.[91] The intervention of the CSWB appears to have allowed the government to step back considerably from its previous involvement in the issue of illegitimate

---

88 Alice Litster, 'Unmarried Mothers, in Great Britain and at Home', p. 2. DH&C, Clandillon papers.

89 Ewart, 'Caring for Migrants', p. 43. It is unclear how many cases the Guild dealt with separately.

90 Ibid. Dulanty arranged an informal conference of Catholic social welfare societies in London in November 1931. DH&C, Clandillon papers.

91 See Redmond, 'In the Family Way'.

pregnancy and emigration, as there is an absence of correspondence in the government files at this time, in contrast to the 1930s, before the CSWB was established. After the time period examined in this book, a small number of women appear to have been involved in the official repatriation scheme, averaging 140 to 180 Irish women per annum from 1955 to 1970.[92] Most (two-thirds) came from 'the Westminster and Southwark Diocesan Crusades of Rescue, around 15 per cent came from Birmingham and the remainder from rescue societies in a range of English cities, including Portsmouth, Leeds, Manchester, Northampton and Liverpool'.[93] Clearly a small number of women either wished to return to Ireland or failed to find alternative options in Britain and, as Ewart has outlined, many may have been unaware of their rights to state-funded care in Britain under the 1948 National Assistance Act.[94]

In the 1950s, the Commission on Emigration and Other Population Problems examined the issue of illegitimacy as part of its research on demographic patterns in Ireland and women's emigration to Britain. Reflecting on rates over previous decades, it reported that the illegitimacy rate in Ireland was below the European average, but this was probably due to an under-reporting of such births and to the emigration of pregnant Irish women. Regarding its enquiries with English organisations that dealt with emigrants, the report stated that their evidence could not be 'regarded as representative'. An estimate of '250 illegitimate births to young women who had become pregnant in Ireland (Thirty-Two Counties)' were recorded by eighteen Catholic rescue societies in London, Liverpool, Birmingham and Lancashire as well as parts of Wales in 1947.[95]

This data differs widely from Litster's data obtained for the same year. Which figures can be considered more accurate? A few possible explanations can be posited for the discrepancy, although none definitively so. Either the Commission and Alice Litster were talking to different societies, or the same societies were offering conjectured statistics rather than actual ones. However, the more apposite point appears to be that, considering the thousands who left in that year alone, most female emigrants did not experience illegitimate pregnancies either in Ireland or in Britain.[96]

92 Ewart, 'Caring for Migrants', p. 281.
93 Ibid.
94 Ibid., p. 280.
95 Commission on Emigration and Other Population Problems, *Majority Report*, para. 216.
96 A total of 18,727 women were issued with new travel permits and passports in 1947, reflecting those who emigrated via official channels, although permits may not have been used. The figures demonstrate that recorded numbers of known women facing pregnancy outside of marriage who sought help from Catholic organisations were a small percentage of the total female emigrant cohort.

The question as to where the pregnancy took place, and thus where the problem lay, was constant and prone to differing conclusions. The evidence from English rescue societies suggests that most pregnancies occurred after emigration. However, by 1953, the Department of External Affairs enquiries into the matter revealed that the vast majority (75 per cent) of unmarried mothers dealt with by English rescue associations had pregnancies that originated in Ireland.[97] Was there a monumental shift in behaviour in the post-war period? Or were the figures collected by the charities simply too high?

Conclusion

National and religious newspapers in Ireland established a version of 'truth' about women and their alleged behaviour that painted them in the worst light. Affected by fashions, trends and frivolity, there was little in these popular depictions that reflected the economic basis of women's migration. When assessing Gertrude Gaffney's journalistic pieces, it is interesting to consider Yuval-Davis's idea of older women acting as 'reproducers of "the nation"' being 'empowered to rule on what is "appropriate" behaviour and appearance and what is not'.[98] While Gaffney's role as a journalist may not fully fall within this definition, her actions do accord with the idea that such commentary was 'very often [...] the main source of social power allowed to women'.[99] In Gaffney's case, it is ironic because she was regarded by many as a feminist, often writing articles challenging de Valera's views, particularly with regard to the 1937 Constitution. What is also ironic is the fact that Gaffney appeared to think she was writing from an empathetic perspective.[100]

It was a woman's responsibility to deal with the crisis of illegitimate pregnancy by vanishing from the community to protect her own and her family's reputation. The repatriation scheme of the 1930s was meant to deal with the 'problem' of unmarried mothers fleeing to Britain, but this was 'motivated by shame and a desire to ensure that Protestant families in Britain did not adopt Irish infants'.[101] As such, it was not focused on the needs or wishes of the woman, and was not successful in eliminating the problem. In the 1950s, the Commission on Emigration and Other Population Problems

97 Letter from Professor Murphy to Mr W. Fay, Department of External Affairs, 8 July 1953, NAI, DFA 402/218/1.
98 Nira Yuval-Davis, *Gender and Nation* (London: Sage, 1997), p. 37.
99 Ibid.
100 For example, in one of her articles Gaffney states: 'I was writing from the maid's point of view'. *Irish Independent*, 12 December 1936, p. 13.
101 Lindsey Earner Byrne, '"Moral Repatriation"', p. 224.

recognised the need to change social conditions better to help unmarried mothers and lessen their emigration rates so that 'many young women who, under present conditions, leave Ireland and never return' may stay at home instead.[102] Unfortunately, as with many other of their recommendations, this was ignored.

The perception that Britain was a sexually advanced place in which looser morals were common appears to have been widespread, if inaccurate. As nurse Mary Morris found, she had to persist in her assertions that Britain was not one of Dante's circles of hell when it came to her moral safety: 'It took me a long time to persuade my relatives and friends that I was not returning to a hornets' nest of evil, danger and Godlessness'.[103] It did offer less scrutiny, and this is perhaps why this perception persisted, as did the question of whether emigration was used as a form of 'escape' from family ties and obligations. While some historians have posited women's emigration as an expression of independence and self-empowerment, my analysis would suggest that this is too modern a construct to explain the migration of most Irish women.[104] Lambert's hypothesis seems more apposite: 'it seems that as an Irish woman's identity was defined by her role within the family she was less likely to sever family ties than to adopt strategies of maintaining them from a distance'.[105] Continuity of behaviour would be expected far more than radical change; as Brenda Collins has argued, 'Irish immigrant women carried their cultural baggage with them'.[106] Irish women's propensity was to marry, have families and form strong alliances within their communities. Their social activities in Britain, the practice of their faith and how these were thought to affect their marriage and mothering as immigrants in Britain, are explored in the next chapter suggesting that 'cultural baggage' or mores were actively preserved by Irish immigrant women in twentieth-century Britain.

102 Commission on Emigration and Other Population Problems, *Majority Report*, para. 219.

103 Mary Morris, *A Very Private Diary: A Nurse in Wartime*, ed. Carol Acton (London: Weidenfeld & Nicolson, 2014), p. 18. Mary is referring to her return to Britain from a trip back to Ireland in 1940.

104 Rejection of patriarchal attitudes to women is cited by some historians as a reason why women emigrated from Ireland. See, for example, Gray, *Women and the Irish Diaspora* and O'Carroll, *Models for Movers: Irish Women's Emigration to America*. The strength of family expectations was referred to by Arensberg and Kimball as being to such an extent that an individual's ambitions would be thwarted if they did not coalesce with what was best for the family as a whole. See *Family and Community in Ireland*, pp. 388–390.

105 Lambert, 'Irish Women's Emigration to England, 1922–60', p. 152.

106 Quoted in Akenson, *The Irish Diaspora*, p. 174.

5

'Bride Famine', 'Empty Cradles' and 'Leakage': Irish Women Emigrants, Motherhood, Marriage and Religious Practice

A nation's greatness is gauged by the percentage of God-fearing, church-going, home-loving wives and mothers. Its decay may be measured by the proportion of pleasure seeking, maternity-dodging, half-dressed bachelor women who, like bats, owls, and lemurs, turn night into day.

Fr Degen, 'Pointers' column, *Irish Catholic*,
15 November 1930, p. 3.

Twentieth-century Ireland was a place where womanhood revolved around motherhood and marriage. In the quotation from Fr Degen, above, women set the standard for the nation, and in the 1930s they were, in his view, doing less than well.[1] In the case of emigration, it was often argued that it was immoral to leave Ireland and abandon this 'national' duty. Lamenting the lack of marriages in Ireland, the *Standard* quoted the late Arthur Griffith: 'If you can do nothing else for your country ... get married', thus positing marriage as a fulfilment of nationalist principles.[2] The discourses on non-economic motivations for women's emigration specifically referred to women's interests in marriage opportunities, but to what extent was this a motivating force for women to leave?

Kerby Miller has argued that marriage and the status it gave became a goal for most Irish women in the nineteenth century partly because of 'the

---

1 Degen returned to this topic many times in newspapers throughout the 1930s and the 1940s.
2 *Standard*, 8 February 1930, p. 10.

enhanced and sanctified roles of wife/mother/houseworker, and because the waged alternatives for women in post-Famine Ireland were so few and bleak'.[3] While Irish women may have been influenced by such ideology, it seems the equation of emigration with a means to marriage misrepresented their motivations. Yet, within public discourses, Irish emigrant women's 'betrayal' was portrayed as a double one – depriving Ireland of families while populating another country. Paradoxically, as Kennedy pointed out, there were far higher proportions of single Irish men in rural areas than there were women, so 'if young Irish women were migrating simply to find a husband, they were going in the wrong direction'.[4]

To assert that Irish women maintained traditional ways of feminine behaviour and links with their families, which may have been patriarchal in nature, is not to denigrate such women as mindless dolts, blindly following societal expectations. As Akenson has argued, most female emigrants

> had not broken free [of family ties], but that is no failing on the part of the emigrants. By not abrogating family ties, but instead using them to help themselves to slide into a new life in a new land, the hundreds of thousands of unmarried Irish emigrant women were being shrewd and self-preserving, and that is no weakness.[5]

The evidence does not allow for a definitive answer to the question as to whether female emigrants were using emigration as a tool to gain independence or not. There will always be private decisions and private emotions that have not left their mark in archival holdings. However, to view emigration by women as *primarily* motivated by anything other than economic imperatives is to posit their migration outside of the context of the time period. In this, my findings coalesce with Akenson's observations in the American context:

> whether or not emigration was a big step towards emancipation for most Irish migrant women, or merely the method by which they obtained in a New World what they could not have in the old – a husband and family – is something we cannot know. The great danger for us as modern observers is to draw simple correlations based on modern assumptions – such as the idea that unmarried non-dependent women were emancipated from their Irish past, but that the ones who married and had children were not [...] Economic independence and

3 Miller, *Ireland and Irish America*, p. 312.
4 Kennedy, *The Irish*, pp. 71–72.
5 Ibid., pp. 179–180.

the abandonment of social and cultural networks derived from the Old World were not at all the same thing.[6]

The movements of Irish emigrants were frequently within the nexus of familial and community relations, thus it makes sense that relationships would be maintained, not only from a sense of loyalty or affection, but also because they were key resources. The reciprocal nature of female emigrants' bonds with their families is commonly reported. For example, many sent remittances home but also received gifts in times of need; many went home with their children for whole summers but also returned when they were needed to care for sick or dying relatives.

The high numbers of single people in Ireland was commented upon regularly in the press. There was much speculation, particularly after the publication of census statistics, as to why the marriage rate was not higher. In the 1930s, 55 per cent of women and 74 per cent of men between the ages of 24 and 34 years in Ireland were single. This compared with 47 per cent of women and 55 per cent of men in Northern Ireland of the same age.[7] In Britain, the contrast was even starker: just 33 per cent of women and 35 per cent of men in this age category were single.[8] The behaviour of singletons in Ireland came under scrutiny. The *Irish Press*, for example had articles after every Census report was published. In 1931, it reported comparative statistics for England and Wales, indicating that Irish people were acutely aware of their anomalous demographic status.[9] In 1942, Anna Kelly in the *Irish Press* queried the low marriage rate in Ireland when she thought most women would believe that: 'marriage is a man's duty and a woman's goal'.[10] In the context of the emigration debates, this could be interpreted as meaning that Irish men may marry out of obligation, but women *wanted* marriage and thus may emigrate to achieve this.

Women's connection to the reproduction of the nation has been emphasised as the most important aspect to their identity in Ireland, particularly in nationalist discourses. This rhetoric maintained women's position as dependent and embedded within the family structure. As Walter has observed:

> The trope of the family is widespread in the figuring of national narratives – homeland, motherland, fatherland, daughters and sons of the nation. This imagery serves to naturalise a social hierarchy

---

6 Akenson, *The Irish Diaspora*, p. 186.
7 Ibid., Table 48 (p. 141).
8 Ibid. The figure for England includes Wales.
9 *Irish Press*, 15 September 1931, p. 6.
10 *Irish Press*, 17 September 1942, p. 2.

within an apparent unity of interests so that its gendered formation is unquestioned.[11]

Extending Walter's analysis, the female emigrant from Ireland contravened the national order by removing herself from the traditional schema, transgressing the physical and psychological boundaries of the state. However, Irish women did not necessarily abandon their traditional expectations as Nolan has argued in the context of migration to the USA: 'The legions of young women leaving rural Ireland in the late nineteenth and early twentieth centuries were discarding their newly subservient and marginal positions, not their traditional expectations'.[12]

The 'fact' that Irish women were rejecting marriage chances at home in favour of seeking them abroad was often referred to. A Cork County Councillor, T. O'Donoghue, claimed that there were 'farmers over the whole of West Cork, but girls of the type who used to marry them won't marry them now'. Such girls 'would insist on going to England for work, no matter what public opinion would say, rather than stay at home and get married to farmers'.[13] As with the discourses on 'fussy' domestic servants outlined in the next chapter, there appears to be some anger in these statements that women would not simply stay in Ireland and accept their lot. O'Donoghue was not alone in expounding the idea that women were abandoning marriage in Ireland for work in Britain.

In evidence given by members of the Irish Housewives' Association (IHA), the Commission on Emigration and Other Population Problems repeatedly asked the delegation to agree that marriage prospects may be a consideration, if not the sole motivating factor in some circumstances, for women's migration, particularly domestic servants.[14] Mrs Lloyd of the IHA answered a question on the matter from Dr Geary, a statistician and member of the Commission, which clearly showed a gendered bias in his views on migrants:

11 Bronwen Walter, 'Irishness, Gender, and Place', p. 37, *Environment and Planning D: Society and Space*, 13 (1995), pp. 35–50.
12 Nolan, *Ourselves Alone*, p. 92.
13 Quoted in the *Irish Press*, 16 December 1936, p. 1.
14 The Irish Housewives Association was represented at the interview by the following members: Mrs Skeffington, Mrs Lloyd, Mrs White, Mrs McGregor and Miss Swanton. Miss Swanton is stated as having gone to England to nurse for four years before having to return for 'domestic reasons'. Arnold Marsh papers, Trinity College Dublin MSS 8307–8308/3. Hilda Tweedy was not present at the meeting and appears to have attached little significance to it in her memoirs, as reference to the submission of a memorandum simply appears among a chronological list of such at the end of her book, *A Link in the Chain: The Story of the Irish Housewives Association 1942–1992* (Dublin: Attic Press, 1992).

Dr. Geary: It is probably true that a large number of men are forced through unemployment and poverty to emigrate. In the case of women, emigration is largely just the result of a desire for change or to make more money. Farmers' daughters sometimes do not give Ireland a fair chance or trial as a place of employment. They prefer to go to England than to Dublin.

Mrs Lloyd: Ireland does not give them a fair chance either. I think it is a difficult thing to go into an Irish homestead as a wife. It often means very hard work and poverty.[15]

Thus, according to Dr Geary, men are forced, but women are flighty. It is also noteworthy that such a highly respected statistician would draw upon unqualified assumptions in his arguments: Geary, more than many of the Commissioners, would have been intimately acquainted with the kind of data available on emigrants and aware there was no recorded evidence on *why* emigrants were leaving.

Questioning of the IHA continued in this vein. Andreé Sheehy-Skeffington, a founding member of the IHA, refuted claims of migration for marriage in a number of her answers. Referring to studies they had conducted on employment conditions and opportunities for women in Ireland, the IHA contended that females were being forced to leave. The Commissioners, however, sought to establish the more social factors and the following exchange gives an indication of the style of questioning:

Chairman: Even with better pay and amenities in Ireland is there not a likelihood that they will still go because of better prospects of marriage in Great Britain?

Mrs Sheehy-Skeffington: No, I do not think so. We have not considered that particular aspect of the question, but personally I would not think that would really enter into consideration very much.

Chairman: Have you met maids who left for that reason only?

Mrs Sheehy-Skeffington: No.[16]

Although wages and conditions were posited by the IHA as the most important 'pull' factor, marriage is referred to elsewhere as part of the spectrum of appeal of domestic service in Britain as opposed to Ireland. For

15 Arnold Marsh papers, Trinity College Dublin MSS 8307–8308/3. The difficulties of a woman going into a rural household are also described by Arensberg and Kimball. See *Family and Community in Ireland*, chap. 7.

16 Arnold Marsh papers, Trinity College Dublin MSS 8307–8308/3. The transcript is not dated but it appears to be from 1948.

example, a letter from a domestic servant that appeared in the *Irish Times* – an unusual occurrence itself – highlighted the all-round improvement in women's lives offered by domestic service in Britain. The letter, signed simply 'Domestic', refuted previous editorial commentary stating it was 'snobbishness which makes service more honourable when it is done abroad' or it was the 'freedom from wholesome control which young people gain when they work far from the eyes of their elders' that prevented Irish women engaging in domestic service at home.[17] Her letter put it bluntly – higher wages offered in Britain was the reason women left: 'I myself have £65 yearly and I am offered a paltry £36 here [in Ireland]'.[18] Second were the conditions of employment: many domestic servants in Britain could expect their own living room and a radio along with certain amounts of daily leave. Although 'Domestic' recognised the fact that wages and conditions could be remedied by appropriate legislation, she claimed:

> there is, unfortunately, one point that no legislation could touch – that is, the snobbery not of young women but of young men. In England young men actually marry domestic servants, and are proud of them. In Ireland the young men, if they marry at all, choose anyone other than a domestic. Since most women want to marry, is it surprising they go where they are most honoured?

The multiple levels of irony in this quotation are poignant. Some women did not feel they had a place in Ireland either to earn a living or to be wives and mothers, despite the special recognition for this role in the ideology of the time and the 1937 Constitution in particular that was being formulated at that very moment.[19] The letter demonstrates that status and the fulfilment of the

17 Editorial column, *Irish Times*, 18 December 1936, p. 8.

18 From letters to the Editor, *Irish Times*, 22 December 1936, p. 4. There had been legislation in May 1936 to ensure the conditions of employment of domestic workers (S.I. No. 160/1936 – Conditions of Employment (Women Cleaners) (Exclusion) Order, 1936). Under section 4, work could not commence before 6.30 a.m. or go longer than 10 p.m. or for longer than nine hours in one day. Domestic workers were also limited to a forty-eight-hour work week. Given the oral history accounts recalling long hours, it seems unlikely that these rules were strictly adhered to, and no mechanism was contained within the act whereby employers would be inspected.

19 Article 41.2 of Bunreacht na hEireann (the Irish Constitution) of 1937 specifically values women's place within the home: 'In particular, the State recognises that by her life within the home, women gives to the State a support without which the common good cannot be achieved'. This article remains in the Constitution to the present day. For more on the importance of high fertility for Irish women, see David Fitzpatrick, 'The Modernisation of the Irish Female', in Patrick O'Flanagan, Paul Ferguson and Kevin Whelan (eds), *Rural Ireland 1600–1900: Modernisation and Change* (Cork: Cork University Press, 1987), pp. 162–80.

'normal' roles of wife and mother *did* play a part in the decision-making of some women, but this cannot be rationally viewed as the *primary* motivating factor for most or all women. 'Domestic' was not alone in espousing these views about attitudes towards domestic servants. A breach of promise case taken by Elizabeth Feeney against Michael Mulvey (both of Roscommon) in 1946 hinged partially on her alleged misrepresentation of herself as a fully qualified nurse when he claimed she was a domestic servant; she was in fact a children's nurse, a position in between those two categorisations.[20] So much like motherhood, not just anyone was fit to be a wife. The paradoxical tension between valorising domestic roles yet denigrating unmarried women who did them for pay is evidence of the contradictory attitudes towards women and work in wider Irish society at the time.[21]

The focus on non-economic motivations has another curious dimension: marriage prospects are mentioned in nationwide surveys undertaken by the Commission that state the desire to marry as a motivating factor for young *men* who see no way of achieving this without obtaining steady employment. Some of these young men had rejected employment in Ireland, going so far as to say they would not stay even if wages they could obtain in Britain were matched. For example, Case C (R. Gallagher), aged 23, single, and interviewed in Portarlington, was summarised in the following report by the Secretariat to the Commission:

> He wants to emigrate to see England for himself and would prefer to do so than accept a permanent job at home at even £4 a week. He does not intend to come back if he finds conditions to his liking in England – stated that his prospects of marriage in England are much brighter than in Éire.[22]

This stated desire to improve marriage prospects does not emerge as a dominant trope for men, although it does get mentioned at times in relation to Irish couples in the Commission's surveys. In fact, in some reports, it was stated that a mutual decision was made by young people to emigrate to marry as economic conditions and the lack of housing prevented them from starting married lives at home.[23]

Some of the Commissioners' conclusive connections between marriage

---

20 'Farmer to Pay Breach Damages', *Irish Times*, 3 December 1946, p. 4.
21 For further discussion, see, for example, Louise Ryan, 'Leaving Home: On Female Employment, Domesticity and Emigration to Britain in the 1930s', *Women's History Review*, 12.3 (2003), pp. 387–406.
22 Rural Surveys, Arnold Marsh papers, Trinity College Dublin MS 8306/S17.
23 For evidence of this from County Mayo, see, for example, Rural Surveys, Arnold Marsh papers, Trinity College Dublin MS 8306/S1.

rates and emigration were based on a gender-biased and judgemental view of women's roles and ambitions. However, it would be incorrect to say this was the view of all members. James Meenan, also a Commissioner, later wrote that 'emigration (and the low marriage rate) should be regarded as a rational response to a particular economic and social situation. It should not be described in value terms as something that is "good" or "bad"'.[24] Not all commentators demonstrated such nuance on the matter.

There was deep unease about the loss of future mothers in post-independence Ireland, or 'national breeding stock', as Gray has termed it.[25] Irish female emigrants were single and at marriageable age which led to hyperbolic discourses on 'the empty cradle' in Ireland, or, as King and O'Connor phrase it, a 'bride famine' whereby Ireland was facing a demographic catastrophe.[26] Dr Casey, Bishop of Ross, captured the tone of panic when he exclaimed: 'One may well ask where the Irish mothers of the future are to come from'.[27] The Irish Bishops thought emigration of women to be so serious a danger to future motherhood in Ireland that they drafted a joint statement at their annual meeting in 1947 for private transmission to the Taoiseach:

> The Bishops view with great alarm the continuous drain on the womanhood and future motherhood of the country as the result of the present wave of emigration, and they consider it contrary to the spiritual and temporal welfare of the nation that foreign agents should be allowed to enter the country to attract girls abroad with promises of lucrative employment, the fulfilment of which no one in this country could control.[28]

Thus women, their marital status and their activities were markers not only of the tone of the nation but its very success. Their 'flight' was thus of serious national concern. No parallel concern for the lack of husbands or fathers in Ireland was evinced, despite high levels of male migration. The value placed on motherhood within the Constitution has been much commented upon as one of the means by which an ideology of Irish womanhood was established in Éire, yet, as Sawyer has commented, it was not an idea that met with mass objection and 'in the Catholic Free State, it was a very small minority of psychologically

24 James Meenan, *The Irish Economy Since 1922* (Liverpool: Liverpool University Press, 1970), p. 344.
25 Gray, *Women and the Irish Diaspora*, p. 2. This did not include concern about the loss of mothers of illegitimate children.
26 Russell King and Henrietta O'Connor, 'Migration and Gender: Irish Women in Leicester', *Geography*, 81.4 (1996), p. 312.
27 *Irish Independent*, 20 November 1936, p. 8.
28 Department of the Taoiseach files, NAI, S 13598A.

liberated women who reacted vociferously. The majority, had they been greatly interested, would have welcomed such a clear exposition of Catholic values'.[29] Irish female emigrants cannot be presumed to be any different from other Irish women in their general acceptance of religious ideologies about woman's role. Indeed, many carried these ideas with them to Britain.

Emigration and Marriage: Irish Women's Marriage Practices in Britain

There was much querying, particularly within the Catholic press, as to whether Irish women who migrated to Britain would become forever lost to Ireland and the faith because they would marry English Protestants. This seems to be a fear again based on supposition rather than fact. Numerous instances of endogamous marriage are contained both within the secondary literature and in oral history accounts. Mixed marriage was a controversial topic in Free State Ireland with commentary in both Catholic and Protestant newspapers condemning it for different reasons, most notably because of the demands of *Ne Temere*.[30] Extending the issue to emigrants was thus no great leap, but what is evident is a greater focus on Irish women's, as opposed to Irish men's, marriage practices.

The fact that many Irish women married while in Britain was simply the continuation of social practices in Irish society that had become distorted by post Famine trends of delayed marriage and enforced celibacy. Emigrants viewed it as entirely normal that they got married and had families; the fact that they did is often not elaborated on in any detail in their accounts, it was simply an expected part of life: 'I suppose in the main I would say that nine out of ten Irish people that have come here have more or less the same story. Came, worked, married, brought up a family, and you did it, you didn't ask too much'.[31] Lambert views many female emigrants as upholding traditional 'criteria' of suitable marriage partners when they chose to marry in Britain, often choosing Irish Catholics of whom their parents would approve.[32]

Endogamous marriages are the reported experience of the majority of those in the various oral history collections. This is not surprising given that many report socialising almost exclusively within the Irish community. Irish clubs and dance halls provided the opportunity for Irish people to mix and were the

---

29 Roger Sawyer, *'We Are But Women': Women in Ireland's History* (London: Routledge, 1993), p. 104.

30 This is the Papal decree issued by Pope Pius X in 1908 that reinforced the concept that children of mixed faith marriages must be raised as Catholics.

31 Nancy Lyons, in Lennon *et al.*, *Across the Water*, p. 176.

32 Lambert, *Irish Women in Lancashire*, p. 77.

venue for numerous matches. John Munally met his wife in the Irish dance hall in Hammersmith after asking 'her out for the siege of Ennis'.[33] Nancy Lyons met her husband in an Irish dance hall in London and went home to Kerry be married.[34] A Pioneer Club in Manchester was reported to have provided 'a most excellent means of match-making as quite a number of marriages have resulted among members'.[35] There was even a Catholic Introductions Bureau in London which claimed 42 marriages in its first year of operation.[36]

In O'Connor's study of Irish women in Leicester, many 'of the women had known their husbands before going to Britain but had only become serious in Britain when they "re-met", often at Irish clubs and dances in the city'.[37] A number of women in Walter's study of Bolton married Irish men: Mary, a Galway woman married a man from Mayo; Eileen, also from Galway, married a Sligo man; Bridie, from Tipperary, married a man from Clare she met at an Irish club.[38] Anne O'Grady also found many Irish people who had met their spouses through social activities provided by the Church.[39] Many interviewees articulated a sense of being more fully understood by Irish people and hence it is not surprising that many chose to marry fellow country people. Of the travel permit applications made during the Second World War by 3,715 married Irish women, 2,682 were married to fellow Irish men, with 1,008 married to British men, a ratio of over 2 to 1.[40] The Newman Demographic Survey, conducted between 1948 and 1954, found that 71 per cent of Irish-born Catholics married Irish Catholics in a review of thirty-seven parishes in the Westminster Archdiocese.[41] Available evidence therefore shows a high preference for marrying one's own kind, although regional differences have been noted.[42]

---

33 Interviewed as part of Schweitzer's collection, *Across the Irish Sea*, p. 138.
34 In Lennon *et al.*, *Across the Water*, p. 175.
35 Quote from Fr James Cosgrove, SJ, Spiritual Director of the Centre attached to the Church of the Holy Name in Manchester in the *Irish Catholic*, 21 September 1944, p. 4.
36 Reference is made to the Bureau in the Archbishop Downey papers, Catholic Diocesan Archives Liverpool, DOW.S.1.11.A.44. Liverpool Catholic Action Auxiliary Societies Catholic Introduction Bureau. Archbishop Downey rebuffed the invitation to set up a Bureau in Liverpool. Results were for the 1948–49 period.
37 Henrietta O'Connor, 'Women Abroad: The Life Experience of Irish Women in Leicester' (MLitt thesis, Trinity College Dublin, 1993), p. 83. O'Connor's study was on fifty Irish women resident in Leicester, originating from all parts of Ireland who had arrived between the 1930s and the 1980s.
38 Walter, *Outsiders Inside* (see chap. 7).
39 Anne O'Grady, *Irish Migration to London in the 1940s and 50s*, Irish in Britain Research Forum papers (London: PNL Press, 1988), p. 13.
40 Calculations made from author's database of NAI, DFA, travel permit applications.
41 A.E.C.W. Spencer, *Arrangements for the Integration of Irish Immigrants in England and Wales*, ed. Mary Daly (Dublin: Irish Manuscripts Commission, 2012), p. 43 n. 17.
42 Ewart notes these in her thesis, 'Caring for Migrants'.

Mixed marriages were greatly feared as contributing to the 'leakage problem'. Within oral history collections there were no instances of Irish emigrant women who went into mixed marriages. This may be explained by a number of possibilities. If Irish women married English Protestants, or those of no or other religious beliefs, they may have abandoned their own faith. As the Church provided links with the Irish community, such women may have severed their connection to other Irish emigrants and may not have been able to be sourced by historians who use Irish associations to find participants. It may also be that the incidence of mixed marriage was not as common as was thought, although further research is needed for any firm conclusions to be made. Walter's study of Irish women in Bolton uncovered the stories of women married to English men, although in each case the story differs from the traditional narrative in oral histories. Kathleen from Mayo married an English man and had previously rejected an Irish match at home with a postman in favour of working in Britain, an example of the 'fussy' women much maligned in Ireland. Margaret, from Dublin, met her English husband while she was still in Ireland, while Bernadette married a Catholic man who seemed to have Irish ancestry but knew little about it.[43]

Walter has asserted that Irish women in Britain from the nineteenth century may have married British men and 'after several generations are part of the diaspora space of Britain, intertwined in complex ways but not unidirectionally assimilated into an homogeneous British identity'.[44] Exogamous marriage did not result in an assimilation or 'disappearance' of Irish women; lesser visibility does not mean they vanished. Research on Irish people's marriage practices in Britain has been hindered by the difficulties posed by the source material. It is, however, a topic in need of further exploration.

Dedicated Faith or 'Leakage': Irish Female Emigrants and Religious Practice in Britain

The parks of alien London
Are schools for unchristian mind
To sow the seed of their godless
Creed
'Mongst weaklings who list
behind.[45]

---

43 Walter, *Outsiders Inside* (see chap. 7).
44 Ibid., p. 161.
45 Extract from 'An Irish Exile's Litany', poem by Joseph O'Connor, published in the

The term 'leakage' was used frequently to describe the perceived problem of emigrants losing their religious faith upon migrating to Britain. The issue of religious practice by Irish citizens in Britain appears to have been a sensitive one, intimately linked to the national identity of the new state. As argued in Chapter 1, emigration itself was problematic for the new Free State leaders who sought to establish a legitimate, independent state. Both Cumann na nGaedheal and the subsequent Fianna Fáil administration sought to base the new state on Catholic principles in opposition to what was viewed as a secular, British national ethos. Smith has argued that in their rivalry in the early years of the state 'Cosgrave and de Valera each attempted to out-Catholic each other'.[46] The perceived ease with which emigrants were thought to abandon their religious faith suggested that the pious identity cultivated by the state was not entirely authentic. This interplay is noted by Ewart: 'Leakage could both result from and lead to social problems in England but it had its roots in Ireland'.[47]

Within these discourses emigrants are spoken of as if they are all members of the Roman Catholic Church, and little attention was paid to the practices of members of the Church of Ireland. Because of this contemporary blindness (or bias), research on Irish Protestants in Britain has been scarce, and, as Walter has observed, since post-Famine times, the equation of Irish immigrants with Catholicism has masked the existence of a consistent Protestant minority amongst Irish migrants.[48] Wills also suggests that, during the Second World War, the Catholic Church feared 'loss of control over the war workers' and hence the emphasis on finding out where they were going and what they were doing.[49] The religious welfare of Protestant migrants was also of concern to the Church of Ireland, and the Society for the Promotion of Christian Knowledge deemed it 'the duty of the Church to care for all those who transfer themselves within our Empire, or to other lands'.[50] The system of welfare supports given to emigrants through voluntary organisations fulfilled

Irish Catholic, 7 September 1939, p. 2. The newspaper often carried poems on the Irish emigrant as exile.

46 James M. Smith, 'The Politics of Sexual Knowledge', p. 210 n. 5.

47 Ewart, 'Caring for Migrants', p. 71.

48 Walter, *Outsiders Inside*, p. 86. For a comprehensive analysis of Protestants in Ireland, including their migration practices, see David Fitzpatrick, *Descendancy: Irish Protestant Histories since 1795* (Cambridge: Cambridge University Press, 2014).

49 Wills, *That Neutral Island*, p. 321.

50 Quote taken from letter by George L. Gosling, Secretary of the SPCK, *Church of Ireland Gazette*, 12 April 1929, p. 208. The work of the Society for the Promotion of Christian Knowledge (SPCK) is referred to frequently in the columns of the *Church of Ireland Gazette* and illustrates an attitude held by some that Ireland was a fundamental part of the British Empire and an assumption that Church of Ireland members wanted to be part of empire settlement projects.

this purpose somewhat as the ICGPS, the GFS and the CSWB all attempted to provide follow up contact with emigrants through local volunteers and clergy. Emigrants were not required to give any details of their religious affiliation on Irish travel permit applications or anywhere else, and thus the religious composition of the Irish migrant community can only be revealed through Census data which is not wholly reliable.

Indeed, much like the nature of emigration statistics, there is no quantitative measure of the extent to which Irish emigrants either continued or ceased to practise their religion, whatever this was. Nor is there a measure of the frequency of participation in religious rites or activities, or the depth of belief and whether this changed upon migration.[51] Non-practice of religion by emigrants was cited by the CSWB as a concern in 162 special cases in 1959, but this tells us little of the specific issue and is a small fraction of the number of emigrants overall.[52] Despite this, there was a widespread belief in the early decades of independence that Irish immigrants in Britain were falling away from their faith in large numbers.[53] There were various estimates as to how bad the leakage problem was in public statements and articles. For example, Rev. Eugene Hopkins in 1948 stated that 50 per cent of Irish male emigrants did not go to Mass regularly in England, and though girls were better they 'need watching'.[54] However, other studies show that mass attendance remained strong in certain areas. In Birmingham, in 1967, 'Rex and Moore found that 89 per cent of their sample of eighty-nine Irish interviewees was Roman Catholic and weekly Mass attendance was high, at 57 per cent. This compared with 25 per cent weekly Mass attendance among English Catholic interviewees' in the same suburb.[55] So perhaps the conclusion should be that heterogeneity was characteristic of Irish immigrant religious practice in Britain and that rates of devotional practice were often above the native born population.

There were differing perceptions of the religious practices of working- and middle- class Irish immigrants. As Delaney has noted:

A recurring undercurrent in much of the public discussions was the seeming inability of the working classes to maintain and uphold the

---

51 As Jackson commented, 'conflicting opinions in the church are based on little empirical knowledge', *The Irish in Britain*, p. 147.
52 Spencer, *Arrangements for the Integration of Irish Immigrants*, Table 15 (p. 58).
53 T.P. French, Catholic Young Men's Society, speculated in the *Irish Catholic* that perhaps fewer than half of all Irish emigrants lost their faith upon emigrating. *Irish Catholic*, 28 October 1937, p. 5.
54 See Hopkins, 'Irish Workers in England', *Christus Rex*, April 1948, pp. 17–24. No evidence is given in the article as to what the statistics are based on.
55 Ewart, 'Caring for Migrants', p. 8.

morals of a 'respectable' Catholic country whilst living abroad. Much
ink was spilt on the problem of 'leakage', that is, Catholics who failed
to maintain strict 'Irish' norms of religious observance in Britain.[56]

There is little evidence of negative discourses on professional, middle-class
emigrants such as teachers in relation to their moral behaviour. Such emigrants
were not viewed as problematic in terms of the leakage problem or in any
other way.[57] F.X. Martin, in a letter on Irish emigrants sent to Archbishop
McQuaid, stated that the problem of leakage only affected those emigrants
of the 'half-educated type'.[58] Those of professional status were 'actually a
godsend to Catholic parishes' in Britain because they had an 'intellectual
basis for their faith' and were 'a source of consolation to an otherwise harassed
clergy'. In other words, they were not the kind of parishioners who troubled
priests with their social, emotional or economic problems. Martin tempered
his assertions somewhat with the acknowledgement that many clergy were
themselves Irish. Martin further asserted that the problems caused by the
working classes could be attributed to three main causes: lack of adequate
religious instruction in Ireland, the attitude of English Catholics to Irish
emigrants and the social conditions that Irish immigrants found themselves
in, such as poor accommodation, which allowed them to drift. Thus the
leakage problem was due to a number of factors working either independently
or sometimes in combination, with the effect that once-regular Mass-goers
would become lost to the Church.

Other factors that emerged as contributory to the leakage problem
were: new work practices that would prohibit one from going to Mass on
Sundays;[59] a sense of new-found freedom experienced by migrants that
would allow them to abandon the habit of Mass going; and a moral corrupt-
ibility or degeneracy that occurred upon emigration, a sort of pagan osmosis.
There was also the assumption that Britain was not a place where faith was
valued, or religion practised. The newspaper, the *Irish Catholic*, even quoted
Pope Pius XII as fearing that 'this leaving of Ireland might [...] weaken
the Faith or injure the morals of those young people reared in a Catholic
atmosphere and now transferred to places where Catholic principles do not

---

56 Delaney, *The Irish in Post-War Britain*, p. 7.
57 See the next chapter for further discussion of middle-class emigrants.
58 Undated letter from F.X. Martin to Archbishop McQuaid. McQuaid papers, Emigrants'
     Welfare 1, General Correspondence 1939–61, Dublin Diocesan Archives, AB8/B XXIX.
59 Under this category, men were included because of their opportunities to work overtime.
     Reference was made to men living in poor accommodation with access to beds only on a
     shift basis. Such homes were generally not run by Catholics and hence did not foster a
     spirit of religious devotion. Undated letter from F.X. Martin to Archbishop McQuaid,
     McQuaid papers.

operate'.[60] Living and working in an atmosphere that promoted the Catholic faith was therefore thought imperative to avoiding its loss. The impossibility of this in Britain is obvious, hence the leakage problem. Was the constant reinforcement of religious principles necessary to preserve Irish emigrants' Catholicism? Cardinal McRory also questioned the reasons as to why some Irish emigrants were falling away from the Church, asking: 'Is their falling away due merely to human frailty or because they were not sufficiently grounded in the teachings of the Faith?'[61]

Clearly, being part of a minority rather than a majority religion was feared to have a detrimental effect on emigrants, which suggests that religious devotion was seen largely as a cultural practice rather than a genuine expression of faith. Rev. M. Lydon, on a visit back to his native Connemara, warned of the dangers to 'weak' Catholics in Britain in a sermon given in 1941: 'In England scarcely one person out of every fourteen they would meet was a Catholic and with the force of bad example it was the easiest thing in the world for a weak Christian to lose his Faith'.[62] Rev. Lydon's remarks, like so much of this commentary, assumes that Irish emigrants did not have strong beliefs or religious knowledge if they could be so easily swayed in giving up what was supposed to be an inherent part of their national and personal identity. Gaffney's articles in the *Irish Independent* refer to this issue, particularly in relation to those she regards as a 'lower class type' of domestic servant. Gaffney quoted one 'very fine woman' who mistrusted girls who had stopped going to Mass: 'I sometimes think … that with many of them religion is a social act, not a spiritual one; they go to Mass at home in their village because they know that if they stay away everybody will know and remark on it'.[63] Gaffney claimed this opinion was continually repeated to her throughout her time in Britain and applied to those from all counties in Ireland. Indeed, as was asserted by a 'Special Correspondent' to the *Irish Catholic*, 'it would be extremely difficult to name an Irish locality that is not the birthplace of at least one apostate emigrant girl'.[64]

Jackson also questioned the true faith of the Irish emigrant in *The Irish in Britain*, although his arguments appear to be largely androcentric and came in the wake of the Emigrant Chaplaincy Scheme of the 1950s, which particularly targeted men working in camps, usually far away from churches.[65] While Jackson's comment may not apply to many men, it is worth

60 *Irish Catholic*, 13 November 1947, p. 3.
61 Lenten Pastoral, *Irish Catholic*, 19 February 1942, p. 3.
62 *Irish Catholic*, 31 July 1941, p. 5.
63 *Irish Independent*, 9 December 1936, p. 7.
64 *Irish Catholic*, 8 August 1936, p. 8.
65 For a recent appraisal of the work of the Scheme, see Patricia Kennedy, *Welcoming the*

considering some of the points he raised, arguing that 'the Catholicism of the Irishman is internalised only to a very slight degree' and that:

> In general his religious life is made up of social and ritual forces which through the person of the priest bind him to God. He may understand little of his faith and is not trained to discuss or justify it. In addition in many of the rural communities from which the immigrants come the pressures of conformity and the central role of the priest in the community may have served to inhibit a revolt which may well develop in a situation where anonymity can be achieved.[66]

Did the anonymity of English cities provide the catalyst for loss of faith or religious devotion? Or did the anonymity allow for the expression of previously held feelings of 'revolt' that emigrants dare not utter while living in their small home towns? Whilst no conclusive evidence can be offered to support either argument, it seems that the leakage problem was *perceived* to be a significant one, despite the lack of hard evidence.

'Leakage' is referred to as a particularly female problem in numerous letters to the editor and special articles in the *Irish Catholic*. In 1934, for example, in a letter outlining the difficulties for the moral welfare of Irish women, 'One who knows' referred to two key factors that led to moral ruin: the distance an emigrant often found themselves from other Catholics and a church and the preponderance of non-Catholic men in Britain. This led to discussion of 'the inevitable mixed marriage'.[67] The crux of the matter, however, seemed to be this: 'Even if a non-Catholic young man is willing to inquire about Catholicity, how many girls can answer intelligent questions about their religion no matter how faithfully they may have fulfilled their duties at home?' This comment is extremely revealing. It implies that knowledge and practice of faith are entirely separate things, and lack of the former may contribute significantly to the leakage problem. John Healy, writing in the 1960s, concurred with this opinion as he felt that sermons would ill-prepare the emigrant in maintaining their religion:

> Our Church talked of pagan England and its dangers in its Sunday sermons but the Sunday voices never reached out beyond the four walls

Strangers: Irish Migrant Welfare in Britain Since 1957 (Dublin: Irish Academic Press, 2015).

66 Jackson, *The Irish in Britain*, p. 149.

67 *Irish Catholic*, 22 December 1934, p. 5. Other articles appeared which critiqued both men and women for their knowledge of the Catholic religion.

of those chapels and there was no reflection in the school curriculum of how we might survive in 'pagan Godless England'.[68]

The impression was given in some articles that better knowledge was needed to answer tricky questions that may be posed by non-Catholics. For example, the editor of the *Irish Catholic* stated that an 'intelligent Catholic must be armed with adequate knowledge to meet the various specious sophisms of non-Catholics and to refute false charges and erroneous vices'.[69]

In 1936, a special correspondent for the *Irish Catholic*, quoting an unnamed English Catholic ecclesiastic, referred to 'disgraceful' lapses in faith by Irish women. A direct, and unflattering, contrast was made between men and women:

> The Irish boys in England are usually very fine fellows, staunch Catholics, and a credit to Ireland and the Church, but I'm very sorry to say that the majority of Irish girls who come over here to work are the direct opposite, and the cause of considerable anxiety and trouble to the clergy. Far better [...] that their mothers would put them in their graves before allowing them to emigrate to England.[70]

Dr Gilmartin at the Cathedral in Tuam quoted this 'fact' in a sermon the next week where he argued that 'girls must be protected from themselves'.[71]

The fear that women emigrating to jobs in Britain may be prohibited by employers from going to Mass every week was articulated constantly between the 1920s and the 1950s. In another letter to the editor of the *Irish Catholic*, Arthur Canon Jackman of Watford identified what he saw as the female leakage problem with regard to nurses in his area who 'as we all know, if they ever missed Mass they would never hear the end of it' and would get 'the shock of their lives when they find Mass is not provided for, but, unfortunately, after a time they get over the shock, and are thus cut away from the most important part of their spiritual life'. The result was an undermining of 'their faith and spiritual fabric, as the gash they receive is, indeed, a mortal wound, for, after all, it is the Mass that matters'.[72]

Thus, the slippery slope started with missing Mass and ended with the unravelling of all principles of morality. Jackman argued that as Irish women were greatly in demand in Britain they should simply insist on being allowed

---

68 Healy, *The Death of an Irish Town*, p. 70.
69 *Irish Catholic*, 11 September 1941, p. 4.
70 *Irish Catholic*, 8 August 1936, p. 8.
71 *Irish Catholic*, 15 August 1936, p. 6.
72 *Irish Catholic*, 17 September 1936, p. 4.

to go to Mass, but this was not always practicable or realistic, as many female emigrants articulated. Furthermore, being able to attend Mass or not may not have borne any relation to their true beliefs or religiosity. Agnes, a participant in Sharon Lambert's study, recalled her mother's concern over this issue:

> My mother had an awful thing about being allowed to practise your religious duties and we were always called on Holydays of Obligation for Mass. We were on the wards at half-seven so the Mass was usually at half-six and we were called for it. I was very glad to be able to devote one page of a letter to tell my mother that we were called for Mass.[73]

Concern was for women in all types of work as it was felt that English employers would not respect their faith, even if they were otherwise respectable and good employers. The 1937 Lenten Pastoral by Most Rev. Dr MacNamee of Ardagh and Clonmacnoise argued for careful investigation by girls before emigration in case 'Mass and the Sacraments may be impossible for them and without those supernatural aids the Catholic life is apt to wilt and wither and evil influences grow in power'.[74] Ten years later, similar advice was given by the Rev. J. Boland, National Chaplain of the Catholic Nurses' Guild of Great Britain: 'We would warn girls applying to hospitals in England, Scotland and Wales to make sure that they have Sunday Mass every week. When replying to an advertisement offering facilities for Catholic Nurses, they must make sure that this means every Sunday and no less'.[75]

Rev. Boland recommended that a central agency be set up to investigate whether girls were able to practise their religion at their intended hospital to ensure 'there will be a congenial atmosphere and opportunities for the practice of their Faith'.[76] Despite the assumption in this quotation that emigrants would find it difficult to reconcile their work and religious practice, there is ample evidence to suggest that many did find ways to do so. In fact, for many, maintaining religious practices was vital in validating their sense of themselves as Irish while away from their homeland for many years. Patricia was regarded by Lambert as being typical of many of her respondents' views on the importance of faith:

> I think you just grew up and there was something in your mind was just driving you to say your prayers. I never now went on my knees in

73 Lambert, *Irish Women in Lancashire*, p. 36.
74 *Irish Independent*, 8 February 1937, p. 6.
75 *Irish Catholic*, 18 December 1947, p. 1.
76 Ibid.

the morning, it was nearly always at night. Not just as I'd go into bed but sometime in the evening, when I'd be upstairs, I'd just kneel down and say a few prayers. It just comes more-or-less automatic now, and if I didn't do it I'd think there was something missing.[77]

Clearly, the vast range of experiences of religious feeling and practice are both personal and dependent upon circumstances. Complexity was rarely reflected in public commentary, but, for many, Catholicism was a fundamental part of their Irish identity, regardless of frequency of mass attendance.

Catholicism and Irish Emigrant Identity

In common with other immigrant communities, religion was important for Irish people as a point of contact with home, and as a source of community feeling on arrival. It offered a familiar point on an otherwise strange landscape. It was also a way of marking difference and separateness from the host community.[78] There is a long-standing, multifaceted relationship Irish emigrants have had with the Catholic Church in Britain. Fitzpatrick has argued that Irish emigrants in Australia drew closer to the Church to affirm their identity: 'Religion was perhaps the most common context for affirmation of cultural continuity in a menacing environment'.[79] It appears this was also true for many Irish in Britain, despite the 'leakage' rhetoric. Many Irish emigrants articulated a sense of their Irishness through their continued devotion to the Catholic Church in Britain. Brigid Keenan was emphatic about the importance of religion to her and its centrality to her sense of Irish identity:

An Irish identity is very important to me and to my children. They were very proud of it. And I am involved with a prayer group over here based at St. Aloysius which is a very Irish church near Euston. I go to Westminster Cathedral every Friday evening. Religion has always been very important to me. It has been my life and I don't know where I would have been without it. I always thank God for the faith my father and mother gave me. No matter what was going on in my life, I could flash back to my childhood. Day in and day out, my faith has never left me.[80]

---

77   Lambert, *Irish Women in Lancashire*, p. 51.
78   Lennon *et al.*, *Across the Water*, p. 17.
79   Fitzpatrick, '"That Beloved Country, That No Place Else Resembles"', p. 336.
80   Schweitzer, *Across the Irish Sea*, p. 98. The importance of religion in imparting a sense

Here a sense of Irishness is intermingled with religious practice and devotion. O'Grady also found this in her interviews describing the Catholic Church as 'a point of continuity for life in the homeland'.[81] Similarly, O'Connor's study of women in Leicester found that 74 per cent of the respondents stated that 'religion influenced their daily lives' and many were 'emphatic about this'.[82]

Many female emigrants were concerned with passing on a sense of Irishness and this seems to be intertwined with religion.[83] Fourteen of the seventeen women in Mary Daniels's cohort of Irish nurses said they were still 'very devout church goers'.[84] Daniels asked her interviewees, 'Do your children have a sense of Irish identity?' They gave the following answers:

> Three replied that their children would describe themselves as 'half-Irish' or 'English and Irish'; one that they felt some sense of Irishness, another that her daughter felt 'distinctly' Irish, and *seven* that their children's sense of Irish identity was 'very' or 'extremely' strong. Amongst these last, the daughter of one had already gone to live in Ireland, and the son of another was planning to do so.[85]

These women had not adopted any particular strategy for passing on a sense of Irish ethnicity, but one of the key elements seemed to be religion, as well as the prevalence of spending entire summers in Ireland. Interestingly, one of the participants (MD11) stated that her sons did not have an Irish identity specifically because they were not actively religious: 'Irish identity? No, my sons have not kept up their religion'.[86] Mary Burke, interviewed as part of the documentary, 'I only came over for a couple of years', expressed a sense of regret that her children don't go to church because it has always been very important to her.[87] In some ways this behaviour can be seen as an extension

of Irishness to second-generation children is also articulated by some men; for example, Kevin Casey mentions this in Dunne's study, *An Unconsidered People*, p. 65.

81 O'Grady, *Irish Migration to London*, p. 13.
82 O'Connor, 'Women Abroad', p. 85. Of the remaining women in the study, some had renounced religion completely and the rest were the younger respondents in the survey who did not display such an attachment.
83 It is also connected to cultural practices such as the cooking of traditional foods, as Moya Kneafsey and Rosie Cox have outlined in 'Food, Gender and Irishness: How Irish Women in Coventry Make Home', *Irish Geography*, 35.1 (2002), pp. 6–15.
84 Mary Daniels, *Exile or Opportunity? Irish Nurses and Midwives in Britain*, Occasional Papers in Irish Studies No. 5 (Liverpool: University of Liverpool, 1993), p. 17.
85 Ibid.
86 Ibid., p. 19.
87 '"I only came over for a couple of years …": Interviews with London Irish Elders', documentary by David Kelly in collaboration with the Irish Studies Centre, London Metropolitan University, 2003.

of the gendered practices that had developed within the state. Valiulis has argued that, in the 1920s and the 1930s, by consigning women to the home, 'the government assigned to women the responsibility for insuring the "Irishness" of the new state, that is, of preserving and transmitting traditional Irish culture'.[88] Inglis has also identified the empowered role Irish women have played in transmitting religion within their households in Ireland: 'She became the sacred heart of the Irish home'.[89] Irish women actively continued the project of the State even outside its national boundaries.

While religious devotion was undoubtedly important to many Irish emigrants, on a practical level, the Catholic Church provided an important social outlet for them to mix with one another. Similar to the clubs for working girls mentioned earlier, the Church provided numerous social occasions such as dances, sodalities, confraternities, retreats, lectures and fundraising events attended by Irish people in Britain. Indeed, Mass itself provided an opportunity to mix with fellow country people. Susan Clark reported socialising with Irish people after Mass after living in Britain for over sixty years.[90] Church clubs provided family events, Irish dancing lessons and St Patrick's Day celebrations.[91] F.X. Martin advised McQuaid that the social events provided by the Church were good examples of the ways in which emigrants could be encouraged to maintain connections with the Catholic Church in Britain:

> That the Irish can be got together, and prefer to be so, is evident from the success of the Augustinian social halls at Hoxton and Hammersmith to which the Irish come in crowds from distant parts of London. In the process they are hooked in for religious duties: they willingly fall in with the programme – they feel the Irish priests understand them and give them a fair hearing.[92]

Being affiliated with the Church and maintaining their routine of worship thus helped many emigrants ease their loneliness and homesickness, such as Hannah Raynor, who spoke to the priest on her days off and said: 'I was

---

88 Valiulis, 'Power, Gender and Identity in the Irish Free State', p. 129.
89 Tom Inglis, *Moral Monopoly: The Rise and Fall of the Catholic Church in Modern Ireland* (Dublin: UCD Press, 1998), p. 248.
90 Susan Clark (née O'Connell) came from Clare to England in 1937 and married an English farmer. Life story included in Anne Jones (ed.), *The Scattering: Images of Emigrants from an Irish County* (Dublin: A. & A. Farmar, 2000), p. 238.
91 See Dunne, *An Unconsidered People*, pp. 65–66 and Lambert, *Irish Women in Lancashire*, pp. 61–62.
92 Undated letter from F.X. Martin to Archbishop McQuaid. McQuaid papers.

always in the church, the church always helped me to cope'.[93] Raynor worked
for a Jewish family, which, according to the rhetoric, would have been viewed
as a job that precluded any Catholic religious worship. Yet Raynor was
actively encouraged to go to the Church for support.[94] She also attributed
her faith as keeping her 'safe' from moral danger. Referring to a Cork girl,
also in service, who became pregnant, Raynor explained her own sense of
moral purity resulted from her religious devotion: 'What kept me safe and
sound was prayers. Thank God, and his Blessed Virgin Mother, the Lord's
taken me all the way through up to today'.[95] The evidence suggests that many
emigrants remained faithful to the Church throughout their lives, despite the
prominence of rhetoric on the leakage problem.

Lapses of Faith and Renegotiation

Lapses of faith are referred to within oral histories and in the public
commentary of the period. Kennedy asserted that 'the most disaffected
Catholics were likely to be found among the Irish abroad', although this claim
is difficult to prove.[96] The Catholic Truth Society pamphlet, *Handbook for
the Catholic Emigrant*, asserted that lack of real knowledge about religious
principles would leave Irish emigrants vulnerable to 'attack' by people
who asked them to explain their faith: 'only those who have a strong faith
and a sound knowledge of what their religion means have remained good,
practising Catholics'.[97] This was also Gaffney's conclusion; she felt that lack
of education overall, and religious instruction in particular, in Ireland left
many emigrants with only a 'social' commitment to their faith.[98]

For those who did lapse in their religious beliefs, there is evidence that
they were not simply accepted as 'lost' by the English Catholic Church.
Frank Boyce interviewed a woman who recalled a rather vigilant priest in the
Liverpool area who made it his mission to rouse the 'Mass-missers':

> Father Newsham had a big walking stick with a brass knob on the end
> of it. Every Sunday morning from eight o'clock he would parade up
> and down our street knocking at doors and banging on windows with
> his stick, trying to get people up out of bed. Most people were terrified

---

93 Schweitzer, *Across the Irish Sea*, p. 153.
94 Similar support is reported in other oral history collections. O'Grady, *Irish Migration
    to London*, p. 10.
95 Schweitzer, *Across the Irish Sea*, p. 156.
96 Kennedy, *The Irish*, p. 8.
97 Catholic Truth Society, *Handbook for the Catholic Emigrant to England*, p. 5.
98 Gaffney, *Irish Independent*, 14 December 1936, p. 5.

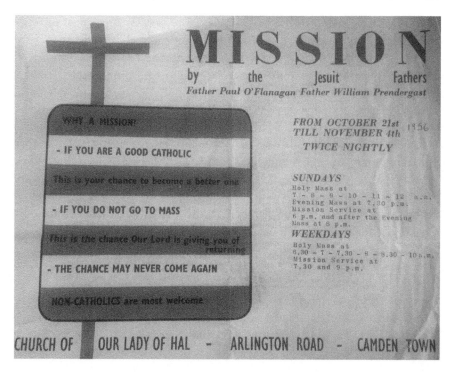

Figure 5.1   A pamphlet advertising the Jesuit mission at the Church of Our Lady of Hal, Arlington Road, Camden Town, London, 21 October–4 November 1956. Reproduced with permission of the Irish Jesuit Archives, Dublin.

of him, and would jump out of bed and across to the church for mass, just to keep him away from their door. Yet, when he died, even though many people hated him, they named a street after him![99]

All clergy may not have followed this rather zealous approach, but the English hierarchy were no less concerned than the Irish about potential loss of faithful parishioners. By the 1950s, a series of missions were embarked on throughout Britain to bring back those who had been aberrant in their religious duties.[100] This decade also saw an expansion of services for Irish emigrants including the Irish Overseas Chaplaincy scheme, the advent of County Associations and the setting up of community bases such as the London Irish Centre.[101]

99 The quotation here is from an interview Boyce conducted with a Mrs J.K. in Frank Boyce, 'The Irish in Liverpool', p. 93.
100 For more information on the activities of priests involved in missionary work with emigrants in England, see, for example, the papers of Fr Leonard Sheil, J16, Irish Jesuit Archives, Dublin.
101 The County Associations provided social events and welfare services for Irish

For some, emigration to Britain meant a process of negotiation with their faith rather than a complete abandonment and some have argued that this process began in Ireland. Kearns has contended that women in Ireland may have had an ambiguous relationship with the Church: 'Though Mother Church was often feared, she was profoundly loved. And very much needed. For most mothers, it was a relationship characterised by ambivalence and contradictions: trust–fear, adoration–anger, belief–disillusion, security–insecurity'.[102] Lennon *et al.* suggest the ambivalence many Irish women emigrants may have felt about their faith relates primarily to moral issues; for example, in negotiating the option to use birth control.[103] Phyllis Izzard recalled being wracked with guilt over her decision to use contraception after having two children within eighteen months.[104] However, she remained a devoted Catholic throughout her life and expressed the opinion that religious observance was more genuine in Britain:

> I think religion was a matter of location, in some ways. Here, it was a very different thing from at home in Ireland. I felt that here people went to Mass of their own accord, whereas at home, in those days, people went to Mass because they would have been talked about if they didn't.[105]

Lambert found three Irish women married to Irish men who were described as more devout than they were, although the majority (thirty-four in total) had rarely missed Mass throughout their time in Britain. For others, the Church remained important, although they now felt the freedom to make more choices about how they conducted their personal lives:

> I don't think the practice of religion fell off in those days – we were more or less brainwashed. I did fall a bit myself – it didn't disturb me if I didn't go to Mass. I didn't give up, but I didn't have a conscience about it. It was often very funny listening to people worrying about contraception, but my decisions were private ones.[106]

immigrants in London. For more on County Associations, the GAA and Irish immigrant social life in the 1950s, see Delaney, *The Irish in Post-War Britain*, pp. 171–174 and Miriam Nyhan, 'Comparing Irish Migrants and County Associations in New York and London: A Cross-Cultural Analysis of Migrant Experiences and Associational Behaviour circa 1946–1961' (PhD thesis, European University Institute, Florence, 2008).

102 Kearns, *Dublin's Lost Heroines*, p. 156.
103 Lennon *et al.*, *Across the Water*, p. 17.
104 Dunne, *An Unconsidered People*, p. 47.
105 Ibid., p. 48.
106 Mary Walker (pseudonym), quoted ibid., p. 103. Walker emigrated in 1959.

These examples suggest that religiosity in Britain cannot be understood in terms of the binary of complete devotion or complete abandonment of belief. Rather, a much more complex picture of female emigrant Catholicity emerges which reflects many of the changes in religious practices that occurred throughout the twentieth century in Ireland too.

Paradoxical Pride:
Irish Emigrants and the 'Spiritual Empire'

As with many of the discourses on emigrants, there were contradictions about migrants and religious practice. While there were calls on people to recognise the seriousness of the leakage problem, there was a paradoxical pride that Irish people, through emigration, could be propagators of the faith in what was disrespectfully regarded as a 'pagan' country. Jackson has commented that articles in Church publications warning of the leakage problem appeared at the same time as statements 'praising the faith and Catholicity of the Irish in Britain'.[107] Mary Daly's analysis of 'Ireland's spiritual empire' has found that it 'was a theme much favoured by Irish political leaders after 1922, since it implied that emigration brought substantial benefits to the nation by giving Ireland an international influence that was disproportionate to its small size'.[108] This was a popular theme in Lenten Pastorals of the Irish Bishops, such as Dr Fogarty's admonition that 'Our people going to England, could, if true to themselves, be an immense source of edification to their non-Catholic neighbours over there'.[109] The aforementioned Catholic Truth Society pamphlet aimed to encourage emigrants to keep their faith but also to 'help you to be an apostle to others by bringing back those who have drifted away from their service of God'.[110]

Much of this may have been influenced by the growth in missions work by Irish religious, which, according to McKenna, epitomised Ireland's success in maintaining 'the strength of the faith amongst the Irish people and its potential to influence Catholicism world-wide'.[111] As a counter to overarching depictions of Irish women as sexually active, immoral and lacking in religious devotion, it is worth noting that many single Irish women became involved in church sodalities and Catholic lay organisations as well as becoming members of religious orders in Britain. In Dunne's study, Kathleen Morrissey joined the Children of Mary and educated her six children as

107 Jackson, *The Irish in Britain*, p. 148.
108 Daly, *The Slow Failure*, p. 13.
109 *Irish Catholic*, 19 February 1942, p. 3. Dr Fogarty was Bishop of Killaloe.
110 Catholic Truth Society, *Handbook for the Catholic Emigrant to England*, p. 5.
111 Yvonne McKenna, *Made Holy: Irish Women Religious at Home and Abroad* (Dublin: Irish Academic Press, 2006), p. 182.

Catholics.[112] Sheila Dillon (a pseudonym) was a nurse who became involved in rescue work with the Legion of Mary, meeting Irish girls off the trains in London.[113] Noreen Hill recalls receiving regular visits to her house by the Legion of Mary to check if she was going to Mass. They knew her address because she had received a reference from the local priest to get her job.[114] Clearly, there were some Irish women on the other side of the issue.

An article in the *Irish Catholic* in 1932 had a boastful air when it reported that the Rev. P.J. Cassidy had established a 'little bit of Ireland in the very heart of England' by building a Church and other amenities for the Irish Catholic community in Northfield, a new suburb of Birmingham.[115] This generosity may have been to some immigrants' cost. Boyce has commented on the disparity between the wealth of the Liverpool diocese and the parishioners, many of whom were Irish immigrants, arguing that the 'large and spacious' Churches 'furnished with the best Italian marble sanctuaries, altars and pulpits' stood 'in marked contrast with the level of poverty, slum housing, and general social conditions of the parishioners'.[116] Nonetheless, identity was imbricated with religion for many Irish Catholics, particularly in some areas of Liverpool where people 'tended to identify with their own parish to such an extent that if they were asked the question, "Where do you live?" they were likely to name their parish before naming their street'.[117] Women in Liverpool also supported religious fundraising through their consumerism, as outlined in Charlotte Wildman's work on the inter-war period.[118] Women formed the backbone of fundraising committees, sent their children to Catholic schools and joined sodalities. Rossiter has highlighted women as providing the core of the faithful who assisted the Catholic Church in Britain throughout the twentieth century:

> Through fund-raising for vast church building programmes, parish devotional associations, sodalities, guilds, confraternities, welfare organisations and, not least, Catholic schools, the Church established

112 Dunne, *An Unconsidered People*, p. 83.
113 Ibid., p. 155. She specialised in helping pregnant women: 'I used to know if they were pregnant just by looking at them. Even at six weeks, I could tell by the shape of the nose. I had an eye for that. Helping those young pregnant girls became my mission in life'.
114 In Lennon *et al.*, *Across the Water*, p. 96.
115 *Irish Catholic*, 27 February 1932, p. 8.
116 Frank Boyce, 'Irish Catholicism in Liverpool: The 1920s and 1930s', in Patrick Buckland and John Belchem (eds), *Irish Labour History* (Liverpool: University of Liverpool, 1993), p. 91.
117 Ibid., p. 95.
118 Charlotte Wildman, 'Irish-Catholic Women and Modernity in 1930s Liverpool', pp. 72–91.

strong links with immigrants. While men dominated virtually all the secular organisations, women formed the backbone of the church-based activities, and [...] the magnitude of their work is, as yet, hidden from history.[119]

As one of Catherine Dunne's interviewees pithily remarked: 'Women tended to join the Church: men went to the pub'.[120]

According to the Catholic Truth Society, the Irish emigrant as apostle represented not only the Catholic faith but the Irish nation: 'Remember, too, that the Catholic Church, as well as Ireland, is being judged by the way in which you work'.[121] The rhetoric in such pamphlets is slightly patronising, as though Irish Catholics are needed both to show English Catholics how to be faithful and to 'bring back' Irish Catholics who lapsed on their 'watch', or, in Healy's memory of Mayo: 'I would hear a priest say that God worked Himself in many ways, and that the Irish exodus was bringing the Faith back to pagan England'.[122] The growth and wealth of the Catholic Church in Britain was greatly facilitated by Irish immigrants, both as clergy and parishioners. This fact Gaffney admitted as she heard evidence that workers in a new suburb contributed most of the £11,000 to build Catholic schools in the area and that the Churches were regularly packed with Irish building site workers and domestic servants.[123]

Lambert also found that, out of the thirty-nine Catholic interviewees in her study, all continued the practice of decorating their houses with religious pictures and statues as had been done in their family homes.[124] The greater religious devotion of women may have been widely perceived within the Church itself despite contradictory assertions in the press. Indeed, Mary Collins, a second-generation Irish woman, recalled the perception in her community that men needed rousing by the local priest to go to Mass but that 'women always go to church, women are religious, naturally, men are not, which you probably know'.[125]

When the Archbishop of Westminster, Cardinal Hinsley, wrote to High Commissioner Dulanty and the Irish government of his concern at the

---

119 Rossiter, 'Bringing the Margins into the Centre', p. 193.
120 Quote from Kathleen Morrissey in Dunne, *An Unconsidered People*, p. 83.
121 Catholic Truth Society, *Handbook for the Catholic Emigrant to England*, p. 14.
122 Healy, *The Death of an Irish Town*, p. 51.
123 After writing this, Gaffney stated: 'That's the other side of the story, the side with which I am not concerned, but always I would have you bear it in mind', *Irish Independent*, 14 December 1936, p. 5.
124 Lambert, *Irish Women in Lancashire*, p. 49.
125 Interview by Reg Hall with Mary Collins (née Moriarty), C903/420, Reg Hall Archive Collection, BLSA. Collins's mother was born in Ireland while her father was second-generation Irish.

number of ill-prepared female emigrants within his diocese, he also admitted that 'the situation is not so serious as has been represented. A very large proportion of Irish girls who come to work in this country do in fact settle down to a happy and successful career either in service or in marriage, and remain faithful to their religion'.[126] Hinsley repeated this in his letter to de Valera in 1939, stating that the 'large majority of the Irish who reach London are credits to their country and to their religion'.[127] However, by focusing on those who had lapsed in their religious duties rather than those who maintained them, the impression – at the very highest levels – was given that the leakage problem was at epidemic proportions.

Conclusion

Marriage was a cultural expectation many Irish emigrants, both male and female, grew up with. In fact, it was part of the cultural fabric of Irish life, much like emigration itself. It is therefore unsurprising that many emigrants married while in Britain, although this was a disappointment to those who wished to see Catholic families grow in Ireland rather than abroad. Despite being resident elsewhere, Irish women immigrants were often the lynchpin of transnational families. Remittances, regular holidays in Ireland, chain migration and the incidence of return migration were all ways in which contact between families across the Irish Sea was maintained, and women were fundamental to all of these.[128] All Daniel's interviewees, working as nurses in Britain, had maintained contact with their home places in Ireland by regular return visits 'to a varying but always remarkable degree over so many years'.[129] Lambert's interviewees were similar, with some in nursing reporting the resentment they felt from English colleagues that they got their fare paid to visit home.[130] Lambert sees the only halt in this behaviour for some as being when they had children and could no longer afford to leave, although many others spent whole summers in Ireland with their children, their husbands joining them for a week or two. This was largely dependent on their financial

---

126 Letter, late 1937, from Cardinal Hinsley, Archbishop of Westminster, to J.W. Dulanty. DH&C, Clandillon papers.
127 Letter from Cardinal Hinsley, to de Valera, 25 May 1939. DH&C, Clandillon papers.
128 Chain migration involving family members and friends is often reported. O'Connor's study of fifty Irish women in Leicester found that the presence of family members in Leicester influenced their decision to emigrate there and they were sometimes brought back with relatives after holidays home to Ireland. See O'Connor, 'Women Abroad', pp. 79–81.
129 Daniels, *Exile or Opportunity?*, p. 18.
130 Lambert, *Irish Women in Lancashire*, p. 42.

circumstances. Some reported the financial hardship they faced in making trips home with their families because this always involved new clothes and putting on a good appearance.[131] They still made the trips though, showing that family obligations remained strong for many. The Commission on Emigration and Other Population Problems also identified this trend:

> Emigration of some members of the family has become almost part of the established custom of the people in certain areas – a part of the generally accepted pattern of life. [...] Such a custom is kept alive by the connection which former emigrants retain with the home country and there is little doubt that these family connections will continue to exercise an influence, even if substantial improvements are effected in economic conditions and social amenities at home.[132]

A study by the Irish Liaison Unit of the London borough of Haringey 'highlighted the fact that most elderly Irish migrants have maintained close connections with their home country: 74 per cent said they made trips to Ireland and 52 per cent said that they in fact visited the country every year. Nearly three-quarters indicated that they still had family or friends in Ireland'.[133] This suggests that many emigrants sustained links with home throughout the course of their lives and runs counter to discourses about the 'forgotten Irish', although this generally refers to men who worked 'on the lump' and became susceptible to alcoholism and homelessness in later years.

Despite the prevalence of 'worst-case scenario' studies of female emigrants in Britain, their direct testimony paints a different picture: many found strength in their faith and the Catholic community in Britain, exhibiting lifelong dedication to the Church. The fact that Irish people were willing to contribute to the building and maintenance of the Catholic Church in Britain suggests many continued in their dedication to the Catholic faith, although it may also be viewed as a sign of their 'institutionalised' religious behaviour in that they were simply conditioned to contribute money and to attend Mass. Whether their behaviour was due to genuine piety or continued cultural conformity, it demonstrates that emigrants, for the most part, did not radically alter their behaviour across the water. They used opportunities provided through their employment as outlined in the next chapter, to live lives often remarkably similar to their peers at home.

131 Nancy Lyons, in Lennon *et al.*, *Across the Water*, p. 176.
132 Commission on Emigration and Other Population Problems, *Majority Report*, para. 301.
133 Elizabeth Malcolm, *Elderly Return Migration from Britain to Ireland: A Preliminary Study* (Dublin: National Council for the Elderly, 1996), p. 49. The study was based on 100 Irish people aged sixty and over living in the London borough of Haringey.

6

Jobs for the Girls:

Discourses on Irish Women's Employment

Why do people migrate? Some go for economic reasons, some
to escape from political or religious conditions which they find
intolerable, some from a desire for adventure, some for various
other reasons, but the most important cause of all is economic.
Emigrants go from countries with a lower standard of living
to countries with a higher standard, or they go because their
particular occupation is overcrowded and prospects in it are
bad.

D. Tait Christie, 'International Aspects of Migration',
Journal of the Royal Institute
of International Affairs, 6.1 (1927), p. 37.

Dramatic language was often used in newspaper reports on women's
employment prospects in Britain, evocative of the rhetorical titillation
we observed in Chapter 3 over the menace of the white slave trade.
It seems that many could not abjure the theatrics in discussing emigration,
and simple, dispassionate observations such as that of D. Tait Christie of the
International Labour Office (ILO), quoted above, were few and far between.[1]
This chapter juxtaposes public discourses and personal recollections in
exploring women's emigration and employment. The predominance of Irish
female immigrants in occupations such as domestic service and nursing is
mirrored by a dearth of research on the spectrum of Irish women's working
experiences. This chapter explores alternative sources of information to

---

1 In a memorandum to the government by the Department of External Affairs, the
statutes of the International Labour Office (ILO) are referred to as representing 'the
pagan sociologist' point of view. Memorandum dated 9 May 1944, NAI, DTS 11582B:
'New Proposals Regarding Restrictions on Travel Permit Issues to Workers'.

sketch a broader picture of female emigrant employment in Britain while recognising the primacy of these occupational groupings by mining new source material on both.

Delaney has cogently argued that emigration was undertaken within the context of knowledge on available options and opportunities, including economic ones, something that was not only rational but also entirely normal:

> Individual decisions were taken within a broader economic, social, and cultural environment, as migrants were not insulated from the wider society: in simple terms, they were influenced by what other people were doing, saying, planning, and discussing. Leaving home was a shared response to the situation in which young people found themselves, and was far from being deviant or abnormal behaviour, as so often was assumed by politicians and civil servants.[2]

Within this rhetoric by 'politicians and civil servants', among others, assumptions based on gender also emerged, with many recognising the legitimacy of male economic migration but denying such motives for women. This is perhaps a result of the increasing dominance of the male 'navvy' as an all-encompassing image of Irish emigration, which diminished the visibility of women's work. Louise Ryan has argued that 'women were simply forgotten', but they may not have been recognised even at the time as workers.[3] There was also a certain discomfort about recognising the economic aspects of emigration as this reflected upon – and essentially critiqued – the economic policies of successive governments of Ireland. As Daly observed, 'Emigration posed a fundamental policy dilemma: whether to abandon deeply held cultural and social ideals and aim at replicating British living standards in order to deter emigration, or to continue to uphold traditional rural society'.[4]

Accusations of frivolous behaviour on the part of women abounded, with women allegedly attracted by 'the fascination of the garish distractions of the city and by the hectic life of the great world as displayed before their wondering eyes in the glamorous unrealities of the films'.[5] The cinema occupied many column inches, its influence widely deplored, and, as Delaney has argued:

> Contemporaries often alleged that females were especially influenced by such glamorous portrayals of American life, although this tells

---

2 Delaney, *The Irish in Post-War Britain*, p. 19.

3 Louise Ryan, 'Aliens, Migrants and Maids: Public Discourses on Irish Immigration to Britain in 1937', *Immigrants and Minorities*, 20.3 (2001), p. 37.

4 Daly, 'The Economic Ideals of Irish Nationalism', p. 98.

5 Lenten Pastoral given by Dr McNamee, Bishop of Ardagh and Clonmacnoise, *Irish Independent*, 8 February 1937.

us more about the gendered nature of discourse and the lack of understanding of the rising aspirations of young women than about any innate differences [between men and women].[6]

By positing women's motivations to emigrate as being imprudent responses to Hollywood portrayals of modern life, the government could disclaim all responsibility. It was not their fault if 'featherhead females succumbed to the glossy image of foreign lands portrayed by the advertisers, despite the dutiful warnings of those who had their true welfare at heart'.[7]

The position many faced – poor working conditions, low pay, and lack of stability – meant that a desire for adventure was a luxury, surely a secondary consideration behind secure wages. This is not to say that the desire for adventure was *completely* absent among the reasons for emigrating, but it was certainly not the predominant one for most working-class emigrants.[8] This was the conclusion of the Commission on Emigration and Other Population Problems:

> Those who have steady and reasonably well-paid employment are much less likely to migrate than those whose employment is of a seasonal, intermittent, temporary or casual nature – *of a kind, in short, which does not enable a man to plan reasonably for his future.* Employment offering prospects of advancement, greater security and continuity, higher wages and better conditions of employment will inevitably be an attraction to the worker whose pay is low or whose job is insecure. In particular, the average unskilled worker from this country has in recent times been able to secure in Great Britain a greater material return for his labour.[9]

The idea that men might wish to plan for their future indicates contemporary notions of women as passively waiting for marriage and reliant on men's employability. Examining women's economic position in Ireland reveals much about why they may have wanted to leave.

6 Delaney, *The Irish in Post-War Britain*, p. 23.
7 J.J. Lee, *Ireland, 1912–1985: Politics and Society* (Cambridge: Cambridge University Press: 1990), p. 376.
8 Specific references to the desire for adventure as a reason to emigrate are rare within oral history testimonies. See Dunne, *An Unconsidered People*, p. 94. For more on social class and emigration, see also Beale, *Women in Ireland*.
9 Commission on Emigration and Other Population Problems, *Majority Report*, para. 296. My emphasis.

Women's Economic Position in Ireland

In 1926, C.H. Oldham wrote: 'Ireland is not a place where adult women can find a living'.[10] The idea of women working outside the home was in many ways antithetical to the foundational ideas of the state. The vision of 'home-identified' women had long standing in Ireland, supported by many sections of society. Yet the erosion of opportunities for women, particularly rural women, throughout the nineteenth century, meant that ways they had previously contributed economically to the family had vanished or diminished. This narrow vista sparked women's migration and is recounted in oral narratives by women who eschewed this confining life.[11]

The lack of opportunities provided by farming life for non-inheriting children arose in the short case histories taken by members of the Commission on Emigration and Other Population Problems. Other oral history collections give an alternative view. Josephine, for example, interviewed by Anne Lynch, stated, 'I would have stayed at home on the farm, but my father always said I prefer all of you to do something else because this farming is awful'.[12] Apart from farming, women could be found in many occupations, although women's overall participation in the workforce was low. In 1926, men counted as being in work outnumbered women by a ratio of 2.7:1;[13] in 1936, this ratio remained stable at just less than 2.7:1;[14] by 1946, the ratio had increased slightly to 2.8:1.[15]

Table 6.1 details the range of occupational categories where Irish women were to be found in the census, showing their proportionate percentage of each grouping. The only category of employment in which women overwhelmingly predominated throughout the post-independence era was in 'personal service', which included domestic service in private households and hotels. While the detailed statistical breakdown of each occupational category is not shown here, women were represented in almost every sub-category of work within the groupings.

As Table 6.1 shows, women engaged in a variety of occupations throughout the 1920s to the 1950s. Their participation, however, was generally as a minority

10 C.H. Oldham, 'Reform of the Irish Census of Population', *Economic Journal*, 36.141 (1926), p. 119.

11 This is mentioned by Jane Bruder, an emigrant from Wicklow in Schweitzer, *Across the Irish Sea*, p. 16 and by Kathleen Ruth from Donegal in an uncatalogued interview which is part of the Smurfitt Archive, London Metropolitan University.

12 Anne Lynch, *The Irish in Exile: Stories of Emigration* (London: Community History Press, 1988), p. 11.

13 Calculation made from *Census of Population 1926*, vol. 7 (Industries), Table 1 (p. 1).

14 Calculation made from *Census of Population 1946*, vol. 7 (Industries), Table 1 (p. 1).

15 Ibid. It must be noted that the figures may not have captured women engaged in casual employment for which they did not pay taxes; for example, in cleaning or washing work which oral histories suggest was a vital form of economic activity for many.

Table 6.1   Numbers and percentages of women in occupational groups in the 26 counties, according to the Census Reports, 1926–1951

Occupational Group	1926		1936		1946		1951	
	Total number of women	Total group (percentage)	Total number of women	Total group (percentage)	Total number of women	Total group (percentage)	Total number of women	Total group (percentage)
Agricultural occupations	122,081	18.8	106,442	17.5	81,209	14.2	67,578	13.7
Fishermen	23	0.4	12	0.3	16	0.5	13	0.4
Mining and quarrying occupations[1]	21	1.2	15	0.5	49	1.5	168	1.7
Manufacturing industries[2]	31,868	20.3	43,827	22.1	47,939	23.4	61,613	22.0
Transport and communication	1,181	3.0	1,187	3.1	1,587	3.7	5,483	9.7
Commerce and finance[3]	34,311	30.0	41,089	32.3	42,504	33.2	51,212	34.2
Public administration and defence	19,798	26.0	23,987	30.9	26,686	29.9	7,574	18.7
Professions	18,209	46.7	21,025	47.9	24,895	49.1	45,211	54.7

Occupational Group	1926		1936		1946		1951	
	Total number of women	Total group (percentage)	Total number of women	Total group (percentage)	Total number of women	Total group (percentage)	Total number of women	Total group (percentage)
Personal service	99,130	77.5	96,195	78.7	89,811	79.6	68,402	80.9
Entertainment and sport	1,114	23.3	1,579	23.5	3,624	37.5	4,150	38.3
Other industries or industry not stated	1,668	18.3	1,122	24.0	3,158	29.2	3,224	34.8

[1] In the 1951 Census there is a slight alteration in categories, and it is specified that this includes turf production.

[2] The 1951 Census shows those in construction and in electricity, gas, water and sanitary services in separate categories, whereas in previous reports they are included in manufacturing. Thus, for consistency, I have added in the figures under these headings in 1951 to the 'manufacturing' occupational group category.

[3] The 1951 Census shows commerce and insurance, banking and finance in separate categories, but, for consistency, I have added them to the total for commerce and finance.

Source: Central Statistics Office, *Census of Population Reports, 1926, 1936, 1946 and 1951* (Dublin: Stationery Office).

cohort, apart from certain exceptions: women obtained relative parity in what was classed as 'professions'.[16] Women also predominated in personal service, though the number of women involved in this work reduced by a third in this time period due to emigration and unattractive working conditions.[17] This is perhaps due to the predominance of very young girls in service in Ireland who were (as shown in Chapter 1) the age group chiefly emigrating.[18] The effect of the public service ban on married women can be seen in the reduction in their numbers in the 'public administration and defence' category.[19] Women's employment in this category dropped from 19,798 (26 per cent) in 1926 to just 7,574 by 1951 (or 18.7 per cent). According to Joyce Padbury, this ban, coupled with the restrictions on women in industrial employment, led to 'the inclusion of the Free State on a League of Nations black list of countries with legislation against women's interests'.[20] In addition to the reduction in women in clerical or office work through legislative measures, these jobs often had to be obtained through personal contacts or favours which meant they were positions outside of the social scope of most working-class women.[21] It is no wonder that many Irish women were attracted by the prospect of obtaining such work in Britain when their opportunities were so limited at home.

Caitriona Clear has argued that the decades from independence onwards saw momentous changes in Irish women's economic status and the areas in which they were employed, reflecting social as well as industrial changes:

16　This category included, for example, religious, law occupations, accountants, vets, dentists and teachers.

17　Though the number of women in domestic service categories decreased, as may be expected, the number of men in this work did not increase – men did not rush to take up the opportunities for employment left open by female servants.

18　For more discussion of the profile of domestic servants in Ireland, see Mona Hearn, *Below Stairs: Domestic Service Remembered in Dublin and Beyond, 1880–1922* (Dublin: The Lilliput Press, 1993).

19　The marriage bar came into effect through a regulation instituted by the Minister for Finance, Ernest Blythe, to Section 9 of the Civil Service Regulation Act (1924) on 26 April 1924 whereby it was decreed that 'Female Civil Servants holding established posts will be required on marriage to resign from the Civil Service' (Unnumbered Statutory Rules and Orders). The subsequent Civil Service Amendment Act banned women from taking exams for certain civil service positions. See Cullen Owens, *A Social History of Women in Ireland*, pp. 241–243 and 265. Ireland was not unique in passing legislation limiting the number of married women in employment. See also, Redmond and Harford, '"One Man One Job"'.

20　Joyce Padbury, 'Mary Hayden (1862–1942): Feminist', *Studies: An Irish Quarterly Review*, 96.390 (2009), p. 153.

21　This is, of course, outside of public administration where examinations had to be sat to gain entry to employment. The system of favours was not confined to women's employment and applied generally to obtaining professional office work. Elizabeth Kiely and Máire Leane, *Irish Women at Work, 1930–1960: An Oral History* (Dublin: Irish Academic Press, 2012), p. 55.

These forty years wrought great changes in women's working lives. Going by the census, the average working (i.e. gainfully occupied) woman in 1926 and 1936 was a single or widowed woman working on a farm (not, it must be repeated, a farmer's wife, who was not deemed to be gainfully occupied), or a domestic servant. In 1961 she was more likely to be a clerk-typist or a factory worker.[22]

However, it seems that the changes were slower to manifest themselves and may have mainly occurred in the 1950s, as up to the 1951 census, the rates of female employment in most sectors remained static. The most dramatic rise was a threefold increase in the number of women in the 'transport and communications' category. This still only brought their rate up to 9.7 per cent. The only other significant increase was in the number of women not stating their category of employment. Women's industrial employment saw limited growth, due not only to the lack of economic development but also to the fact that such employment was created and framed as 'male' employment, hence the limitations imposed by legislation such as the Conditions of Employment Act (1936).[23] Industrial employment was condemned as harmful to women and the family in Ireland, with the term 'factory girl' carrying 'all sorts of negative connotations in rural Ireland'.[24] The vociferous Aodh de Blácam even argued that factories were 'the greatest evil that had come to this country' and the employment of women in them meant that 'womanhood was being de-naturalised and turned into something it was never intended for'.[25] Louie Bennett of the Irish Women Workers' Union (IWWU), however, countered his assertions by arguing that factory work in Ireland was a way to prevent rural depopulation and emigration, with its attendant dangers: 'Personally, I would much prefer to see them employed for eight hours daily in a local industry and in contact with home and friends, than drifting away to the uncertainties and loneliness of domestic employment in Dublin or Britain'.[26]

22 Caitriona Clear, *Women of the House: Women's Household Work in Ireland, 1922–1961* (Dublin: Irish Academic Press, 2000), p. 18.
23 Mary McAuliffe, 'The Irish Woman Worker and the Conditions of Employment Act, 1936: Responses from the Women Senators', *Saothar*, 36 (2011), pp. 37–48.
24 Delaney, *The Irish in Post-War Britain*, p. 32.
25 Speech given to Muintir na Tire conference, quoted in Louise Ryan, 'Leaving Home: Irish Press Debates on Female Employment, Domesticity and Emigration to Britain in the 1930s', *Women's History Review*, 12.3 (2003), p. 394. Aodh de Blácam made other public announcements on the topic; see, for example, 'Letter to the Editor', *Irish Times*, 5 December 1936, p. 5.
26 Letter responding to letter from Aodh de Blácam, *Irish Times*, 9 December 1936, p. 4. For further discussion of the image of the factory girl, see Jennifer Redmond, 'The Largest Remaining Reserve of Manpower: Historical Myopia, Irish Women Workers and World War Two', *Saothar*, 36 (2011), pp. 61–72.

Unemployment for working-class women was a significant problem. The rates of those counted on the live register reveal that there were never fewer than 36,000 women during the 1920s to the 1950s claiming unemployment relief, with the highest figure recorded for 1942 with an average of 80,215 women and 9,345 girls unemployed in each year.[27] Domestic servants in private households were not counted as they were not covered under the national insurance schemes and hence ineligible to claim unemployment relief if they lost their job.[28] Given there were far more women employed in service than any other category, the figures thus do not include a significant number of women who may have experienced unemployment. There are further problems with these figures when examining the position of women: the rates for those counted as 'unoccupied' included women such as farmers' wives who were engaged solely in home duties. The figures may also include some who did not declare their employment. The overall picture is one of women predominantly occupying low-skill, temporary and poorly paid employment. Indeed, in the case of agricultural occupations, they may not have received any financial remuneration at all.[29] Women were not provided with as many opportunities for relief work schemes, apart from a small number employed in turf cutting during the Emergency who were 'paid less than the daily rate for hiring a donkey'.[30]

How women were categorised is therefore important to consider. Clear maintains that the language used to describe women who were not paid for their labour is as important to reflect on as the actual statistical data:

By describing this work as 'duties' and including those who performed it under the 'not gainfully occupied' heading along with students,

27 In 1929, 36,274 women were on the live register. The peak in 1942 saw 166,127. The opposite trend can be seen for girls – the lowest number on the live register was in 1943, when 3,835 girls were counted; the highest rates were recorded in 1927, with 12,376 girls. There were also more dramatic fluctuations in the numbers of women and girls on the live register. The lower number of girls during the war years may be evidence that they were availing themselves of the loophole that allowed under-sixteens to travel on their parents' permit although further research is needed before this could be posited conclusively. Data taken from *Statistical Abstracts*, as above.

28 As well as domestic service, those in agriculture were not included under the Unemployment Insurance Acts, thus the figures may obscure both men's and women's actual rates of unemployment. Lee asserts that the government's rejection of the Inquiry into Workmen's Compensation allowed it to delay calculating accurate employment statistics. For more on this, see Lee, *Ireland, 1912–1985*, p. 126.

29 Delaney has sketched the disadvantaged state of male agricultural workers in comparison with skilled workers in Ireland, and thus, theoretically, even if women did receive a wage for their farming work, they would have found themselves in 'acute hardship' during this time. See *Demography, State and Society*, pp. 51–53.

30 Daly, *The Slow Failure*, p. 59.

invalids, retired people, pensioners, and the unemployed, and by giving it a certain 'weighting', the census was, effectively, expressing an opinion about the work.[31]

Kearns has also argued that the defective nature of statistics on women's work is one of the strongest reasons for the use of qualitative methods to sketch their histories.[32]

Terms such as 'duties' and 'not gainfully occupied' to describe occupational status counter Ryan's argument that 'women/girl emigrants embody the failures of the state to tackle problems of unemployment, rural deprivation and emigration'.[33] Contemporary discourses centred frequently on actively *denying* women's right or need to work in Irish society, as evinced in successive Irish legislation to limit women's economic opportunities.[34] As Valiulis has argued, within such areas as the civil service, 'women could be limited to the lower ranks because this was not their primary vocation in life'.[35] Thus, women's emigration served to highlight the lack of 'space' for women's work in Irish society at this time, as well as the triviality attached to women's employment and the absence of cultural recognition or acceptance of women's work.[36] Muldowney found this view in her oral history study of women during the Second World War: 'You'd be looked down, if he hadn't work, like that, a woman would, oh yes. It'd be: she married that fellow there and she has to go out and work for him'.[37] A dichotomous falsehood was thus perpetrated in cultural attitudes to women's work: a simultaneous denial of working women's existence alongside a bourgeois attitude that women did not *need* to be economically productive, their apposite sphere being that of hearth and home.

Historians of Irish women in the twentieth century hold up the Conditions of Employment Act of 1936 as one of the most restrictive pieces of gendered

---

31 Clear, *Women of the House*, p. 26.
32 Kearns, *Dublin's Lost Heroines*, p. 20.
33 Ryan, *Gender, Identity and the Irish Press*, p. 112.
34 Reference is to such legislation as the 1925 Civil Service Regulation Act and the 1936 Conditions of Employment Act, which regulated the type of industries women were allowed to be employed in and the number of women allowed in such industries.
35 Maryann Valiulis, 'Neither Feminist Nor Flapper: The Ecclesiastical Construction of the Ideal Irish Woman', in Mary O'Dowd and Sabine Wichert (eds), *Chattel, Servant or Citizen? Women's Status in Church, State and Society* (Belfast: Queen's University of Belfast Press, 1995), p. 178.
36 For more on this point, see Jennifer Redmond, 'Gender, Emigration and Diverging Discourses: Irish Female Emigration, 1922–48', in Maryann Valiulis (ed.), *Gender and Power in Ireland* (Dublin: Irish Academic Press, 2009), pp. 140–158.
37 Quote taken from interview with Letty and Josie in Muldowney, 'The Impact of the Second World War on Women in Belfast and Dublin', vol. 2, p. L&J2.

legislation to affect women's employment in the post-independence era. It gave the Minister for Industry and Commerce (under Section 16(1)) the power to prohibit women from certain kinds of industrial work or to fix the proportion of women to be employed in any factory. The Fianna Fáil government's intention can be surmised that where industrial development occurred, it would be directed towards providing employment for male breadwinners, not women. This was to avoid what Lemass saw as a future in which technology made men redundant in industrial life, which he pointed to as a problem in northern counties:

> That tendency to transfer employment from men to women in consequence of mechanical development may take place in any industry at any time, and it is desirable that we should not get altogether into the position in which, I am told, the city of Derry is, where the great bulk of the men stay at home minding the children and the women go out to earn the daily bread.[38]

Fears of the feminisation of men through women's increasing employment were far-fetched to say the least. These fears, however, also emerged in the investigation by two members of the Commission on Emigration and Other Population Problems, who raised the spectre of parental authority 'becoming proportionate to the contribution to family budget' when daughters were working but their father was not.[39] This disruption of conventional gender and familial dynamics was evidently disapproved of by these Commissioners, yet the simple fact was that in many households Irish women's income was necessary to maintain even basic standards of living. In the absence of employment opportunities for women in Ireland it was necessary for women to emigrate to maintain households overburdened by multiple children and inadequate incomes.[40]

In contrast, the economy in Britain had an emphasis on female-oriented service sector occupations.[41] Irish women could also apply for clerical positions in the public service in Britain, engage in work as teachers at all levels (the secondary school sector in Ireland was heavily dominated by religious), and were specifically in demand for domestic, factory and hospital work. Irish women thus had access to a much wider array of jobs in Britain than in their own country. Wage differentials between Ireland and Britain were also an

38 Seán Lemass, *Dáil Éireann Debates*, vol. 56, col. 1282, 17 May 1935.
39 Rural Survey of Drogheda by Mr Byrne and Mr O'Leary (undated), *c.*1948. Arnold Marsh papers, Trinity College Dublin MS 8306/S13.
40 Redmond, '"Sinful Singleness?"'
41 See Delaney, *Demography, State and Society*, chap. 4.

influential factor for both men and women in the emigration process. In the 1930s and the 1940s, there was an increasing disparity between British and Irish wages for similar work.[42] For women, the situation was even more drastic, with female rates of pay in Ireland throughout the 1940s up to the 1960s between 53 per cent and 57 per cent of those of men.[43] Wage differentials also existed between men and women in Britain, but the rates of wages were still higher than most women could secure in Ireland. During the years of the Second World War, Litton found wage differences between Britain and Ireland rose from 8 per cent to 31 per cent for women.[44] Although gendered wage differentials existed in most countries for which data is available at this time, as Daly has highlighted, they were more *extreme* in Ireland.[45] Where women did have work, they often found themselves relegated to the lowest paid, lowest status, least secure jobs, leading Mary Cosgrave of the Women Citizens and Local Government Association in 1928 to bemoan the fact that the 'equal citizenship guaranteed under the Constitution of An Saorstát still remains an ideal'.[46]

Within domestic service, and nursing in particular, the stark difference in wages must be viewed as a strong motivating factor to leave. According to investigations by the Irish Housewives' Association, resident maids with some experience received £1 17s.6d. per week in Britain compared with 25 shillings in Ireland in the late 1940s.[47] Such facts were at times disputed by those who saw emigration as an 'evil' or a particularly dangerous undertaking for women. Dr Gilmartin, Bishop of Galway, stated that the 'wages which an untrained girl can get in Ireland is as good, if not better, than she can get in England'; evidently he had no clear idea of the situation.[48] In fact, the government had investigated the issue of wages in 1946, finding that an annual wage for domestic servants amounted to between £30 and £35 in Ireland, while they could get the same work for £50 per annum in Britain.[49] Whilst a lower figure than found by the IHA, this could perhaps

---

42 Diarmaid Ferriter, *Judging Dev: A Reassessment of the Life and Legacy of Éamon de Valera* (Dublin: Royal Irish Academy, 2007), p. 283.

43 King and O'Connor, 'Migration and Gender', p. 313.

44 Litton says that, for men, the wage differences between Ireland and Britain during the Second World War rose from 16 per cent to 32 per cent. See Helen Litton, *The World War Two Years; The Irish Emergency: An Illustrated History* (Dublin: Wolfhound Press, 2001), p. 107.

45 Mary E. Daly, *Women and Work in Ireland* (Dublin: Irish Economic and Social History Society, 1997), p. 53.

46 *Irish Independent*, 6 October 1928.

47 Memo submitted by the Irish Housewives Association relating to 1948. Arnold Marsh papers, Trinity College Dublin MS 8305/9.

48 *Irish Catholic*, 15 August 1936.

49 See Department of External Affairs, Memorandum dated 30 August 1947, NAI, DFA 402/25.

reflect the disparity in skills in the domestic service sector and nevertheless demonstrates the difference in wages for the same work in Britain and Ireland. Gilmartin's main point seemed to be that 'the big difference [is] that she is safe in our home surroundings, whilst the dangers to friendless girls in English cities are simply appalling'.[50] It was further argued that the benefits of higher wages would be outweighed by higher costs of living, but this did not act as a deterrent to the many thousands of emigrants.[51]

In nursing, the fact that free or low-cost training was provided and probationer nurses were paid while completing it ensured that the British medical system exerted a consistent 'pull' on Irish women eager to enter the profession.[52] While the evidence on significant wage differentials is compelling, other significant factors include the stability of employment and 'income uncertainty and relative deprivation', as Stark has argued.[53] These factors apply equally to men and women, yet there was a complete absence of any discourses on decent or appropriate wages for women to help them meet their financial commitments. Delaney defines relative deprivation as the process by which 'people assess their own "deprived" position in the economic hierarchy relative to the reference grouping around them, usually the local community'.[54] In the Irish context, relative deprivation may have been assessed not only in relation to the local community but also in comparison with friends and family members in Britain due to frequent contact between Irish emigrants and their home communities.

According to the Rev. Cornelius Lucey, Roman Catholic Bishop of Cork and Ross, adult unmarried daughters would not be tempted to 'postpone marriage through fear of finding themselves economically worse off as a result of giving up their job' if the focus was on decent wages for married men.[55] The report of the Commission on Emigration and Other Population Problems advocated that 'wage standards should be sufficient to enable a

50 *Irish Catholic*, 15 August 1936.

51 There was a steady rise in the cost of living in Ireland throughout the 1930s, which peaked during the Emergency. See Appendix 8 in Muldowney, *The Second World War and Irish Women*.

52 For more on Irish women working in the British medical profession, see Jennifer Redmond, 'The Thermometer and the Travel Permit: Irish Women in the Medical Profession in Britain during World War II', in MacPherson and Hickman, *Irish Diaspora Studies and Women* and Jennifer Redmond, 'Migrants, Medics, Matrons: Exploring the Spectrum of Irish Immigrants in the Wartime British Health Sector', in David Durnin and Ian Miller (eds), *Medicine, Health and Irish Experiences of Conflict, 1914–45* (Manchester: Manchester University Press, 2016).

53 Oded Stark, *The Migration of Labor* (Oxford: Basil Blackwell, 1991), p. 3.

54 Delaney, *Demography, State and Society*, p. 13.

55 Cornelius Lucey, 'The Problem of the Woman Worker', *Irish Ecclesiastical Record*, 48 (July–Dec. 1936), p. 457.

man to marry and rear a family without hardship'.[56] This was critiqued at the time for its unrealistic assessment of Ireland, such as Donal Nevin's comment, 'I must point out that on any interpretation of this statement very large numbers of Irish workers are even now in receipt of grossly inadequate wages'.[57] Despite critiques of the realism or otherwise of the Commission's assertion, attitudes privileging the idea of a family wage for men continued unchallenged throughout this period and beyond. This is perhaps unsurprising, but it still ignored the reality for many working-class families. This is not to suggest that economic opportunities for men in this era were idyllic. As Delaney has rightly pointed out, opportunities for lower class men and women were limited and unstable, with men facing 'intermittent employment ... punctuated by long spells of underemployment'.[58] This is, in fact, why female wages were needed to keep families afloat.

Ryan's study of eleven women who migrated to Britain in the 1930s concurs with Delaney's finding that 'the decision to emigrate was usually presented in terms of the need to earn more money and to send as much as possible home to their families'.[59] This shift in focus from looking at individual decisions to family decisions to migrate fits well with Irish women's experiences, particularly in relation to remittances.[60] Irish women's remittances were essential for keeping some families from becoming a burden on the state and they helped keep rural households on unprofitable farms on their land. Some have also suggested that women could be better relied upon to send remittances than men, thus they were 'the best emigrants'.[61] No systematic gender breakdown of senders of remittances to Ireland is available, and this assessment is based on perceptions of gendered behaviours.

The Department of Industry and Commerce undertook an analysis of remittances in 1942 comparing pre-war and contemporary levels of income derived from this source. Remittances totalled over £1 million in each year, rising to over £2 million in 1942 as war workers sent back large proportions of their wages.[62] Such was the scale of the money sent home by migrants that from 1936 to 1942 total postal and money orders received in the Free

56 Commission on Emigration and Other Population Problems, *Majority Report*, para. 433.
57 Donal Nevin, 'Symposium on the Report of the Commission on Emigration and Other Population Problems', *Journal of the Statistical and Social Inquiry Society of Ireland*, 29.4 (1956), p. 117.
58 Delaney, *The Irish in Post-War Britain*, p. 31.
59 Ryan, 'Moving Spaces and Changing Places', p. 72.
60 Stark, *The Migration of Labor*, p. 3.
61 Luddy and McLoughlin, 'Women and Emigration from Ireland from the Seventeenth Century', p. 568.
62 Department of Industry and Commerce Memorandum, 'Remittances from Great Britain and Northern Ireland', Department of the Taoiseach files, NAI, S12865, June 1942.

State amounted to £8,019,950. This doesn't include money that may have been sent as cash or delivered by hand on visits home. By the 1950s, net remittances contributed £12 million of Ireland's Gross National Product[63] or the equivalent of between €635 million and €952 million each year by a calculation made in 2001.[64] The governments of the time were acutely aware of the benefits of remittances, taking care to monitor and count them. The Commission on Emigration and Other Population Problems saw both positive and negative effects of remittances, but underlined their importance:

> Emigrants' remittances are an important item in the national economy; they partly redress the adverse balance of trade; they may stimulate production, or in certain circumstances they may have a limited inflationary effect. Their social effect is to bring about greater equality in the distribution of wealth.[65] The Commission also heard evidence from the Congested Districts Board which reported the real impact that was seen from remittances in country life: home improvements, the buying of new farm equipment, dowry payments, bank savings and debt diminution.[66]

Allusions to remittances are in almost every oral history collection. Women refer to them as a means of keeping in touch with family and an unquestionable duty. Mary Henry, for example, 'recounted how she saved money from her wages to send home to the farm. She had to be thrifty (a trait she had all her life), so she had egg and chips every day for her lunch – not because she particularly liked that meal but because it was the cheapest one'.[67] Similarly, Noreen Hill stated that the 'minute I'd get my wage packet I'd put the money into an envelope and send it to my mother. And then I felt better ... And I felt I was actually with my mother when I sent the money'.[68] Examples of this kind are also contained in Lambert's study of Irish women in Lancashire[69] and in testimony from Tilda in Ryan's study of 1930s emigrants: 'I got paid the first of the month and straight down to the post office and then the next morning I'd be thinking "the money is there

---

63 Lennon *et al.*, *Across the Water*, p. 25.
64 *Mayo News*, 2001 quoted in Dunne, *An Unconsidered People*, p. 4.
65 Commission on Emigration and Other Population Problems, *Majority Report*, para. 313.
66 Summaries of Memoranda, Arnold Marsh papers, Trinity College Dublin MS 8301.
67 From a life history relating to Mary Henry (née McKavanagh) given to the author by her daughter, Patricia Marsh.
68 Lennon *et al.*, *Across the Water*, p. 94.
69 As part of her study, Lambert interviewed forty women who had emigrated between 1910 and 1946 from many different parts of Ireland to Lancashire. See Lambert, *Irish Women in Lancashire*.

now", the postman bringing mammy the pound. It was great to be able to help her'.[70] Remittances can be viewed, therefore, as an extension of the normal practice for unmarried women (and men) to 'hand up' their wages to their mothers every week.[71]

Benefits of emigration such as remittances were rarely alluded to in public by the government. Nor was there specific recognition within contemporary discourses that women's capabilities for producing remittances may have influenced a *family* decision for the woman to emigrate. This is important because their position is different from male emigrants, who, as theorists such as Stark argue, may be motivated to send remittances back to their family due to inheritance aspirations.[72] Given the preference for sons (usually, but not always, the eldest) to inherit farms at this time rather than daughters, we can interpret the high level of remittances as emanating from altruistic desires or strong family connections that survived the emigration process.[73] Why then were there competing discourses that posited women as being motivated by desires other than financial stability?

Emigration for Employment or Emigration for Enjoyment? Competing Discourses on Irish Female Emigration

Although successive governments failed adequately to tackle unemployment in Ireland, the theme of 'men need jobs' was a familiar trope in government debates and the press. Yet private narratives of female emigrants almost unanimously claim that their emigration was because of unemployment or irregular or poorly paid employment, which forced them to seek more stable jobs in Britain and elsewhere.

To those sceptical of the claim of economic necessity, the 'legitimacy' of economic motivations may have been a strategy used by interviewees to justify their emigration against the memory of negative public discourses that denied their need for economic emigration. However, the constancy of this argument within oral history narratives in different collections over the last few decades, and the fact that the economy performed so poorly,

---

70 Tilda (a pseudonym) was paid £1 8s. 4d. a month of which she sent home £1. Louise Ryan, 'Family Matters: (E)migration, Familial Networks and Irish Women in Britain', *Sociological Review* (2004), p. 360.

71 This practice is referred to by interviewees in the Kiely and Leane book, *Irish Women at Work*, and also by Muldowney in *The Second World War and Irish Women*.

72 See, for example, Stark, *The Migration of Labor*, pp. 238–240.

73 For more on inheritance patterns in Ireland, see Cormac Ó Gráda, 'Primogeniture and Ultimogeniture in Rural Ireland', *Journal of Interdisciplinary History*, 10.3 (1980), pp. 491–497.

provide justifiable reasons for viewing the *majority* of Ireland's emigrants in the time period as economic migrants *primarily* motivated by the necessity to support themselves and their families. This is particularly true for women who had limited economic opportunities and lower chances of marriage (and thus economic support) available to them in post-independent Ireland. As Ó Gráda has argued, non-economic motivations for migration can generally be discounted as primary ones because, 'on the whole, cross-county evidence shows that as living standards improve emigration slows down and return migration begins'.[74]

A memorandum circulated by the Department of External Affairs in 1947 claimed that:

> there is a significant difference between male and female emigrants: the former usually proceed in groups to factory or building work where arrangements are made for their moral and religious welfare and often for the maintenance of an Irish atmosphere, whereas the bulk of the female emigrants who are engaged in domestic service or allied work take up employment individually and are scattered singly throughout Great Britain, the moral atmosphere of which young and inexperienced girls are only too often unfitted to withstand.[75]

No evidence, however, was provided to prove that working in groups would preserve moral character to a higher extent than working individually. Furthermore, evidence which will be presented below on Irish women recruited to group schemes demonstrates that many women were migrating within organised, protected programmes provided by the British ministries in charge of factories. Yet, as with other strands of negative discourse on young women, the issue persisted.

Women's economic necessity to migrate was a topic hotly debated in the hearings of the Commission on Emigration and Other Population Problems. Contrasting views were put forward with evidence presented from both sides. There is a general tone in many of the drafts, memos and transcripts of interviews with witnesses that some members of the Commission wanted to prove that women and men were motivated by different reasons. The final report stresses this difference:

> Although female emigration, like male, is the result of a variety of causes, the purely economic cause is not always so dominant. For

---

74 Ó Gráda, *A Rocky Road*, p. 217.
75 Department of External Affairs, Memorandum dated 30 August 1947, NAI, DFA 402/25, p. 4.

the female emigrant improvement in personal status is of no less importance than the higher wages and better conditions of employment abroad and some of the evidence submitted to us would suggest that the prospect of better marriage opportunities is also an influence of some significance.[76]

This, however, was not only refuted by some witnesses, but was based on a serious lack of evidence. As Daly convincingly argues, the Commission's assessment that women were motivated less by economic factors than by personal factors was a flawed assumption 'because they failed to interview women emigrants about their reasons for emigrating'.[77]

Evidence from oral history collections and small-scale studies has shown the importance of economic motivations for Irish female emigrants. Of King and O'Connor's sample of fifty women originating from all over Ireland and settled in Leicester in the 1940s to the 1980s, the highest scoring motivations were for employment, community links and proximity to Ireland.[78] King and O'Connor also questioned their interviewees as to why they were leaving Ireland (as opposed to why they chose Britain). High unemployment and a lack of career opportunities were rated as more important motivating factors than discrimination against women, narrow-minded attitudes in Ireland, low incomes, high taxes and family or personal problems.[79] These categories are subjective, as are any self-assessments of behaviour, but the results indicate that in the view of women themselves the most pressing reasons given both for leaving Ireland and coming to Britain were economic, correlating with Ravenstein's theories, as discussed in Chapter 1.

The 'Dangers' of Answering 'Innocent-Looking' Advertisements

Long before the government banned job advertisements during the Emergency on the grounds of neutrality, there were calls in the Catholic

---

76 Commission on Emigration and Other Population Problems, *Majority Report*, para. 303.

77 Daly, *The Slow Failure*, p. 168.

78 King and O'Connor, 'Migration and Gender', Table 2 (p. 317).

79 Lack of career opportunities and high unemployment were cited by 24 and 17 interviewees respectively as 'very important'. In contrast, discrimination against women was ranked as 'unimportant' by 41 of the women, as were family or personal problems (suggesting the women were not fleeing to escape family control or conflict). Furthermore, narrow-minded attitudes were ranked as 'unimportant' by 35 of the women. The data posits economic motivations firmly as primary to the women in the sample.

press for the restriction or monitoring of British agencies or individuals seeking Irish domestic servants through newspapers. To some people's minds, advertisements could be snares, and agencies covers for criminal gangs, or simply unscrupulous businesses that did not adequately check the calibre of their clientele. Advertisements relied on individual contact being made between interested applicants and employers, thereby circumventing any help – or intervention – those concerned for the welfare of Irish girls might wish to assert.

In May 1926, a British publication, *St Mary's Magazine*, was quoted in the *Irish Catholic* under the heading 'A "Domestic" Problem'. The authors referred to the rural origin of many girls answering advertisements, who 'are not used to city life [and] they have not previously handled much money of their own' and thus were in need of 'kindly words of help and guidance'.[80] They also suggested that publications in which advertisements appeared should keep in touch with girls who answered them. This request was gently rebuffed by the editor of the *Irish Catholic* who outlined the impracticalities of such a plan, arguing instead for 'admonitions published from time to time, addressed to both maids and mistresses', which the editor believed more effective and which were already a regular feature.[81]

The idea that advertisements may be 'snares for the unwary'[82] was one that persisted because it was felt that many Irish women were totally unprepared for living in Britain and, more controversially, that they lacked domestic skills altogether. There were references again to the potential of becoming involved in the 'nefarious business' of the 'white slave trade' through the answering of false advertisements.[83] This commentary appears to have had an effect as the NVA in Britain reported that it investigated advertisements by employers on behalf of girls who wrote to them. Mr Sempkins of the NVA wrote to the *Irish Independent*: 'The girls should understand that if those enquiries are made and information is sent to Ireland, it is sent in the strictest confidence and must not be divulged to third parties. I have already had one case where a girl has been foolishly indiscreet'.[84]

Concerns over this issue appear to have been particularly acute throughout the 1930s. The Most Rev. Dr Morrisroe, Bishop of Achonry, in 1936 warned of the dangers of registry offices in Britain that advertised in the Irish press

80   *Irish Catholic*, 29 May 1926, p. 2.
81   Ibid.
82   Lenten Pastoral of the Most Rev. Dr MacNeely, Bishop of Raphoe, extracts of which appeared under the heading 'Warning to Girls Who Emigrate', *Irish Catholic*, 8 March 1930, p. 8.
83   *Irish Catholic*, 'Our Social Myopia', 31 December 1936, p. 5.
84   Letter dated 26 November 1936, Women's Library, File 4NVA/04/02 Box FL098. The NVA appears to have been concerned with the possibility of being sued for slander.

as they 'occasionally prove to be veritable pitfalls'.[85] Furthermore, as a result of applying through the agencies 'some few applicants [...] found themselves in the toils of white slave traffickers, from whom they were rescued with difficulty'. Although the message within the pastoral letter seems to be motivated by a genuine concern for the welfare of emigrant women, the admission that this related to 'some few', and that the need to rescue women happens 'occasionally', again demonstrates the tendency to generalise from the exceptional occurrence to the common experience: this warning is directed to *all* girls who are emigrating and using employment agencies or answering advertisements.

The message was repeated in the *Irish Catholic* later in 1936 in a report of a sermon given by Dr Gilmartin, Bishop of Galway, in which he spoke of advertisers 'getting hold of Irish girls for unmentionable purposes': and the 'dangers' of answering 'innocent-looking' advertisements.[86] In an editorial piece it was argued that answering advertisements for employment left little time for checking its authenticity, with the implication being that women would be so carried away by 'elation – even a sense of new-found freedom' that they would not care about the peril they were almost certain to face.[87] The consequences of such lust for freedom were dire: 'The notices may not emanate from genuine sources at all, and the unsuspecting girl may be lured across the sea to suffer degradation and dishonour'.[88]

While publicly appearing to ignore the issue, the Irish government was active in investigating the employment agencies and advertisements appearing in Irish newspapers. High Commissioner in London Dulanty was involved in verifying the credentials of English employment agencies. This behind the scenes work was brought to a head, however, when the English Catholic hierarchy decided to bring the welfare problems associated with Irish female emigration directly to the Irish government's attention. In 1937, Cardinal Hinsley of Westminster wrote directly to de Valera and Dulanty about the problems his diocese was encountering in trying to meet the welfare needs of Irish women who became pregnant in Britain, as outlined in Chapter 4. Cardinal Hinsley's purpose was to secure the welfare of girls coming to employment, but he was primarily anxious to tackle the problem of unmarried Irish mothers in Britain. Facing the embarrassment of the situation, the Irish government decided to act.[89]

Hinsley's advice was to get the newspapers to agree to publish advertisements only from agencies approved by the Catholic Church, and

85   *Irish Catholic*, 4 July 1936, p. 8.
86   Report of a sermon by Dr Gilmartin, Bishop of Galway, *Irish Catholic*, 15 August 1936, p. 6.
87   Ibid., p. 4.
88   Ibid.
89   Document E171. DH&C, Clandillon papers.

to encourage the Irish hierarchy to act. Such agencies had to promise to cooperate with a new scheme to distribute leaflets to women that gave details of the Welfare Officer of the Catholic Girls' Society and had a portion that could be detached and sent on so that women could be tracked and looked after. The Irish hierarchy were immediately alerted, and a series of letters ensued as to how best to respond. On the government side, the responsibility seems to have fallen not to any cabinet ministers but to high-ranking civil servants. They initiated the process of securing the Irish hierarchy's approval of the scheme. In this regard, it seems that Sean Murphy and J.P. Walshe, of the Department of External Affairs, and James Hurson, Secretary of the Department of Local Government and Public Health, were chiefly involved. Hurson was responsible for approaching the editors of the *Irish Press*, the *Irish Times* and the *Irish Independent* to secure their cooperation. All agreed to distribute leaflets and to make them available in areas in their offices where prospective employees may come in. The pamphlets urged women to seek help, even if they had relatives already living in Britain, and it emphasised that a girl who practises her religion 'is respected in any company', linking religious devotion with respect and status.[90]

One stumbling block, however, appears to have been the fact that individuals, not companies, placed most advertisements and the *Irish Times* was not willing to abandon taking advertisements from them. The general manager, J.J. Simington, seems to have taken a much stronger line than the other editors and asserted that, while they would be happy to distribute leaflets to private advertisers, it was the responsibility of the Catholic organisations in London to ensure that the employment offices that placed advertisements were *bona fide*.[91] Thus, the Irish government, the newspapers and, to a certain extent, the English hierarchy believed that the proper responsibility for ensuring that Irish women were safeguarded in their efforts to find work in Britain lay with the Irish Catholic Church.

Clearly, warnings from the hierarchy and the Catholic press were ignored as many women obtained employment by answering private advertisements, some of which appeared in Catholic newspapers themselves. A letter written from an Irish woman (signed simply 'MCB, London') who obtained a teaching post at an English boarding school, however, concurred with the warnings:

Irish girls should not trust advertisements or agencies, even those published in irreproachable papers. Neither the newspaper nor the

90 Ibid.
91 Letter from Hurson to Walshe, September 1937; Document E114. DH&C, Clandillon papers.

Table 6.2   Analysis by Department of Social Welfare of
advertisements in the *Irish Independent* by type of job
advertised (1947)

Gender	Nurses, probationers and student nurses	Industrial workers	Domestics for institutions
Male	0	0	3
Female	286	30	23
Total		342	

Source: Arnold Marsh Papers, Trinity College Dublin MS 8304/46.

agencies guarantee their notices, written by the prospective employer, are all that they lead one to expect.[92]

MCB's complaints were related to the poor conditions and standards she and others experienced at schools that were much lower than advertised. The case of MCB demonstrates that despite the focus on domestic servants false advertising was a problem that could potentially affect all classes of women.[93]

In 1947, the Department of Social Welfare conducted an analysis of seventy-six issues of the *Irish Independent* for the three months ended 31 December 1947 to assess whether advertisements were acting as an inducement to emigrate. Table 6.2 details the range of employment they found in larger advertisements, which were in addition to the small personal ones. The Department's memo noted that the increased demand for female labour was due to the post-war deregulation of women's employment in Britain and the abandonment of the travel permit system for them, as outlined in Chapter 1. The memorandum laid out who placed the advertisement, with examples of the language used. The memorandum does not specify what action was taken, but it is likely that it related to the proposed ban on female emigration contained in a memorandum in 1948. This was suggested by the office of the Minister for External Affairs and circulated by D.J. O'Donovan from the Employment Branch of the

92 *Irish Catholic*, 16 January 1947, p. 3.
93 This is the only letter I have found in the *Irish Catholic* that relates this experience to women teachers rather than domestic servants, and while it shows that this was a potential problem for women engaging in all types of work, the issue of conditions for emigrant teachers needs to be further investigated to judge whether this problem was widespread.

Department of Social Welfare to the Commission on Emigration and Other Population Problems.[94]

The public perception that the government was doing nothing about advertisements for jobs in Britain was revealed in evidence given to the Commission by the playwright Michael Molloy.[95] Molloy reflected on the reasons Ireland was now experiencing a population 'crisis' and claimed that:

> infinitely more deadly were the advertisements which swarmed in every newspaper, especially the provincial newspapers, which are bought in every farmhouse. What farmer would give his daughter £150 of his hard-earned money [for a dowry] when he could get rid of her for nothing to a respectable job worth £4 or £5 a week? What farmer would, or could, keep even one son on his small holding when he could go to England and earn £6 a week? [...] It was this unceasing barrage of financially irresistible advertisements which gradually seduced into madness and suicide the Irish countryside. What is one to say about the politicians who have allowed this barrage (now entering upon its tenth year) when, at any time, they could have stopped it with a stroke of a pen? Seemingly they are prepared to see the last young man or woman in rural Ireland go rather than run the risk of antagonising their newspapers which are waxing rich on the Extermination through Advertisement Campaign.[96]

Molloy's angry accusations indicate that the government's tentative steps in investigating or trying to control emigration without formally regulating it went unnoticed. It is also no surprise – given the tone – that he names Aodh de Blácam in the memorandum as someone he admires for his stance on emigration.

Ironically, in Britain, exasperation was expressed that Irish women often came over *without* having secured employment through answering advertisements. Within Catholic circles there was much sympathy and support, but outside this group some took a harsher view. Ryan has highlighted

---

94 See Arnold Marsh papers, Trinity College Dublin MSS 8300/12/1 and 8300/12/2.

95 Molloy had written a three-act comedy, *The Old Road*, staged at the Abbey Theatre, about the crisis of rural depopulation in 1943. It referred to the impact the war was having on life in Galway. See Wills, *That Neutral Island*, pp. 309–310 and *The Best are Leaving: Emigration and Post-War Irish Culture* (Cambridge: Cambridge University Press, 2015).

96 Memorandum, 'Origin and Development of the Present Emigration Mania and Catastrophe', submitted by the playwright Michael J. Molloy, Milltown, Co. Galway, to the Commission on Emigration and Other Population Problems, undated (c.1948). Arnold Marsh papers, Trinity College Dublin MS 8305.

the Lord Mayor of Liverpool's references to women who came over without having lined up a job through an advertisement as 'absolutely simple' and 'foolish'.[97] Clearly there were opposing views as to what was 'dangerous' for Irish women in their pursuit of employment in Britain.

Employment Agencies and Emigration

Women were regularly recruited to jobs in Britain through employment agencies between the 1920s and the 1940s. As mentioned earlier, the Irish government, through the auspices of the Irish High Commissioner in London, engaged in regular correspondence with the NVA to check their credentials. The first evidence of contact is a letter by Annie Baker, then Honorary Secretary to the NVA, to Margaret Fletcher of the Catholic Women's League. Baker reported with joy that she had been approached by the Irish High Commissioner, James MacNeill.[98] The focus of the interview appears to have been welfare work for Irish women who became destitute and/or pregnant. It is interesting to note here that, even at the very beginning of the Free State, the High Commissioner's office was aware of problems and active in sourcing information about Irish women in Britain, even if it did little with this information.

In 1932, Mr Hynes, the Private Secretary to the High Commissioner, contacted Mr Sempkins of the NVA to check on the credentials of the Anglo-German Agency, who had approached them about sourcing Irish women for domestic employment.[99] The agency had given the NVA as a reference. Sempkins stated his opinion that the woman who ran it was respectable, although they would not vouch for her entirely in relation to Irish girls as her previous experience was with German women.[100] In another letter, dated 21 June 1932, Sempkins wrote to the Irish High Commissioner's office (no name is given but it is most likely a reply to Hynes) detailing the international agreements that existed for the protection of women and the suppression of trafficking. Sempkins appears to be answering a query about Ireland's lack of legislation in this regard.[101] The agreements were referred to particularly in relation to Irish women going to domestic employment;

97 Ryan, 'Aliens, Migrants and Maids', p. 39.
98 Letter dated 7 July 1923, Women's Library, File 4NVA/04/02 Box FL098.
99 Letter from High Commissioner' Secretary, Mr Hynes, to Mr Sempkins dated 16 June 1932, Women's Library, File 4NVA/Folder Co34a, 'Irish Free State'.
100 Letter from Sempkins in reply, 21 June 1932, Women's Library, File 4NVA/Folder Co34a, 'Irish Free State'.
101 The original letter from Hynes is not extant and this may have been destroyed due to sensitivity around the issue.

hence the inference is that, of all emigrants, this was the most vulnerable group. Domestic servants also used employment agencies, which should have brought them under the protections of Article 6 of the International Convention for the Suppression of the Traffic in Women and Children, which stated:

> The High Contracting Parties agree, in case they have not already taken legislative or administrative measures regarding licensing and supervision of employment agencies and offices, to prescribe such regulations as are required to ensure the protection of women and children seeking employment in another country.[102]

Sempkins was eager to stress that he was writing in a personal regard, and this may have been to temper the tone which pointed out the Free State's shortcomings in its protection of women going to employment in Britain: 'May I respectfully venture that a wrong impression may be given in other countries by the fact that the Free State is not a party to these conventions'.[103] Sempkins also told them that the NVA journal he edited had made reference to this in its forthcoming issue. This seems to have provoked a panicked reaction from the High Commissioner's Office. In a note dated 27 June, Sempkins wrote:

> Mr. Hynes, Private Secretary to the High Commissioner of the Irish Free State called at office to-day. They are very perturbed at the thought of their statement being published, of the laxity on the part of the Irish Free State in signing the Conventions. They promised to have the Conventions signed and brought before Parliament, and ask for a revised version to go into the Vigilance Record. I agreed to this on the understanding that the High Commissioner sent me an official letter [o]n the matter.[104]

Unfortunately, neither the original letter nor the 'official letter' Sempkins refers to is extant in the files, and there was no legislative action on the issue.[105]

102 League of Nations, International Convention for the Suppression of the Traffic in Women and Children, 1921. Available from http://ec.europa.eu/anti-trafficking/ legislation-and-case-law-international-legislation-united-nations/1921-international-convention.

103 Letter from Sempkins, 21 June 1932, Women's Library, File 4NVA/Folder Co34a, 'Irish Free State'.

104 Note dated 27 June 1932, Women's Library, File 4NVA/Folder Co34a, 'Irish Free State'.

105 The *Vigilance Record* is not contained in the file.

Communications continued, suggesting genuine concern despite the lack of official action. In October 1932, Hynes again wrote to Sempkins stating that his Minister (presumably the Minister for External Affairs) had requested he obtain 'a list of the local representatives throughout Great Britain of the National Vigilance Association, so that Employment Exchanges in the Irish Free State may have this information at hand in the event of inquiries being made by applicants'.[106] This information, however, was only going to be released on a 'need to know basis' as it was stated that the lists 'will not be publicly displayed as this might have the effect of inducing Irish people, who would not otherwise do so, to seek employment in Great Britain'. The letter indicates the hypersensitivity with which the matter of emigration had to be treated within the public sphere. The leap being made here between the simple provision of welfare information and the encouragement to emigrate is reminiscent of the Dáil debates of the period.

The NVA was used by both Catholic and Protestant organisations to check the respectability of agencies and employers. For example, in response to a letter by Mrs Gregg, wife of the Church of Ireland Archbishop of Dublin, directed through the GFS, Mr Sempkins indicated frustration at the use of the NVA in enquiries about employers by Irish agencies:

we have had to decline to make enquiries on behalf of registry offices, and I am sure that you will readily understand that there is a distinction to be made between making enquiries on behalf of parents, or of an individual girl, and acting as a sort of unpaid subsidiary to a registry office. A number of such offices have tried to get us to do work which they should properly do themselves.[107]

There were numerous organisations involved in trying to safeguard Irish women who took up employment through British agencies. As mentioned in Chapter 3, the International Catholic Girls' Protection Society (ICGPS) was deeply interested in placing women in employment. They also wanted to ensure that any work women had organised independently was of a 'respectable' nature. In reporting on the work of the ICGPS, an article in the *Standard* stated that: 'In most of the cases where the girls took domestic or hospital work, careful enquiries were made beforehand, and when the answers were satisfactory, the girls were *allowed to accept* the situations offered'.[108] While this seems to be an overstatement of the powers of the ICGPS it

106 Letter from High Commissioner' Secretary, Mr Hynes, to Mr Sempkins dated 28 October 1932, Women's Library, File 4NVA/Folder Co34a, 'Irish Free State'.
107 Letter dated 9 March 1935, Women's Library, File 4NVA/04/02 Box FL098.
108 *Standard*, 23 June 1928, p. 16. My emphasis.

indicates the degree of influence it wished to portray it possessed, reflecting perhaps an acceptable degree of social control over young, working-class women. Certainly, there were no follow up letters published in the *Standard* objecting to the ICGPS's reported system on the grounds of privacy or liberty. Furthermore, this system of 'checking up' was not just particular to the Irish branch of the ICGPS, but was part of their remit internationally. Their report on trafficking in women to the League of Nations described local committees as 'carrying out useful enquiries into employment and the investigation of advertisements, which are frequently traps for the unwary'.[109]

The ICGPS also ran its own employment registry office for domestic servants in Rutland Square, Dublin and it encouraged girls to take posts in Dublin, but helped them when applying for jobs abroad, including Europe and the USA.[110] Their *modus operandi* was explained in one of their advertising leaflets: the ICGPS 'does not seek so much to rescue her from the harm she has fallen into, but rather strives to carry out the old adage, "A stitch in time saves nine"'.[111] The ICGPS saw its *raison d'être* as arising from the flippant behaviour of emigrants when accepting employment abroad:

> For those forced to leave home to think they have nothing further to do than to gather the price of their ticket, bid adieu to their friends and relations, and trust themselves to the unknown is to court moral danger and much anxiety of mind.[112]

The ICGPS, like the NVA, undertook enquiries on behalf of female emigrants as to the respectability of British employment agencies the women had accepted jobs with, but went one step further, employing covert tactics to try to catch employers out. In 1935, for example, Assistant Secretary Miss O'Donohue sent an urgent, detailed letter to Archbishop Byrne of Dublin describing their investigations into the activities of a British employment agency that had sent a representative to recruit domestic servants at the County Hotel in Harcourt Street, Dublin.[113]

The ICGPS sent one of its station workers, a Miss Mount, to the recruiter, posing as a potential employee. After checking her credentials, they established

109 Trafficking in Women and Children Committee, Annual Report 1933, by S. de Montenach, President of ICGPS, dated 8 January 1934, Women's Library, File 3AMS/B/11/02, Box Number 071, League of Nations 2, 1934–44 folder.
110 *Irish Catholic*, 27 November 1947, p. 7.
111 Undated advertisement pamphlet in ICGPS folder, uncatalogued file, Down and Connor Diocesan Archives, Belfast.
112 Ibid.
113 Letter dated 7 January 1935, in ICGPS folder, uncatalogued file, Down and Connor Diocesan Archives, Belfast.

that not only was she a properly licensed employment agent, but she was also a Resident District Agent of the Association for Moral Hygiene in Britain. They also established she had visited the potential mistresses and checked that their character was respectable. Thus, while they conceded that she was operating perfectly legally and morally, their concern lay in the fact that she was arranging for them to be met by their employers at Euston Station rather than providing them with hostel accommodation from where they could be picked up. The ICGPS would therefore not know whether the girls were truly safe, or perhaps that the agency would not ensure they were all met. Hence the urgent letter to Archbishop Byrne, with the following closing lines: 'the girls fall into the trap easily. There is an amount of energy and business about her, admirable! if there was not a question of souls' (emphasis in original). No follow-up correspondence exists within the files to indicate what action, if any, Byrne took. Unfortunately, too little of ICGPS archival material is extant to judge whether this type of correspondence was typical, or whether they regularly employed the use of incognito station workers in their investigations. They did, however, use an extensive list of contacts to ensure the respectability of employment and a woman's ability to practise her religion.[114]

Despite all the efforts of the Irish and British hierarchy and the work of lay organisations, concern about women obtaining employment through agencies persisted. The advice to female emigrants was to tell their local clergy of their destination before they sailed so they could inform the clergy in Britain. The Catholic Church in Britain was ready to assist emigrants and was heavily involved in ensuring their safety and well-being. However, in the 1940s, the government privately seemed to feel that the efforts of lay welfare organisations were insufficient to cope with the multitude of dangers that Irish female workers experienced. A memorandum of 1947 appears specifically to reference the ICGPS, although, predictably, given their lack of profile, it gets the name wrong:

There are Catholic Girls' Protection and Welfare Societies in Great Britain, which occasionally have come to the aid of Irish girls in distress in the past but it is felt that these organisations are totally inadequate for combating the dangers to and protecting the interests of the numbers of young girls, who are now being suddenly released from their home environment and who have not the sense to look after themselves.[115]

114 This was judged by whether there was a Catholic church nearby and whether their employer would allow them to attend Mass.
115 Department of External Affairs, Memorandum dated 30 August 1947, NAI, DFA 402/25.

The memorandum opines that little can be done once the emigrants are in Britain as, even if their employment was initially controlled, there was nothing to stop them from changing jobs. Their solution, however, was not to institute a programme of state aid for welfare organisations concerned with female emigration, such as the ICGPS or the CSWB, but rather to ban women from emigrating altogether.

Conclusion

The desire for steady and well-paid (or, indeed, any) employment fuelled emigration from Ireland in every decade under examination in this book. For women in Ireland, employment opportunities were often scarce, and little effort was made to provide new ones. Public discourses, including the report of the Commission and newspaper accounts that hypothesised male migration within a 'rational' and 'legitimate' economic framework and women outside of this, also led to a division between women and men in terms of their 'calibre': while the *best* male workers were leaving the country, the *worst* types of women were leaving to satisfy their 'immoral' desires for 'luxury' lifestyles.

There had been an assumption that independence would automatically improve Ireland's economic position, its citizens' living standards and diminish its population losses 'without anyone actually having to do anything about them'.[116] Delaney's work shows that this malaise prevailed, with de Valera's mind-set reflecting an attitude that viewed emigration as 'fuelled by unrealistic (and irrational) expectations on the part of the poorer sections of Irish society'.[117] In contrast to this, Delaney posits, was an alternative view, forwarded by de Valera's colleague and successor Seán Lemass, who believed that 'in order to reduce emigration Irish living standards needed to be increased over time, rather than hoping that the populace would [...] lower their expectations'.[118] While both attitudes may have coexisted, de Valera's was more prevalent in public assertions on the topic, particularly in relation to women. De Valera often presented emigration as a quest for luxury and, to some extent, a rejection of what was viewed as a 'Christian' conception of 'good' standards of living. This was also phrased by de Valera as a 'more rational standard' as opposed to 'international standards', indicating he

116   Bartlett, *Ireland: A History*, p. 425.
117   Delaney, *The Irish in Post-War Britain*, p. 36. The desire for unrealistically lavish standards of living is also addressed by Lee who asserts that the emigrants of the poorer classes were not 'flying from "reasonable" Irish prospects. They were flying from nothing'. See Lee, *Ireland, 1912–1985*, p. 384.
118   Delaney, *The Irish in Post-War Britain*, p. 36.

thought there was something superior about pursuing prudent economic policies so that the Irish populace had 'just enough' rather than 'plenty'.[119] Given these attitudes towards emigration were at the highest level of government, it is no surprise, as Lee has argued, to find similar sentiments in the popular newspapers of the period.[120]

Sharon Lambert, in her qualitative study of Irish female immigration to Lancashire, has concluded that the 'traditional view' of emigration as motivated by economic reasons 'is now being revised because it was based only on male emigrant experiences and the probability that women left Ireland for social *as much as* economic reasons is now being acknowledged'.[121] The *equation* of social and economic motives is, in my assessment, too narrow and perhaps too modern a description of women's emigration motivations. The immediate imperative was undoubtedly financial for the majority, with wages contributing to the family income through remittances. If this also allowed the opportunity to be trained, marry and have a family (or escape the pressures to do so), socialise, gain independence or other 'social' motives, these were *secondary* in the decision-making process for the majority, if thought of at all.

---

119 Moynihan, *Speeches and Statements by Eamon de Valera, 1917–73*, p. 158.
120 Lee, *Ireland, 1912–1985*, p. 378.
121 Lambert, *Irish Women in Lancashire*, p. 15. My emphasis.

Types of Employment
for Irish Women in Britain:
More than Just Nurses and 'Skivvies'?

T he most common referents many people have when thinking about Irish women's employment in Britain are nursing and domestic service. As with most stereotypes, there is an element of truth, as many Irish women worked as servants and nurses, and in fact specifically sought out these areas of employment. There is also a larger body of evidence on these employment types, and oral history collections always include women in these occupations. This chapter examines the rhetoric and evidence on the experience of Irish women who worked as nurses and servants, but will also broaden out to discuss other occupations that Irish women participated in using new evidence from the travel permit files from the Second World War. Irish women often experienced greater career mobility than men, with many able to obtain white-collar jobs inaccessible to them in Ireland, and which continued to be unavailable to their male immigrant peers.[1] They also engaged in some daring and exciting occupations during the Second World War that have so far remained outside the broad perception of Irish women's lives in Britain.

Throughout the years 1939 to 1945, the number of Irish women going to Britain to domestic service jobs greatly outnumbered those going to agricultural, nursing and factory work. Table 7.1 details the breakdown by gender and occupational group of emigrants regulated through the travel permit system in the 1940s.[2] For men, the most common occupation was as unskilled workers,

---

1 Irish travel permit applications made to the Irish High Commissioner in London reveal that whilst many women obtained permits initially to work in service, they often managed to access better-paid and higher-status work in factories, the transport system and in offices.

2 As noted in Chapter 1, these statistics are not definitive; there are different estimates contained in different documents. For example, from 1943 to 1947, a total of 42,098

Table 7.1   Numbers of persons from the 26 counties receiving
new travel permits and passports to go to employment,
by gender and occupational group, 1941–1948

Occupational group	1941	1942	1943	1944	1945	1946	1947	1948
			Males					
Agriculture	1,733	4,767	3,588	1,361	3,148	2,418	4,607	5,442
Food, drink and tobacco	200	377	368	34	189	188	178	204
Textiles, clothing	191	279	213	21	154	116	141	301
Wood workers	1,448	1,231	754	141	425	193	131	266
Metal workers	1,402	1,734	1,147	186	308	229	226	425
Building	2,655	1,172	1,473	226	632	402	210	534
Clerks and other skilled workers	3,165	3,873	3,468	1,414	2,085	1,367	1,468	2,997
Unskilled workers (excluding builders' labourers)	21,035	23,830	18,310	4,340	6,244	5,916	5,550	11,553
Total males	31,829	37,263	29,321	7,723	13,185	10,829	12,511	21,722
			Females					
Agriculture	176	657	422	307	466	322	205	201
Nursing	785	2,233	2,838	1,125	3,523	3,893	2,531	912
Domestic service and housekeeping	1,343	6,037	9,125	2,760	4,719	12,077	13,166	12,353
Clerical work	179	461	363	107	207	254	292	429
Other	789	5,060	6,255	1,591	1,694	2,659	2,533	4,458
Total females	3,272	14,448	19,003	5,890	10,609	19,205	18,727	18,353
Total males and females	35,101	51,711	48,324	13,613	23,794	30,034	31,238	40,075

Note: As from the 5 January 1948, travel permits were discontinued, and Police identity cards were substituted.
Source: Central Statistics Office, *Statistical Abstract of Ireland 1949* (Dublin: Stationery Office), Table 32.

with a total of 96,788 men in this group. There were 61,580 female domestic servants who emigrated between 1941 and 1948, representing 56 per cent of the total (109,507) recorded number of women issued travel documentation. Nursing accounted for 17,840 women obtaining travel permits, representing only 16 per cent of the female cohort, although it is likely that many women emigrated to take up this work rather than being trained already: it was noted that many emigrants 'put down the occupation which it is hoped to follow abroad rather than the occupation actually followed at home'.[3] In oral history collections, it is revealed that many men and women had no experience of working in their chosen occupation before emigrating.

Silvia Pedraza has shown that these occupational groupings are common to many immigrant women entering the labour market in their new country: 'most of them cluster in just a few occupations. They become domestic servants, work for the garment industry, donate their labour to family enterprises, or most recently, work in highly skilled service occupations, such as nursing'.[4]

Information on women leaving for Britain is, for many reasons, less rich than that which details their return during the Second World War. The return application forms for travel permits required women to state their occupation (even if they were not working outside the home). The forms also capture female religious, working in various roles in convents across Britain, a group rarely classified as emigrants but who nonetheless also had to comply with the wartime rules for leaving Britain. Furthermore, specific titles for people's work are given, as defined by the applicant, and while this makes it more difficult to group them it reveals a rich array of nuanced detail in every sector. Women describe themselves as 'housewives', 'on home duties' and as 'householders' in the forms; they reveal their specialisations in nursing or the different roles in domestic service they occupy, such as daily domestic, linen maid, parlour maid or lady's companion (a role it might have been assumed had fallen away by the early 1940s). The extant records, as detailed in Chapter 1, consist of a greater number of female applications, most particularly due to the prevalence of evacuating children or visiting children previously sent to Ireland,[5] but also because women applicants occupied jobs that allowed them time off, such as in nursing or in state-regulated factory work.

women went to domestic service jobs compared with 1,675 to agricultural jobs, 12,772 to nursing and 9,863 to factory work. Calculations are made from Department of External Affairs, Memorandum dated 30 August 1947, NAI, DFA 402/25: 'Female Workers to Great Britain and Northern Ireland', Table (p. 4).

3 Meenan, *The Irish Economy Since 1922*, p. 211.

4 Silvia Pedraza, 'Women and Migration: The Social Consequences of Gender', p. 314, *Annual Review of Sociology*, 17 (1991), pp. 303–325.

5 Jennifer Redmond, 'Immigrants, Aliens, Evacuees: Exploring the History of Irish Children in Britain During the Second World War', *Journal of the History of Childhood and Youth*, 9.2 (2016), pp. 295–308.

As Table 7.2 shows, a remarkable array of occupations were reported by Irish women working in Britain, a spectrum ranging from the unskilled and temporary (daily domestic worker) to the highly specialised (doctors, dentists and radiographers, to name just a few in the medical field). This cache of records broadens our understanding of the places Irish women occupied in the British economy, but it also confirms and expands our evidence base on what we already know: Irish women worked in significant numbers in both nursing and domestic service, each of which will be discussed next.

Table 7.2   Occupational sectors of Irish women applicants for return travel permits (1940s)

Occupation category	Numbers of women	Self-described job titles
Actor/artist/ musician/writer/ collector	16	Actress, journalist/writer, artist, musician, antique dealer/art collector
Agriculture	89	Farmer, farm labourer, milk trade, poultry attendant
Air Raid Protection/ Home Defence	33	Air raid protection, ambulance attendant, ambulance driver, First Aid, Post worker
Business owner	31	Hotel/boarding house owner, licensed victualler, off-licence proprietor
Clerical and office work	402	Book keeper, civil service, clerk, insurance agent/worker, office supervisor, receptionist, secretary, shorthand typist/typist, stenographer, postal worker
Cooking and catering work	579	Assistant cook, baker, buffet attendant, canteen worker, cook, counterhand, NAAFI worker, refreshment room attendant, attendant (unspecified)
Domestic and personal service	3,203	Chambermaid, children's nurse/nursemaid/ mother's help, companion, daily domestic/ char woman, domestic servant, general maid, kitchen maid, ladies' maid, linen maid, laundry worker, nursery worker, pantry maid, parlour maid, sewing maid
Education	198	Governess, lecturer, student/school girl, teacher/assistant school teacher

Occupation category	Numbers of women	Self-described job titles
Factory work	933	Aircraft worker, barrage balloon maker/operator, capstan operator, factory inspector/supervisor, factory worker, food production/packaging, foreman/supervisor, machine operator/machinist, metal worker, mill worker, munitions worker
Government employee	84	Bus conductress, policeman [sic]
Independent means	11	Private means/independently wealthy
Managerial	64	Hotel manageress, manageress
Medical field	4,421	ARP/Civil Nursing Reserve/First Aid/Red Cross, dentist, doctor, maternity (midwife/pupil midwife), Matron, Nurse probationer, specialist, State Registered or Staff Nurse, Ward sister, Nurse assistant, Nurse companion, Orderly, Private nurse
Religious	163	Religious in nursing, religious in teaching, religious in training, religious sister
Retired	28	No details are given as to former occupations
Sales and service industry	1,122	Bar attendant, barmaid, caretaker, commercial traveller, cashier, chauffeur, chemist's assistant, cinema operator, cloakroom attendant, grocer/grocer's assistant, hairdresser, hotel worker, masseuse/beautician, porter in hotel/warehouse/railway, security guard, shop assistant, storekeeper/warehouse storekeeper, telephone operator, usherette, waitress
Textiles	161	Clothing/textile worker, dress maker, spinner, tailor
Unemployed	47	No previous occupation given
Unpaid work in the home	2,869	Caring for a relative, home duties, householder, housewife, unpaid domestic duties
Manual work	63	Brewery worker, carpenter, carpenter and joiner, council worker (manual work), dumper/tractor/heavy machine operator, electrician, engineer, fitter/fitter's mate, ganger, general labourer, skilled labourer, motor mechanic, painter/painter and decorator, railway worker, telephone manual worker, wood worker, chemical worker

Occupation category	Numbers of women	Self-described job titles
Women's Auxiliary Services	14	Women's Land Army, Women's Royal Navy Service
Miscellaneous	135	This category is composed of applicants who gave unclear job titles, or those that could not be categorised with other occupational groupings and also includes the following for the purposes of this table: horse trade worker, photographer/ photographic/ lithographic worker, missionary/ religious charity worker, social worker
Missing information	586	This category encompasses those forms that failed to include any information on occupation
Total	15,252	

Note: In creating the categories in Table 7.2, I have used my own judgement as to how to classify self-described employment titles, and at times a subjective approach had to be taken to interpret the information. For example, a number of women claimed to be an 'attendant', without specifying to what they attended. I had seen multiple examples of 'refreshment room attendant' and decided they meant in some way they were attending to food or refreshments, although others could interpret this to mean another occupation. *Source*: Figures calculated from Department of Foreign Affairs Travel Permit Files.

Irish Women in Nursing

Nursing was an area of employment that opened the possibility for Irish women emigrants of a lifelong career, rather than merely a job, and Irish nurses continue to constitute a large proportion of Ireland's 'medical diaspora'.[6] The British and Irish nursing bodies cooperated so that a nurse trained in either country could transfer to the register of the other, a continuation of arrangements established in 1919.[7] This allowed women

6 Redmond, 'The Thermometer and the Travel Permit', p. 93.
7 Information in the transcript of evidence given by Miss Healy (President), Miss Grogan (Secretary) and Mrs Nix (Member of the Executive) on behalf of the Irish Nurses' Organisation, 14 January 1948. Arnold Marsh papers, Trinity College Dublin MSS 8307–8308/11. The Irish Free State seceded from the General Nursing Council set up for Ireland in 1919 but the similarity of the standard of training in both countries meant qualifications were recognised in each. See Political and Economic Planning, *Report on the British Health Services: A Survey of the Existing Health Services in Great Britain with Proposals for Future Development* (London: Political and Economic Planning, 1937), p. 167.

the option of returning to Ireland with a skill should they wish. Daniels has highlighted the 'special economic and cultural niche occupied in Britain by Irish nurses', illustrating the importance of this sector as well as the higher visibility Irish women had in this occupation.[8] According to Ewart, the 'image of the nurse in both England and Ireland was bound up with ideals of femininity including self-sacrifice' and duty, thus ideological beliefs about the appropriateness of nursing as an occupation for women were shared in both countries.[9] It was also an area of employment that prevented 'the formation of a strong working-class stereotype such as attaches to Irish males' or to Irish women in domestic service.[10] The opportunities provided by nursing were thus not only economic but also related to improvements in status, skills and lifelong career opportunities. The idea of 'betterment' is neatly encapsulated in a quotation from Dr Doolin in a transcript of evidence of the Commission on Emigration and Other Population Problems: 'Recently my wife had some trouble with a recalcitrant maid who threatened to go to England to take up nursing'.[11] The maid was signalling to her employer that she did not have to put up with her job as a servant; nursing is used here as the epitome of superior status.

Nursing was a profession that required fees to complete training in Ireland, but was free in some hospitals in Britain, attracting Irish women excluded from such an opportunity at home:

> You might say why didn't I try to get into [nursing in] Ireland, but you had to pay a big fee. I thought I might as well be paid something rather than pay a big fee, and I didn't have it anyway.[12]

According to one Dublin matron in 1946, this fee was 20 guineas (£21).[13] While the matron described this fee as 'nominal', it may still have been out of the reach of many working-class women. The fact that women were given just a small stipend whilst training was also a barrier. In Britain, between £40 and £100 a year could be expected in the first three years of

---

8   Daniels, *Exile or Opportunity?*, p. 4.

9   Ewart, 'Caring for Migrants', p. 284.

10 Ibid. See also Bronwen Walter, 'Irishness, Gender, and Place' and *Outsiders Inside*; and Louise Ryan, '"I Had a Sister in England": Family-Led Migration, Social Networks and Irish Nurses', *Journal of Ethnic and Migration Studies*, 34.3 (2008), pp. 453–470. Ryan's study is based on interviews with twenty-six Irish women who went into nursing in Britain.

11 Transcript of evidence of the Irish Nurses' Organisation, Friday, 14 January 1948. Arnold Marsh papers, Trinity College Dublin MSS 8307–8308/11.

12 Quote from Josephine who left Clare in 1936 to train as a nurse, in Lynch, *The Irish in Exile*, p. 11. See also Muldowney, *The Second World War and Irish Women*.

13 Quoted in *Irish Times*, 12 October 1946.

training along with free uniform, followed by higher wages and access to a pension for trained staff.[14] There was more to the issue than money, however. The attractions of working in British hospitals under the new Rushcliffe scheme[15] were not simply the better pay and conditions but also the culture of discipline and control, perceived as less restrictive than in Ireland. In the words of one anonymous commentator, one 'of the greatest grievances of nurses in training in Ireland is what has been described as the "ridiculous red tape, pin-pricking and schoolroom discipline" employed in hospitals' in Ireland.[16] This is not to say that British hospitals were discipline free, however, as is discussed below.

Irish women were recruited to fill the shortage of nurses in Britain, driven by the development of the welfare state and publicly funded health care in Britain. Evidence of Irish nurses from return travel permit files has revealed a diverse range of jobs and levels of seniority. Women reported working as the following: air raid protection nurse, civil nursing reserve, First Aid nurse, Red Cross nurse, maternity ward nurse, midwife, pupil midwife, matron, nurse (state registered/staff nurse), nurse assistant, nurse probationer (trainee), private nurse, religious in nursing, specialist nurse (e.g., TB) and ward sister.[17] Some of these specialisms, and the particular context of the Second World War, may have provided Irish women with career opportunities unavailable to them at home, and added to the draw of British hospitals. One such emigrant was Mary Nugent from County Wicklow who worked at the South Lodge hospital during the war, pictured in Figure 7.1 in her travel permit.

Gertrude Gaffney's series of articles in 1936 specifically addressed the dangers to Irish women entering mental hospitals to be trained as psychiatric nurses. She stated dramatically: 'I don't believe there was a rescue worker in either Liverpool or London who did not tell me to beg Irish girls not to take positions as nurses in English mental hospitals'.[18] One of the objections to this work for women was because many mental hospitals were located some distance from Catholic churches and thus women were in danger of 'losing' their faith. This was also an area of the profession that saw greater numbers

14 Ibid.
15 Throughout the 1940s, there were efforts made to improve pay and working conditions for nurses in Britain to increase recruitment. The Rushcliffe Committee, established in 1941, examined pay and conditions and the 1943 Nurses Act initiated a Roll of Assistant Nurses with a two-year training requirement. The National Health Service was established on 5 July 1948.
16 *Irish Times*, 12 October 1946.
17 See Redmond, 'The Thermometer and the Travel Permit'.
18 *Irish Independent*, 12 December 1936. A report by an official from the Ministry of Labour in June 1942 refers to a visit made by them to Dublin. Gertrude Guffney [*sic*] of the *Irish Independent* is mentioned in a list of those met with. TNA PRO LAB 26/9.

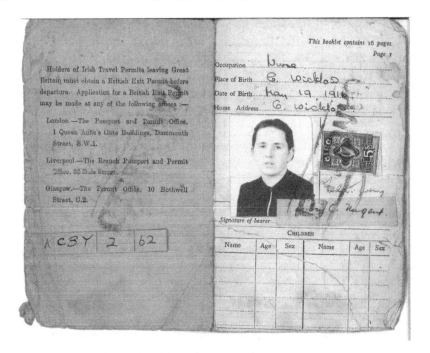

Figure 7.1   Travel permit belonging to Mary Nugent.
Reproduced with permission of her grandson, Joe Glennon.

of male nurses and orderlies working alongside women.[19] As Gaffney noted, lonely, isolated Irish girls may find themselves 'a ripe victim for a bored and unscrupulous attendant'.[20] Fears about women's safety working as nurses in Britain appear to be overblown given the evidence from both Irish and British women on the protections offered by the regime of training and the special concern and attention that was often shown to Irish women. As Nancy Lyons (who left Kerry in 1943) recalled, she and other girls who were newly arrived received specific consideration:

> We were very protected really. I think they did have a conception of the young girl leaving home for the first time, y'know. There was such a lot of staff looking after you, who were very protective towards you. They were really very patient people and they were very good.[21]

---

19 Dónall Mac Amhlaigh, author of the famous memoir, *An Irish Navvy: The Diary of an Exile* (London: Routledge & Kegan Paul, 1964) emigrated to England to work first in a psychiatric hospital before leaving for the more lucrative career of labouring.
20 *Irish Independent*, 12 December 1936.
21 Lennon *et al.*, *Across the Water*, p. 172.

Irish women trained and worked with other Irish female emigrants; indeed, they were often in the majority in training schools.[22] This may have made them feel less alienated.[23]

Gaffney also stated that the girls who went as wardsmaids may have found the job too physically demanding and quit to go to domestic service. Given the widespread accounts of the arduous nature of domestic service in this era this seems a rather strange assertion, and, again, no concrete evidence was offered. Gaffney also referred to the fact that many girls pretended they were nurses in their letters home when in fact they were lowly wardsmaids 'deriving a snobbish satisfaction from her small deception', which depicts female emigrants as prideful. Whether this was snobbish satisfaction or mere excitement, it seems harsh to criticise them for it.

Networks were key in nursing. Several of Lambert's interviewees emigrated with their sisters to take up nursing positions in Britain. Theresa's sister was already a nurse and wanted a companion, so Theresa emigrated with her in 1948. Agnes got a post in a hospital, but her mother insisted she didn't go alone:

The War was on and my mother was very much against us going to England ... I had applied to this hospital, Birch Hill in Rochdale, Lancashire and got accepted. But me mother was determined that we both go. I don't really know did my sister want to go that much: she kinda drifted into it because I was going.[24]

This 'chain migration' phenomenon characterised much Irish emigration and is verified by Ryan's more recent study of Irish nurses in Britain.[25] Familial networks played a significant role in instigating emigration, but also in keeping women protected.

Lack of education is also referred to and Gaffney asserted that, of those who trained as nurses, 'few of them survive any length of time, as they have not the education to absorb the theoretical portion of the training and take examinations'.[26] This commentary suggests that women without education (that is, working-class women) should perhaps limit their 'snobbish' aspirations and accept work more 'fitting' to their abilities. This language is typical of Gaffney's articles, which do not include the voices of women who are

---

22 Daniels, *Exile or Opportunity?*, p. 15.
23 Kathleen Ruth reports that there were mainly Irish women training to be nurses during the war because many English women had been conscripted. Uncatalogued oral history interview, Smurfitt Archive, London Metropolitan University.
24 Lambert, *Irish Women in Lancashire*, p. 24.
25 See Ryan, "'I Had a Sister in England'".
26 Ibid.

themselves emigrants, but rather discusses them from the point of view of expert opinions (both hers and others). In Ireland, recruits were required to have a Leaving Certificate, and while many of the teaching hospitals in Britain also required high levels of education, many regional hospitals were prepared to take women without these.[27] As one of Daniels's interviewees remarked, this was her only chance to enter the profession: 'I had had to leave school at 14 ... even if my father could have found the fees, you needed a bike – the convent school was miles away so the British hospitals were the only ones open to someone without qualifications'.[28] Lack of money rather than a lack of intellectual ability thus drove many women to pursue nursing in Britain.

Evidence from British oral history collections is also interesting to consider. Mrs Maden, an English woman interviewed as part of a project on British nursing, had worked in a hospital after her training that was commonly referred to as the 'Irish Hospital' due to the predominance of Irish women and the heavy influence of a Roman Catholic matron.[29] The Matron appears to have been a zealous convert to Catholicism and Mrs Maden recalls her proselytising. The Matron went on missions to Ireland, and located 'Irish farm girls and girls from convents you know, all mad keen to get to London', through priests. The religious culture engendered by the control of this matron seems to have thoroughly infused this hospital:

> She would have liked to staff the whole hospital with Roman Catholics, she was really fanatical, you know, she had very little patience even with Protestant patients you know, 'cos if they were Roman Catholic they had, you know, their red disc, red disc on the bed, the Protestants had yellow.

As I have argued elsewhere, Mrs Maden's anecdotal evidence suggests a particular hospital environment imbricated with both Irishness and fervid religiosity, but her account provokes questions of how the presence of so many Irish nurses and doctors in Britain may have impacted or influenced hospitals in Britain.[30] It also offers a counterpoint to contemporary fears that Irish women were prevented by hospitals from practising their religion.

27 Daniels, *Exile or Opportunity?*, p. 10.
28 Ibid.
29 Interview by Christopher Maggs with Mrs Maden, Royal College of Nursing History Group Interviews, British Library Sound Archive, C545/21/01. Kathleen Ruth was of the opinion that 'Invariably the Sister Would be Irish' in many English hospitals. Smurfitt Archive, London Metropolitan University.
30 Such questions could be best answered by detailed comparative local studies of British hospitals that employed Irish and other ethnic minorities and is beyond the scope of this book.

Discipline was seen to be an essential part of the training for a professional nurse, and despite claims of life being easier in British hospitals there are numerous examples of discipline being imposed on trainee nurses. An anonymous writer to the *Irish Times* wished to reveal the reality behind false 'pictures of a milk-and-honey existence' she thought were being circulated as debates comparing pay and conditions in Ireland and Britain raged in the Autumn of 1946:

> We can never take a phone call here. We can under no conditions have visitors ... Just imagine, I can't ask my uncle ... to see me, nor can I ever ask my brother to call on me if he ever came on a short trip to England ... We never have a Sunday off, and we work 66 hours in the week.[31]

Other instances of discipline and control emerge from oral histories. Frances was chastised for going to the cinema with a married soldier patient, despite it being a platonic relationship.[32] Maira Curran's experience appears to be fairly standard in terms of the imposition of curfew rules: 'When you stay out the night, you have to sign a book to say that you are not coming back, but the following evening you have to be in before ten'.[33] Her previous experience of convent life prepared her for these rules, but after a while she finally experienced some rebellious feelings and ignored them, resulting in her being dismissed from her job. Similarly, Mrs Pearce reported that the rules were simple and were automatically obeyed: 'Lights out at a certain time, you didn't talk back ... you didn't go off duty, you walked quietly down the corridors'.[34]

The experience of previously being in a convent or a boarding school is common to accounts of women in nursing and was reported by some as helping them cope with the confines of nursing life. Mrs Maden, for example, stated this explicitly: 'Being a nurse was like being in a convent, it was a very enclosed world'.[35] While her lack of experience of Catholic life may have coloured her view (she was a Protestant), this analogy resonates with the testimony of Irish Catholic women also. The restrictions associated with nursing referred to by many interviewees serves to create the impression that women were protected while training and working as nurses, and many were in the care of religious orders who ran hospitals or provided housing.

31 *Irish Times*, 16 October 1946.
32 Muldowney, 'The Impact of the Second World War on Women in Belfast and Dublin', vol. 1, p. 163.
33 Schweitzer, *Across the Irish Sea*, p. 61.
34 Interview by Christopher Maggs with Mrs Pearce, Royal College of Nursing History Group Interviews, British Library Sound Archive, C545/26/01-02.
35 Interview by Christopher Maggs with Mrs Maden, Royal College of Nursing History Group Interviews, British Library Sound Archive, C545/21/01.

While it would be wrong to suggest a universal picture of strict regimes and dour matrons (there is much evidence of mischief making and illicit fun in memoirs from the period), the idea of protection and discipline was strong, which counters popular ideas of women in nursing as being morally vulnerable. Domestic service, however, was viewed almost universally as quite a dangerous undertaking.

Irish Women and Domestic Service

Domestic service provided employment opportunities for Irish women emigrants in the nineteenth and twentieth centuries in America and Great Britain where Irish women filled the gap left by native women turning away from this work, much like Irish women were in their own country.[36] Two opposing strands of discourse emerged on the issue of Irish women emigrants' involvement in domestic service. On the one hand, it was claimed Irish women would not be safe in English homes, particularly because they would generally be Protestant or Jewish (that is, not Roman Catholic). On the other, a contrary discourse emerges from accounts from emigrants themselves. Personal testimonies detail the lack of freedom that often went with service jobs, as well as recollections of great care and facilitation from employers specifically because they were inexperienced at both work and living away from home. Few articles commented on domestic service from a more realistic standpoint – that Irish women were attracted by better conditions and wages for similar work that allowed them to send home remittances. Not even the existence of what Hearn terms 'Biddyism', or the lampooning of Irish women in domestic service, seemed to deter women from entering service in Britain.[37]

Irish women were far more willing to respond to the need for service work in Britain than they were in Ireland. Why was this so? The answer appears to have had financial as well as psychological or emotional aspects. Women earned more at this type of work in Britain; there were more avenues of employment (for example, in hospitals, hotels, boarding schools, restaurants and the more expansive British service sector as well as private homes); conditions were often better; fares were often paid by employers;[38] and Irish women seemed to feel that they attained a higher social status in Britain for engaging in this work than they did in Ireland. Whether this was actually the

36 In this regard it is interesting to note that in 1947 the government considered the possibility of bringing foreign women into the country to fill the shortfall in domestic workers. See *Dáil Éireann Debates*, vol. 105, cols. 1690–1691, 30 April 1947.

37 Hearn, *Below Stairs*, p. 103.

38 Sometimes fares were paid outright and sometimes they were taken back week by week through wages.

case was a disputed matter as the discussion of marriage prospects in Chapter 5 indicated. Even those who advocated reducing the number of female emigrants admitted that the conditions of domestic work in Ireland were driving women away. As a contributor to the *Irish Catholic* stated:

> Some wealthy employers think that a fire in the kitchen is quite unnecessary, even in winter. Club life and the restaurant habit of many employers nowadays often meant that the servant, for five days out of seven, is not properly fed.[39]

Loneliness and the lack of personal warmth between servants and employers are also alluded to in many sources.

Aversion to domestic service in Ireland received much coverage in the press. There were frequent admonitions against the negative images perpetrated of domestic work in modern society. Father Degen, for example, argued that service should not be viewed as lower in status than factory jobs because 'the training in household duties and the discipline which domestic service imparts would contribute much to a girl's future efficiency as a wife and to her happiness as a mother'.[40] This valorisation of domestic skills overlooks the drudgery many felt was involved in the job. It also implied that being a servant was similar to being a wife and mother, despite the fact that the reality involved 'a complete break with home, friends and a familiar way of life' and 'entailed living in a dependent and subordinate position in the home of people who were not only strangers, but who were also of a different social class with different habits, values and lifestyle'.[41]

Father Degen was not alone in his glorification of domestic service training. Up to the 1940s, there were 'constant recommendations by government commissions and women's organisations [...] that girls be trained as domestic servants, when it should have been clear that Irish girls and women were forsaking this kind of work in huge numbers'.[42] The idea that women were rebelling from their domestic roles emerged frequently within newspapers, although Ireland did not experience a mass movement for women's emancipation and equality until much later. This indicates a certain paranoia regarding women's acceptance of traditional roles that centred on domestic instruction and whether this should be taught more rigorously in schools. The concern in newspapers about the domestic 'prowess' of young girls seemed twofold: first,

39 *Irish Catholic*, 31 December 1936.
40 Fr Degen was the author of the 'Pointers' column in *Irish Catholic*. *Irish Catholic*, 2 March 1929.
41 Hearn, *Below Stairs*, p. 3. Interestingly, the importance of domestic skills to attain a respectable post was also stressed in Magdalen asylums for unmarried mothers.
42 Clear, *Women of the House*, p. 2.

that they did not value a role in the home; and second, that they emigrated unprepared and unskilled, running the risk of only finding employment that 'endangered their morals', a somewhat coded reference to employment in 'low-class' establishments (such as hostels and cheap hotels) where Irish women may have run the risk of becoming involved in prostitution.[43] Father Degen represents the most extreme end of the spectrum of opinion when he wrote in 1931: 'It is better for a girl not to be educated, if the price to be paid for education is a revulsion against housework and motherhood'.[44]

Another issue was whether the state should be involved in educating or training people to *facilitate* their emigration. Cork appears to have been at the centre of much of the debate as initiatives were taken in the city and county to respond to the alleged need for domestic training. In 1923, it was announced that the Midleton Technical Instruction committee were awarded funds from the Ministry of Commerce and Industry[45] to provide full-time courses on domestic subjects for unemployed women between eighteen and thirty-five years of age 'with a view to fitting them to accept situations in indoor domestic service'.[46] The women were to receive a maintenance allowance of £1 per week during training with financial penalties incurred if they were late or failed to attend.

It is interesting to note the anticipated apathy; the scheme would go ahead if they could find women willing to undertake the training. Given that the course was designed for just thirty-one women, and that it was being provided at a time of unemployment in the area, it seems odd there was any question that women would enrol.[47] The issue of domestic training persisted in Cork. In 1935, TD for Cork West, Eamonn O'Neill, asked the Minister for Education, Thomas Derrig, whether he would 'undertake, in connection with the local vocational committees, to increase the facilities for the instruction and training of such girls so as to equip them properly to take up domestic positions abroad'.[48] The Minister replied:

> I agree that it is very desirable to provide suitable instruction and training for girls who take up domestic service [...] but I do not accept

---

43 Nolan has argued that prostitution, along with domestic service, was one of the only avenues open to unskilled women at home in Ireland, thus limited economic opportunities always implied this 'moral risk' for women, regardless of emigration. Nolan, *Ourselves Alone*, p. 63.

44 *Irish Catholic*, 5 September 1931.

45 This was the name of the department at the time – it later changed to the Department of Industry and Commerce.

46 *Irish Times*, 23 January 1923.

47 See also *Irish Independent*, 24 January 1923.

48 *Dáil Éireann Debates*, vol. 55, cols. 1239–1240, 21 March 1935.

the view expressed in the latter part of the question that training facilities should be increased specially to equip girls to take up domestic or other positions abroad rather than at home.[49]

The spectre of the 'emigration agent' rose again.

The Irish Women Workers' Union (IWWU) also pushed for the training of domestic servants at a conference in 1936 in response to newspaper commentary on the issue (most notably, Gaffney's articles).[50] The conference proposed a Training School for domestic servants. The effect, conference participants felt, would be that 'the task of keeping Irish girls at home would be rendered more practicable' and would avoid what the Cork Chamber of Commerce claimed was the experience of the majority – that they were 'ill-equipped to earn a decent livelihood' should they leave Ireland.[51] Training, it seemed, was also the way to avoid moral danger: 'Untrained workers are no more wanted in another country than they are at home. And note that it is only the untrained that become the unwanted. The capable, industrious girl makes good anywhere'.[52]

The idea that women were not properly trained and were domestically incompetent is an element of the discourses that is paradoxical to say the least – if Irish women were the ideal homemakers, as evoked in the 1937 Constitution and elsewhere, why were they not passing these skills on to their daughters? Interestingly the Bishop of Achonry viewed the responsibility to ensure girls were properly trained as lying not with the government but with her parents and warned:

the parents of those girls who intended to go abroad [of] the absolute necessity of being properly fitted and trained for whatever work they meant to engage in. They should endeavour, as far as they could, to see that they got a course of training in domestic science and general household management.[53]

It is notable that, unlike other commentary, he does not single out mothers as responsible, but both parents. Dr Gilmartin also warned that girls must be qualified if they were to avoid joining the 'waifs and strays in city squares'.[54] This, he argued, was in direct contrast to their male counterparts: 'Boys on the whole do well enough abroad, but this cannot be said for a

---

49 Ibid.
50 *Irish Catholic*, 2 January 1937; The Irish Independent, 22 January 1937.
51 *Irish Independent*, 22 January 1937.
52 *Irish Catholic*, 31 December 1936.
53 *Irish Catholic*, 4 July 1936.
54 *Irish Catholic*, 15 August 1936.

large percentage of girls'.[55] This is despite the fact that the majority of male emigrants were also unskilled workers and thus also ran the risk of being unsuitable for the job they were hired for.

Negative perceptions of domestic work in Ireland are recounted in personal testimonies. Noreen Hill, a Cork migrant interviewed as part of Lennon *et al.*'s study, was one of the women who rejected domestic service in Ireland:

> there was nothing there [Cork] for us at all. We couldn't find any work, unless you went to scivvy, scrub floors or something like that, you know. That's the only kind of work, and that was very poorly paid. But no way would I do that, I was always very proud, you know, and I wouldn't go down on my knees for anybody.[56]

Hill's disgust at this work reflects the status it was accorded in Ireland. Hill blames her own pride, but would her pride have been as prohibitive if the work was regarded more positively?

This attitude can also be found in the surveys of migrants made as part of the Commission on Emigration and Other Population Problems. Commissioners Geary and O'Leary commented that 'Girls whose pride would not let them go to domestic work in Ireland have no such feeling about such work in Britain'.[57] Thus pride, and not economic motivations, aspirations for a better quality of life or the fulfilment of personal ambitions, is attributed as the sole reason why women will not take similar jobs in Ireland.

Despite the fact that Irish women flocked to domestic service jobs in Britain because they were seen as higher status, some have argued that Irish women were perceived as lower in social and racial terms in Britain. Holden has revealed that Irish women were often given rough jobs that English women would not do[58] and Rossiter has argued that 'Irish women were considered unsuitable for work which brought them into close contact with their employers' when working in service.[59] Two women in Ryan's study stated they were consistently mocked by British servants in their households

55 Ibid.
56 Lennon *et al.*, *Across the Water*, pp. 93–94.
57 'Survey in Emigration Areas', Report prepared by Dr R.C. Geary and Mr F. O'Leary, Carrick-on-Shannon, 23 September 1948. Arnold Marsh papers, Trinity College Dublin MS 8306/S4.
58 Katherine Holden, 'Personal Costs and Personal Pleasures: Care and the Unmarried Woman in Inter-War Britain', in Janet Fink (ed.), *Care: Personal Lives and Social Policy* (Bristol: Policy Press, 2004), p. 58.
59 Ann Rossiter, 'In Search of Mary's Past: Placing Nineteenth-Century Irish Immigrant Women in British Feminist History', in Joan Grant (ed.), *Women, Migration and Empire* (Stoke-on-Trent: Trentham Books: 1996), p. 16.

for not knowing about 'exotic wines and cheeses and fine foods' thereby reinforcing the cultural stereotype of Irish people as ignorant and backward.[60] The move away from domestic service by British women created opportunities for Irish women, but the discourses reveal that they were viewed by some as inferior for taking them. The *Irish Independent* reported on the British Labour Ministry's committee to investigate the 'servant problem' in 1923. They found that British women were choosing unemployment rather than domestic service as they regarded it as 'a degrading occupation'. When questioned as to why she would not undertake employment in service, one girl was reported as replying that 'all her family had always been respectable'.[61] Irish women therefore fulfilled the lower status jobs within a low status occupation. Despite all this, domestic service in Britain appears to have been preferable to engaging in similar work at home.

Allusions to moral dangers for Irish women engaged in domestic service in English cities were made repeatedly. Dr MacNeely warned in his Lenten Pastoral of 1930: 'Those who knew modern cities could easily imagine how such girls [domestics] might be led to ruin'.[62] Thus the city *and* the job posed risks for women. The *Irish Press* entered the debate by proclaiming in 1931 that:

Pitfalls await the unwary, and girls going direct from an Irish village to the teeming life of an industrial centre, do not realise that they are in peril. The shocking death of Annie Haughney, a young Irish girl, who was found impaled on the railing of a building called the Derby Hotel, Marylebone Road, London, recently, brings this aspect of emigration vividly to public notice. 'Unfortunately, she did not make her presence in London known to any recognised organisation, so far as can be learned, otherwise she would not have found herself in an hotel of questionable repute, a fact which was revealed at the inquest'.[63]

The quotation within this excerpt appears to be from an unnamed social worker connected with the ICGPS, and reiterates their message that girls would not be safe if they did not go through the 'proper' channels. There was no hegemonic experience of domestic service. It should not be presumed that all women working in domestic service were in danger because the evidence shows that many others had either the opposite experience of that posed by Gaffney and others, or a far more mundane one.

60 Ryan, 'Moving Spaces and Changing Places', p. 75.
61 *Irish Independent*, 16 May 1923.
62 *Irish Catholic*, 8 March 1930.
63 *Irish Press*, 16 October 1931.

Unsurprisingly, messages about the dangers of the city permeated the consciousness of emigrants. Some of Ryan's interviewees described being nervous walking around by themselves on their days off. Molly specifically referred to the dangers of the white slave trade, reporting two stories about girls she knew of that she thought were related to this phenomenon.[64] Regardless of fears for their own safety, oral history interviews with Irish women often reveal they had little freedom in their employment, which in itself acted as a form of 'protection'. Molly Allsop, interviewed as part of Pam Schweitzer's *Across the Irish Sea* collection, left Fermoy in 1929 in response to an advertisement her aunt found. She states that it was both the rigidity in terms of her employer's standards of behaviour and concern for her as a young woman from Ireland that restricted her:

> I think I missed my freedom most of all. When you're working in place for a living, you've got to abide by their times. You can't just down tools and go off. You can't just say, 'I'm going off for a couple of hours'. Anyway, I had nowhere to go on my afternoons off. I'd go and sit on the common on my own. I didn't make any friends at all outside the job. You don't get a chance when you work for these real old fashioned people. They didn't believe in that at all. I think they were worried in case I'd go off the rails and they were responsible for me, bringing me over from Ireland, you see.[65]

Molly's loneliness in the house led her to go and talk to some Irish men who were doing repairs to the road outside, but a neighbour told her employer and she was told that she 'wasn't to go outside that door while they were out there. Oh she was very strict'.[66] Molly eventually left that job to work in a boarding house where she didn't live in and much preferred the busyness of the place, which distracted her from her homesickness. The irony is that the greater 'protections' offered by her live-in situation made her feel isolated; therefore she shunned the respectability of such a job to take up work in a friendlier environment. A similar experience is reported by Teresa Burke, an unusual case in that she turned down clerical work in Ireland to take a job as a domestic servant in Britain at the request of her mother to assist an older sister who had just given birth. Burke's mother allowed her to emigrate because her job as a parlour maid 'was a living in job and my mother allowed me to stay for the simple reason that she felt that I'd have

64 Ryan, 'Moving Spaces and Changing Places', p. 77.
65 Schweitzer, *Across the Irish Sea*, p. 7.
66 Ibid., p. 6.

to behave myself, that I'd be fed and clothed and that'.[67] Teresa had to be back at her house by 10 p.m. if she went out, and on Sundays, when she would go to a local ceilidh, this meant she had to leave early to get home. Burke comments of this: 'You couldn't have a boyfriend because nobody would leave at nine thirty!'[68]

There is further evidence that parents were comfortable when their daughters lived in their employment. Julia Griffin came to Britain in 1943 to work in service at a convent and reported that her parents 'were not too worried about letting me come, because they felt I would be looked after'.[69] Similarly, Frances was sent to a Catholic girls' boarding school in Birmingham by her mother at the age of fifteen because she was thought to be 'a bit cheeky' and the restrictions provided by domestic service in such an environment might calm her down.[70] Not all women who emigrated felt restricted by the rules on their behaviour and free time. Brigid Keenan started as a housemaid in a hotel and was told by the head housekeeper that 'When you're in this hotel, you're a member of my own family', which she enjoyed.[71]

Gaffney's criticism of domestic service blended class and religious biases in her series of special articles in 1936, particularly the 'realities' of life for Irish maids in poorer Jewish households:

These districts are thickly populated with the foreign Jews to whom I alluded in yesterday's article; in themselves in all probability quite good people, but because of their outlook on life and the conditions of employment they offer, not desirable employers for a Catholic girl brought up in the simplicity of the countryside.[72]

Gaffney asserted that 'Christian' women in the same poor economic circumstances would not employ a maid, but that Jewish women had an objection to doing housework and instead helped their husbands in their business. Although Gaffney commended the industry of such Jewish families, she clearly sees their households as unfit places for Irish women to work. There is a rather judgemental tone in this commentary that associates Irish women as the 'proper' maids of middle-class Christian women, rather than lower

---

67 Ibid., p. 35.
68 Ibid., p. 38.
69 Ibid., p. 81.
70 Muldowney, 'The Impact of the Second World War on Women in Belfast and Dublin', vol. 2, p. FS1.
71 Schweitzer, *Across the Irish Sea*, p. 94.
72 *Irish Independent*, 11 December 1936.

middle-class or working-class Jewish mistresses.[73] Despite her references to the poor standards of the Jewish household and hard domestic work, the impression is given that it is more the 'alien' cultural aspects that she is objecting to. She comments on the lack of pork in such families, referring to the need for maids to be properly nourished, disregarding the fact that they may have received other nutritious food.

Gaffney also claimed that maids in Jewish houses might sometimes be paid in clothing rather than money, making it difficult for them to leave. While this may have been true, and may have been experienced as a hardship, we don't know what such servants personally thought of that arrangement. Furthermore, Gaffney referred to the 'violent scenes' that often occurred in the houses of 'Continental Jewish people', relying on anecdotes and commonly held prejudices rather than evidence to make her point. The Jewish mistress is painted as lacking in refinement, poor and with a violent temper, the 'embodiment of the squalid, unhealthy, frightening city'.[74] This derogatory typecasting differentiates from the overall stereotype of women who employed household help, who were seen to have a benevolent and refining influence on servants. Indeed, as Ryan has argued, Gaffney's reports on such households appear to suggest 'that living among Jews may prove to have a de-nationalising influence on Irish girls', a suggestion that would have appealed to those who viewed emigration itself as an inherently anti-nationalist act.[75]

The 'degradation' resulting from employment by Jewish families was a theme that persisted. In 1948, in interviews held by the Commission on Emigration and Other Population Problems, Aodh de Blácam accused the Irish Housewives Association of spreading falsehoods by suggesting that Irish women enjoyed better conditions in Jewish rather than Irish households:

Aodh de Blácam: Would you like to see any girl you know, a daughter or a sister, go into domestic service in a decent typical Irish home where she would be treated as a member of the family, and living in exactly the same conditions and with the same material and spiritual circumstances as the family, or would you like to see that girl going to England where she will be treated (to use a vulgar expression) 'like a dog'? Would you like to see any girl in whom you had any interest going into a Jewman's [sic] house in the English slums? That is where

73 Although Ryan argues that Gaffney was 'careful to differentiate between these immigrant Jews who lived in the East End of London and other, more affluent Jews who ran very decent households in other parts of the city' (*Gender, Identity and the Irish Press*, p. 120), I do not think that Gaffney sufficiently stressed the point that there were many types of Jewish mistresses.

74 Ryan, *Gender, Identity and the Irish Press*, p. 122.

75 Ibid.

the girls are going, while they would be well treated in Ireland. In England, the 'Irish scivvy' is spoken of. That is how they regard the domestic servants, while in Ireland they are treated as one of the family. Any woman that has lived in the country towns will bear me out; if a girl goes to work in one of our Irish country homes she is treated as one of the family and nobody can hope for more.

Mrs [Andrée Sheehy] Skeffington: That is the condition in the ideal home but many are not like that.

Aodh de Blácam: That is the typical decent Irish home.

Mrs Skeffington: That is not what the Irish Housewives' Association have been led to believe.[76]

This exchange clearly reflects de Blácam's nationalistic rural bias which construed Irish households as idyllic to work in, an opinion that did not reflect the experiences of many domestics. One of Ryan's interviewees went so far as to describe her time in domestic service in Ireland as 'slavery'.[77] Furthermore, in a survey of seven intending emigrants in Galway city, Commissioner Mr McElhinney reported that the 'girls have very hard things to say about Irish employers of domestic workers, long hours of duty, bad food, and above all, lack of respect. They are treated as inferior beings who have very few rights'.[78] The qualitative evidence thus refutes de Blácam's cosy picture of life as a servant in Ireland. It also sheds light on the reasons why many left such employment to take up opportunities created by the Second World War.

Irish Women and Employment in the Second World War

The Second World War, or the Emergency, was an important moment in women's migration from Ireland: they faced the simultaneous push of unemployment in Ireland and the pull of a vastly expanded employment sector in Britain. Irish women were directly recruited by the British government through the Irish Labour Exchanges as noted in Chapter 2, many going to work in munitions factories and industries directly supporting the war effort, such as food and aircraft production.[79] They were also targeted to join the British Army's women's auxiliary forces, although this is less well known in

---

76 Transcript of evidence of Irish Housewives' Association (undated), c.1948. Arnold Marsh papers, Trinity College Dublin MSS 8307–8308/3.

77 Ryan, 'Moving Spaces and Changing Places', p. 73.

78 Rural Surveys, Arnold Marsh papers, Trinity College Dublin MS 8306/S11.

79 Redmond, 'The Largest Remaining Reserve of Manpower'.

the story of Irish migration to Britain. While this section cannot claim to be
a comprehensive history of Irish women in the British war effort, evidence
from multiple sources has been drawn together to sketch the multitude of
areas Irish women could be found in throughout the war years.[80] Connolly
has argued that the Second World War had a strong impact on Irish female
emigration and in some cases it was transformative.[81] The popularity of war
work for Irish women is understandable in the context of the added bonuses,
such as provision of accommodation and 'settling in' grants, the latter being
increased during the war period to make the work even more attractive.[82]

According to Wills, Peadar O'Donnell estimated in 1945 that 250,000 Irish
workers were in Britain, in addition to seasonal migrants.[83] Such large numbers
were an embarrassment to the neutral Irish government and, as Ó Drisceoil
observed, censorship officials were adamant that pictures of 'thousands of
starving Irish workers flocking across to the bombed areas of England or to
join the British forces' would be suppressed so that public morale was not
too 'hopelessly compromised'.[84] Throughout the war the civilian working
population and military in Britain were boosted by Irish participation on a
voluntary basis. Doherty discussed the varying evidence on the numbers of
Irish men and women involved in the British forces, which range widely from
over 42,000 to 250,000.[85] These estimates do not supply reliable breakdowns
by gender, thus it is unknown exactly how many Irish women were directly
involved in auxiliary support work for the British defence forces. They were,
however, significantly recruited to work in factories taken over to produce
both war-related technologies and consumer goods.

Women working in war-related industries were billeted in hostels or on
farms according to their occupation. Irish women in group labour schemes
were part of this movement of female labour power, yet they are not generally
highlighted in the vast literature on women's experiences of the Second World
War. Dawson's research found that hostels provided for conscripted women

---

80 For further studies of women in war work, see Enda Delaney, *Demography, State and
    Society*; Muldowney, *The Second World War and Irish Women*.
81 See Tracey Connolly, 'Irish Workers in Britain during World War Two', in Brian
    Girvin and Geoffrey Roberts (eds), *Ireland and the Second World War: Politics, Society
    and Remembrance* (Dublin: Four Courts Press, 2000), pp. 121–132.
82 The increase in 'settling in grants' in 1943 was made to facilitate the British Ministry
    of Labour and National Service in moving workers to essential duties as needed. The
    grant was for 25s. for the first week, decreasing to 10s. in the fourth week of work.
    Ministry of Labour Circ. 7/107, in TNA PRO AVIA 22/1185.
83 Wills, *That Neutral Island*, p. 314.
84 Donal Ó Drisceoil, "Whose Emergency is it?' Wartime Politics and the Irish Working
    Class, 1939–45', in Lane and Ó Drisceoil, *Politics and the Irish Working Class*, p. 267.
85 Richard Doherty, *Irish Men and Women in the Second World War*, p. 22 (Dublin: Four
    Courts Press, 1999).

workers were described as 'dreary beyond description' and lacked any organised activities for the workers' spare time.[86] Hostels were strictly managed and men (even relations) were forbidden from entering them to avoid any scandalous accusations of sexual impropriety. While Dawson's research on hostels breaks new ground concerning the lives of wartime women workers and Muldowney's work on Irish women during the war is the most thorough examination of this issue to date, yet more research is needed to investigate whether Irish women objected as strongly to the hostels as did their British counterparts.[87] As Dawson notes, many women left the hostels and commuted to work from home. This alternative was not available to Irish women, so how did they cope with isolation and boredom? Were their religious needs catered to?

Henrietta Ewart's doctoral thesis serves partially to fill the lacunae in our knowledge of Irish women's contribution to the war effort. In 1943, the British Ministry of Labour employed 1,585 female and 3,649 male Irish workers in Birmingham. Although health and leisure facilities had been set up, it was noted that the Irish did not avail themselves of them.[88] In conjunction with the Catholic Archdiocese, a new club in Selly Oak was created. This catered for the recreation and welfare needs specifically of Irish women war workers who paid 2 shillings per week to become members. The Ministry of Labour's intentions in involving themselves were not entirely pastoral; the high rate of workers around the country leaving war work because of poor conditions and homesickness was detrimental to the war effort. The club was deemed a success based on high usage and a membership of over 100. This is the only dedicated Irish club of its kind found by Ewart, but it demonstrates a recognition that transferrable Irish women workers were an important part of the British home front factory scene, and others may have existed elsewhere.

Irish Women in Wartime Factory Work

Irish women emigrated in significant numbers to engage in factory work in Britain, either continuing trades they had previously worked in or engaging in industrial work for the first time. The negative stereotypes associated with factory work for women were prevalent in Ireland but not unique. The moral appropriateness of factory work was often debated in public discourses and the

---

86 Sandra Trudgen Dawson, 'Busy and Bored: The Politics of Work and Leisure for Women Workers in Second World War British Government Hostels', *Twentieth Century British History*, 21.1 (2010), p. 30.

87 See Muldowney, *The Second World War and Irish Women*.

88 Ewart, 'Caring for Migrants', p. 258.

issue concerned not only members of the hierarchy, but also the Irish Women Workers' Union.[89] Their Annual Report for 1941–42 put the matter bluntly:

> Your Executive have made very careful inquiries concerning arrangements made by the Government to safeguard the position of such migrants, and are satisfied that care is taken to ensure as far as possible that only reputable firms may recruit Irish workers. Your executive do, however, deplore the necessity for such an exodus of our people and they sincerely hope that voluntary organisations are at work in Britain to provide safeguards for the moral and physical health of our people.[90]

The implication in this quotation is that moral and physical health were threatened by working in Britain. There is also the assumption that an English organisation of some sort will look after any problems, without any regard for the responsibilities of the Irish government in such arrangements. Workers flocked to Britain throughout the war period, largely unaware of the dramatic rhetoric on their moral welfare.

The delicate arrangements that existed between the Irish and British governments during this period were to the benefit of approximately 30,000 unemployed or underemployed women and men in Ireland who managed to navigate the new bureaucratic procedures for travelling and accessing regulated employment.[91] As A.V. Judges, official historian of the conflict observed:

> Irish workers were found to display so considerable a familiarity with the finer points of official requirements, and so ingenious a knowledge of the limits of tolerance which official routine was accustomed to observe, that a constant watch was needed to prevent the evasion of the rules.[92]

Emigrants in the group labour schemes had to be medically examined before being accepted for work and this proved to be a traumatic experience for some.[93] Mary Anne, interviewed by Lynch, described the process of being examined in Dublin after a long journey from Kerry:

> When we got to Dublin, we were met there and taken to this hotel. I'll never forget that experience, it was terrible. The way they looked at

---

89 Redmond, 'The Largest Remaining Reserve of Manpower'.

90 IWWU, Annual Report 1941–42, p. 2, Irish Labour History Archive.

91 Peggy Inman, *Labour in the Munitions Industries* (London: Her Majesty's Stationery Office, 1957), p. 56.

92 A.V. Judges, *Irish Labour in Britain, 1939–1945*, p. 15, TNA PRO LAB 8/1528. This was the official British history of the labour arrangements during the war period.

93 For a fuller description of the arrangements, see Wills, *That Neutral Island*; Delaney, *Demography, State and Society*.

Table 7.3   Numbers and percentages of women from the
26 counties recruited through the British Ministry of Labour
Group Recruitment Scheme

Year	Number of female workers	Total workers recruited	Percentage of female workers recruited
1942	3,867	31,659	12%
1943	7,653	37,604	20%
1944	2,670	14,000	19%
1945*	2,287	8,157	28%

*Figures for January to June only.
Note: The percentage is calculated as an expression of the total number of workers recruited for that year.
Source: Adapted from Enda Delaney, "'Almost a Class of Helots in an Alien Land'", Table 10.2 (p. 254).

you, we had to strip, take all our clothes off and they looked at every bit of us, at our hair and everything, before they gave us a cup of tea even. … I'll never forget that night. You can imagine, after leaving home and travelling all day to get to Dublin, first time away from home.[94]

Unfortunately, no oral history evidence exists from those who were deemed to be contagious with scabies or other ailments. This was a concern at the time as Irish people were blamed for bringing outbreaks of such diseases to Britain. In a letter from the Regional Controller, dated 16 November 1942, it was stated that due to the poor health and sometimes hygiene conditions of Irish emigrants, they would be more likely to *contract* scabies when in Britain rather than to be the source of it.[95]

Women constituted a minority of workers recruited under official group schemes, as men were mostly sought for heavier industrial work.[96] However, as Table 7.3 reveals, thousands of Irish women were recruited each year for government-controlled factory work. Between 1942 and 1945, Irish women constituted 38 per cent of Ministry of Supply and 28 per cent of Ministry of Aircraft Production workers. By 1944, over 40 per cent of those recruited to

94 Anne Lynch, *The Irish in Exile*, p. 15.
95 'Arrangements for the reception and accommodation of workers travelling to this country from Eire', TNA PRO LAB 26/9.
96 The data does not include those going into domestic service or other privately arranged engagements. The data thus represents women solely engaged in factory employment or industries directly related to the war effort.

Ministry of Supply positions were women.[97] The peak year for recruitment for women was 1945. Many were recruited for factory work in Britain right up to the end of the war and continued to be sought after wartime recruitment restrictions were relaxed.[98]

The files of the Commission on Emigration and Other Population Problems show that factory work for women was thought not to suit all workers, as the case of 'C', who was turned down for employment, illustrates:

> Ballinlaw, Westport; aged 39; single; daughter of a farmer with 90 acres in comfortable circumstances; three brothers and one sister (unmarried) at home and one sister (married) in Manchester; house has only two bedrooms despite background of 28 cattle, 3 horses and 10 acres of tillage; wishes to go to Howlett's of Birmingham who advertised locally for female labour to manufacture brass and clay components for public lighting, etc; has never been away from home and does not know anyone in Birmingham; does not seem to know her own mind and seeks advice; a queer type; Liaison Officer discouraged her as he considers her mentally deficient, unsuitable for factory life and too easily influenced.[99]

Commissioner Beddy made no comment on the decision of the Liaison Officer. The opinion of the officer, however, may have been influenced by the experiences of British factory welfare officers who found some Irish girls ill-prepared for industrial conditions. The Mass Observation studies of factories in Birmingham and Aston show that the work was dirtier and more physically demanding than some of the Irish girls had expected.[100] As one welfare assistant reported: 'So much of the work is smoothing the girls down when they first come. They're not told that it's heavy dirty work when they're in Ireland – it's left to me to deal with smoothing that down at this

---

97 Inman, *Labour in the Munitions Industries*, p. 173.

98 For example, Bridget Dantu migrated from Limerick to London in 1945 to work in a shoe factory, something she had previously done in Limerick. Dantu was put on piece work making black suede shoes and she was such a good worker she earned more than the men, which caused trouble. Dantu's recollections of the experience of factory life invokes the freedom and independence this industry afforded women, a reason why it was thought of as 'dangerous'. Interview by Matthew Linfoot, Millennium Memory Bank Interview Collection, C900/05026 C1, BLSA.

99 Report by Dr Beddy, Co. Mayo and Co. Sligo (undated), c.1948. Rural Surveys, Arnold Marsh papers, Trinity College Dublin MS 8306/S1.

100 This appears to have also been the case for male workers as suggested by a letter from a male worker to the *Irish Catholic* (7 February 1946, p. 4), who wrote to warn those emigrating that 'If you come here you will get the dirtiest job going. The English have no love for us and so they keep for themselves any decent jobs that crop up'.

end'.[101] Such commentary is not surprising given the low level of industrialisation in Ireland and the lack of any experience working with heavy-duty machinery. It was also, as Lunn has commented, an experience shared by many: 'There were numerous complaints of dissatisfaction at work, with wages and conditions not matching those promised on recruitment' but 'this represented a general dissatisfaction among workers over war-time employment conditions and was not unique to the Irish'.[102]

While complaints weren't unique, Summerfield has argued that Irish women *did* experience some direct prejudice, particularly in terms of racial stereotyping and discrimination. The views of a Birmingham labour manager, who wanted to replace two male welders, are revealing:

At Labour Exchange I see Female Vacancies Supervisor, ask for women for the job. She says the sort they get now are either afraid of the blow pipe and the sparks or don't like the dirt and heat ... I see a girl there who looks intelligent enough to be trained. Supervisor goes over to her. Comes back and says 'She's an Irish girl – domestic servant.' I say hastily, 'No thank you!'[103]

The reasons behind the emphatic 'No thank you!' are not spelled out, although the impression is given that once he realised she was Irish he reassessed his earlier idea that she would be 'intelligent enough to be trained'. Further evidence of prejudicial attitudes towards Irish women is given in Mass Observation's own report, *People in Production*. A detailed diary extract is included from a welfare manager at a Midlands factory in which a woman from Ireland was reluctantly taken on as a worker:[104]

January 1st 1942: A Labour Supply Officer phones me he has a woman

101 Dorothy Sheridan (ed.), *Wartime Women: A Mass-Observation Anthology, 1937–45* (London: Phoenix Press, 2000), p. 168.
102 Kenneth Lunn '"Good for a Few Hundred at Least": Irish Labour Recruitment into Britain during the Second World War', in Buckland and Belchem, *The Irish in British Labour History*, p. 109.
103 Penny Summerfield, *Women Workers in the Second World War: Production and Patriarchy in Conflict* (London: Croom Helm, 1984), p. 59.
104 It is interesting to note that the woman was recruited from Belfast, although no record is made as to whether she is from Northern Ireland or from Éire. Given the evidence (see Chapter 3) on many southern Irish women using the services of the Belfast branch of the ICGPS, the woman could have come from either side of the border. Throughout the report, reference is only made to 'Irish workers' without distinction of their origins in quotes from managers and workers and in writings by Mass Observation, indicating that many either were not aware of the political border or the political sensitivities of referring to workers from both the North and South as Irish.

worker (untrained) he can offer me. She's Irish (I groan), she also has a baby about 18 months old (I thank him fervently). However, I daren't refuse her.[105]

Other evidence from Mass Observation, however, suggests that some managers felt Irish women were good workers overall and did not predominantly engage in 'bad' behaviour. The welfare assistant in Aston commented:

We're very lucky with our Irish girls on the whole – they're exceptionally nice. We've only had one or two complaints from landladies about dirt and drunkenness. Some of them do take time to settle into billets and in the end prefer to find their own.[106]

The stereotype is, however, still evident in the use of the word 'lucky', suggesting that it could have been a very different experience.[107]

There seems to have been a widespread perception that Irish female factory workers were a welfare liability needing more assistance than other workers – although why this should have been surprising when they were new to the country is strange. An example can be seen in the commentary of another welfare assistant in a war factory in Aston when she stated in July 1942 that the 'job just grew of its own accord ... Of course it is the Irish girls that form the greatest part of the work'.[108]

During her time in shoe factories, Bridget Dantu also reported experiences of both racist and sexist comments from co-workers. She appears to have countered remarks with force and humour: 'They hated me as soon as I arrived! One of them said to me "is it true you sleep with the pigs?" I said, "of course, and we eat with them, if the pig isn't at the table we don't sit down!"'[109] She did, however, report excellent experiences of working for Jewish employers, contrary to popular discourse. Other oral history evidence supports more positive experiences of factory work, particularly because of

105 Mass Observation, *People in Production: An Enquiry into British War Production, Part 1* (London: John Murray, 1942), p. 87.
106 Sheridan, *Wartime Women*, p. 168.
107 Gail Braybon and Penny Summerfield maintain that Irish women had to overcome both sexist and racist stereotypes 'of Irish drunkenness, unreliability and immorality' during the war. See Braybon and Summerfield, *Out of the Cage: Women's Experiences in Two World Wars* (London: Pandora, 1987), p. 157.
108 Ibid.
109 Ibid. It is interesting to note in this regard that a secret memorandum by the British government in 1937 classed Irish workers as accustomed to living 'at a slight remove from the pig-sty stage'. Backward, rural stereotypes employed here about factory workers reflected wider cultural attitudes towards Irish immigrants. Reference taken from Ryan, 'Aliens, Migrants and Maids', p. 37.

the conditions. Letty, an interviewee of Muldowney, worked in munitions after being laid off from a sewing factory in Dublin. She reported being housed in a hostel 'she described as being extremely comfortable, with every convenience'.[110] Thus factory work is reported within diverse oral history collections in largely positive terms.

Mass Observation reports from British employers and managers detail surprise that Irish people were not filled with the same sense of national pride in being part of the war movement, but rather viewed the work simply as work. There may have been greater suspicion of Irish workers due to the IRA bombing campaign which began in January 1939. The campaign involved 'over 200 explosions and ... culminated in the notorious Coventry explosion on 25 August 1939 when five people were killed and 70 others were injured'.[111] Webster has also outlined the British press criticism of Ireland's neutrality from 1940, 'particularly for its refusal to allow the use of its ports as British bases – a refusal that was seen as causing the deaths of British and allied seamen in the Atlantic war'.[112] Despite criticisms by some employers that Irish women were doing factory work without an accompanying home front patriotic spirit, Irish women engaged directly in the British women's supplementary army organisations, often in order to make a contribution to fighting Nazism.

Irish Women in the British Auxiliary Forces

Accounts appear in almost every oral history collection of Irish women engaged in one of the women's army auxiliaries in Second World War Britain. This is particularly the case for involvement in the Women's Land Army (WLA) (Table 7.4) and the Auxiliary Territorial Service (ATS).[113] Muldowney's *The Second World War and Irish Women* also contains personal experiences of women who were in the Women's Auxiliary Air Force (WAAF), the ATS in Britain and Northern Ireland and the Queen Alexandra's Imperial Military

---

110 Muldowney, 'The Impact of the Second World War on Women in Belfast and Dublin', vol. 1, p. 139.

111 Enda Delaney, '"Almost a Class of Helots in an Alien Land": The British State and Irish Immigration, 1921–1945', *Immigrants and Minorities*, 18.2–3 (July–Nov. 1999), p. 251.

112 Wendy Webster, 'Enemies, Allies and Transnational Histories: Germans, Irish, and Italians in Second World War Britain', *Twentieth Century British History*, 25.1 (2014), p. 64.

113 Although there were other organisations for women in the war, such as the Voluntary Aid Detachments (VADs) and the Red Cross, the WLA and the ATS are the two that appear most commonly within oral history accounts of Irish emigrant women.

Table 7.4 Profile of Irish women (from the 26 counties) applying for a travel permit who are in the Women's Land Army

File reference number	Place of birth	Age at application	Date of application for travel permit	Place of present residence in Britain	Destination in Ireland
19130	Dublin	24	28 November 1940	London	Belfast[1]
22624	Cork	20	28 January 1941	Charfield, Gloucestershire	Cork
25045	Donegal	21	18 March 1941	Shaftesbury, Dorset	Donegal
25761	Tipperary	29	31 March 1941	Plumpton, Sussex	Tipperary
28126	Waterford	25	5 December 1941	Lincoln	Waterford
28266	Wicklow	19	16 May 1941	Portishead, Somerset	Tipperary[2]
29306	Leitrim	20	24 May 1941	Salcombe, Devon	Leitrim
32866	Donegal	22	28 June 1941	Sevenoaks, Kent	Donegal
32998	Tipperary	33	4 June 1941	Ivor, Buckinghamshire	Tipperary
37213	Meath	22	8 June 1941	Kington, Herefordshire	Meath
39300	Kilkenny	20	20 September 1941	Loxwood, Sussex	Kilkenny
39301	Kilkenny	19	20 September 1941	Loxwood, Sussex	Kilkenny
39334	Laois	26	9 September 1941	Sutton, Surrey	Laois

[1] Applicant was returning permanently to Ireland. No explanation was given as to why she was going to Belfast when she is recorded as having been born in Dublin.
[2] Applicant stated that she had previously lived in Tipperary, so it can be assumed she was returning to her family.
Source: Department of Foreign Affairs Travel Permit Files, National Archives of Ireland.

Nursing Service (QAIMNS).[114] I have found just two recorded oral histories related to service in the Women's Royal Naval Service (WRNS), often called the 'WRENS', which will be discussed below. The qualitative evidence highlights individual Irish women's stories, yet most women report working with other Irish women during the war. This suggests that the full extent of Irish women's involvement in the auxiliary military services was more significant than research has heretofore revealed.

Irish women were directly targeted to join the supporting military services through the Irish Labour Exchanges. Noreen Hill recounted the posters: 'Then the posters went up, at the Labour Exchange – 'JOIN THE WRENS', 'JOIN THE ATS', 'PLENTY OF WORK IN ENGLAND', 'COME TO ENGLAND AND SEE THE WORLD' – and all that sort of thing'.[115] Noreen tried to join the WRNS but failed the medical due to a weak chest. Her sister was successful in getting into the ATS. It is interesting to note that the posters Noreen recalls did not try to appeal to any kind of patriotic or jingoistic spirit, the message simply being that this was work. This indicates, perhaps, that government departments responsible for issuing such posters were sensitive about Irish workers' involvement in war work. The frequency of these references makes it difficult to judge whether this kind of war work was undertaken in higher numbers than has previously been thought, or whether oral history collections tend to include narratives from such persons, or, finally, whether persons who engaged in such work are more likely to want to share their story. Lunn has commented that the 'dilemma of having to deal with a 'hidden history' is that, during the process of its uncovering, we never know whether we have the tip of the iceberg or its entirety'.[116] While this section does not propose to solve this dilemma, evidence will be highlighted here that demonstrates the need for further exploration of the topic.

Irish women joined their British peers in the Women's Land Army (hereafter WLA), more commonly known as 'land girls'. The British Government needed to revitalise home agriculture as food shortages were feared, thus they reformed the original WLA, set up in 1917 when similar food shortages arose during the First World War. The WLA provided the

---

114 The QAIMNS was a special military nursing unit. Muldowney's interviewee, Hilda, is the only case I found of an Irish woman in QAIMNS. Muldowney also has the only example I have found of an Irish woman, Ethel, who joined the WAAF. Ethel joined in Belfast and went to Britain after she had trained as an electrician. Ethel's evidence suggests there were many more Irish women in the WAAF. Given that there is just one example of each kind in the qualitative evidence, I have not included this in the main text. See Muldowney, *The Second World War and Irish Women*, pp. 107–108.

115 Lennon *et al.*, *Across the Water*, p. 93. Capitalisation in the original.

116 Kenneth Lunn, '"Good for a Few Hundred at Least": Irish Labour Recruitment into Britain During the Second World War', in Buckland and Belchem, *The Irish in British Labour History*, p. 107.

extra labour needed as men were conscripted. In 1939, farmers were offered incentives to grow grain, which necessitated greater help on the land and women stepped in due to the simultaneous need for soldiers.[117] The WLA was officially resurrected on 1 June 1939, with Lady Gertrude Denman as its Director, after much procrastinating about the appropriateness of women engaging in this work.[118] While the Imperial War Museum gives estimates of up to 75,000 women out of 204,000 land workers in total,[119] Nicola Tyrer states that the WLA constituted 80,000 women at its peak, with a quarter of a million women engaged over its eleven-year lifespan.[120] Clearly, regardless of exact figures, they made up a significant force engaged in the British home front war effort. Women in the WLA were girls who 'had often left school early and came in the main from modest backgrounds where daughters were expected to work for their living, just like sons'.[121] This indicates that Irish female emigrants would have fitted in well in terms of class background with their British counterparts. Women were paid on average £1 8s. 0d. per week during the first years of the war, which was 10 shillings below the rate for male agricultural workers. This rose to £2 8s. 0d. in 1944.[122]

Bridget joined the WLA while on holiday in Britain. Her farming background gave her an advantage over some of the other girls:

> The war had just broken out and being a farmer's daughter, land greatly appealed to me. I knew so much about it, cattle and everything, so I joined the Land Army … One or two of the women was used to farming, but the others used to say to me: 'It's all right for you, because you can handle the cattle, but we can't. We want to see the back of those cows as soon as we can!'[123]

Women involved in the auxiliary services were required to obtain travel permits, unlike Irish men enrolled in the British army. Thirteen women who

---

117 Nicola Tyrer, *They Fought in the Fields. The Women's Land Army: The Story of a Forgotten Victory* (London: Sinclair-Stevenson, 1996), p. 4. Note that this book does not go into any detail about Irish women in the WLA, despite the fact that collections on Irish emigration contain many examples.

118 Lady Denman had been involved in the first incarnation of the WLA in the First World War and had been instrumental in setting up the Women's Institutes in Great Britain, whose membership she used to roll out the WLA across the country. Ibid., p. 5.

119 Information obtained from the Imperial War Museum Collection at https://www.iwm. org.uk/history/what-was-the-womens-land-army.

120 Tyrer, *They Fought in the Fields*, p. 16.

121 Ibid., p. 23.

122 Ibid., pp. 17 and 64.

123 Pam Schweitzer, Lorraine Hilton and Jane Moss (eds), *What Did You Do in the War, Mum?* (London: Age Exchange Theatre Company, 1985), p. 5.

applied for return permits from Britain in my research reported working in the WLA. Of these women, a general profile can be drawn. Only one of the thirteen women was married (to a Welsh man) and none had children; most were returning home on leave (one was returning permanently) and we may assume they were planning to return to work. The average age of the women was twenty-three years, the youngest being nineteen and the oldest being thirty-three.[124]

The Women's Royal Navy Service, like the ATS and WLA, was reformed in the Second World War to cope with the shortage of manpower.[125] In 1939, Mrs Vera Laughton Mathews, who had served with the WRNS during the First World War, became its Director, and by 1944 the service numbered 74,000 women undertaking 200 different jobs. The 'Wrens' were involved in many aspects of wartime naval operations. During the course of this research just two personal recollections of Irish women working in the WRNS in secondary or oral histories were found and just one recorded applicant in the travel permit files. The first is Elizabeth Chamberlain, who migrated to Britain specifically to join the WRNS (they would not accept applications directly from Ireland). After first training in England and Scotland in 1942 she spent time in Italy where she was involved in cipher duties.[126] The second example is Bridget McKenzie (née Richardson), from Tipperary, who moved to Britain initially as a nanny.[127] After her Scottish fiancé (later husband) was called up to the army she says boredom motivated her to respond to an advertisement to join the WRNS in 1940. She was sent to Scotland for training where she worked as a porter's assistant, cooking and serving food. After completing training, she was one of the first 200 Wrens to go to the Pacific. McKenzie spent nearly six years in the WRNS before the war ended and she was demobilised. Applicant 39035 in the DFA travel permit application files was a twenty-four-year-old native of Cork who was returning to her parents for a holiday in January 1941 from her base in London. No other details are

---

124 All information derived from travel permit applications in the National Archives of Ireland collection.

125 Information on the WRNS obtained from the Royal Navy Museum website https://www.nmrn.org.uk/pioneers.

126 See Doherty, *Irish Men and Women in the Second World War*, p. 261. Chamberlain's experience fits with Doherty's thesis that many Irish men and women joined the British forces out of a sense of duty to fight Nazism. Chamberlain was clearly from a middle-class background and thus financial motives did not form part of her decision making.

127 Her story is included as part of the King's Cross Voices Collection. Permission to access the database and refer to the interview was provided by Leslie McCartney, former project coordinator. The King's Cross Voices Oral History Project is now looked after by the Camden Local Studies and Archives in the Holborn Library in London. See https://voices.kingscross.co.uk/ for further details.

given, and we can only assume that her trip was for a simple holiday. These three accounts may well be just the 'tip of the iceberg' that Lunn referred to, as many more may have served. Elizabeth Chamberlain reported that she met Irish people everywhere she went, including three from Dublin when she was in Naples.[128] Further research is needed to determine the extent of Irish women's involvement in the WRNS and other auxiliary services. Of interest is whether economic or other motivations were of primacy to Irish women who joined the British forces. Doherty asserts that not many were influenced by the wages, because they were generally low. However, wages could be poor for many women's jobs, so what prompted their decisions to join up may have been different from that of the men.

Irish women also joined the Auxiliary Territorial Service (ATS). The ATS was formed as a women's auxiliary to the army and, like the WLA, was revived in 1938 from an earlier version in the First World War.[129] At its peak in June 1943, 210,308 officers and auxiliaries served.[130] Women worked as office, mess and telephone orderlies, drivers, postal workers, butchers, bakers, ammunition inspectors, military police, gun crews and many other operational support tasks as well as the first aid sections that provided most of the ATS transport. Romie Lambkin, a Dublin woman who joined via Belfast, trained to be a driver, resisting attempts to get her into office work that she had done before joining.[131] Unlike the WLA, where there was only one rank, the ATS had ranks similar to the army and was directed by women from upper-class families. It is likely that Irish women in the ATS made up the general rank and file rather than the commanding class, but no conclusive research exists on this.

There is one example given in the Commission on Emigration and Other Population Problems rural surveys of a woman who had been in the ATS:

Case 'K' (Female) Returned emigrant aged 21; member of A.T.S. July, 1945–March, 1948; no other experience of employment; intends to return to England; no suitable work in Mullingar area.[132]

There is no extra commentary devoted to this entry by members of the Commission, indicating that they did not regard 'K' as particularly unusual

---

128 Doherty, *Irish Men and Women in the Second World War*, p. 266.

129 The ATS was directed by Dame Helen Gwynne-Vaughan. For more details on the set up of the ATS, see Muldowney, *The Second World War and Irish Women*, p. 105.

130 The Auxiliary Territorial Service in the Second World War, Information Sheet No. 42, Imperial War Museum.

131 Romie Lambkin, *My Time in the War: An Irishwoman's Diary* (Dublin: Wolfhound Press, 1992).

132 Mullingar, Rural Surveys, Arnold Marsh papers, Trinity College Dublin MS 8306/S14a.

in having been in the ATS. In Muldowney's study, Pat recounted four weeks of drilling and training in cold conditions where the women were paid 2 shillings per day, plus food and board. Thereafter she was paid approximately 25 shillings per week, with full board and lodging. Pat recalled a specific dislike for the conditions. The arrangements do, however, reveal a structured and relatively safe environment:

> It was a dreadful time. We all thought we were crazy for volunteering because to go from comfortable homes to chalets, yes, wooden chalets. You'd go into the ladies room [laughs] and there'd be all the hand basins and you'd get on and get washed. Oh, we often cried at night because you couldn't do anything. The last weekend, I think, we went to Edinburgh and that was the highlight.[133]

Pat's parents were worried for her safety but she was not prohibited from going, which counters the assertion within newspapers – particularly Catholic publications – suggesting women were wilfully disobeying parents in migrating.[134] Although Pat admits to wanting to 'Spread my wings' by joining the ATS, her comment that they 'couldn't do anything', and the fact that their accommodation and daily lives were routinely managed, and to some extent policed, suggests that this form of structured employment was relatively 'safe' in terms of moral and physical welfare.

There were rumours, however, that women engaged in both the ATS and in WLA work were morally suspect, and this is at odds with the reported experience of the closely controlled work. In the example above from the Mass Observation report regarding the Irish woman who reported for an interview at a factory with her eighteen-month-old baby, it was recorded that she had previously been in the ATS:

> She was once in a clothing factory and had joined the A.T.S. from which she was discharged on 'Medical Grounds' (crossed out and 'Compassionate Grounds' substituted). Checking certain dates seems to show that the little stranger started his voyage to this vale of tears just about the time his mother joined the A.T.S. Point this out to my assistant and she says 'Well, she isn't wearing a wedding ring'.[135]

---

133 Muldowney, 'The Impact of the Second World War on Women in Belfast and Dublin', vol. 1, p. 162.
134 See, for example, Ryan, *Gender, Identity and the Irish Press* and her article 'Leaving Home'.
135 Mass Observation, *People in Production*, p. 87.

Mass Observation themselves felt compelled to comment upon the rumours and negative discourses surrounding the ATS: 'the greatly exaggerated but widely believed stories, of immorality in the A.T.S. – a form of public opinion unfavourable to A.T.S. recruiting and to the war effort which has little factual basis, and quite a lot in common with some of the public opinion that has grown up over war industry'.[136]

Awareness of such attitudes within the ATS is evident from an account by Kath O'Sullivan of the training regimen. O'Sullivan recalled being given moral advice on sexual behaviour as part of their Hygiene classes: 'We were lectured on the perils of venereal disease and told to value our virginity'.[137] Throughout this research, only one example of an Irish woman becoming pregnant after joining the ATS emerged, although given the under-researched nature of this cohort it is probable that there were others. Noreen Hill's sister (she is not named), got pregnant by an Englishman and put the child in an institution. The pregnancy was hidden from the family apart from Noreen and her mother as it would ruin her chances of meeting anyone else and her mother was extremely concerned about the neighbours at home. While Muldowney has highlighted that the ATS were viewed by some as the 'groundsheet of the army' her interviewees did not mention being worried about being seen to be immoral for joining up.[138] This was perhaps part of the English rather than Irish discourses on women's war work.

It seems that the widely perpetuated rumours about the 'land girls' stemmed from a negative reaction to their freedom, the perception being that they were rather *too* free. Such speculations are contained in *Betty's Wartime Diary*, in which the diarist, Betty (a pseudonym), notes some speculation about a girl she was friendly with in the WLA who 'liked her gin' and had colleagues who were 'a bit on the loud side'.[139] Tyrer's research on the WLA echoed this: some of the women recounted tales of being banned from the house by the farmer's wife or being made the subject of teasing or sexual harassment. While it is impossible to conclude anything definitive about the behaviour of any women in the WLA or ATS, many also experienced strict housing conditions akin to those for nurses, requiring them, for example, to be in by 10 p.m. or risk being shut out for the night. Tyrer has asserted that the sexy reputation of land girls was unfounded, arguing that such rumours 'contained more than a dash of wishful thinking spiced with a dollop of

136 Ibid., p. 33.
137 'Remembering the 1940's': 1940s Society websitewww.1940.co.uk. Elizabeth Chamberlain also recalled being given lectures about 'not getting involved with foreign men, not getting pregnant and so on' in her Wren training. Doherty, *Irish Men and Women in the Second World War*, p. 265.
138 Muldowney, *The Second World War and Irish Women*, p. 107.
139 Nicholas Webley (ed.), *Betty's Wartime Diary, 1939–1945* (London: Thorogood, 2006).

malice'.[140] Tyrer does mention one example, however, of an Irish matron of a WLA hostel who could be persuaded to give late passes in exchange for flowers – this is in fact the only time that Irish women are specifically mentioned in the book, and ironically in this instance the inference is that the matron was unconcerned about imposing strict guidelines. Such anecdotal evidence, while interesting, does not provide any decisive evidence about Irish women's behaviour or that of women in the WLA in general.

Irish Female Emigrants and Career Mobility

Many Irish women who migrated to Britain enjoyed greater social and career mobility than men through 'respectable' employment not only in nursing but also in clerical work, including the civil service. This was often achieved by moving from lower status jobs after spending some time in Britain. In this way, women could access better-paid jobs unlike many men who worked 'on the lump' on building sites across Britain and who became vulnerable once their bodies could no longer sustain such hard, physical labour. While it is unclear how many Irish women in Britain were part of the one in three, never-married women in Britain aged over forty, who owned homes by 1961, their participation in professional jobs allowed for this to be a possibility at least.[141]

Margaret Smith, from Cork city, left for London in 1946 to work as a servant in the home of an Irish woman. After working there for over a year, she became a cashier with Lyons and Company teashop in Oxford Street, where she experienced significantly better working conditions and pay, allowing her to 'buy a bit of clothes or something for yourself and send a few pounds home to my mother'.[142] Similarly, Marie Maberley got a job in a hotel in Birmingham in 1939 as a waitress/domestic servant, which she found difficult. After a year she moved to her sister's house in London and took up work as a 'daily' in a house that gave her far more money and free time.[143] In the 1930s, Molly began working as a maid but later passed a Post Office exam, getting a job in the Sorting Office.[144] This kind of career mobility may have been an incentive to emigrate in the first place. Stanley Lyon, in his interviews with eleven returned emigrants as part of his work on the Commission on Emigration and Other Population Problems, concluded that:

140 Tyrer, *They Fought in the Fields*, p. 161.
141 A.E. Holmans, *Historical Statistics of Housing in Britain* (Cambridge: The Cambridge Centre for Housing and Planning Research, 2005), Table A7 (p. 17).
142 Ryan, 'Moving Spaces and Changing Places', p. 75.
143 Schweitzer, Hilton and Moss, *What Did You Do in the War Mum?*, p. 3.
144 Ryan, 'Family Matters', p. 358.

Employment as factory hands, hotel and café waitresses, is very much sought after. A certain social distinction (or, better, perhaps, lack of social stigma) attaches to these occupations, permitting a higher holding of the head, especially when affairs of the heart crop up. The metropolitan boy-friend is apparently allergic to the domestic servant. In addition, the factory hours and the changing faces in cafés and hotels are attractive to the female workers.[145]

Lyon's quotation does not fully recognise the economic motivations for changing work as well as the higher social status, but it is true that many women did not wish to stay in service and enjoyed the increased social status other jobs had in Britain.

There is far less evidence on Irish women who emigrated directly to clerical work. It seems that Irish women in clerical or professional occupations, perhaps due to their skills and socio-economic status, were not the subject of concern for the government or members of the hierarchy. They also rarely appear in the records of welfare organisations that helped unmarried mothers, for example. Many Irish women moved into office work after spending some time initially in domestic service or other unskilled occupations.[146] Women in white-collar or skilled employment were not subject to the same degree of negative commentary on their welfare, moral behaviour or safety as women as domestic servants or factory workers. Although they were perhaps a small minority in the total female emigrant cohort, they nevertheless were present, as seen in the travel permit files – a total of 419 applicants, or just 2.7 per cent of the women who applied to return to Ireland in the early 1940s.[147]

The case of Mary Henry is a rare example of an Irish woman migrating directly to a professional office job (Figure 7.2). Mary had learned shorthand and typing at home in Ireland and thus was qualified to a much greater extent than many Irish women emigrants. Mary followed her sister Bridie to London in 1938 where she worked for a solicitor and then for a Jewish-owned company before she eventually got a better paid job in the typing pool of the Civil Service in a department dealing with National Savings Bonds.[148]

---

145 Returned Emigrants Survey, 1948. Arnold Marsh papers, Trinity College Dublin MS 8306/S20.
146 Catherine Dunne's book, focusing mainly on the 1950s, is an exception, with some of her female participants having engaged in clerical work and hairdressing.
147 This figure has been calculated by adding the totals for the following job titles given on the forms: book keeper (29); civil service (61); clerk (143); insurance agent/worker (7); office supervisor (2); postal worker (21); receptionist (19); secretary (37); shorthand typist (79); stenographer (4); telephone operator (17). All data collated from Department of Foreign Affairs collection, National Archives of Ireland.
148 Reference is made here to the life history given to me by Patricia Marsh.

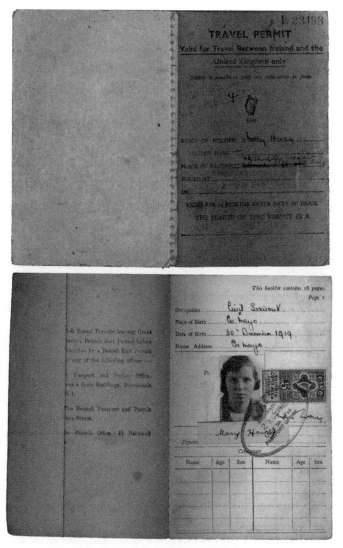

Figure 7.2   Mary Henry's travel permit.
Courtesy of Mary Henry's family.

It is interesting to note that Mary's application had been held up initially because one of her references, her local priest, had not returned a letter for her. Upon enquiring, she was told he was too busy to write one. It seems not all clergy were enthusiastic in their concern for female emigrants.[149]

149 Irish female emigrants were advised to use their parish priests for references and as a way to communicate with the local priest and welfare societies in their intended area of employment. *Irish Catholic*, 4 July 1936.

Catherine Ridgeway, an emigrant from Dublin interviewed by Lennon *et al.*, started work initially as a chambermaid in a London hotel. She later progressed to linen keeper, which gave her her own room for the first time in her life. Her manager, seeing that she was ambitious, let her learn book-keeping and typing in her spare time and then gave her the next opening as receptionist and book-keeper. The outbreak of the Second World War gave Catherine the professional opportunity she had dreamed of: 'I thought, this is my opportunity to get out of hotels ... The war gave me a break too, yes I do feel that I would never have got into the Civil Service in peace time. I wouldn't have had sufficient educational background, but because of shortages I got in'.[150]

Ridgeway would not have qualified for the civil service in Ireland; thus, the opportunities provided by the war were significant. These opportunities were completely out of the grasp of women like Ridgeway without migration. As may be expected, this rather positive outcome of female emigration does not feature in public discourses.

Conclusion

Irish women often left low-paying, insecure and low-status jobs in Ireland to pursue better ones in Britain. The idealistic visions painted of Irish women's employment as servants in Ireland were exposed as fallacious by the number of women leaving for similar employment in Britain. As this chapter has demonstrated, Irish women clearly fulfilled vital roles in the British economy. While some of these were of a low status, such as domestic service, the new evidence provided in this chapter shows that this archetype does not represent the heterogeneity of Irish immigrant employment. Even within the familiar occupation of nursing, Irish women developed different specialisms, attained a variety of credentials and held roles of responsibility that are not reflected when we refer simply to 'Irish nurses'. As noted, the shared cultural mores surrounding the vocational nature of nursing meant that it was viewed positively by most as an appropriate occupation for women. The dramatic language used at times, connecting work with the 'leakage' problem, doesn't appear to have a basis in reality. There are other facets of this history that have been less researched, such as the roles fulfilled by women in the Second World War; the silences surrounding the employment of women outside the well-known areas of nursing and service may reflect the fact that many quietly got on with taking up the new opportunities presented to them.

---

150 Lennon *et al.*, *Across the Water*, p. 51.

For many, the Second World War was a watershed moment as they first entered Britain to take up roles left vacant by men, or switched careers as the demands on the home front increased.

For some historians, there is still a question mark as to whether migration was really a positive move for women. Clear has argued against the perception that, for women, emigration for jobs in Britain was better than staying in Ireland, claiming that migration was 'often lonely and confusing, and marriage was not always a happy ending. [...] many emigrants remained prisoners of the values and expectations of their families in Ireland, without the everyday support and companionship that normally goes with such bonds'.[151] Were they prisoners or fellow believers? Countless women emigrants' personal narratives detail fulfilled lives similar to those they would have lived at home. Moreover, it seems that many female emigrants *did* feel they were better off because migration allowed them to be economically productive and to have at least the *opportunity* for marriage, unavailable to many at home. It is true that many women were homesick, but they emigrated specifically with family support and within kin networks, thereby ensuring they had support, either from a distance or directly from living with or near family and friends. There is no one, homogeneous experience, but rather a multiplicity of individuals, acting and reacting to the economic situation and the emigration culture of twentieth- (and, indeed, twenty-first-) century Ireland. Each woman experienced her own migration journey.

The historiography of Irish people's involvement with the Second World War has up to this point focused on the broader issues of employment schemes, the policy of neutrality and British–Irish relations during and after the conflict.[152] Research utilising oral histories with Irish people (with the exception of Muldowney's work) tends to emphasise their military achievements and to focus on men's involvement in the forces to the neglect of scholarship not just on women, but on the more ordinary experiences of citizens from a neutral state working in a belligerent one. Girvin has observed that those who volunteered 'returned to an Ireland uneasy with them and often unwelcoming' and this may explain some of the silences that have developed over their wartime experiences and contributions.[153] Nonetheless, Irish women contributed vitally to the landscape of work in wartime Britain, and, combined with their work in many other areas, demonstrated that migration was often an economically empowering move for Irish women.

---

151 Clear, *Women of the House*, p. 203.

152 For example, the edited collection by Girvin and Roberts, *Ireland and the Second World War*, has no contributions specifically on women or on the daily lives of Irish wartime workers.

153 Brian Girvin, *The Emergency: Neutral Ireland, 1939–45* (London: Macmillan, 2006), p. x.

Conclusion

I regard the emigration of our young people as an open gash in the nation's main artery, through which the nation is bleeding to death. Nevertheless, I do not hold that the way to stop emigration is [...] by a ruthless coercion measure prohibiting our people from leaving.

Deputy Bernard Butler, Fianna Fáil, *Dáil Éireann Debates*, vol. 97, col. 2437, 13 July 1945.

M igration is a perennial feature of Irish life, part of the nexus of low marriage and high fertility rates of the Irish population which are peculiar in demographic terms. As Coleman stated, 'Ireland's demography challenges demographic theory'.[1] It is doubtful that anyone in the 1950s could have conceived that within fifty years Ireland would become a site of immigration; some were predicting the end of the Irish race. The upsurge in twenty-first-century emigration may have caused less surprise, but perhaps more dismay, as the discourses reveal in many cases an earnest desire that Ireland cease to be an 'emigrant nursery' for larger economies.[2] Although not on the scale of migration from the 1920s to the 1950s, we have seen a return flow of people in recent years as outward migration has been recorded again in the 2016 Census.[3]

1 D. A. Coleman 'The Demographic Transition in Ireland in International Context', in J.H. Goldthorpe and C.T. Whelan (eds), *The Development of Industrial Society in Ireland* (Oxford: Oxford University Press, 1994), p. 53.
2 Jim Mac Laughlin, *Ireland: The Emigrant Nursery and the World Economy* (Cork: Cork University Press, 1994).
3 The total net migration for the period 2011–16 is estimated at 22,500, the first time an outward flow has been recorded since the 1986–91 period. See Central Statistics Office, *Census 2016 Summary Results, Part 1* (Dublin: Central Statistics Office, 2017), p. 10.

Metaphors drawing upon water and blood, evocative of life itself, as referred to in the Introduction, have persisted. In the post-Second World War era there were fears of losing a particular kind of quality in the population, or, in Wills's analysis, the 'Gaeltacht stock' regarded as '"very fine" because it was hardy and robust, strengthened through frugal and simple living'.[4] What 'type' of person was leaving and what 'stock' remained vexed interested parties. Wills has argued that literary depictions of life in the 1950s hinted at the notion that 'the population will become too soft to cope with rural Ireland' due to modernity and the concomitant rising expectations for quality of life.[5] It seems, however, that the concern was not so much for the people – their fitness, their desires, their material needs – as with modernity itself. Ideas of 'frugal comfort', of Ireland being somehow above modern concerns with technology, progress and material ease, were referenced by de Valera and in Catholic social teaching (and the connection between the two is not coincidental). The idea was formulated that to be Irish was to be simple, pure, outside the realm of avarice and wealth; the emigrant, framed as seeking such things, was castigated. This had particular implications for women: lust for glamorous lives, make-up, hairstyles and fashions were speculated as sustaining their desire to leave their communities. They were denied the legitimacy of being economic actors, reacting to market forces that drove them from unemployment in rural Ireland to jobs in the cities of Britain. Ewart's analysis confirms this conclusion: 'whereas male migration was seen as a regrettable but understandable response to economic pressures, female migration was seen as much less rational or necessary'.[6] Paradoxically, without the material success of emigrants, particularly women who were anecdotally regarded as the more reliable remittance senders, rural Ireland may have collapsed completely.

Part of the problem was the Irish defiance of global migration norms. Where other cultures have experienced migration ebbs and flows, with returning countercurrents bringing back fortunes made in new lands, the predominant trend of migration has been one way, out, for us, with very few returning apart from brief episodes when Ireland's economic fortunes looked, briefly, brighter in the 1970s and the 1990s and 2000s. In the wake of the recent recession, the strong outflow of young people led to answers again being sought as to why and where people were going and to what extent the government and its policies were culpable. Since 2014, Ireland has had a Minister for Diaspora Affairs, marking a clear shift in policy and focus, although it remains to be seen what long-term impact this will have. It *does* mark a significant shift in thinking about migrants – out of sight is no longer out of mind, at the very least.

4 Wills, *The Best Are Leaving*, p. 45.
5 Ibid., p. 31.
6 Ewart, 'Caring for Migrants', p. 254.

Migration attests to the cyclical view of history. Reflecting on the first decades of independence, this book focused on narratives constructed about women's migration to Britain during a time of hope for the country that lifting the yoke of colonialism would arrest or reverse the well-established migration tradition. There were many issues at play in how migration was discussed. In an era where the strength of Catholic identity was being asserted, the flight of so many from the land, from the traditions and communities that kept Catholicism strong, was deeply problematic. As Delaney has observed, these are twinned stories, and whether 'Irish migrant culture can be separated from Irish Catholic identity is an open question'.[7]

Emigration from Ireland to Britain has a long history, yet it has received less attention in research than the more epic and exciting migrations to America. Women have consistently been a part of the flow, or the flight, from the land. The gender of emigrants was variously highlighted and ignored when the topic arose and there are many instances of parliamentary rhetoric in which the needs and desires of male migrants are conflated with those of Irish women when they neither occupied the same sectors of the economy nor enjoyed the benefit of government-provided labour schemes. Alarm was expressed over women's feminine vulnerability whilst men were ignored in such gendered analyses. Many reports on the condition of Irish migrants in Britain relied on hearsay and opinion and few contained detailed or empirical evidence. The tendency of reports conducted by the Catholic Church to speak of 'the Irish' as one homogeneous group also meant that 'proposed solutions' were 'unworkably vague and untargeted' and 'based more on the preferences and interests of the potential providers than on objective assessment of need' of the emigrants themselves.[8]

The familiarity of Britain was part of its continued draw, yet it was the reason why emigration was cast in such negative terms. The spirit of 'pulling together' for the sake of the nation was keenly felt at the birth of the Free State, with commentary coming from many quarters, including the *Church of Ireland Gazette*: 'Ireland needs the maximum from every one of her sons and daughters, if she is to survive'.[9] The evocation of Ireland on the brink of extinction, and the casting of emigrants as children abandoning their needy parent were axioms that frequently emerged. Abandonment and ungratefulness were sentiments shared across the confessional divide. For women, an emblem of the nation, their distinctive Irish purity, beauty and religious fervour were thought to be compromised through emigration. The loss of

---

7 Enda Delaney, Review of Clair Wills's *The Best are Leaving: Emigration and Post-War Irish Culture*, *Irish Times*, 6 June 2015.

8 Ewart, 'Caring for Migrants', p. 83.

9 'Carry On', Editorial, *Church of Ireland Gazette*, 22 December 1922, p. 730.

a woman's name through sexual misconduct was one of the worst fates she could face, and this was posed as a corollary to taking the boat to England.

Despite their reputation as excellent remittance senders, a concomitant and more negative discourse existed about women as sexually profligate emigrants, liable to 'get into trouble' easily. As with many archetypes, there is a kernel of truth. Such fears of impropriety were based on a hidden history that saw Irish women leave to conceal crisis pregnancies. Earner Byrne and Garrett's research has revealed a steady trickle of women seeking to 'risk destitution in Britain rather than institutionalisation in Ireland', yet there is evidence to suggest that the claims regarding Irish women's illegitimate pregnancies were often overstated by certain Catholic welfare societies.[10] It is also the case that when official investigations were made, either by the Irish government or by associations such as the NVA, there were relatively few Irish women in the care of religious maternity homes. It appears that the *idea* of female sexual transgression took hold in the Irish imagination to such an extent that the conflation of female emigration with illegitimate pregnancy was easily believed. As Sharpe and Yuval-Davis, among others, have argued, women migrants are used symbolically to define the collective community and its boundaries, thus their transgressive behaviour can be viewed as transgression of national ideologies.[11] Far more common than premarital sex was the experience of traditional courtships leading to marriage, particularly within the Irish emigrant community. The fact that early marriages were taking place in Britain among Irish emigrants rather than at home led to rather bitter discourses on the 'disloyalty' shown by emigrants who left their struggling home communities. However, the focus was yet again on women, with claims that they were specifically motivated to leave Ireland to get married, rather than because they needed to work.

Women were often spoken of as in need of guidance and the special protection offered by welfare associations in their journeys. The 'white slave trade', or what we would now refer to as trafficking, may seem very far from the Irish emigrant experience, yet a considerable proportion of the discourses emanating from a moral perspective on Irish women's emigration to Britain centred on their travel arrangements in light of this nefarious trade in women. It was widely thought that gangs of men and women involved in international prostitution rings would lure unsuspecting women travelling through train stations and major ports into a life of debauchery, often under the pretext of genuine work or through the power of seduction by a particularly charming

10 Quote from Earner Byrne, referring to the findings of the Carrigan Report, in '"Moral Repatriation"', p. 157.

11 See Pamela Sharpe, 'Gender and the Experience of Migration', in Sharpe, *Women, Gender and Labour Migration*, pp. 1–14; Yuval-Davis *Gender and Nation*.

man. Moral welfare groups acted as chaperones to deter this scheming and to protect women while they were transiting through these areas of danger by offering practical advice and physical accompaniment. The evidence suggests that fears for Irish women's safety were exaggerated, relying as they did on stereotypical notions of Irish women as exceptionally vulnerable in comparison with their male peers and an exaggeration of the extent of the problem, at least in Ireland and Britain. The International Catholic Girls' Protection Society, the Girls' Friendly Society, the Irish Women Police Patrols and the Catholic Social Welfare Bureau (incorporating activities by the Legion of Mary) were all involved in providing information, assistance and at times shelter for women travelling through Dublin to the ports of Great Britain, in the main Liverpool. No such dedicated organisations existed to help men.

Although these societies had no support at state level for their work, they operated on a professional philanthropic basis and were highly networked with similar organisations in Great Britain and throughout Europe, such as the Catholic Women's League, the Port and Station Rescue Work Society, the National Vigilance Association (later the British Vigilance Association) and the local branches of the Legion of Mary among others. As with other charitable concerns, the cause of protection for emigrant women was taken up by lay organisations established in the nineteenth century along religious (and sectarian) lines. These groups were run predominantly by women, as were other initiatives to help the 'deserving poor'. Contemporary notions of women's sensitivity and benevolence as well as a belief in a sort of feminine morality meant that women were regarded as the appropriate givers of this aid. This was also an area where lay women as opposed to religious could make their mark; while increasingly throughout the nineteenth century religious-run services were housed at institutions within convent walls, the requirement for active engagement with emigrants where and when they needed help meant services of a different kind were required. Industrious lay women inclined to social work therefore found their niche.

Emigration as an exit from judgemental Ireland also emerges as a reason women left, although to a lesser extent than was feared. It seems that the most common recourse for women who found themselves pregnant and who decided to go to Britain to preserve their 'character' was to enter a home and have the baby adopted. Sandra McAvoy has investigated the incidence of Irish women obtaining abortions in this period and concludes that while no definitive statistics will ever be known 'it is likely that there was a high level of awareness of the possibility of obtaining "backstreet" abortions in Britain. For those with that knowledge and sufficient funds, or contacts they could visit in Britain, it was an option'.[12] There is no anecdotal evidence related

12 Sandra McAvoy, 'Before Cadden: Abortion in Mid-Twentieth Century Ireland', in

to Irish women seeking abortion within oral history collections analysed in this research. This is unsurprising given the highly sensitive nature of this topic and the illegality of the act itself up to 1967 in Britain. Small, liminal traces of this darker part of migration history infrequently occur in the secondary literature; Wills, for example, has examined the impact of the Emergency period on the incidence of illegitimacy and infanticide. She found just a few cases whereby migration played an indirect role. In one, a woman who wanted to return to England to work after having an illegitimate child in Ireland, strangled her infant. In another, a woman whose husband was working in England killed her newborn baby with her lover so that her husband would not find out and stop sending her remittances.[13] While it is unlikely a definitive history will ever be written on Irish migrants' sexual behaviour, the point to emphasise is that there were far more Irish women migrants who did *not* experience pregnancy outside of marriage than those who did. Immigration and immorality did not go hand in hand.

Welfare agencies, despite their infantilising discourses on female emigrants, did provide a vital service in assisting Irish women who were unused to the realities of city life. The findings on the vast networks of emigrant welfare organisations is counter to Mary Daly's assertion that the efforts of welfare associations were ad hoc. They managed admirably given the lack of government support; and, as Delaney has noted, the Catholic Church's efforts through the Legion of Mary and the CSWB were 'energetic and well-organised efforts [which] starkly contrasted with the limited involvement of the state with the Irish in Britain'.[14]

Interestingly, the assistance societies such as the ICGPS gave to women did not lead to them being branded as 'emigration agents' as was the case in the political arena outlined in Chapter 2. The ICGPS, and later the CSWB, were perceived as simply fulfilling a need to help women travel safely. The 1924–25 Annual Report of the ICGPS put it plainly: 'We regret as much as anybody the loss to Ireland of her young people, but if they must go, we would like to make that going as safe as possible'.[15] These organisations were satisfying a pastoral need that the government was unwilling to undertake despite its

Keogh, O'Shea and Quinlan, *The Lost Decade*, p. 154. Rattigan has found that Irish women were aware of the availability of abortion in Britain and has identified at least two cases of Irish women who died as a result of abortions and another who attempted to self-abort in Dublin before leaving for London. See Cliona Rattigan, '"Crimes of Passion of the Worst Character": Abortion Cases and Gender in Ireland, 1925–1950', in Valiulis, *Gender and Power in Ireland*, pp. 115–139.

13 Wills, *That Neutral Island*, p. 326.

14 Enda Delaney, 'Emigration, Political Cultures and the Evolution of Post-War Irish Society', in Brian Girvin and Gary Murphy (eds), *The Lemass Era: Politics and Society in the Ireland of Seán Lemass* (Dublin: University College Dublin Press, 2005), p. 57.

15 ICGPS, Annual Report 1924–25, Down and Connor Diocesan Archives, Belfast, p. 1.

concerns about emigrants. Welfare-related services of all kinds were viewed as within the remit of the Catholic Church. This had specific consequences for women as any services offered for their care – for example, for unmarried mothers – were controlled and funded by religious institutions and not by the state. This meant that Catholic ideologies of women prevailed in welfare services that often regarded them as wayward and in need of control.

The evidence presented on welfare work associated with Irish women going to employment in Britain has often been ignored in narratives of Irish emigration. Documentation from the Women's Library archives reveals the constant help Irish women received from British welfare organisations, and the interest the Irish government took behind the scenes. The lack of funding and public acknowledgement of this assistance appears to have worn upon the patience of the Secretary of one of the key organisations involved, the National Vigilance Association. In a letter of 1938, Mr Sempkins wrote:

> The position as I see it is this: Irish girls coming to this country receive a great deal of assistance and preliminary supervision which is given, so far as I know, to no other community in this world. The amount of work we can do is strictly limited by the amount of money which we receive and certainly the funds of the N.V.A. in London would not permit them to do more than is done – that is, to inform the appropriate Roman Catholic authorities of the arrival of particular girls, to meet and assist those girls, and deal with particular cases which are brought to our notice.[16]

The lack of action – despite promises from the Irish High Commissioner's office in London – must have been particularly dispiriting, and it is likely that the NVA and other such organisations had little faith that the Irish government would ever do anything either to support their work or to stem the flow of Irish women coming to Britain to work.

Irish emigration was variously ignored, berated, researched and discussed by successive governments in Ireland between the 1920s and the 1950s. Such attention did not, however, result in action. Even the mammoth investigation of the Commission of Emigration over a six-year period was allowed quietly to disappear almost instantly. Perhaps the increasing rates of emigration were too symbolically and politically sensitive for governments after independence. Akenson's apt observation epitomises this feeling well: 'To successive twentieth-century Irish governments emigration has been a

---

16 Letter from Sempkins to Edith Rose of Liverpool Port and Station Work dated 14 January 1938, Women's Library, File 4NVA/04/02 Box FL098.

very touchy topic, a symptom of national failing'.[17] This sensitivity to the issue may explain some of the vitriol directed at times towards emigrants, framing them as unpatriotic.

The stance taken by political parties about the role of the government in providing employment – and hence stopping or significantly reducing emigration – appeared to fluctuate depending on whether they were in power or opposition. This is true both for Cumann na nGaedheal/Fine Gael and Fianna Fáil. For the former, however, it must be recognised that as well as the problem of emigration and unemployment it had to contend with the substantial issues of restoring law and order in the 1920s, establishing an independent democracy and managing a new relationship with Britain. Despite understanding the difficulties of stemming the migrant flow, once in opposition after 1932, Fine Gael deputies never lost an opportunity to question Fianna Fáil ministers on the size of the population or migration rates. The metric of population size– how many people in the twenty-six counties, where they were located, how many were leaving – seemed to be a commonly held scale of worth for the country. Bigger was better. Recouping a pre-Famine population would be a victory for those who doubted the viability of the independent Irish state. The Commission on Emigration and Other Population Problems articulated this view: 'a steadily increasing population should occupy a high place among the criteria by which the success of national policy should be judged'.[18] Emigration was therefore recognised – both at the time and by historians – as a significant marker of failure for consecutive Irish governments; Delaney has gone so far as to say that it was the 'acid test' by which Lemass judged the entire success of the nation.[19] None of this rhetoric paid attention to the conditions in which people were living, the strain large families put on impoverished city and rural dwellers, or the crushing weight of disappointment that many, unable to fulfil their ambitions and desires in Ireland, experienced.

Fianna Fáil made it a mantra on pre-election platforms to question emigration and the lack of employment whilst in opposition, but did not follow through with their rhetoric once in power. For example, in a speech entitled 'A Constructive Policy' given by Éamon de Valera on 22 August 1927 at Blackrock Town Hall, he issued a dire warning to the Cumann na nGaedheal administration on their duties to their citizens:

17 Akenson, *The Irish Diaspora*, p. 10.
18 Commission on Emigration and Other Population Problems, *Majority Report*, para. 472.
19 Delaney, 'Emigration, Political Cultures and the Evolution of Post-War Irish Society', p. 62.

Unemployment and emigration, if allowed to continue, will so cripple this nation that there can be little hope for it, in the immediate future at any rate. Work must be found. I have repeatedly stated that I hold it is the primary duty of a modern state to ensure that every man who is able and willing to work will have work, so that he may earn his daily bread.

This quotation raises two interesting points – first, it was made in an election year and hence represents a populist approach designed to appeal to both the unemployed and underemployed. De Valera's speech also succeeded in making the criticism without, however, distinguishing how Fianna Fáil would do things differently. Second, the quotation refers to 'every man' who needs work, and while the use of the male referent is usual in speeches made in this era to refer to all peoples of a nation, the conspicuous lack of reference to both male and female emigration and the equal need of men and women to earn a livelihood indicates a disregard for women's financial needs, independent of men. Women were part of a nation that expected better as independence progressed and despite gendered rhetoric about the family wage the reality was that most households in Ireland were dependent on men's *and* women's incomes, or remittances in the case of emigrants.

Why did successive governments not try to formulate a national policy on population? Could it have intervened in the marriage practices of its populace by giving dowries, as advocated by M.J. Molloy? Should the government have paid more attention to female employment opportunities? The lack of coherent government policy to tackle what was perceived as a national problem begs the question: why? When so much rhetoric was expounded on the 'evils' of emigration, and harsh censure invoked when any inference was made to positive aspects of migrating to Britain, it seems curious that no administration attempted to tackle it. The answer, perhaps, lies simply in political pragmatism. No politician wished explicitly to promise something they knew they could not deliver. The fact that migration patterns changed may also have had an influence. Migration to Britain was not as conspicuous as to the USA, for example, requiring little documentation (apart from during the Emergency).

Failure adequately to address emigration was not limited to any particular political party. As Delaney noted, 'despite the fact that emigration was a politically charged issue, no party developed a distinct policy on emigration but rather they anticipated that a reduction in emigration could be brought about by a successful economic policy'.[20] Emigration was viewed as a 'by-product' of unemployment, a secondary problem, not an issue to be tackled with a specific, strategic, dedicated policy of its own. It therefore

20 Delaney, *Demography, State and Society*, p. 296.

remained an issue used as a political jibe rather than a subject of serious debate, and its use as a political tool and an emblem for marking progress continued beyond the period under study here. After the election of 1948, de Valera confidently announced to a luncheon given by the United Irish Societies in San Francisco: 'I have no doubt that we can say soon that no man or woman need leave Irish soil because of economic necessity'.[21] Quite how this was planned was not addressed and 'soon' was never to come.

By failing to develop economic policies that would successfully tackle unemployment, emigration was doomed to the exigencies of economic circumstances that saw Ireland act as a recruitment pool for Britain. The setting up of the Commission on Emigration and Other Population Problems may have seemed the first step towards developing such policies. However, the results and recommendations of the Commission were studiously ignored, despite the political rhetoric surrounding the body. The obsession with emigration as a topic led many at the time, and many more historians since, simply to refer to the Commission as the 'Commission on Emigration', thereby forgetting that it had a wider remit. Perhaps if attention had been paid to the other categories of demography that were discussed in the report – illegitimacy, marriage rates, rural depopulation, urban immigration – greater efforts could have been made to produce 'joined up' thinking in policy. If the government had also taken the bold step of developing more employment for women, for example, this may also have lessened their emigration rates.

It is unlikely, however, that women would have been fully considered within any national economic plans given the conservative political climate at this time. Irish legislation of the period restricted women's access to employment in favour of developing opportunities for men. This may have meant, ironically, that despite overt concern for female emigrants, their rates of emigration would not have been substantially affected by the introduction of specific economic policies to combat emigration. Members of the Dáil and Seanad, male or female, rarely took a proactive view on lessening the need for female emigration. Even if some had objected to the discourses or wished to implement legislation, women's low representation in the Oireachtas meant that a critical mass was not achieved for women's issues to emerge. Even on the Commission, ostensibly a body meant to influence policy, the female members (Mrs Agnes McGuire and Mrs Frances Wrenne) do not feature as strong figures of controversy or influence and as argued in Chapter 2. They do not come across as having a role in representing a 'female point of view' on emigration and may have been appointed simply as a token gesture. This view may be influenced because of the lack of alternative archival material relating to the Commission. It is more likely, however, that the women adopted

21 *Irish Independent*, 17 March 1948.

positions similar to those of women TDs and Senators at the time in being less vocal than their male counterparts in the political arena. Hilda Tweedy's comment on 'silent sisters' in public life may be apposite here; the extant records suggest neither woman had a strong impact on the eventual report.[22]

Arguments over civil rights to travel, and thus the inevitability of some form of migration, were raised periodically. While some TDs were obviously serious when they argued for citizens' rights to freedom of movement, it is also the case that this line of reasoning allowed the government justification for not introducing restrictions on emigration. As Deputy Coburn argued in 1945, viewing emigration as an exciting escapade for some did not ring true: 'There is no use getting up and saying that young men leave this country in a spirit of adventure. That is a new saying of Fianna Fáil Deputies, very different from what they said prior to the advent of a Fianna Fáil government'.[23]

While restricting citizens' movements could only legitimately be sanctioned in crisis situations such as the Emergency, bans or strict controls on emigration would not have been the most effective way in any case for reducing emigration rates due to the resourcefulness of those who wished to leave the country. Emigration could have been more effectively controlled or reduced through national policy. This needed backing up by significant financial resources for employment schemes in rural areas that would have kept people on the land, and support for urban industries in need of protectionist controls or the fostering of fledgling industries. This may appear to be too modern a solution, relying on notions of benign government intervention in the private lives of its citizens to ensure quality of life. It is worth remembering, however, that other radical economic solutions to the demographic problems Ireland faced at the time were raised. These included the decentralisation of government departments in the 1950s to arrest the depopulation of rural areas[24] and the introduction of a marriage allowance,[25] and though the allowance was not given to all it was gifted to women retiring from the civil and public sector upon their marriage.

Wills has written of the sense of 'moral failure, or national "defeatism"' that enveloped Ireland in the 1950s resulting from the return to emigration on a large scale.[26] She argues that the Catholic Church began to adopt a more realistic attitude to emigration during this decade, evidenced by a decline in speeches 'exhorting emigrants to remember their national duty' and an

22 Hilda Tweedy, *A Link in the Chain*, p. 22.
23 *Dáil Éireann Debates*, vol. 97, col. 2466, 13 July 1945.
24 See, for example, John D. Sheridan, 'We're Not Dead Yet', in O'Brien, *The Vanishing Irish*, p. 183.
25 This was suggested in the submission of the playwright M.J. Molloy to the Commission on Emigration and Other Population Problems, but was rejected.
26 Wills, *The Best Are Leaving*, p. 14.

acceptance of 'the economic laws which were forcing people to leave'.[27] However, this presupposes an acceptance of all emigrants as primarily economically motivated, a premise that was not universally accepted, as an examination of female emigrants establishes. Furthermore, when looking specifically at the case of women's emigration, it seems this mood of moral failure was imbricated with a concern about the future sustainability of the nation and a desire to control the sexual behaviours of those who left. This is another example of how a specific focus on women, their motivations and experiences is essential to appreciate fully the qualitative differences between male and female migrants in the past, differences that have been erased by radical changes in women's status in society in the decades since the 1970s. The 1950s and the 1960s also saw a marked change in immigration to Britain with the rise in Commonwealth immigration that may have significantly changed the Irish experience as a white migrant grouping, differentiated yet more similar to the host community than the 'new wave' emigrants.

Histories which treat of emigration in a broad sense seem to be drawn to the image of the navvy, the 'men who built Britain', rather than the women who married them, cooked for them, reared children with them and often had working lives outside the home. Indeed, the image of the navvy appears to be paramount in the collective memory and cultural iconography of migration to Britain. There are, however, other histories to be told. Charlotte Wildman's research on the active religious lives of Irish women in Liverpool reveals interesting details of the ways in which women used a catholic identity as a focus of leisure pursuits such as shopping.[28] More generally, greater research is needed into Irish women's leisure activities, their engagement with religious-based organisations attempting to offer entertainment, and their views on the social aspects of immigrant life in Britain.

Focusing only on men reinforces the ideology of that male employment and men's reasons for emigrating were more serious topics than the concerns of women. Researching women's lives, putting them centre stage as the subject of this book, challenges the historiography of modern Ireland which has in many cases marginalised their experiences to special chapters or fleeting references. Despite the excellent work completed by historians who have traced and interrogated the gendered nature of the state, its legislation and institutions, the discursive practices that helped to shape such phenomena have yet to be fully understood in the context of emigration. From a feminist perspective, it is important to acknowledge the past struggles of women, and with regard to Irish women's emigration, the ungrateful treatment they received in the public

---

27   Ibid.
28   Charlotte Wildman, 'Irish-Catholic Women and Modernity in 1930s Liverpool', pp. 125–159.

domain when they sustained their homes and families through remittances. Connolly has observed that at the same time as remittances were welcomed there was a simultaneous 'obscure opposition' to emigration.[29] This is a good paradigm for understanding objections to female emigration itself.

It would be short-sighted not to acknowledge a key benefit to women because of the cultural and gendered stereotypes that emerged about Irish women emigrants in this period. Emigration, despite its negative connotations, provided positive outcomes for many emigrants, particularly women: being female, white, English-speaking and a professional (in the case of the many nurses in Britain) allowed Irish women to avoid the narrow stereotype of the drunken navvy or Celtic rogue. Unlike their counterparts in America in an earlier era, there was no cultural equivalent of the 'Bridget' domestic servant archetype, a coarse, brutish, clumsy and violent rendition of the Irish female, drawn in opposition to the WASP (white, Anglo-Saxon Protestant) mistress. Further research is required to understand experiences of discrimination, particularly in light of the intriguing argument by Rossiter that Irish women were given servant roles in houses that did not bring them into contact with the family.[30]

Women's low levels of influence in public debates or in shaping public policies must be acknowledged as a factor in why an organised, collective female emigrant voice failed to emerge in the early years of the Irish Free State. Mary Kettle, one of the few prominent feminists and public activists in independent Ireland, lamented this in a letter to Mary Hayden: 'Irish women are hopeless as regards all feminist activities'.[31] Indeed, it was not until the 1970s and the 1980s that organisations such as the London Irish Women's Centre were established, bringing to light the impact of women's emigration on both Irish and British society. It is significant that this awakening came from women outside rather than inside Ireland and that it was within the larger context of the Second Wave Feminist Movement, tying these issues to demands for equality for women in all areas of society.

Moving Histories offers an analysis specifically of women. It is by no means an exhaustive work, with many paths needing further exploration by future scholars, and it is hoped there will be many. The importance of continuing to highlight women's emigration experiences cannot be taken for granted given that collections are still produced about 'the Irish' that fail to include chapters on women. Yet women are essential to the story. It has been

29 Connolly, 'Emigration from Independent Ireland', p. 82.
30 Rossiter, 'In Search of Mary's Past', p. 16.
31 Undated letter from Mary S. Kettle to Mary Hayden, letters and postcards addressed to Mary Hayden, 1908–38. Mary Hayden papers, University College Dublin Archives, MS 24009.

important in this book to take up the challenge set implicitly by Mary Cullen in *Telling it Our Way* to create a multidimensional narrative that is capable of complexity and inclusion of multiple perspectives:

> History, in the sense of the closest approximate reconstruction of what really happened that can be achieved, will always need the convergence of as many different stories from as many different points of view as possible.[32]

This book ends its temporal analysis at a significant juncture in the history of emigration. The declaration of an Irish republic in 1948 fuelled a sense of patriotism and a feeling of new beginnings.[33] The subsequent establishment of the Commission on Emigration and Other Population Problems in the same year may have held hope for some that the continuing demographic anomalies in Ireland would be finally explained and overcome. Meanwhile, 'emigration took on a "new lease of life"'[34] and any such hopes were dashed. Increasing numbers of men and women continued to emigrate, and the 1950s became a watershed era in twentieth-century Irish migration. Jackson has estimated that an average of 30,000 Irish people came annually to Britain from 1951 onwards and the number of Irish-born persons in London alone rose by half between 1951 and 1961 to reach a total of 172,493 or 5.4 per cent of the total population of London. Irish-born people in England and Wales totalled 627,021 in 1961 compared with 381,089 in 1931.[35] Not only were there increasing numbers leaving the country, but also new destinations emerged such as Australia, whose government was offering to pay the passage of families willing to immigrate.[36] This again raised the spectre of more permanent whole family migrations as seen in the nineteenth century.

The 1950s also saw a change in strategy by the Catholic Church, which switched from focusing on Irish emigrants at ports and stations at home to the needs of Irish immigrants in Britain. For women, this meant less focus on white slavery; but the moral concerns did not disappear, they simply shifted. Legion of Mary workers reported high numbers of Irish women

---

32 Mary Cullen, 'Telling it Our Way: Feminist History', in Steiner-Scott, *Personally Speaking*, p. 264.

33 Ireland officially became a republic with the passing of the Republic of Ireland Act, 1948 on 21 December 1948.

34 Comment by Professor Liam O Buachalla, in Bielenberg, *The Irish Diaspora*, p. 118.

35 Jackson, *The Irish in Britain*, p. 15.

36 In 1948, the Australian government offered to pay up to £35 for individual passages to Australia which ranged from £60 to £100. See Angela McCarthy, '"The Only Place Worth Thinking About": Personal Testimony and Irish and Scottish Migrants in Australasia, 1921–61', *Social History*, 33.3 (2008), p. 319.

Figure 8.1 Photograph
of an Irish mother
dated 1960, at
Commercial Road, East
London. Reproduced
with permission
of the Irish Jesuit
Archives, Dublin.

involved in street prostitution, particularly in London, and high rates of
Irish women cohabiting and having mixed-race children with newly arrived
colonial immigrants.[37] A photograph of one such family is included in the
papers of Fr Leonard Sheil, SJ, for example, emanating from his mission
work in Britain.[38] The Hotel Chaplaincy scheme was initiated in 1957 in
part to address these concerns as it was felt that many establishments Irish
women worked in were little better than brothels, or, more innocently, that
hotel shift work would keep employees from attending mass.[39] Thus the
period under review here was one of intense change, faltering expectations,
speculation and regulation of emigration that was ultimately to fail to bring
about any significant changes in the numbers of men and women leaving
Ireland.

The 1950s was the era of the 'vanishing Irish', many of whom remain
in Britain to this day and are referred to as the 'forgotten Irish'. The 1950s
was a moment of significance and the beginning of a process for some that
saw migrations conceived of as temporary become permanent. O'Leary has
pointed to the agency of women in Ireland in creating social change from
the 1950s, a time when 'rising levels of individual and collective dissatisfaction at both the cost and standard of living began to undermine national
consensus'.[40] For others, the tide was too slow to change, Ireland too narrow
an economy to find decent, well-paid employment, too restrictive to women's
personal ambitions, and they continued to go. This book is for them all.

37 Ewart, 'Caring for Migrants', p. 266.
38 Undated photograph, 'Irish mother & Jamaican babies' in file entitled 'Missions in
   Britain 1950s'. Irish Jesuit Archives, Dublin, IE IJA/ADMN/3/64.
39 Ewart, 'Caring for Migrants', p. 266; see also Kennedy, *Welcoming the Stranger*.
40 Eleanor O'Leary, 'Desperate Housewives: Social Change and the Desire for Modern
   Lifestyles in 1950s Ireland', in Barr, Buckley and Kelly, *Engendering Ireland*, p. 14.

Select Bibliography

Primary Sources

Collections in Ireland

The National Library
Newspapers
The Advocate
The Catholic Herald and Standard (*The Standard*)
Christus Rex
Church of Ireland Gazette
The Connaught Telegraph
The Freeman's Journal
The Irish Catholic
The Irish Catholic Herald
Irish Farmer's Journal
The Irish Independent
The Irish Press
Irish Review and Annual (*Supplement to the Irish Times*)
The Irish Statesman
The Irish Times
Leitrim Observer
The Meath Chronicle
Sunday Independent
The Tuam Herald

Department of Health and Children
22.4.3, Clandillon papers (489778), UK–Ireland Repatriation Scheme, 1939–50

Down and Connor Diocesan Archives, Belfast
Records relating to the International Catholic Girls' Protection Society (provided in
hard copy by Canon G. Hanlon)

Dublin Diocesan Archives
Archbishop Byrne papers, Minutes of the Hierarchy
McQuaid papers, Catholic Social Welfare Bureau, Box 1, Ref. AB8/B/XIX; Box 2, Ref. AB8/B/XX
McQuaid papers, Emigrant Welfare Box 1, General Correspondence 1939–61, Ref. AB8/B/XXIX
Papers of the International Catholic Girls Protection Society, Irish Branch

Irish Labour History Archives
Archives of the Irish Women Workers' Union (IWWU)

Jesuit Archives, Dublin
Fr Edward Cahill, SJ, private papers
Fr Edward J. Coyne, SJ, private papers
Fr Richard S. Devane, SJ, private papers
Fr Leonard Shiel, SJ, private papers

Military Archives
Office of the Controller of Censorship, Records 1939–45

National Archives, Ireland
Department of External Affairs/Foreign Affairs
Department of the Taoiseach Department of Industry and Commerce
Government Information Service Files

National Folklore Archive, University College Dublin
Anne Sweeney, interview by Helen McCarthy, 1994, Record Number 6563, Tape C0627
Margaret O'Neill, self-recorded life story, undated, Tape C0304
MSS 1407–1411, Irish Emigration

Representative Church Body Library
Reports of the Guardians of the Magdalen Asylum, Leeson Street, Dublin
Girls' Friendly Society papers

Cardinal Tomás Ó Fiaich Library and Archive
Cardinal McRory papers

Trinity College Dublin
Arnold Marsh papers, MSS 8299–8310-12
C.B. McKenna, 'The Depopulation of Ireland', Text of a speech given in Trinity College Dublin, 1930

University College Cork
UCC Women's Oral History Project https://www.ucc.ie/en/appsoc/resconf/res/oralhistory/

University College Dublin Archives
Mary Hayden papers, MS 24009
Richard Mulcahy papers

Government Reports

Census of Population Reports
Department of Industry and Commerce, *Census of Population, 1926* (Dublin: Stationery Office, 1928–34)
Department of Industry and Commerce, *Census of Population, 1936* (Dublin: Stationery Office, 1938–42)
Department of Industry and Commerce, *Census of Population, 1946* (Dublin: Stationery Office, 1949–52)
Department of Industry and Commerce, *Census of Population, 1951* (Dublin: Stationery Office, 1952–54)

Statistical Abstract of Ireland Reports
Central Statistics Office, *Statistical Abstract of Ireland* (for the years 1926–1948) (Dublin: Stationery Office)

Other Government Reports
Report of the Inter-Departmental Committee on Seasonal Migration to Great Britain, 1937–1938 (Dublin: Stationery Office, 1938)
Report of the Commission on Emigration and Other Population Problems, 1948–1954 (Dublin: Stationery Office, 1954)
Mother and Baby Home Commission of Investigation, *Second Interim Report*, September 2016 www.mbhcoi.ie/MBH.nsf/page/LPRN-ALCFND1238712-en/ $File/MBHCOI%202nd%20Interim%20Report.pdf

Collections in the UK

British Library Sound Archive
Interview by Christopher Maggs with Mrs Maden, Royal College of Nursing History Group Interviews, C545/21/01
Interview by Christopher Maggs with Mrs Pearce, Royal College of Nursing History Group Interviews, C545/26/01-02
Interview by Matthew Linfoot with Millennium Memory Bank Interview Collection, C900/05026 C1
Interview by Reg Hall with Julia Clifford, Reg Hall Archive, C903/431 C1
Interview by Reg Hall with Mary Collins, Reg Hall Archive, C903/420 C1

Catholic Diocesan Archives Liverpool
Archbishop Downey papers

King's Cross Voices
King's Cross Voices Oral History Project, online repository available at https://voices.
  kingscross.co.uk/ (permission to access database granted by Ms Leslie McCartney,
  Project Coordinator)

Liverpool Central Library
Liverpool Port and Station Work Society, Annual Report 1923

Liverpool Record Office
Records of the National Vigilance Association, Liverpool Branch
University of Liverpool Social Science Department, Statistics Division, *Migration to
  and from Merseyside: Home, Irish, Overseas*, The University Press of Liverpool, 1938

Museum of London
Interview with Mary Maguire, Ref 93.50, Museum of London https://www.museumo-
  flondon.org.uk/

The National Archives, Kew
Cabinet Office Home Office
Ministry of Labour and National Service Ministry of Supply

National Archives, Scotland
Camps, Hostels, etc.; Accommodation for seasonal workers; Kirkintilloch Burgh; fatal
  accident inquiry DD 13/227
Removal to Ireland of paupers born in Scotland, HH 1/537
Social service policy in Irish Free State: Correspondence with Civics Inst. Government
  Departments, etc. GD 281/82/36

Smurfitt Archive of the Irish in Britain, London Metropolitan University
Interview with Kathleen Ruth, uncatalogued collection of oral histories
Irish Studies Centre, London Metropolitan University. 'I only came over for a couple of
  years ... Interviews with London Irish elders', DVD, 2003

The Women's Library, London
Records of the Association for Moral and Social Hygiene (3AMS)
Records of the British Women's Emigration Society (1BWE)
Records of the International Bureau for the Suppression of Traffic in Persons (4IBS)
Records of the National Vigilance Association (4NVA)

Private Collections

Nestor–Corless Letters
Letter from British Liaison Officer, H. Toms to Paddy Corless, 3 October 1941
Letter and Money Order from McAlpine Brothers to Paddy Corless, 24 October 1944
Travel permit belonging to Patrick Corless, 18 March 1943
Series of four letters from Josephine Nestor to Patrick (Paddy) Corless, all 1944
(all documents provided, with permission to use, by Ms Adrienne Corless, granddaughter

of Josephine and Paddy Corless; now retained at Trinity College Dublin Manuscripts Department)

Life History and Travel Permit of Mary Henry
Provided by her daughter, Patricia Marsh

Contemporary Books, Articles and Pamphlets

Baxter, Patrick, 'A Nation Losing Its Mothers: Tilled Land Going Barren, Irish Lifeblood for England', *Hibernia*, February 1937, pp. 9–10, 12.

Brennan, Joseph, Geary, R.C., O'Brien, George and Lyon, Stanley, 'The Population Problem: A Radio Discussion', *Journal of the Statistical and Social Inquiry Society of Ireland*, 16.1 (1937–38), pp. 112–121.

Brown, Stephen J., SJ, *Emigration from Ireland* (Dublin: The Standard, 1953).

Carter, C.F., 'Symposium on the Report of the Commission on Emigration and Other Population Problems', *Journal of Statistical and Social Inquiry Society of Ireland*, 19.4 (1956), pp. 104–121.

Catholic Truth Society, *Handbook for the Catholic Emigrant to England* (Dublin: CTS, 1953).

Collis, J.S., *An Irishman's England* (London: Cassell and Company, 1937).

Elizabeth, Countess of Fingall, *Seventy Years Young: Memories of Elizabeth, Countess of Fingall, as told to Pamela Hinkson* ([1937] Dublin: The Lilliput Press, 1991).

Elliott, Rev. Spencer H., *A Woman's Honour: A Straight Talk to Men*, Straight Talk Series No. 5 (London: Society for Promoting Christian Knowledge, 1929).

Ellison, Mary, *Sparks beneath the Ashes: Experiences of a London Probation Officer* (London: John Murray, 1934).

Freeman, T.W., 'Migration Movements and the Distribution of Population in Eire', *Journal of the Statistical and Social Inquiry Society of Ireland*, 16.2 (1938–39), pp. 89–104.

—— 'Emigration and Rural Ireland', *Journal of the Statistical and Social Inquiry Society of Ireland*, 17.3 (1945–46), pp. 404–422.

Gaffney, Gertrude, *Emigration to England: What You Should Know About It, Advice to Irish Girls* (Dublin: Irish Independent, 1937).

Gregory, J.W., *Human Migration and the Future: A Study of the Causes, Effects and Control of Emigration* (London: Seely, Service and Co., 1928).

Hanly, Joseph, *National Action: A Plan for the National Recovery of Ireland*, 4th edn (Dublin: The Council of National Action, 1947).

Hopkins, E., Rev., 'Irish Workers in England', *Christus Rex*, April 1948, pp. 17–24.

Inman, Peggy, *Labour in the Munitions Industries* (London: Her Majesty's Stationery Office, 1957).

Lucey, Rev. Cornelius, 'The Problem of the Woman Worker', *Irish Ecclesiastical Record*, 48 (July–Dec. 1936), pp. 449–467.

McQuaid, J.C., Archbishop of Dublin, 'Pastoral Letter of the Archbishop of Dublin, Lent 1942' (Dublin: Browne & Nolan, 1942).

—— 'Pastoral Letter of the Archbishop of Dublin, Lent 1943' (Dublin: Browne & Nolan, 1943).

—— 'Pastoral Letter of the Archbishop of Dublin, Lent 1944' (Dublin: Browne & Nolan, 1944).

—— 'Pastoral Letter of the Archbishop of Dublin, Lent 1945' (Dublin: Browne & Nolan, 1945).

—— 'Pastoral Letter of the Archbishop of Dublin, Lent 1947' (Dublin: Browne & Nolan, 1947).

—— 'Pastoral Letter of the Archbishop of Dublin, Lent 1948' (Dublin: Browne & Nolan, 1948).

Mass Observation, *People in Production: An Enquiry into British War Production, Part 1* (London: John Murray, 1942).

O'Carroll, Rev. Michael, 'The Legion of Mary', *Irish Ecclesiastical Review*, 66 (July–Dec. 1945), pp. 353–359.

O'Doherty, T., Rev., Bishop of Clonfert, 'Catholics and Citizenship', pamphlet (1922), National Library Reference Ir282p179.

Ó Donnabháin, Séamus, 'The Depopulation of Ireland', *Capuchin Annual*, The Father Matthew Record Office, Dublin, 1930, pp. 150–152.

Oldham, C.H., 'Reform of the Irish Census of Population', *Economic Journal*, 36.141 (1926), pp. 118–123.

Political and Economic Planning, *Report on the British Health Services: A Survey of the Existing Health Services in Great Britain with Proposals for Future Development* (London: Political and Economic Planning, 1937).

Rigney, P. Ivers, 'The State as Teacher', *Irish Ecclesiastical Record*, 34 (July–Dec. 1929), pp. 611–623.

Schrier, Arnold, *Ireland and the American Emigration, 1850–1900* (New York: Russell & Russell, 1958).

Strong, Rupert, 'An Englishman Looks at Ireland', *Hibernia*, October 1937, pp. 5–6 and 30 (article split over pages).

Tait, D. Christie, 'International Aspects of Migration', *Journal of the Royal Institute of International Affairs*, 6.1 (Jan. 1927), pp. 25–46.

Toksvig, Signe, 'Why Girls Leave Ireland', *Survey*, 1929, pp. 483–509.

'Vigilans', 'Goings and Comings', *Christus Rex*, October 1947, pp. 56–57.

Waters, J.P.F., 'Diseases of the Social System', *Irish Ecclesiastical Record*, 52 (July–Dec. 1938), pp. 386–395.

Other Primary Sources

Lambkin, Romie, *My Time in the War: An Irishwoman's Diary* (Dublin: Wolfhound Press, 1992).

MacAmhlaigh, Donall, *An Irish Navvy: The Diary of an Exile*, translated from Irish by Valentin Iremonger (Cork: The Collins Press, 2004).

O'Mara, Pat, *The Autobiography of a Liverpool Irish Slummy* (Bath: Cedric Chivers, 1968).

Ravenstein, E.G., 'The Laws of Migration', *Journal of the Statistical Society of London*, 48.2 (June 1885), pp. 167–235.

Secondary Sources

Adams, Michael, *Censorship: The Irish Experience* (Dublin: Scepter Books, 1968).

Akenson, Donald Harman, *The Irish Diaspora: A Primer* (Toronto: P.D. Meany Company Inc., 1996).

—— 'Irish Migration to North America, 1800–1920', in Andy Bielenberg (ed.), *The Irish Diaspora* (London: Longman, 2000), pp. 111–138.

—— *Ireland, Sweden and the Great European Migration, 1815–1914* (Quebec: McGill-Queen's University Press, 2012).

Arensberg, Conrad, and Kimball, Solon T., *Family and Community in Ireland*, 2nd edn (Cambridge, Mass.: Harvard University Press, 1968).

Allain, Jean, 'White Slave Traffic in International Law', *Journal of Trafficking and Human Exploitation*, 1.1 (2017), pp. 1–40.

Arkell, Tom, 'Irish Studies in Coventry: Pilot Project on the Development of Irish Cultural Studies for the Children of Irish Migrant Workers in Coventry', *Irish Studies in Britain*, 1 (Spring 1981), p. 9.

Auchmuty, Rosemary, Jeffreys, Sheila and Miller, Elaine, 'Lesbian History and Gay Studies: Keeping a Feminist Perspective', *Women's History Review*, 1.1 (1992), pp. 89–108.

Baines, Dudley, 'European Emigration 1815–1930: Looking at the Emigration Decision Again', *Economic History Review*, n.s., 47.3 (Aug. 1994), pp. 525–544.

—— *Emigration from Europe, 1815–1930* (Cambridge: Cambridge University Press, 1995).

—— 'The Economics of Migration: Nineteenth-Century Britain', *ReFresh*, 27 (1998), pp. 5–8.

Bardon, Jonathon and Keogh, Dermot, 'Introduction: Ireland, 1921–84', in J.R. Hill (ed.), *A New History of Ireland*, vol. 7, *Ireland, 1921–84* (Oxford: Oxford University Press, 2003), pp. iv–xxxiii.

Barrington, Clare, *Irish Women in England: An Annotated Bibliography* (Dublin: University College Dublin, 1997).

Bartlett, Thomas, *Ireland: A History* (Cambridge: Cambridge University Press, 2010).

Bauer, Elaine and Thompson, Paul, '"She's Always the Person with a Very Global Vision": The Gender Dynamics of Migration, Narrative Interpretation and the Case of Jamaican Transnational Families', *Gender and History*, 16.2 (Aug. 2004), pp. 334–375.

Beale, Jenny, *Women in Ireland: Voices of Change* (Dublin: Gill & Macmillan, 1986).

Beaumont, Caitriona, 'Women, Citizenship and Catholicism in the Irish Free State, 1922–1948', *Women's History Review*, 6.4 (1997), pp. 563–585.

—— 'Gender, Citizenship and the State, 1922–1990', in Scott Brewster, Virginia Crossman, Fiona Beckett and David Alderson (eds), *Ireland in Proximity: History, Gender, Space* (London: Routledge, 1999), pp. 94–108.

Beiner, Guy and Bryson, Anna, 'Listening to the Past and Talking to Each Other: Problems and Possibilities Facing Oral History in Ireland', *Irish Economic and Social History*, 30 (2003), pp. 71–78.

Bermant, Chaim, *Point of Arrival: A Study of London's East End* (London: Eyre Methuen, 1975).

Bhaba, Homi, 'Narrating the Nation', in John Hutchinson and Anthony D. Smith (eds), *Nationalism* (Oxford: Oxford University Press, 1994), pp. 306–312.

Bielenberg, Andy (ed.), *The Irish Diaspora* (London: Longman, 2000).

Bishop, Patrick, *The Irish Empire* (London: Macmillan, 1999).

Bourke, Angela, Kilfeather, Siobhán, Luddy, Maria, MacCurtain, Margaret, Meaney, Gerardine, Ní Dhonnchadha, Máirín, O'Dowd, Mary and Wills, Clair (eds), *The Field Day Anthology of Irish Writing*, vol. 4, *Irish Women's Writing and Traditions* (Cork: Cork University Press in association with Field Day, 2002).

—— (eds), *The Field Day Anthology of Irish Writing*, vol. 5, *Irish Women's Writing and Traditions* (Cork: Cork University Press in association with Field Day, 2002).

Bowen, Kurt, *Protestants in a Catholic State* (Quebec: McGill-Queen's University Press, 1983).

Boyce, D. George and O'Day, Alan (eds), *The Making of Modern Irish History: Revisionism and the Revisionist Controversy* (London: Routledge, 1997).

Boyce, Frank, 'Irish Catholicism in Liverpool: The 1920s and 1930s', in Patrick Buckland and John Belchem (eds), *The Irish in British Labour History*, Conference Proceedings of Irish Studies No. 1 (Liverpool: Liverpool University Press, 1993), pp. 86–101.

Boyd, Monica, 'Family and Personal Networks in International Migration: Recent Developments and New Agendas', *International Migration Review*, 23.23 (1989), pp. 638–670.

Brah, Avtar, Hickman, Mary J. and Mac an Ghaill, Máirtín, *Thinking Identities: Ethnicity, Racism and Culture* (Basingstoke: Palgrave Macmillan, 1999).

Braybon, Gail and Summerfield, Penny, *Out of the Cage: Women's Experiences in Two World Wars* (London: Pandora, 1987).

Bronack, Mairead, *The Curse of Emigration* (London: Excalibur Press, 1989).

Buckland, Patrick and Belchem, John (eds), *The Irish in British Labour History*, Conference Proceedings of Irish Studies No. 1 (Liverpool: Liverpool University Press, 1993).

Buckley, Sarah-Anne, *The Cruelty Man: Child Welfare, the NSPCC and the State in Ireland, 1889–1956* (Manchester: Manchester University Press, 2013).

Burrell, Kathy, *Moving Lives: Narratives of Nation and Migration among Europeans in Post-War Britain* (Aldershot: Ashgate, 2006).

Burton, Antoinette, '"History" is Now: Feminist Theory and the Production of Historical Feminisms', *Women's History Review*, 1.1 (1992), pp. 25–39.

Carty, R.K., 'Women in Irish Politics', *Canadian Journal of Irish Studies*, 6.1 (1980), pp. 90–104.

Carroll, Bernice A. (ed.), *Liberating Women's History: Theoretical and Critical Essays* (Urbana: University of Illinois Press, 1976).

Caslin, Samantha, '"One Can Only Guess What Might Have Happened if the Worker Had Not Intervened in Time": The Liverpool Vigilance Association, Moral Vulnerability and Irish Girls in Early- to Mid-Twentieth-Century Liverpool', *Women's History Review*, 25:2 (2016), pp. 254–273.

Castles, Stephen and Miller, Mark J., *The Age of Migration: International Population Movements in the Modern World*, 3rd edn (Basingstoke: Palgrave Macmillan, 2003).

Chubb, Basil, *The Politics of the Irish Constitution* (Dublin: Institute of Public Administration, 1991).

Clear, Caitriona, *Women of the House: Women's Household Work in Ireland, 1922–1961* (Dublin: Irish Academic Press, 2000).

—— '"Hardship, Help and Happiness", Oral History Narratives of Women's Lives in Ireland, 1921–1961', *Oral History*, 32 (2003), pp. 33–42.

—— '"Too Fond of Going": Female Emigration and Change for Women in Ireland, 1946–1961', in Dermot Keogh, Finbarr O'Shea and Carmel Quinlan (eds), *The Lost Decade: Ireland in the 1950s* (Cork: Mercier Press, 2004), pp. 135–146.

Coleman, D.A., 'The Demographic Transition in Ireland in International Context', in J.H. Goldthorpe and C.T. Whelan (eds), *The Development of Industrial Society in Ireland* (Oxford: Oxford University Press, 1994), pp. 53–77.

—— 'Demography and Migration in Ireland, North and South', in Anthony F. Heath, Richard Breen and Christopher T. Whelan (eds), *Ireland North and South: Perspectives from Social Science* (Oxford: Oxford University Press, 1999), pp. 69–115.

Colum, Padraig (ed.), *A Treasury of Irish Folklore: The Stories, Traditions, Legends, Humor, Wisdom, Ballads and Songs of the Irish People* (New York: Crown Publishers, 1954).

Comerford, R.V., *Ireland: Inventing the Nation* (London: Hodder Arnold, 2003).

Conlan, Patricia, 'Female Emigration from Ireland', in Eberhard Bort and Neil Evans (eds), *Networking Europe: Essays on Regionalism and Social Democracy* (Liverpool: Liverpool University Press, 2000), pp. 175–190.

Connolly, Tracey, 'Emigration from Ireland to Britain during the Second World War', in Andy Bielenberg (ed.), *The Irish Diaspora* (London: Longman, 2000), pp. 51–64.

—— 'Irish Workers in Britain during World War Two', in Brian Girvin and Geoffrey Roberts (eds), *Ireland and the Second World War: Politics, Society and Remembrance* (Dublin: Four Courts Press, 2000), pp. 121–132.

—— 'The Commission on Emigration, 1948–1954', in Dermot Keogh, Finbarr O'Shea and Carmel Quinlan (eds), *The Lost Decade: Ireland in the 1950s* (Cork: Mercier Press, 2004), pp. 87–104.

Cooney, John, *John Charles McQuaid: Ruler of Catholic Ireland* (Dublin: The O'Brien Press, 1999).

Cova, Anne (ed.), *Comparative Women's History: New Approaches* (New York: Columbia University Press, 2006).

Crowley, Una and Rob Kitchin, 'Producing "Decent Girls": Governmentality and the Moral Geographies of Sexual Conduct in Ireland (1922–1937)', *Gender, Place and Culture*, 14.4 (2008), pp. 355–372.

Cullen, Mary, 'Invisible Women and their Contribution to Historical Studies', *Stair* (1982), pp. 2–6.

—— 'Women's History in Ireland', in Karen Offen, Ruth Roach and Jane Rendall (eds), *Writing Women's History: International Perspectives* (Basingstoke: Palgrave Macmillan, 1991), pp. 429–441.

Cullen Owens, Rosemary, *A Social History of Women in Ireland, 1870–1970* (Dublin: Gill & Macmillan, 2005).

D'Arcy, Frank, *The Story of Irish Emigration* (Cork: Mercier Press, 1999).

Daly, Mary E., *Social and Economic History of Ireland Since 1800* (Dublin: The Educational Company, 1981).

—— 'Women in the Irish Workforce from Pre-Industrial to Modern Times', *Saothar*, 17 (1981), pp. 74–82.

—— 'The Economic Ideals of Irish Nationalism: Frugal Comfort or Lavish Austerity?', *Éire-Ireland*, 29.4 (1994), pp. 77–100.

—— 'Women in the Irish Free State, 1922–1939: The Interaction between Economics and Ideology', *Journal of Women's History*, 6.4/7.1 (1995), pp. 99–116.

—— *Women and Work in Ireland*, Studies in Irish Economic and Social History 7 (Dublin: Economic and Social History Society of Ireland, 1997).

—— 'Irish Nationality and Citizenship Since 1922', *Irish Historical Studies*, 32.127 (2001), pp. 377–407.

—— 'Wives, Mothers and Citizens: The Treatment of Women in the 1935 Nationality and Citizenship Act', *Éire-Ireland* (Fall/Winter 2003), pp. 244–263.

—— *The Slow Failure: Population Decline and Independent Ireland, 1920–1971* (Madison: University of Wisconsin Press, 2006).

—— 'Forty Shades of Grey? Irish Historiography and the Challenges of Multidisciplinarity', in Liam Harte and Yvonne Whelan (eds), *Ireland Beyond Boundaries: Mapping Irish Studies in the Twenty-First Century* (London: Pluto Press, 2007), pp. 71–91.

Daniels, Mary, *Exile or Opportunity? Irish Nurses and Midwives in Britain*, Occasional Papers in Irish Studies No. 5 (Liverpool: Liverpool University Press, 1993).

Davis, Graham, 'The Irish in Britain, 1815–1939', in Andy Bielenberg (ed.), *The Irish Diaspora* (London: Longman, 2000), pp. 19–36.

DeLaet, D.L., 'Introduction: The Invisibility of Women in Scholarship on International Migration', in G.A. Kelson and D.L. DeLaet (eds), *Gender and Immigration* (New York: New York University, 1999), pp. 1–17.

Delaney, Enda, 'State, Politics and Demography: The Case of Irish Emigration, 1921–71', *Irish Political Studies*, 13 (1998), pp. 25–49.

—— 'The Churches and Irish Emigration to Britain, 1921–60', *Archivum Hibernicum*, 52 (1998), pp. 98–114.

—— '"Almost a Class of Helots in an Alien Land": The British State and Irish Immigration, 1921–1945', *Immigrants and Minorities*, 18.2–3 (July–Nov. 1999), pp. 240–265.

—— *Demography, State and Society: Irish Migration to Britain, 1921–1971* (Liverpool: Liverpool University Press, 2000).

—— 'Placing Postwar Irish Migration to Britain in a Comparative European Perspective, 1945–1981', in Andy Bielenberg (ed.), *The Irish Diaspora* (London: Longman, 2000), pp. 331–356.

—— 'Gender and Twentieth Century Irish Migration', in Pamela Sharpe (ed.), *Women, Gender and Labour Migration: Historical and Global Perspectives* (London: Routledge, 2001), pp. 209–223.

—— *Irish Emigration Since 1921*, Studies in Irish Economic and Social History 8 (Dublin: Economic and Social History Society of Ireland, 2002).

—— 'The Vanishing Irish? The Exodus from Ireland in the 1950s', in Dermot Keogh, Finbarr O'Shea and Carmel Quinlan (eds), *The Lost Decade: Ireland in the 1950s* (Cork: Mercier Press, 2004), pp. 80–86.

—— 'Emigration, Political Cultures and the Evolution of Post-War Irish Society', in Brian Girvin and Gary Murphy (eds), *The Lemass Era: Politics and Society in the Ireland of Seán Lemass* (Dublin: University College Dublin, 2005), pp. 49–65.

—— 'The Irish Diaspora', *Irish Economic and Social History*, 23 (2006), pp. 35–45.

—— *The Irish in Post-War Britain* (Oxford: Oxford University Press, 2007).

Delaney, Enda and MacRaild, Donald. M., 'Irish Migration Networks and Ethnic Identities since 1750: An Introduction', *Immigrants and Minorities*, 23.2–3 (July–Nov. 2005), pp. 127–142.

Devlin Trew, Johanne, *Leaving the North: Migration and Memory, Northern Ireland 1921–2011* (Liverpool: Liverpool University Press, 2013).

Diner, Hasia R., *Erin's Daughters in America: Irish Immigrant Women in the Nineteenth Century* (Baltimore, Md.: Johns Hopkins University Press, 1983).

Doherty, Richard, *Irish Men and Women in the Second World War* (Dublin: Four Courts Press, 1999).

Downs, Laura Lee, 'From Women's History to Gender History', in Stefan Berger, Heiko Feldner and Kevin Passmore (eds), *Writing History: Theory and Practice* (London: Hodder Arnold, 2003), pp. 261–281.

Drudy, P.J., 'Migration between Ireland and Britain Since Independence', in P.J. Drudy (ed.), *Ireland and Britain Since 1922* (Cambridge: Cambridge University Press, 1986), pp. 107–123.

Duffy, Patrick, 'Literary Reflections on Irish Migration in the Nineteenth and Twentieth Centuries', in Russell King, John Connell and Paul White (eds), *Writing across Worlds: Literature and Migration* (London: Routledge, 1995), pp. 20–38.

—— 'Introduction', in Patrick J. Duffy (ed.), *To and From Ireland: Planned Migration Schemes c.1600–2000* (Dublin: Geography Publications, 2004), pp. 1–15.

Dunne, Catherine, *An Unconsidered People: The Irish in London* (Dublin: New Island Books, 2003).

Dwyer, T. Ryle, *De Valera: The Man and the Myths* (Dublin: Poolbeg Press, 1995).

Earner-Byrne, Lindsey, 'The Boat to England: An Analysis of the Official Reactions to the Emigration of Single Expectant Irishwomen to Britain, 1922–1972', *Irish Economic and Social History*, 30 (2003), pp. 52–70.

—— '"Moral Repatriation": The Response to Irish Unmarried Mothers in Britain, 1920s–1960s', in Patrick J. Duffy (ed.), *To and From Ireland: Planned Migration Schemes c.1600–2000* (Dublin: Geography Publications, 2004), pp. 155–174.

—— 'Managing Motherhood: Negotiating a Maternity Service for Catholic Mothers in Dublin, 1930–1954', *Social History of Medicine*, 19.2 (2006), pp. 261–277.

—— *Mother and Child: Maternity and Child Welfare in Dublin 1922–1960* (Manchester: Manchester University Press, 2007).

Eichengreen, Barry, 'Unemployment in Interwar Britain', *ReFresh*, 8 (1989), pp. 1–4.

Elliot, Bruce S., Gerber, David A., and Sinke, Suzanne M. (eds), *Letters across Borders: The Epistolary Practices of International Migrants* (New York: Palgrave Macmillan, 2006).

Evans, Bryce, 'The Construction Corps, 1940–1948', *Saothar*, 32 (2007), pp. 19–31.

Ewart, Henrietta, 'Protecting the Honour of the Daughters of Eire: Welfare Policy for Irish Female Migrants to England, 1940–70', *Irish Studies Review*, 21.1 (2013), pp. 71–84.

Fanning, Ronan, 'Mr. de Valera Drafts a Constitution', in Brian Farrell (ed.), *De Valera's Constitution and Ours* (Dublin: Gill & Macmillan, 1988), pp. 33–45.

Farrell, Brian, *The Founding of Dáil Éireann: Parliament and Nation Building* (Dublin: Gill & Macmillan, 1971).

—— 'From First Dáil through Irish Free State', in Brian Farrell (ed.), *De Valera's Constitution and Ours* (Dublin: Gill & Macmillan, 1988), pp. 18–32.

Feeney, John, *John Charles McQuaid: The Man and the Mask* (Dublin: The Mercier Press, 1974).

Ferenczi, Imre, *International Migrations*, vol. 1, *Statistics* ([1929] New York: Gordon and Breach Science Publishers, 1969).

Ferriter, Diarmaid, *Mothers, Maidens and Myths: A History of the ICA* (Dublin: FÁS, 1996).

——— *The Transformation of Ireland: 1900–2000* (London: Profile Books, 2005).

——— *Judging Dev: A Reassessment of the Life and Legacy of Éamon de Valera* (Dublin: Royal Irish Academy, 2007).

Fielding, Steven, *Class and Ethnicity: Irish Catholics in England, 1880–1939* (Ballmoor: Open University Press, 1993).

Fitzgerald, Patrick and Brian Lambkin, *Migration in Irish History, 1607–2007* (Basingstoke: Palgrave Macmillan, 2008).

Fitzpatrick, David, 'The Overflow of the Deluge: Anglo-Irish Relationships, 1914–1922', in Oliver MacDonagh and W.F. Mandle (eds), *Ireland and Irish-Australia: Studies in Cultural and Political History* (London: Croom Helm, 1986), pp. 64–80.

——— '"A Share of the Honeycomb": Education, Emigration and Irishwomen', *Continuity and Change*, 1.2 (1986), pp. 217–234.

——— 'The Modernisation of the Irish Female', in Patrick O'Flanagan, Paul Ferguson and Kevin Whelan (eds), *Rural Ireland, 1600–1900: Modernisation and Change* (Cork: Cork University Press, 1987), pp. 162–180.

——— '"That Beloved Country That No Place Else Resembles": Connotations of Irishness in Irish-Australian Letters, 1841–1915', *Irish Historical Studies*, 27.108 (1991), pp. 324–351.

——— 'The Irish in Britain: Settlers or Transients?', in Patrick Buckland and John Belchem (eds), *The Irish in British Labour History*, Conference Proceedings of Irish Studies No. 1 (Liverpool: Liverpool University Press, 1993), pp. 1–10.

——— *Oceans of Consolation: Personal Accounts of Irish Migration to Australia* (Ithaca, NY: Cornell University Press, 1994).

——— *The Two Irelands: 1912–1939* (Oxford: Oxford University Press, 1998).

——— 'Irish Emigration and the Art of Letter-Writing', in Bruce S. Elliot, David A. Gerber and Suzanne M. Sinke (eds), *Letters Across Borders: The Epistolary Practices of International Migrants* (New York: Palgrave Macmillan, 2006), pp. 97–106.

——— *Descendancy: Irish Protestant Histories since 1795* (Cambridge: Cambridge University Press, 2014).

Flanagan, Laurence, *Irish Women's Letters* (Stroud: Sutton Publishing, 1997).

Fletcher, Ian Christopher, 'Opposition by Journalism? The Socialist and Suffragist Press and the Passage of the Criminal Law Amendment Act of 1912', *Parliamentary History*, 25.1 (2006), pp. 88–114.

Fortier, Anne-Marie, *Migrant Belongings: Memory, Space, Identity* (Oxford: Berg, 2000).

Foster, R.F., *Modern Ireland: 1600–1972* (Harmondsworth: Penguin, 1972).

Fowler, Roger, 'Power', in Teun Van Dijk (ed.), *Handbook of Discourse Analysis*, vol. 4, *Discourse Analysis in Society* (London: Academic Press, 1985), pp. 61–82.

Fuchs, Rachel G. and Moch, Leslie Page, 'Pregnant, Single, and Far From Home: Migrant Women in Nineteenth-Century Paris', *American Historical Review*, 93.4 (1990), pp. 1007–1031.

Galway Labour History Group, *The Emigrant Experience: Papers presented at the Second Annual Mary Murray Weekend Seminar, Galway, 30th March–1st April 1990* (Galway: Galway Labour History Group, 1991).

Garfield, Simon, *We Are At War: The Diaries of Five Ordinary People in Extraordinary Times* (London: Ebury Press, 2006).

Garner, Steve, 'Babies, Bodies and Entitlement: Gendered Aspects of Access to Citizenship in the Republic of Ireland', *Parliamentary Affairs*, 60.3 (2007), pp. 437–451.

Garrett, Paul Michael, 'The Abnormal Flight: The Migration and Repatriation of Irish Unmarried Mothers', *Social History*, 25.3 (2000), pp. 330–343.

—— 'The Hidden History of the PFIs: The Repatriation of Unmarried Mothers and their Children in the 1950s and 1960s', *Immigrants and Minorities*, 19.3 (2000), pp. 25–44.

Garvey, Donal, 'The History of Migration Flows in the Republic of Ireland', *Population Trends*, 39 (1985), pp. 22–30.

Gerber, David A., 'Epistolary Masquerades: Acts of Deceiving and Withholding in Immigrant Letters', in Bruce S. Elliot, David A. Gerber and Suzanne M. Sinke (eds), *Letters across Borders: The Epistolary Practices of International Migrants* (New York: Palgrave Macmillan, 2006), pp. 141–157.

Gilje, E.K., *Migration Patterns in and around London* (London: Greater London Council, 1975).

Girvin, Brian, 'Church, State and the Moral Community', in Brian Girvin and Gary Murphy (eds), *The Lemass Era: Politics and Society in the Ireland of Seán Lemass* (Dublin: University College Dublin, 2005), pp. 122–143.

—— *The Emergency: Neutral Ireland, 1939–45* (London: Macmillan, 2006).

Gluck, Sherna, 'What's So Special about Women? Women's Oral History', *Frontiers: A Journal of Women's Studies*, 2.2 (1977), pp. 3–17.

Goldthorpe, J.H. and Whelan, C.T. (eds), *The Development of Industrial Society in Ireland* (Oxford: Oxford University Press, 1994).

Gothard, Jan, 'Space, Authority and the Female Emigrant Afloat', *Australian Historical Studies*, 112 (1999), pp. 96–115.

Gray, Breda, 'Unmasking Irishness: Irish Women, the Irish Nation and the Irish Diaspora', in Jim McLaughlin (ed.), *Location and Dislocation in Contemporary Irish Society: Emigration and Irish Identities* (Cork: Cork University Press, 1997), pp. 209–235.

—— 'Gendering the Irish Diaspora: Questions of Enrichment, Hybridization and Return', *Women's Studies International Forum*, 23.2 (2000), pp. 167–185.

—— *Women and the Irish Diaspora* (London: Routledge, 2004).

Gray, Breda and Ryan, Louise, '(Dis)locating "Woman" and Women in Representations of Irish National Identity', in Anne Byrne and Madeleine Leonard (eds), *Women and Irish Society: A Sociological Reader* (Belfast: Beyond the Pale Publications, 1997), pp. 517–534.

—— 'The Politics of Irish Identity and the Interconnections between Feminism, Nationhood and Colonialism', in Ruth Roach Pierson and Nupur Chaudhuri (eds), *Nation, Empire and Colony: Historicizing Gender and Race* (Bloomington: Indiana University Press, 1998), pp. 121–138.

Gray, Jane, 'Gender Politics and Ireland', Review, *Journal of Women's History*, 6.4/7.1 (1995), pp. 240–249.

Griffin, Gabrielle, and Braidotti, Rosi (eds), *Thinking Differently: A Reader in European Women's Studies* (London: Zed Books, 2002).

Grob-Fitzgibbon, Benjamin, *The Irish Experience during the Second World War: An Oral History* (Dublin: Irish Academic Press, 2004).

Halpin, Brendan, 'Who are the Irish in Britain? Evidence from Large-Scale Surveys', in Andy Bielenberg (ed.), *The Irish Diaspora* (London: Longman, 2000), pp. 89–107.

Hanley, Brian, *The IRA, 1926–1936* (Dublin: Four Courts Press, 2002).

Harte, Liam and Whelan, Yvonne (eds), *Ireland Beyond Boundaries: Mapping Irish Studies in the Twenty-First Century* (London: Pluto Press, 2005).

Hartigan, Maureen and Hickman, Mary J., *The History of the Irish in Britain: A Bibliography* (London: Irish in Britain History Centre, 1986).

Hayes, Alan and Urquhart, Diane (eds), *Irish Women's History* (Dublin: Irish Academic Press, 2004).

Hazard, Mary (with Sweet, Corinne), *Sixty Years a Nurse* (London: Harper Element, 2015).

Healy, John, *The Death of an Irish Town* (Cork: Mercier Press, 1968).

Hearn, Mona, *Below Stairs: Domestic Service Remembered in Dublin and Beyond, 1880–1922* (Dublin: The Lilliput Press, 1993).

Henkes, Barbara, '"Maids on the Move": Images of Femininity and European Women's Labour Migration during the Interwar Years', in Pamela Sharpe (ed.), *Women, Gender and Labour Migration: Historical and Global Perspectives* (London: Routledge, 2001), pp. 224–243.

Herson, John, 'Family History and Memory in Irish Immigrant Families', in Kathy Burrell and Panikos Panayi (eds), *Histories and Memories: Migrants and their History in Britain* (London: Tauris Academic Studies, 2006), pp. 210–233.

Hickey, Donal, 'Emigration', *Sliabh Luacra*, 1.5 (1989), pp. 17–20.

Hickey, Margaret, *Irish Days: Oral Histories of the Twentieth Century* (London: Kyle Cathie, 2001).

Hickman, Mary J., 'Immigration and Monocultural (Re)Imaginings in Ireland and Britain', *Translocations*, 1.2 (2007), pp. 12–25.

Hickman, Mary J. and Bronwen, Walter, 'Deconstructing Whiteness: Irish Women in Britain', *Feminist Review*, 50 (1995), pp. 5–19.

Hickman, Mary J., Morgan, Sarah, Bronwen, Walter and Bradley, Joseph, 'The Limitations of Whiteness and the Boundaries of Englishness: Second-Generation Irish Identifications and Positionings in Multiethnic Britain', *Ethnicities*, 5.2 (2005), pp. 160–182.

Higgins, Bríd and Blackmore, Liz, 'Memories of Emigration: The Folklore Collection as a Genealogical Source', *Galway Roots: Journal of the Galway Family History Society*, 5 (1998), pp. 11–22.

Hill, J.R. (ed.), *A New History of Ireland*, vol. 7, *Ireland, 1921–1984* (Oxford: Oxford University Press, 2003).

Hill, Myrtle, *Women in Ireland: A Century of Change* (Belfast: The Blackstaff Press, 2003).

Hirschman, Albert O., *Exit, Voice, and Loyalty: Responses to Decline in Firms, Organizations, and States* (Cambridge, Mass.: Harvard University Press: 1970).

Hogan, Gerard, *The Origins of the Irish Constitution, 1928–1941* (Dublin: Royal Irish Academy, 2012).

Hogan, Gerard and Whyte, Gerry, *The Irish Constitution*, 4th edn (Dublin: LexisNexis, 2003).

Holden, Katherine, 'Personal Costs and Personal Pleasures: Care and the Unmarried Woman in Inter-War Britain', in Janet Fink (ed.), *Care: Personal Lives and Social Policy* (Bristol: Policy Press, 2004), pp. 43–76.

Holmans, A.E., *Historical Statistics of Housing in Britain* (Cambridge: The Cambridge Centre for Housing and Planning Research, 2005).

Holmes, Colin, *John Bull's Island: Immigration and British Society, 1871–1971* (Basingstoke: Palgrave Macmillan, 1988).

Holohan, Anne, *Working Lives: The Irish in Britain* (Hayes: Irish Post, 1995).

Hornsby-Smith, Michael P. and Dale, Angela, 'The Assimilation of Irish Immigrants in England', *British Journal of Sociology*, 39.4 (1988), pp. 519–544.

Howarth, Ken, *Oral History: A Handbook* (Stroud: Sutton Publishing, 1998).

Howes, Marjorie, 'Introduction: Public Discourse, Private Reflection, 1916–70', in Angela Bourke *et al.* (eds), *The Field Day Anthology of Irish Writing*, vol. 4, *Irish Women's Writing and Traditions* (Cork: Cork University Press in association with Field Day, 2002), pp. 923–930.

Hughes, Eamonn, 'Sent to Coventry: Emigration and Autobiography', in Eve Patten (ed.), *Returning to Ourselves: Second Volume of Papers from the John Hewitt International Summer School* (Belfast: Lagan Press, 1995).

Inglis, Tom, *Moral Monopoly: The Rise and Fall of the Catholic Church in Modern Ireland* (Dublin: UCD Press, 1998).

Jackson, John Archer, *The Irish in Britain* (London: Routledge & Kegan Paul, 1963).

—— 'The Irish in Britain', in P.J. Drudy (ed.), *Ireland and Britain Since 1922* (Cambridge: Cambridge University Press, 1986), pp. 125–138.

Jones, Anne (ed.), *The Scattering: Images of Emigrants from an Irish County* (Dublin: A. & A. Farmar, 2000).

Kearney, Richard (ed.), *Migrants: The Irish at Home and Abroad* (Dublin: Wolfhound Press, 1990).

Kearns, Kevin C., *Dublin's Lost Heroines: Mammies and Grannies in a Vanished City* (Dublin: Gill & Macmillan, 2004).

Kehoe, Karly S., *Creating a Scottish Church: Catholicism, Gender and Ethnicity in Nineteenth-Century Scotland* (Manchester: Manchester University Press, 2010).

—— 'Border Crossings: Being Irish in Nineteenth-Century Scotland and Canada', in Mary J. Hickman and D.A.J. MacPherson (eds), *Irish Diaspora Studies and Women: Theories, Concepts and New Perspectives* (Manchester: Manchester University Press, 2014), pp. 259–288.

Kelly, Kate and Nic Giolla Choille, Triona, *Emigration Matters for Women* (Dublin: Attic Press, 1990).

Kennedy, Conan (ed.), *The Diaries of Mary Hayden*, vols 1–4 (Killala: Morrigan New Century, 2005).

Kennedy, Finola, *Cottage to Crèche: Family Change in Ireland* (Dublin: Institute of Public Administration, 2001).

Kennedy, Liam, *People and Population: A Comparative Study of Population Change in Northern Ireland and the Republic of Ireland* (Dublin and Belfast: Co-Operation North, 1994).

Kennedy, Michael, *Ireland and the League of Nations, 1919–1946: International Relations, Diplomacy and Politics* (Dublin: Irish Academic Press, 1996).

Kennedy, Patricia, *Welcoming the Stranger: Irish Migrant Welfare in Britain since 1957* (Dublin: Irish Academic Press, 2015).

Kennedy, Robert E., *The Irish: Emigration, Marriage and Fertility* (Berkeley: University of California Press, 1973).

Kenny, Kevin, 'Diaspora and Irish Migration History', *Irish Economic and Social History*, 33 (2006), pp. 46–50.

Keogh, Dermot, 'The Irish Constitutional Revolution: An Analysis of the Making of the Constitution', in Frank Litton (ed.), *The Constitution of Ireland, 1937–1987*, special issue of *Administration*, 35.4 (1987), pp. 4–84.

—— *Twentieth-Century Ireland: Nation and State* (Dublin: Gill & Macmillan, 1994).

Kiberd, Declan, *Inventing Ireland: The Literature of the Modern Nation* (London: Jonathan Cape, 1995).

Kiely, Elizabeth, and Leane, Máire, '"What would I be doing at home all day?" Oral Narratives of Irish Married Women's Working Lives, 1936–1960', *Women's History Review*, 13.3 (2004), pp. 427–445.

—— *Irish Women at Work, 1930–1960: An Oral History* (Dublin: Irish Academic Press, 2012).

King, Russell, Connell, John and White, Paul (eds), *Writing across Worlds: Literature and Migration* (London: Routledge, 1995).

King, Russell and O'Connor, Henrietta, 'Migration and Gender: Irish Women in Leicester', *Geography*, 81.4 (1996), pp. 311–325.

Kneafsey, Moya and Cox, Rosie, 'Food, Gender and Irishness: How Irish Women in Coventry Make Home', *Irish Geography*, 35.1 (2002), pp. 6–15.

Kunzel, Regina G., *Fallen Women, Problem Girls: Unmarried Mothers and the Professionalization of Social Work, 1890–1945* (New Haven, Conn. and London: Yale University Press, 1993).

Laite, Julia, *Common Prostitutes and Ordinary Citizens: Commercial Sex in London, 1885–1960* (Basingstoke: Palgrave Macmillan, 2012).

Lambert, Sharon, *Irish Women in Lancashire, 1922–1960: Their Story* (Lancaster: University of Lancaster, 2001).

—— 'Irish Women's Emigration to England, 1922–1960: The Lengthening of Family Ties', in Alan Hayes and Diane Urquhart (eds), *Irish Women's History* (Dublin: Irish Academic Press, 2004), pp. 152–167.

Lane, Leeann, 'Female Emigration and the Cooperative Movement in the Writings of George Russell', *New Hibernia Review*, 8.4 (2004), pp. 84–100.

Lee, Everett S., 'A Theory of Migration', *Demography*, 3.1 (1966), pp. 47–57.

Lee, J.J., *Ireland, 1912–1985: Politics and Society* (Cambridge: Cambridge University Press, 1990).

Lennon, Mary, 'A Haemorrhaging from the Land: A History of Irish Women's Emigration to Britain', *Spare Rib*, 118 (1982), pp. 38–39.

Lennon, Mary and Lennon, Siobhan, '"Off the Boat": Irish Women Talk about Their Experiences of Living in England', *Spare Rib*, 94 (May 1980), pp. 52–55.

Lennon, Mary, McAdam, Marie and O'Brien, Joanne, *Across the Water: Irish Women's Lives in Britain* (London: Virago Press, 1988).

Leppänen, Katarina, 'Movement of Women: Trafficking in the Interwar Era', *Women's Studies International Forum*, 30 (2007), pp. 523–533.

Lerner, Gerda, *The Majority Finds Its Past: Placing Women in History* (Oxford: Oxford University Press, 1981).

Lerner, Gerda, *Why History Matters: Life and Thought* (New York: Oxford University Press, 1998).

Lister, Ruth, 'Citizenship: Towards a Feminist Synthesis', *Feminist Review*, 57 (1997), pp. 28–48.

Litton, Helen, *The World War Two Years; The Irish Emergency: An Illustrated History* (Dublin: Wolfhound Press, 2001).

Locke, Terry, *Critical Discourse Analysis* (New York: Continuum, 2004).

London Irish Women's Centre, *Roots and Realities: A Profile of Irish Women in London in the 1990s* (London: London Irish Women's Centre, 1993).

London Irish Women's Conference, *Irish Women: Our Experience of Emigration* (London: Women in Print, 1984).

Lucey, Donnacha Seán, '"These Schemes Will Win for Themselves the Confidence of the People": Irish Independence, Poor Law Reform and Hospital Provision', *Medical History*, 58.1 (2014), pp. 46–66.

Luddy, Maria, 'Working Women, Trade Unionism and Politics in Ireland, 1830–1945', in Fintan Lane and Donal Ó Drisceoil (eds), *Politics and the Irish Working Class, 1830–1945* (Basingstoke: Palgrave Macmillan, 2005), pp. 44–61.

—— 'Sex and the Single Girl in 1920s and 1930s Ireland', *Irish Review*, 35 (2007), pp. 79–91.

—— *Prostitution and Irish Society, 1800–1940* (Cambridge: Cambridge University Press, 2008).

—— 'The Early Years of the NSPCC in Ireland', *Éire-Ireland*, 44.1–2 (2009), pp. 62–90.

Luddy, Maria and Murphy, Cliona, '"Cherchez la Femme": The Elusive Woman in Irish History', in Maria Luddy and Cliona Murphy (eds), *Women Surviving: Studies in Irish Women's History in the Nineteenth and Twentieth Centuries* (Dublin: Poolbeg Press, 1990) pp. 1–14.

—— (eds), *Women Surviving: Studies in Irish Women's History in the Nineteenth and Twentieth Centuries* (Dublin: Poolbeg Press, 1990).

Luddy, Maria and McLoughlin, Dympna, 'Women and Emigration from Ireland from the Seventeenth Century', in Angela Bourke *et al.* (eds), *The Field Day Anthology of Irish Writing*, vol. 5, *Irish Women's Writing and Traditions* (Cork: Cork University Press in association with Field Day, 2002), p. 569.

Lunn, Kenneth, '"Good for a Few Hundred at Least": Irish Labour Recruitment into Britain During the Second World War', in Patrick Buckland and John Belchem (eds), *The Irish in British Labour History*, Conference Proceedings of Irish Studies No. 1 (Liverpool: Liverpool University Press, 1993), pp. 102–114.

Lynch, Anne (ed.), *The Irish in Exile: Stories of Emigration* (London: Community History Press, 1988).

Lynch-Brennan, Margaret, *The Irish Bridget: Irish Immigrant Women in Domestic Service in America, 1840–1930* (Syracuse, NY: Syracuse University Press, 2009).

McAuliffe, Mary, 'The Irish Woman Worker and the Conditions of Employment Act, 1936: Responses from the Women Senators', *Saothar*, 36 (2011), pp. 37–48.

McAvoy, Sandra, 'Sex and the Single Girl: Ireland 1922–1949', in Chichi Aniaglou (ed.), *In From the Shadows: The UL Women's Studies Collection*, vol. 3 (Limerick: University of Limerick, 1997), pp. 55–67.

—— 'The Regulation of Sexuality in the Irish Free State, 1929–1935', in Elizabeth Malcolm and Greta Jones (eds), *Medicine, Disease and the State in Ireland, 1650–1940* (Cork: Cork University Press, 1999), pp. 253–266.

—— 'Before Cadden: Abortion in Mid-Twentieth-Century Ireland', in Dermot Keogh, Finbarr O'Shea and Carmel Quinlan (eds), *The Lost Decade: Ireland in the 1950s* (Cork: Mercier Press, 2004), pp. 147–163.

McCarthy, Angela, 'Personal Letters, Oral Testimony and Scottish Migration to New Zealand in the 1950s: The Case of Lorna Carter', *Immigrants and Minorities*, 23.1 (2005), pp. 59–79.

—— '"The Only Place Worth Thinking About": Personal Testimony and Irish and Scottish Migrants in Australasia, 1921–61', *Social History*, 33.3 (2008), pp. 317–335.

MacCurtain, Margaret and Donncha O'Corrain, *Women in Irish Society: The Historical Dimension* (Dublin: Arlen House, 1978).

—— *Ariadne's Thread: Writing Women into Irish History* (Galway: Arlen House, 2008).

MacDonagh, Oliver and Mandle, W.F. (eds), *Ireland and Irish Australia: Studies in Cultural and Political History* (London: Croom Helm, 1986).

MacÉinrí, Piaras, 'Introduction', in Andy Bielenberg (ed.), *The Irish Diaspora* (London: Longman, 2000), pp. 1–15.

McIntyre, Perry, *Free Passage: The Reunion of Irish Convicts and Their Families in Australia 1788–1852* (Dublin: Irish Academic Press, 2010).

McKenna, Yvonne, *Made Holy: Irish Women Religious at Home and Abroad* (Dublin: Irish Academic Press, 2006).

Mac Laughlin, Jim, *Ireland: The Emigrant Nursery and the World Economy* (Cork: Cork University Press, 1994).

—— (ed.), *Location and Dislocation in Contemporary Irish Society: Emigration and Irish Identities* (Cork: Cork University Press, 1997).

—— 'Changing Attitudes to "New Wave" Emigration? Structuralism versus Voluntarism in the Study of Irish Emigration', in Andy Bielenberg (ed.), *The Irish Diaspora* (London: Longman, 2000), pp. 55–67.

McNamara, Meadbh and Mooney, Paschal, *Women in Parliament: Ireland, 1918–2000* (Dublin: Wolfhound Press, 2000).

MacRaild, Don, '"Diaspora" and "Transnationalism": Theory and Evidence in Explanation of the Irish World-Wide', in *Irish Economic and Social History*, 33 (2006), pp. 51–58.

Malcolm, Elizabeth, *Elderly Return Migration from Britain to Ireland: A Preliminary Study* (Dublin: National Council for the Elderly, 1996).

Martin, Angela, 'Death of a Nation: Transnationalism, Bodies and Abortion in Late Twentieth-Century Ireland', in Tamar Mayer (ed.), *Gender Ironies of Nationalism: Sexing the Nation* (London: Routledge, 2000), pp. 65–86.

Mass Observation, *Britain in the 1930s* (London: The Lion and Unicorn Press, 1975).

Mass Observation Archive, *Papers from the Mass Observation Archive at the University of Sussex: Part 7 and Part 8* (Marlborough: Adam Matthew Publications, 2006).

Massey, Doreen, *Space, Place and Gender* (Cambridge: Polity Press, 2003).

Meehan, Elizabeth, *Free Movement between Ireland and the UK: From the 'Common Travel Area' to the Common Travel Area*, Studies in Public Policy 4 (Dublin: Policy Institute, 2000).

Meenan, James, *The Irish Economy Since 1922* (Liverpool: Liverpool University Press, 1970).

Megahy, Alan, *The Irish Protestant Churches in the Twentieth Century* (Basingstoke: Palgrave Macmillan, 2000).

Miller, Kerby, *Emigrants and Exiles: Ireland and the Irish Exodus to North America* (New York: Oxford University Press, 1985).

—— *Ireland and Irish America: Culture, Class and Transatlantic Migration* (Dublin: Field Day, 2008).

Miller, Kerby, with Boling, Bruce and Doyle, David N., 'Emigrants and Exiles: Irish Cultures and Irish Emigration to North America, 1790–1922', *Irish Historical Studies*, 22.86 (1980), pp. 97–125.

Miller, Kerby, with Doyle, David N. and Kelleher, Patricia, '"For Love and Liberty": Irish Women, Migration and Domesticity in Ireland and America, 1815–1920', in Patrick O'Sullivan (ed.), *Irish Women and Irish Migration* (London: Leicester University Press, 1997), pp. 41–65.

Mitchell, Martin J. (ed.), *New Perspectives on the Irish in Scotland* (Edinburgh: John Donald Short Run Press, 2008).

Moody, T.W. and Martin, F.X., *The Course of Irish History*, rev. edn (Cork: Mercier Press, 1994).

Moran, Gerard. *Sending Out Ireland's Poor: Assisted Emigration to North America in the Nineteenth Century* (Dublin: Four Courts Press, 2004).

Morris, Mary, *A Very Private Diary: A Nurse in Wartime*, ed. Carol Acton (London: Weidenfeld & Nicolson, 2014).

Moser, Peter, 'Rural Economy and Female Emigration in the West of Ireland, 1936–1956', *U.C.G. Women's Studies Centre Review*, 2 (1993), pp. 41–51.

Moulton, Mo, *Ireland and the Irish in Interwar England* (Cambridge: Cambridge University Press, 2014).

Moynihan, Maurice (ed.), *Speeches and Statements by Eamon de Valera, 1917–73* (Dublin: Gill & Macmillan, 1980).

Muldowney, Mary, 'Women Workers in Dublin and Belfast during the Second World War', in Alan Hayes and Diane Urquhart, *Irish Women's History* (Dublin: Irish Academic Press, 2004), pp. 168–187.

—— 'New Opportunities for Women? Employment in Britain during the Second World War', *University of Sussex Journal of Contemporary History*, 10 (2006), pp. 2–18.

—— *The Second World War and Irish Women: An Oral History* (Dublin: Irish Academic Press, 2007).

Murphy, Colin and Adair, Lynne (eds), *Untold Stories: Protestants in the Republic of Ireland 1922–2002* (Dublin: The Liffey Press, 2002).

Murphy, Maureen, 'The Fionnuala Factor: Irish Sibling Emigration at the Turn of the Twentieth Century', in Anthony Bradley and Maryann Gialanella Valiulis (eds), *Gender and Sexuality in Modern Ireland* (Amherst: University of Massachusetts Press, 1997), pp. 85–101.

Murray, Patrick, 'Obsessive Historian: Éamon de Valera and the Policing of His Reputation', *Proceedings of the Royal Irish Academy*, 101C (2001), pp. 37–65.

Nevin, Donal, 'Symposium on the Report of the Commission on Emigration and Other Population Problems', *Journal of the Statistical and Social Inquiry Society of Ireland*, 29.4 (1956), pp. 104–121.

Nolan, Janet A., *Ourselves Alone: Women's Emigration from Ireland, 1885–1920* (Lexington: University Press of Kentucky, 1989).

O'Brien, John A (ed.), *The Vanishing Irish: The Enigma of the Modern World* (London: W.H. Allen, 1955).

O'Carroll, Ide, *Models for Movers: Irish Women's Emigration to America* (Dublin: Attic Press, 1990).

O'Connor, Kevin, *The Irish in Britain* (London: Sidgwick & Jackson, 1972).

Ó Crualaoich, Gearóid, 'The Primacy of Form: A "Folk Ideology", de Valera's Politics', in John P. O'Carroll and John A. Murphy (eds), *De Valera and His Times* (Cork: Cork University Press, 1983), pp. 47–61.

O'Day, Alan, 'Revising the Irish Diaspora', in D. George Boyce and Alan O'Day (eds), *The Making of Modern Irish History: Revisionism and the Revisionist Controversy* (London: Routledge, 1997), pp. 188–215.

O'Dowd, Anne, *Spalpeens and Tattie Hokers: History and Folklore of the Irish Migratory Agricultural Worker in Ireland and Britain* (Dublin: Irish Academic Press, 1991).

O'Dowd, Liam, 'Church, State and Women: The Aftermath of Partition', in Chris Curtin, Pauline Jackson and Barbara O'Connor (eds), *Gender in Irish Society* (Galway: Galway University Press, 1987), pp. 3–36.

Ó Drisceoil, Donal, *Censorship in Ireland 1939–1945: Neutrality, Politics and Society* (Cork: Cork University Press, 1996).

—— '"Whose Emergency is it?" Wartime Politics and the Irish Working Class, 1939–45', in Fintan Lane and Donal Ó Drisceoil (eds), *Politics and the Irish Working Class, 1830–1945* (Basingstoke: Palgrave Macmillan, 2005), pp. 262–281.

Ó Gráda, Cormac, 'Primogeniture and Ultimogeniture in Rural Ireland', *Journal of Interdisciplinary History*, 10.3 (1980), pp. 491–497.

—— *Ireland: A New Economic History* (Oxford: Clarendon Press, 1994).

—— *A Rocky Road: The Irish Economy Since the 1920s* (Manchester: Manchester University Press, 1997).

O'Grady, Anne, *Irish Migration to London in the 1940s and 50s*, Irish in Britain Research Forum Papers (London: PNL Press, 1988).

O'Halpin, Eunan, *Defending Ireland: The Irish State and its Enemies Since 1922* (Oxford: Oxford University Press, 2000).

—— 'Politics and the State, 1922–32', in J.R. Hill (ed.), *A New History of Ireland*, vol. 7, *Ireland, 1921–1984* (Oxford: Oxford University Press, 2003), pp. 86–126.

—— *Spying on Ireland: British Intelligence and Irish Neutrality During the Second World War* (Oxford: Oxford University Press, 2008).

O'Leary, Eleanor, 'Desperate Housewives: Social Change and the Desire for Modern Lifestyles in 1950s Ireland', in Rebecca Anne Barr, Sarah-Anne Buckley and Laura Kelly (eds), *Engendering Ireland: New Reflections on Modern History and Literature* (Newcastle upon Tyne: Cambridge Scholars Publishing, 2015), pp. 12–31.

O'Sullivan, Patrick (ed.), *The Irish World Wide, History, Heritage, Identity: Patterns of Migration*, vol. 1 (London: Leicester University Press, 1997).

—— (ed.), *The Irish World Wide, History, Heritage, Identity: The Irish in the New Communities*, vol. 2 (London: Leicester University Press, 1997).

—— (ed.), *The Irish World Wide, History, Heritage, Identity: The Creative Migrant*, vol. 3 (London: Leicester University Press, 1997).

—— (ed.), *The Irish World Wide, History, Heritage, Identity: Irish Women and Irish Migration*, vol. 4 (London: Leicester University Press, 1997).

—— (ed.), *The Irish World Wide, History, Heritage, Identity: Religion and Identity*, vol. 5 (London: Leicester University Press, 2000).

O'Tuathaigh, M.A.G., 'The Historical Pattern of Irish Emigration: Some Labour Aspects', in Galway Labour History Group, *The Emigrant Experience: Papers Presented at the Second Annual Mary Murray Weekend Seminar, Galway, 30th March–1st April 1990* (Galway: Galway Labour History Group, 1991), pp. 9–28.

Offen, Karen, Pierson, Ruth Roach and Rendall, Jane (eds), *Writing Women's History: International Perspectives* (Basingstoke: Palgrave Macmillan, 1991).

Padbury, Joyce, 'Mary Hayden (1862–1942): Feminist', in *Studies: An Irish Quarterly Review*, 96.390 (2009), pp. 145–158.

Pašeta, Senia, 'Censorship and its Critics in the Irish Free State 1922–1932', *Past and Present*, 181 (2003), pp. 193–218.

Pedraza, Silvia, 'Women and Migration: The Social Consequences of Gender', *Annual Review of Sociology*, 17 (1991), pp. 303–325.

Pihl, Liz (ed.), *Signe Toksvig's Irish Diaries, 1926–1937* (Dublin: The Lilliput Press, 1994).

Phillips, Nelson and Hardy, Cynthia, *Discourse Analysis: Investigating Processes of Social Construction* (Thousand Oaks, Calif.: Sage, 2002).

Phizacklea, Annie (ed.), *One Way Ticket: Migration and Female Labour* (London: Routledge & Kegan Paul, 1983).

Pooley, Colin G. and Whyte, Ian D. (eds), *Migrants, Emigrants and Immigrants: A Social History of Migration* (London: Routledge, 1991).

Pozanesi, Sandra, 'Diasporic Subjects and Migration', in Gabriele Griffin and Rosi Braidotti (eds), *Thinking Differently: A Reader in European Women's Studies* (London: Zed Books, 2002), pp. 205–220.

Prior, Katherine, *Immigrants from Ireland* (London: Franklin Watts, 2002).

Prittie, Terence, *Through Irish Eyes* (London: Bachman & Turner, 1977).

Pugh, Martin, *State and Society: British Political and Social History, 1870–1992* (London: Edward Arnold, 1994).

Purvis, June, 'Using Primary Sources When Researching Women's History from a Feminist Perspective', *Women's History Review*, 1.2 (1992), pp. 273–306.

Quine, Maria Sophia, *Population Politics in Twentieth Century Europe* (London: Routledge, 1996).

Rattigan, Cliona, '"Crimes of Passion of the Worst Character": Abortion Cases and Gender in Ireland, 1925–1950', in Maryann Valiulis (ed.), *Gender and Power in Ireland* (Dublin: Irish Academic Press, 2008), pp. 115–139.

Ramazanoglu, Caroline and Holland, Janet, *Feminist Methodology: Challenges and Choices* (London: Sage, 2002).

Redmond, Jennifer, 'Gender, Emigration and Diverging Discourses: Irish Female Emigration, 1922–48', Maryann Valiulis (ed.), *Gender and Power in Ireland* (Dublin: Irish Academic Press, 2008), pp. 140–158.

—— '"Sinful Singleness?" Discourses on Irish Women's Emigration to England, 1922–1948', *Women's History Review*, 17 July 2008, pp. 455–476.

—— 'The Largest Remaining Reserve of Manpower: Historical Myopia, Irish Women Workers and World War Two', article for special edition of *Saothar 36: Journal of the Irish Labour History Society*, 36 (2011), pp. 61–70.

—— 'In the Family Way and Away from the Family: Examining the Evidence in Irish Unmarried Mothers in Britain, 1920s–1940s', in Elaine Farrell (ed.), *'She Said She Was in the Family Way': Pregnancy and Infancy in the Irish Past* (London: Institute of Historical Research, 2012), pp. 163–185.

—— 'The Stethoscope and the Travel Permit: Irish Women in the Medical Profession in Britain during WWII', in Mary J. Hickman and D.A.J. MacPherson (eds), *Irish Women and the Diaspora: Theories, Concepts and New Perspectives* (Manchester: Manchester University Press, 2014), pp. 160–194.

—— 'The Politics of Emigrant Bodies: Irish Women's Sexual Practice in Question', in Jennifer Redmond, Sonja Tiernan, Sandra McAvoy and Mary McAuliffe (eds), *Sexual Politics in Modern Ireland* (Dublin: Irish Academic Press, 2015), pp. 73–89.

—— 'Safeguarding Irish Girls: Welfare Work, Female Emigrants and the Catholic Church, 1920s–1940s', in Cara Delay and Christina Brophy (eds), *Women, Reform, and Resistance in Ireland, 1850–1950* (New York: Palgrave Macmillan, 2015), pp. 79–106.

—— 'Immigrants, Aliens and Evacuees: Exploring the History of Irish Children in Britain During the Second World War', *Journal of the History of Childhood and Youth*, 9.2 (2016), pp. 295–308.

—— 'Migrants, Medics, Matrons: Exploring the Spectrum of Irish Immigrants in the Wartime British Health Sector', in David Durnin and Ian Miller (eds), *Medicine, Health and Irish Experiences of Conflict, 1914–45* (Manchester: Manchester University Press, 2016), pp. 206–219.

Redmond, Jennifer and Harford, Judith, '"One Man One Job": The Marriage Ban and the Employment of Women Teachers in Irish Primary Schools', *Paedagogica Historica*, 46.5 (2010), pp. 639–654.

Roberts, Elizabeth, *A Woman's Place: An Oral History of Working Women, 1890–1940* (Oxford: Basil Blackwell, 1985).

Robinson, Mary, 'Women and the New Irish State', in Margaret MacCurtain and Donncha O'Corrain, *Women in Irish Society: The Historical Dimension* (Dublin: Arlen House, 1979), pp. 58–70.

Roddy, Sarah, *Population, Providence and Empire: The Churches and Emigration from Nineteenth-Century Ireland* (Manchester: Manchester University Press, 2014).

Rossiter, Anne, 'Bringing the Margins into the Centre: A Review of Aspects of Irish Women's Emigration from a British Perspective', in Ailbhe Smyth (ed.), *Irish Women's Studies Reader* (Dublin: Attic Press, 1993), pp. 177–202.

—— 'In Search of Mary's Past: Placing Nineteenth Century Irish Immigrant Women in British Feminist History', in Joan Grant (ed.), *Women, Migration and Empire* (Stoke-on-Trent: Trentham Books, 1996), pp. 1–29.

Rowley, Rosemary, 'Women and the Constitution', *Administration*, 31.1 (1989), pp. 42–62.

Rudd, Joy, 'Invisible Exports: The Emigration of Irish Women This Century', *Women's Studies International Forum*, 11.4 (1988), pp. 307–311.

Ryan, Louise, 'Traditions and Double Moral Standards: The Irish Suffragists' Critique of Nationalism', *Women's History Review*, 4.4 (1995), pp. 487–503.

—— 'Constructing "Irishwoman": Modern Girls and Comely Maidens', *Irish Studies Review*, 6.3 (1998), pp. 263–272.

—— 'Aliens, Migrants and Maids: Public Discourses on Irish Immigration to Britain in 1937', *Immigrants and Minorities*, 20.3 (2001), pp. 25–42.

—— 'Irish Female Emigration in the 1930s: Transgressing Space and Culture', *Gender, Place and Culture*, 8.3 (2001), pp. 271–282.

—— 'Flappers and Shawls: The Female Embodiment of Irish National Identity in the 1920s', in Susan Shifrin (ed.), *Women as Sites of Culture: Women's Roles in Cultural Formation from the Renaissance to the Twentieth Century* (Aldershot: Ashgate, 2002), pp. 37–49.

—— *Gender, Identity and the Irish Press, 1922–1937: Embodying the Nation* (Lewiston, NY: Edwin Mellen Press, 2002).

—— '"I'm Going to England": Women's Narratives of Leaving Ireland in the 1930s', *Oral History*, 30.1 (2002), pp. 42–53.

—— 'Sexualising Emigration: Discourses of Irish Female Emigration in the 1930s', *Women's Studies International Forum*, 25.1 (2002), pp. 51–65.

—— 'Leaving Home: Irish Press Debates on Female Employment, Domesticity and Emigration to Britain in the 1930s', *Women's History Review*, 12.3 (2003), pp. 387–406.

—— 'Moving Spaces and Changing Places: Irish Women's Memories of Emigration to Britain in the 1930s', *Journal of Ethnic and Migration Studies*, 29.1 (2003), pp. 67–82.

—— 'Family Matters: (E)migration, Familial Networks and Irish Women in Britain', *Sociological Review* (2004), pp. 351–370.

—— 'Locating the Flapper in Rural Irish Society: The Irish Provincial Press and the Modern Woman in the 1920s', in Ann Heilmann and Margaret Beetham (eds), *New Woman Hybridities: Femininity and International Consumer Culture, 1880–1930* (London: Routledge, 2004), pp. 90–101.

—— 'Passing Time: Irish Women Remembering and Re-Telling Stories of Migration to Britain', in Kathy Burrell and Panikos Panayi (eds), *Histories and Memories: Migrants and their History in Britain* (London: Tauris Academic Studies, 2006), pp. 192–209.

—— '"A Decent Girl Well Worth Helping": Women, Migration and Unwanted Pregnancy', in Liam Harte and Yvonne Whelan (eds), *Ireland beyond Boundaries: Mapping Irish Studies in the Twenty-First Century* (London: Pluto Press, 2007), pp. 135–153.

—— 'Migrant Women, Social Networks and Motherhood: The Experiences of Irish Nurses in Britain', *Sociology*, 41.2 (2007), pp. 295–312.

—— '"I Had a Sister in England": Family-Led Migration, Social Networks and Irish Nurses', *Journal of Ethnic and Migration Studies*, 34.3 (2008), pp. 453–470.

Ryan, W.J.L., 'Some Irish Population Problems', *Population Studies*, 9.2 (1955), pp. 185–188.

Sangster, Joan, 'Telling our Stories: Feminist Debates and the Use of Oral History', *Women's History Review*, 3.1 (1994), pp. 5–28.

Sawyer, Roger, *'We Are But Women': Women in Ireland's History* (London: Routledge, 1993).

Scannell, Yvonne, 'The Constitution and the Role of Women', in Brian Farrell (ed.), *De Valera's Constitution and Ours* (Dublin: Gill & Macmillan, 1988), pp. 123–136.

Schweitzer, Pam (ed.), *A Place to Stay: Memories of Pensioners from Many Lands* (London: Age Exchange Theatre Company, 1984).

—— (ed.), *Across the Irish Sea* (London: Age Exchange Theatre Company, 2001).

—— (ed.), *Mapping Memories: Reminiscence with Ethnic Minority Elders* (London: Exchange Theatre Company, 2004).

Schweitzer, Pam, Hilton, Lorraine and Moss, Jane (eds), *What Did You Do in the War, Mum?* (London: Age Exchange Theatre Company, 1985).

Sexton, J.J., 'Emigration and Immigration in the Twentieth Century: An Overview', in J.R. Hill (ed.), *A New History of Ireland*, vol. 7, *Ireland, 1921–1984* (Oxford: Oxford University Press, 2003), pp. 769–825.

Sharkey, Sabina, Bromley, Michael, Harris, Mary and Hickman, Mary J., *Irish Studies: An Introductory Course Teaching Pack* (London: University of North London Press, 1996).

Sheridan, Dorothy, 'Using the Mass-Observation Archive as a Source for Women's Studies', *Women's History Review*, 3.1 (1994), pp. 101–113.

—— (ed.), *Wartime Women: A Mass-Observation Anthology, 1937–45* (London: Phoenix Press, 2000).

Smith, James M., 'The Politics of Sexual Knowledge: The Origins of Ireland's Containment Culture and the Corrigan Report', *Journal of the History of Sexuality*, 13.2 (2004), pp. 208–233.

Spencer, A.E.C.W., *Arrangements for the Integration of Irish Immigrants in England and Wales*, ed. Mary Daly (Dublin: Irish Manuscripts Commission, 2012).

Stark, Oded, *The Migration of Labour* (Oxford: Basil Blackwell, 1991).

—— *Altruism and beyond: An Economic Analysis of Transfers and Exchanges within Families and Groups* (Cambridge: Cambridge University Press, 1995).

Summerfield, Penny, *Women Workers in the Second World War: Production and Patriarchy in Conflict* (London: Croom Helm, 1984).

Tastsoglou, Evangelia and Dobrowolsky, Alexandra (eds), *Women, Migration and Citizenship Making Local, National and Transnational Connections* (Aldershot: Ashgate, 2006).

Taylor, Seamus, *Smalltown Boys and Girls: Emigrant Irish Youth in London*, Irish in Britain Research Forum Occasional Papers Series 2 (London: PNL, 1988).

Thompson, Paul, *The Voice of the Past: Oral History*, 2nd edn (Oxford: Oxford University Press, 1988).

Tiernan, Sonja, *Eva Gore-Booth: An Image of Such Politics* (Manchester: Manchester University Press, 2012).

Travers, Pauric, '"The Dream Gone Bust": Irish Responses to Emigration, 1922–60', in Oliver MacDonagh and W.F. Mandle (eds), *Irish-Australian Studies, Papers Delivered at the Fifth Irish-Australian Conference* (Canberra: Australian National University, 1989), pp. 318–342.

—— 'Emigration and Gender: The Case of Ireland, 1922–60', in Mary O'Dowd and Sabine Wichert (eds), *Chattel, Servant or Citizen? Women's Status in Church, State and Society* (Belfast: Queen's University of Belfast Press, 1995), pp. 187–199.

—— '"There Was Nothing for Me There": Irish Female Emigration, 1922–71', in Patrick O'Sullivan (ed.), *Irish Women and Irish Migration* (London: Leicester University Press, 1997), pp. 146–167.

Trudgen Dawson, Sandra, 'Busy and Bored: The Politics of Work and Leisure for Women Workers in Second World War British Government Hostels', *Twentieth Century British History*, 21.1 (2010), pp. 29–49.

Tweedy, Hilda, *A Link in the Chain: The Story of the Irish Housewives Association, 1942–1992* (Dublin: Attic Press, 1992).

Tyrer, Nicola, *They Fought in the Fields. The Women's Land Army: The Story of a Forgotten Victory* (London: Sinclair-Stevenson, 1996).

Valiulis, Maryann, '"Free Women in a Free Nation": Nationalist Feminist Expectations for Independence', in B. Farrell (ed.), *The Creation of the Dáil* (Dublin: Blackwater Press, 1994), pp. 75–90.

—— 'Neither Feminist Nor Flapper: The Ecclesiastical Construction of the Ideal Irish Woman', in Mary O'Dowd and Sabine Wichert (eds), *Chattel, Servant or Citizen? Women's Status in Church, State and Society* (Belfast: Queen's University of Belfast Press, 1995), pp. 168–178.

—— 'Power, Gender and Identity in the Irish Free State', *Journal of Women's History*, 6.4/7.1 (1995), pp. 117–136.

—— 'Engendering Citizenship: Women's Relationship to the State in Ireland and the United States in the Post-Suffrage Period', in Maryann Valiulis and Mary O'Dowd (eds), *Women and Irish History: Essays in Honour of Margaret MacCurtain* (Dublin: Wolfhound Press, 1997), pp. 159–172.

—— 'Subverting the Flapper: The Unlikely Alliance of Irish Popular and Ecclesiastical Press in the 1920s', in Ann Heilmann and Margaret Beecham (eds), *New Woman Hybridities: Femininity, Feminism and International Consumer Culture, 1880–1930* (London: Routledge, 2004), pp. 102–117.

Van Dijk, Tuen A. (ed.), *Handbook of Discourse Analysis*, vol. 4, *Discourse Analysis in Society* (London: Academic Press, 1985).

Vaughan, W.E. and Fitzpatrick, A.J., *Irish Historical Statistics: Population 1821–1971* (Dublin: Royal Irish Academy, 1978).

Walsh, Brendan M., *Some Irish Population Problems Reconsidered* (Dublin: Economic and Social Research Institute, 1968).

—— 'Expectations, Information and Human Migration: Specifying an Economic Model of Irish Migration to Britain', *Journal of Regional Science*, 14.1 (1974), pp. 107–120.

—— *Ireland's Changing Demographic Structure* (Dublin: Gill & Macmillan, 1981).

—— *Tests for the Macroeconomic Effects of Large-Scale Migration Based on the Irish Experience, 1947–87*, Centre for Economic Research, Working Paper No. WP88/10 (Dublin: University College Dublin, 1988).

—— 'Irishness, Gender and Place', *Environment and Planning D: Society and Space*, 13 (1995), pp. 35–50.

—— *Outsiders Inside: Whiteness, Place, and Irish Women* (London: Routledge, 2001).

Webley, Nicholas (ed.), *Betty's Wartime Diary, 1939–1945* (London: Thorogood, 2006).

Webster, Wendy, 'Enemies, Allies and Transnational Histories: Germans, Irish, and Italians in Second World War Britain', *Twentieth Century British History*, 25.1 (2014), pp. 63–86.

White, Jack, *Minority Report: The Protestant Community in the Irish Republic* (Dublin: Gill & Macmillan, 1975).

Whyte, J.H., *Church and State in Modern Ireland, 1923–1970* (Dublin: Gill & Macmillan, 1971).

Widdowson, H.G., *Discourse Analysis* (Oxford: Oxford University Press, 2007).

Wildman, Charlotte, 'Irish-Catholic Women and Modernity in 1930s Liverpool', in D.A.J. MacPherson and Mary J. Hickman (eds), *Irish Diaspora Studies and Women: Theories, Concepts and New Perspectives* (Manchester: Manchester University Press, 2014), pp. 72–91.

Wills, Clair, *That Neutral Island: A History of Ireland During the Second World War* (London: Faber & Faber, 2007).

—— *The Best Are Leaving: Emigration and Post-War Irish Culture* (Cambridge: Cambridge University Press: 2015).

Yadgar, Yaacov, 'From the Pluralistic to the Universalistic: National Narratives in Israel's Mainstream Press, 1967–97', *Nations and Nationalism*, 8.1 (2002), pp. 55–72.

Yuval-Davis, Nira, *Gender and Nation* (London: Sage Publications, 1997).

—— 'Women, Citizenship and Difference', in *Feminist Review*, 57 (1997), pp. 4–27.

Theses

Connolly, Tracey, 'Emigration from Independent Ireland: 1922–1970', PhD thesis, University College Cork, Cork, 1999.

Delaney, Enda, 'Irish Migration to Britain, 1921–1971: Patterns, Trends and Contingent Factors', PhD thesis, Queen's University of Belfast, 1997.

Ewart, Henrietta, 'Caring for Migrants: Policy Responses to Irish Migration to England, 1940–1972', PhD thesis, University of Warwick, 2012.

Ferriter, Diarmaid, '"A Peculiar People in their Own Land": Catholic Social Theory and the Plight of Rural Ireland 1930–55', PhD thesis, University College Dublin, 1996.

Graham, Ann Marie, 'Unmarried Mothers; The Legislative Context in Ireland, 1921–79', MLitt thesis, Maynooth University, 2012.

Leane, Máire, 'Female Sexuality in Ireland 1920–1940: Construction and Regulation', PhD thesis, University College Cork, 1999.

Muldowney, Mary, 'The Impact of the Second World War on Women in Belfast and Dublin: An Oral History', 2 vols, PhD thesis, Trinity College Dublin, 2005.

Nyhan, Miriam, 'Comparing Irish Migrants and County Associations in New York and London: A Cross-Cultural Analysis of Migrant Experiences and Associational Behaviour circa 1946–1961', PhD thesis, European University Institute, Florence, 2008.

O'Connor, Henrietta, 'Women Abroad: The Life Experience of Irish Women in Leicester', M.Litt thesis, Trinity College Dublin, 1993.

Websites/Digital Publications

Buckley, Sarah-Anne, 'The Catholic Cure for Poverty', available from the Jacobin website https://www.jacobinmag.com/2016/05/catholic-church-ireland-magdalene-laundries-mother-baby-homes. Published 27 May 2016.

Centre for Advancement of Women in Politics www.qub.ac.uk/cawp/Irish%20bios/TDs_2.htm.

Emigrant Advice www.emigrantadvice.ie.

Imperial War Museum https://www.iwm.org.uk/.

Irish Newspaper Archives https://www.irishnewsarchive.com/.

Irish Statute Book http://www.irishstatutebook.ie/.

King's Cross Voices Oral History Project http://camden.gov.uk/ccm/content/leisure/local-history/kings-cross-voices.en.

Museum of London https://www.museumoflondon.org.uk/museum-london.

Parliamentary Debates (Ireland) https://www.oireachtas.ie/en/debates/find/.

Royal Navy Museum www.royalnavalmuseum.org.

Index